I Can
Read It
All by
Myself

I Can Read It All by Myself

The Beginner Books Story

Paul V. Allen

University Press of Mississippi / Jackson

The University Press of Mississippi is the scholarly publishing agency of
the Mississippi Institutions of Higher Learning: Alcorn State University,
Delta State University, Jackson State University, Mississippi State University,
Mississippi University for Women, Mississippi Valley State University,
University of Mississippi, and University of Southern Mississippi.

www.upress.state.ms.us

The University Press of Mississippi is a member
of the Association of University Presses.

First printing 2021
∞

Library of Congress Control Number: 2021930599

Hardback: 978-1-4968-3404-1
Trade Paperback: 978-1-4968-3405-8
E-pub Single: 978-1-4968-3406-5
E-pub Institutional: 978-1-4968-3407-2
PDF Single: 978-1-4968-3408-9
PDF Institutional: 978-1-4968-3409-6

British Library Cataloging-in-Publication Data available

publication funding provided by a child
Figure Foundation

To my grandmother, Lauretta Allen, for signing me up for the Beginning Readers' Club when I was three years old

Contents

Part 1: The Beginner Books Story

Part 2: The Beginner Books Encyclopedia

I Can
Read It
All by
Myself

Introduction

Beginner Books (and its spin-off line, Bright and Early Books) comprise over 150 books and counting, done by nearly ninety different authors and illustrators. Collectively they've sold over 100 million copies, placing 20 books on *Publishers Weekly*'s All-Time Bestselling Children's Books list (11 of them in the top 50). An odds-defying number of them are still in print, in many cases decades after their original publication.

The legacy of the line is immense. It's nearly impossible to enter a school, library, or bookstore and not see at least one book with that brightly colored spine featuring a smiling Cat in the Hat at the top. Look at any list of the greatest children's books of all time and you're going to find at least one, but more likely two, or three, or more of them.

Many young readers came away from their Beginner Book experience forever changed. Many of them went on to make books themselves, people like Lisa Yee, John Sciezeska, Jon Klassen, Christopher Paolini, Gary D. Schmidt, Stephen Pinker, and Anna Quindlen.

Beginner Books have been around for over sixty years now, so long that it's difficult to imagine a world without them. It's even more difficult to imagine that there haven't always been books like them. Parents, teachers, and librarians now take for granted the fact that a child just beginning to read has a huge menu of books to choose from that are at her level. Books where the sentences are short, the vocabulary is either known or easily decodable, and the pictures do a large part of the storytelling. Before the late 1950s this wasn't at all the case. While some books that came before may have accidentally fit the definition, early readers didn't exist before Beginner Books.

Few can claim to have created their own category in publishing, but that's exactly what Ted Geisel, Helen Geisel, and Phyllis Cerf did when they decided to model a series of books after *The Cat in the Hat*. They took a research-based pedagogical approach and combined it with an anarchic form of storytelling that Ted dubbed "logical insanity" to make carefully designed chaos. In the process, the founders of Beginner Books invented the rules and parameters of the form that are still in use today.

Beginner Books are often cited, indeed even many times by Ted himself, as being an antidote for the Dick and Jane stories found in school primers. And while *The Cat in the Hat* and Beginner Books were a clear reaction to the perceived deficiencies in those types of stories (and indeed gently parodied and mocked them on more than one occasion), they didn't actually get rid of or replace Dick and Jane. Those stories continued to be used in schools well after 1957.

But Beginner Books addressed an arguably bigger problem. As reading expert Jeanne Chall put it, school reading basals like Dick and Jane were not designed to address every reading need; they were a teaching tool. The big missing ingredient in early literacy before the late 1950s was a book that could be used for independent practice. Beginner Books were meant to be not only—as their motto stated—stories that kids could read by themselves, but by virtue of being engaging and funny, stories kids would *want* to read by themselves.

But the innovation of Beginner Books wasn't just in their motivational or pedagogical properties. Aesthetically, there was nothing else like them. To bring the texts to life, Ted often looked outside the children's books world, discovering talents with backgrounds more in line with his own: cartoonists, animators, and advertising and magazine illustrators. These artists brought a modern graphic sensibility that made the books' settings and characters look less like paintings in a museum and more like comic books and cartoons. The drawings used vivid colors and bold lines, overwhelmed the page, and drew young eyes right inside of them. They reversed the typical hierarchy of the illustrations being there to enhance the text. In many Beginner Books the pictures tell the whole story while the text provides embellishment. In the days before the proliferation of kid-friendly graphic novels, this was the best it got.

A common misconception about Beginner Books is that they're all essentially Dr. Seuss books. Robert Lopshire, author and/or illustrator of five Beginner Books, once complained in a letter, "I've grown weary of saying, 'No, I don't write the Dr. Seuss books . . . you see there is this series and Dr. Seuss writes his own books and I blah, blah . . . '" Superficially, this is an easy mistake. Afterall, the Cat in the Hat is on the cover of every book. And Ted wrote and drew nearly twenty books in the line, and wrote over a dozen more using the pseudonym Theo LeSieg. There's no doubt that Ted's absurd humor and visual inventiveness defined the Beginner Book sensibility. As president and editor of the line, from its inception to 1980, there was scarcely a creative decision that happened without his approval.

But to attribute the whole line to him is false. He was inspired, encouraged, and aided by a colorful, talented, and highly accomplished group of editors, writers, and artists. The line never would have existed in the first place without the clever forward-thinking of Phyllis Cerf, who recognized an opportunity and seized on it. It would have never lasted without the steady guiding hand of Helen Palmer Geisel, who provided a necessary counterpoint to her husband's flights of fancy and anxiety. And it would not be remembered without the words and images created by artists and writers such as P. D. Eastman, Roy McKie, Al Perkins, Stan and Jan Berenstain, Michael Frith, Eric Gurney, Fritz Siebel, and the many, many others you'll read about in the pages ahead. Ted may have been the face of and the brain behind Beginner Books, but he wasn't the heart.

Beginner Books writers and artists made monumental contributions to twentieth-century popular culture, either creating or fostering the development of *Fantasia, Pinocchio, The Muppet Show, Fraggle Rock*, Mr. Clean, Mickey's dog Pluto, Mr. Magoo, Gerald McBoing Boing, *Schoolhouse Rock, The Little Mermaid*, Amelia Bedelia, Encyclopedia Brown, the Berenstain Bears, the Black Stallion, Arthur the Aardvaark, Underdog, and the Trix rabbit.

It was never easy. As an editor Ted was exacting, uncompromising, and blunt. He sometimes struggled to communicate what he wanted, preferring instead to take over and do it himself, alienating many writers and artists in the process. He clashed epically and brutally with Phyllis Cerf, eventually forcing her out of the company that had been her idea. And after losing Helen to a tragic suicide, he took over the line, nearly running himself and Beginner Books into the ground. But the series has survived and thrived, even after Ted's final Beginner Book, 1987's *I Am Not Going to Get Up Today!* The same month I finished researching and writing this book, Random House released the 107th and 108th books in the series.

I count myself among the authors whose love of reading was sparked by Beginner Books. When I was three years old, my maternal grandmother signed me up for the Beginning Readers' Program. This meant that a new Beginner Book or Bright and Early Book arrived at my house each month, titles like *I'll Teach My Dog 100 Words, Put Me in the Zoo, The Big Honey Hunt.* This, along with a small collection of original Beginner Books (*The Cat in the Hat Comes Back, A Fly Went By, Sam and the Firefly*) that had once belonged to my uncle John, served as the basis of my earliest listening, looking, and reading experiences. As I look back now it was the two-page spreads that really got me: the dogs all in bed at night and in the morning in *Go, Dog. Go!*; the explosion of bears, tigers, and apples in *Ten Apples Up on Top!*; the millions of thumbs drumming on drums in *Hand, Hand, Fingers, Thumb*.

When my first son, Peter, was born, I dusted off my collection of Beginner Books. I was delighted to learn that not only were they still great fun for me to read, but that Peter was just as enraptured by them as I had been as a child. By the time Peter's brother Theo came along, our library of Beginner Books had grown, and as a family we discovered new favorites—*Bennett Cerf's Book of Riddles*, *The Bike Lesson*, *Snow*, *Wacky Wednesday*, *The Many Mice of Mr. Brice*. Beginner Books became a staple of a bedtime reading routine, with rollicking laughter at "Oh, you are not my mother. You are a Snort" and repeated choruses of "Yes, they dare!" Soon, Peter took over reading them to us. As both a parent and a teacher who focuses on early literacy, I can tell you that this is the ideal early reading experience.

At the same time as I was reveling in Beginner Books with my sons, I made a shift in my career. After several years as an elementary classroom teacher and a middle school English teacher, I transitioned to focus on early literacy, working with first graders just learning to read. That meant spending my days with reading material produced by educational companies: usually awkwardly written, stilted books with bland illustrations. It made the effervescence of Beginner Books seem like even more of a miracle.

So it was from those three perspectives that I wrote and researched this book:

With the wide-eyed wonder I felt looking at Beginner Books when I was a child.

With the appreciation of a parent being able to share laughter, joy, and a true sense of connection while reading with my children.

With the analytical mind of a reading specialist determined to uncover the inner workings of the books to see what makes them tick.

Ultimately it's my hope that this book serves as a proper examination, explanation, and exaltation of Beginner Books, as a way to honor what they have given to me and so many other readers through the years: the empowering cry, "I can read it all by myself!"

Part 1

The Beginner Books Story

1

A Crisis Arises (1954)

Beginner Books started with a war of—and about—words.

In 1954, *Life* magazine published an article by *Hiroshima* author John Hersey titled "Why Do Children Bog Down on the First 'R'?" Hersey was writing not as a journalist, but as a father concerned with the flaws in the US educational system. He was a member of a committee at the Citizens' School in Fairfield, Connecticut, charged with investigating the question of reading achievement. The *Life* article was a summary of the committee's findings up to that point. Though it was more of a call to awareness than a set of firm conclusions, the article argued for a more authentic and motivational approach to reading in schools. A year later, Rudolf Flesch, an Austrian-born author and proponent of plain English, published *Why Johnny Can't Read*. He shared Hersey's distress about the state of reading instruction, but his proposed solution was that schools return to a phonics-only regimen. His book became a best seller.

John Hersey and Rudolf Flesch were not educators, and yet they brought forth a discussion that had for decades been held only in elementary schools and on college campuses. Suddenly the debate about the best way to teach reading was fodder for coffee shop conversations and newspaper headlines. Policymakers and parents alike became aware and involved. And with that the Reading Wars ignited.

What prompted such a strong response in this particular time in history? The population was rising rapidly with the post–World War II baby boom, so schools were more stuffed than ever with learners at varying levels of reading skill. Television was on its way to becoming a ubiquitous home appliance, and along with it fear that it would ruin young minds. School integration was looming, thanks to the 1954 *Brown v. Board of Education* decision that ruled that racial segregation of public schools was unconstitutional. The Cold War was also heating up (the Russian launch of *Sputnik 1* happened in 1957), and that put pressure on schools to turn out the best and brightest minds in the world, or at least better and brighter than the Russians.

The definition of functional literacy was also on the rise. In the 1940s the baseline was considered to be a fourth-grade reading level (this was generally a condition of military enlistment, though that was thrown aside as the United States became involved in World War II). In 1952 the US Census Bureau raised it to a sixth-grade level. Then, in the early '60s, the US Board of Education raised it again, this time to the eighth-grade level. Teachers of older struggling readers were aiming at a moving target.

It was in this climate of anxiety in which Hersey and Flesch wrote their respective works. Both were addressing a general audience, so their writing was largely absent of in-depth statistical evidence of the supposed reading crisis. Instead they told stories and presented opinions that, while anecdotal, were compelling and tapped into their audiences' generalized sense of worry. As celebrated reading expert Jeanne Chall wrote in *Learning to Read: The Great Debate*, it was a case of "emotion where reason should prevail." Flesch and Hersey did agree on two major points. One was that there was a literacy crisis, and the other was that the stories in the school primers of the time were woefully inadequate.

Here's where a brief digression into the history of school reading materials might be worthwhile. The earliest individual reading aid was the horn book, essentially a single sheet of paper affixed to a rectangular piece of wood. The paper typically contained the alphabet, sometimes accompanied by digraphs (two-letter sound combinations like "th" and "ay") and prayers or proverbs. Students were first taught the names of the letters, then the sounds; spelling was a prerequisite to reading. Horn books remained in use through the eighteenth century, but eventually gave way to primers, which were also religious by nature. Early versions were used in churches, and often contained the Apostles' Creed, the Lord's Prayer, the Ten Commandments, and Psalms. When the printing press began to make mass production possible (and inexpensive), the horn book and primer were combined into a school text designed to teach students to read, as well as provide theological instruction.

The New England Primer, first published in Boston in the late 1600s, served as the template and exemplar of this type of textbook. It would dominate reading instruction in the colonies for the next 150 years. It was followed by similarly constructed books such as Noah Webster's popular *American Spelling Book* (a.k.a. the Blue-Backed Speller), and the *McGuffy Reader*. Both of these, like the *New England Primer*, contained religious material, at least initially. The transition to secular stories (fairy tales, myths, fables) and non-spiritual morality lessons was gradual, but steady, from the mid-1800s into the twentieth century. All through this time, reading was viewed as a passive process. Partly out of the necessity of a multiage one-room schoolhouse, a child was taught to read by listening and reciting. She didn't engage with, challenge, or discuss the merits of what she was reading, as it was assumed to be ironclad wisdom.

This changed gradually as well, actually flipping to the opposite approach, in which the teacher now served as a guide to help the child discover her own interpretation of a text's message. This coincided with a shift toward scaffolding the reading process. In the 1930s the growth of educational psychology led to new notions about child development (and indeed a view of there being such a thing as "childhood"). This in turn revolutionized the way reading was taught. With the advent of the *Elson-Gray Reader*, published in 1936 by Scott Foresman, came the idea of a complete basal reading instruction system. The curriculum aimed to teach reading fundamentals, including phonics (though not in isolation, the way Flesch advocated). There were exercises for children to practice skills, and texts aimed at a child's grade level. This meant that the very early stories were simple enough to encourage students to dive in, even perhaps without solid knowledge of letter sounds, instead relying on the pictures, context, and the child's knowledge of a handful of words to guide them through. Though the texts were no longer religious in nature, they nonetheless presented characters and situations that were "wholesome" and "harmless." The stories almost always concerned children and their pets capering through various domestic situations. Dick, Jane, and Spot.

It's exactly those stories that Rudolf Flesch and John Hersey found so appalling. Hersey wrote that the children in the Elson-Gray readers were unnaturally well behaved and cheerful, and that the books presented a view of life "that does not correspond with reality." He also felt that pedagogy behind the books was suspect, with little to no sense of curricular design or philosophy, instead presenting literacy concepts "higgledy-piggledy."

One instructional fundamental of these readers was the sight word method, where a burgeoning reader receives repeated exposure to common words such as see, like, you, go, up, and so forth. This is where Flesch's complaint mostly lay. He felt the overreliance on sight words resulted in material that didn't feel genuine: "They are artificial sequences of words—meaningless, stupid, totally uninteresting to a six-year-old child or anyone else," he wrote. The text was comprised of excessive unnatural repetition along the lines of,

Jane said, "Oh, look!
See it go.
See it go up."
"Up, up," said Sally.
"Go up, up, up."

Flesch said, "This sort of strung-out prose has no resemblance any more to normal English."

Hersey's article also railed on the brightly painted illustrations that accompanied the Dick and Jane stories. These pictures, by the likes of Eleanor Campbell, Keith Ward, and Robert Childress, were a vital element of the books, providing heavy visual support for the text. They also featured a clean suburban setting and characters that were all middle class and white. Hersey labeled the illustrations "uniform, bland, idealized, and terribly literal." He stated a wish for "pictures that widen rather than narrow the associative richness the children give to the words they illustrate" and mentioned John Tenniel, Howard Pyle, Dr. Seuss, and Walt Disney as exemplars of this sort of approach.

Of these, only Seuss and Disney were alive in 1954, and only the former was personally involved in creating books for children, so it's unlikely that Hersey had any true expectation of his call being taken literally.

And yet it was. His mention of Dr. Seuss would turn out to be both prescriptive and prescient, and the world of early reading would never be the same.

2

How William and Bennett Got Their Book (1957)

When a piece of art is wildly successful, people always want to know how it came about. The creator is asked about it repeatedly, from journalists and fans and friends alike, and in the repeated tellings, a myth gets created. Or, if Dr. Seuss is involved, multiple myths get created. Ted Geisel never quite told the story behind *The Cat in the Hat* the same way twice. In some versions, he blithely fabricated; in others, he stretched the truth like so much oobleck. But it's a worthwhile endeavor to attempt to extricate the truth, because doing so reveals the experiences that informed both *The Cat in the Hat* and Beginner Books.

Nearly every aspect of Theodor Geisel's school and professional life before 1957 was preparation for the writing of *The Cat in the Hat* and his role as editor of the series of books that followed. He had an interest in education (his initial ambition upon graduating college was to be a professor of English literature); he had directed and overseen the creative work of others (he was editor-in-chief of Dartmouth's humor magazine, the *Jack-O-Lantern*); he knew how to use humor both to sell things and to teach (he spent several years in advertising, and three years during World War II making educational films, cartoons, and pamphlets for soldiers); and by 1958 he had thirteen children's books published (his very first, *And to Think I Saw It on Mulberry Street*, could be considered a prototype Beginner Book, and in fact became one retroactively). And then there's the fact that many of the people he'd met along the way would eventually become involved with Beginner Books.

Of these, the one that looms most largely over Beginner Books is Ted's time in the US Army (1943–1946), when he was stationed in Hollywood, California, under the command of the director Frank Capra (*It Happened One Night, Mr.*

Smith Goes to Washington, It's a Wonderful Life). They were part of a Signal Corps unit—the Information and Education Division—assigned to create materials that informed and entertained their fellow soldiers. It was the first military unit ever to be comprised of only creative types. Ted joined a formidable group of talented people: authors John Cheever, Irving Wallace, James Hilton, William Saroyan, and Lillian Hellman; director John Huston; composer Meredith Wilson; screenwriter/producer Carl Foreman; Disney animators Philip Dey (P. D.) Eastman and Gene Fleury; and children's author W. Munro Leaf. They worked out of a leased movie studio near Sunset Boulevard and Western Avenue that they dubbed Fort Fox.

Ted was made head of the animation department and charged with producing content for biweekly newsreels that ran as part of the Army-Navy Screen Magazine. It was important to the military institutions that their soldiers and sailors knew why they were fighting, as well as how to approach various situations surrounding health and self-discipline. The unit came up with a way to entertain the troops while also educating them. They created a character named Private Snafu, a soldier who would teach the right way to do things by doing everything wrong. Working with civilian animators Chuck Jones, Friz Freling, Bob Clampett, and Frank Tashlin (all of whom worked on Leon Schlesinger's madcap Looney Tunes shorts before and after the war), the writers and artists created twenty-eight Private Snafu cartoons.

Given the talent that brought him to life, Private Snafu was very familiar. As writer Christopher Klein described him, Snafu had "the looks of Elmer Fudd and the voice of Bugs Bunny" (Looney Tunes actor Mel Blanc performed both characters). There's evidence of Ted's involvement in approximately ten of the shorts, most notably "Gripes," "Spies," "The Home Front," and "It's Murder, She Says" (which he wrote with Munro Leaf as an adaptation of an antimalaria pamphlet Ted had drawn). Nine of the Snafu shorts were presented in verse, and all of these came from Ted, with "Chow Hound" likely being a collaboration with Eastman.

In his Snafu cartoons, just as he would with Beginner Books, Ted combined entertainment and pedagogy. The soldiers who served as the audience for the Snafu shorts came from varied educational backgrounds, some of them having little to no schooling, so it was essential that the lessons be clear and easily digestible (through limited vocabulary, exaggeration, and slapstick humor). Ted also gained insights about storytelling that he would carry with him throughout the rest of his career, primarily learned from Capra himself. One was the importance of knowing your story: "The first thing you have to do in writing," he reported Capra telling him, "is find out if you're saying anything."

Statuettes of Private Snafu were "the Fort Fox version of an Academy Award," according to Judith and Neil Morgan's book *Dr. Seuss and Mr. Geisel*. This particular one belonged to Phil Eastman. Courtesy Tony Eastman.

The other was how to work out a story visually. "He taught me conciseness, and I learned a lot about the juxtaposition of words and visual images," Ted recalled. Indeed, from this point forward, all of Ted's books would be storyboarded in the way a film was.

Ted's experience with these shorts and his subsequent work creating documentary films *Your Job in Germany* and *Our Job in Japan* (later expanded into the 1948 Oscar-winning documentary *Design for Death*) were formative and essential in the eventual development of *The Cat in the Hat* and Beginner Books. He learned what worked and what didn't (in 1974 he told writer Carolyn See about at anti-VD film he'd helped create that ended up making "no sense whatever" and was never shown). And his experiences traveling in Japan and Germany had given him a unique perspective on educational philosophy. He saw firsthand the dangers of educational systems that valued rote learning and conformity over all else. His conclusion was that children—just like the soldiers—learned best through fun, play, and nonsense.

Another way Ted's World War II experiences fostered Beginner Books was more pedestrian, but no less impactful. In his travels, he'd met William E. Spaulding, also in the Information and Education Division but stationed in Washington, DC. Spaulding's army stint was just a brief aside in what would prove to be a long tenure at Houghton Mifflin. By 1954 Spaulding was director of the publisher's educational children's books division. When he read John

Hersey's *Life* article and saw his former colleague's name, the proverbial light-bulb appeared above his head.

Spaulding had an educational pedigree. His father, Frank Spaulding, had served as superintendent in several large school districts around the country before settling in as chair of the Yale school of education. William himself had graduated from Harvard in 1919. He set up a meeting with Ted in Boston in the spring of 1955, and over dinner he explained his vision of an early reader that would both teach and engage, just as the Private Snafu shorts had informed and amused. Spaulding figured that if Ted could apply his energy and inventiveness within the confines of a book with a limited vocabulary, the result would be early reading magic. "Write me a book that first-graders can't put down!" Ted reported Spaulding as saying.

Ted was intrigued, both by the challenge of severely limiting his writing vocabulary and by the idea of doing something in the realm of education. Though he had quickly abandoned a post-college ambition to be a teacher, his interest in education kept manifesting itself—he had already pitched two educational book ideas to Random House unsuccessfully. One was a textbook for teachers, and the other was a book about the ridiculousness of spelling rules called *I Don't Spelk Very Welk*.

Ted had also been thinking about writing a book for a younger audience than he normally did. In the summer of 1949, Ted had participated in the University of Utah's second annual Writer's Conference, giving lectures and teaching workshops over a ten-day span. The experience was formative. Lecturing about his work had given him one of his first chances at articulating his philosophy of creating books for children, manifesting most prominently in his address "Mrs. Mulvaney and the Billion Dollar Bunny." In this talk, Ted gave a "satirical account of the origin and subsequent swift acclaim" of a cutesy, fatuous tome called *Bunny, Bunny, Bunny, Bunny, Bunny, Bunny, Bunny*. As with the Snafu shorts, he was teaching by showing what not to do.

He met his fellow speakers, including Wallace Stegner and Vladimir Nabokov (he is said to have gotten along famously with the latter), but also a Salt Lake City teacher named Libby Childs, who introduced herself to Ted after his first lecture. Ted ended up going along on a swimming outing to the Great Salt Lake with Libby, her husband, Orlo, and their three-year-old son, Brad. On the drive, Brad recited what was then Ted's most recent book—*Thidwick the Big-Hearted Moose*—from memory. Astonished, Ted is reported to have incredulously commented, "I don't write for kids that young. How does he do it?" Seuss expert Charles Cohen posits that this experience happening while

Ted was in the midst of formulating his writing philosophy started him on the path of considering writing for an even younger audience (as we'll soon see, Cohen's theory is supported by the fact that Ted ended up using Orlo's name in an article describing how he came to write *The Cat in the Hat*).

But Ted didn't commit to Spaulding then and there. By that point Ted had been working with Random House and its publisher Bennett Cerf for over fifteen years, and he enjoyed great creative freedom there. Doing a book at a publisher other than Random House would have been akin to betrayal. Cerf would have to agree to it, and Ted didn't think that was likely.

Spaulding didn't give in. He got in touch with Cerf, and the two managed to work out a deal: Ted would do the first-grade reader, and Houghton Mifflin would get the rights to sell the book to schools while Random House handled bookstore sales. Spaulding had his experts work up three lists of 220 words each, the first comprised of sight words that most first graders would know, the second of groups of "family" rhyming words such as make, rake, and take; and the third of phonetically decodable words. This was not just guesswork; Spaulding was well aware of Rudolf Flesch's drum-beating about phonics. By including sight words *and* decodable words, the three lists cannily acknowledged both sides of the reading wars.

Ted got the lists from Spaulding, but didn't start in on them until finishing up work on his thirteenth children's book, *If I Ran the Circus*. What happened when he did finally pick up the lists is where it becomes difficult to separate the truth from the exaggeration from the outright fabrication.

Much of the confusion comes from the fact that Ted published two separate accounts of *The Cat in the Hat*'s creative genesis in two separate newspapers on the very same day. On November 17, 1957, eight months after the book had been published to wide acclaim, "How Orlo Got His Book" appeared in the *New York Times*, and "My Hassle with the First Grade Language" in the *Chicago Tribune*. Despite the facetious nature of both essays, a comparison of the similarities between the two results in a fairly clear picture of Ted's process.

Both articles are centered around six-year-old boys—Orlo and Norval—who are desperately in need of books that they are both able and have a desire to read. Ted presents Orlo more as a catchall everychild than an actual person, whereas in "My Hassle . . ." Norval is a specific child, Ted's nephew, he says, though Ted's actual nephew—Teddy Owens—was only one year old in 1957. Both essays briefly and humorously reference the reading wars before speaking to the low quality of books the boys have available at their reading level (in "Orlo" it's the fictional *Bunny, Bunny, Bunny*; in "My Hassle" it's "old dull" Dick and Jane). Both pieces mention television, but less as a rival to books than as something that widens a child's vocabulary and worldliness. Thanks to television, he writes, "Orlo, at 6, has seen more of life than his great-grandfather had seen when he died at the age of 90."

When it comes to the writing process, the similarities between the two accounts continue, but fascinating differences also emerge. In "Orlo," Ted was so distressed by the problem of first-grade readers that, he claims, "I put on my Don Quixote suit and went out on a crusade" to fix the problem (Quixote's name, of course, is synonymous with lost causes). But in "Hassle," Ted claims to have been "flung into the mixer [of the reading wars], quite by accident." Both are true in their own way; once the problem was brought to his attention, Ted threw himself behind the cause, but he hadn't sought it out on his own, nor did he quite know the extent of the debate. Things start to line up again when Ted writes about the overconfidence and naiveté with which he initially tackled the task (in "Orlo," he predicts he'll knock the thing out in two weeks), followed by the grim reality of wrestling with the word list (in "Hassle," he says, "I saw the word sick and that's how I felt.").

Both essays detail his early, unsuccessful attempts to produce a viable story from the words on the list, but here another key difference emerges. In "Orlo," he details a book called *Queen Zebra*, which he abandoned after realizing neither word from the title was on the list, followed by a story about a bird, though he claims he couldn't use the word "bird." In "Hassle," his first thought was to write a nonfiction book about climbing Mount Everest, while his second was about king and queen cats. Judith and Neil Morgan's biography of Ted reports that he did work on a book called *Queen Zebra* and that the words of the title were favorites of his from childhood, but it's hard to know if Ted told them that, they saw the unfinished manuscript, or if they were simply repeating the account from "Orlo." If it's true, that means only the account in "Orlo" is true, which would mean "Hassle" was a fabrication. The writing and publication of two separate accounts is strange enough as it is (though it certainly fits with Ted's prankster nature), but it would be even odder to have one of them actually be the "right" one.

What we do know for sure—and what both essays detail—is that it took Ted a very long time to create *The Cat in the Hat*, over a year in fact. Indeed, the punchline of "Hassle" is that by the time Ted finishes his first-grade reader, little Norval has long since graduated first grade and is studying calculus.

Part of the protracted process was coming up with an idea. In later interviews, Ted liked to say that his breakthrough came from finding the first two words on the list that rhymed, "cat" and "hat." But this telling ignores the fact that Spaulding had given Ted three word lists, and that Ted had some leeway to add his own words if they were given proper context or illustrative support (surely "bird" and "zebra" fall into that category).

What seems more likely is that this was the abridged version of the true story. In a 1957 *Saturday Evening Post* profile by Robert Cahn, Ted claimed that the idea arrived after six months of failed attempts. Near his breaking point, he began rifling through a pile of sketches in hopes of finding inspiration. He was arrested by one of a cat wearing a stovepipe hat, quickly searched his lists for "cat" and "hat," found both, and joyfully began working from there. Dr. Philip Nel, author of *The Annotated Cat: Under the Hats of Seuss and His Cats*, believes this account to be more plausible than the word-list version, especially considering that several of Ted's other books arose from drawings. In a 1989 *Horn Book* interview, Ted said of his books: "Mine always start with a doodle."

As to where that doodle came from, well, we can only speculate, but Charles Cohen, in his *The Seuss, the Whole Seuss, and Nothing but the Seuss*, shrewdly examines some of the possible inspirations for the mischievous feline's aesthetic and personality, including Felix the Cat cartoons and Howard R. Garis's Uncle Wiggily stories. Judith and Neil Morgan add that during Ted's elevator ride at Houghton Mifflin for that first meeting with William Spaulding, he was struck by the operator, who wore "a leather half-glove and a secret smile." He ended up giving his cat those same attributes. In recent years Philip Nel has explored the connections between blackface minstrelsy and the Cat in the Hat's appearance and demeanor.

Having mercifully arrived at what seemed like a workable idea for the book, Ted next got bogged down by the word list. "There are no adjectives!" he's reported to have wailed to his wife, Helen, as he worked. Accounts vary on how many words he chose from Houghton Mifflin's lists. There are 236 different words in *The Cat in the Hat*; various tellings place the number of words he used from the lists between 199 and 225, with Seuss himself claiming 223.

In any case, the word list was a huge impediment to Ted's writing process, but the problem was exacerbated by his perfectionism. Ted held himself to extremely high standards, and this was at least partially because of his philosophy of writing for children. He believed that, because children's books were so much shorter than adult books, each word and sentence held that much more weight. He'd attribute this way of thinking to his first Random House editor, Saxe Commins: "He helped me to realize that a paragraph in a children's book is equivalent to a chapter in an adult book." Ted also felt that kids were harsher critics than grown-ups. He told Digby Diehl in 1972 that "children catch on more quickly when you're doing sloppy writing than adults do. They just walk away. Kids are a much more demanding audience, because they don't have to be polite."

He was known to revise repeatedly and obsessively, sometimes coming close to throwing out fully completed manuscripts. He constructed his books, both words and pictures, extremely carefully and thoughtfully. For a sixty-page book he claimed he'd often write five hundred pages, and that he'd throw away 90 percent or more of his drawings. When a book was done, he was often so full of self-doubt that he wouldn't sleep the night before hand-delivering it to Random House. "The 'creative process' consists for me of two things—time and sweat," he said. Bennett Cerf was fond of labeling Ted as "the only genius on my list," but Ted's response was, "If I'm a genius, why do I have to work so hard? I know my stuff looks like it was all rattled off in 28 seconds, but every word is a struggle and every sentence is like the pangs of birth."

As for the story itself, Ted seems to have drawn inspiration from the very reason he was given the assignment to write the book, namely that children were bored with the books they were being given. And so we start with two bored kids. The boy is not named, since he's the narrator, but his sister is called Sally (which Nel points out was the name of Dick and Jane's younger sister). Their mother is out on an errand, and it's raining. In June 1955, as he was just beginning to stew over ideas for *The Cat in the Hat*, Ted was presented with an honorary doctorate from Dartmouth. In the accompanying speech, it was said that "As author and artist, you single-handedly have stood as Saint George between a generation of parents and the demon dragon of exhausted children on a rainy day." He never said as much, but it seems very likely that an idea fired in Ted's subconscious when he heard those words.

Another way the book directly assaults Dick and Jane is in its rejection of their hermetic, placid world. Dick, Jane, and friends weren't bored children, but they certainly were boring. Ted knew that to appeal to his audience he'd have to have some naughty behavior. "I think a youngster likes to read about someone who is bad for a change . . . kids respond to a little humor, to a crazy situation . . . ," he told *Parents* magazine in 1960. And this is where the Cat's personality began to develop. He wanted his Cat to bring a spirit of anarchy without being malevolent, which is a difficult balance to maintain. Michael Frith shared a handwritten letter from Ted that expands on who the Cat is (and isn't):

> He is not a smartass. He is not loud. He never yells. He never shows off in a bragging manner. He is glib, suave, well-educated. He gets carried away with his enthusiasm. However he does an occasional pratfall. He may break an occasional

dish . . . Always gentle. He is always surprised whenever he messes anything up. His gestures, although flamboyant, are not braggadocios. They are boulevardier.

Ironically, the philosophy of humor to which Ted subscribed came from Dick and Jane's creator, May Hill Arbuthnot. In her 1947 book *Children and Books*, she laid out a list of what children find funny: sounds, surprise, grotesque, incongruous, falling down, absurdity, and horseplay. The Cat is the epitome of all of these. Maryann Weidt, in her 1994 biography of Seuss, mentioned the fact that one of Ted's favorite books as a child was Peter Newell's *The Hole Book* (1908) in which young Tom Potts fires a bullet that improbably travels through the town, inciting a series of humorous mishaps. One wonders if subconsciously Ted was trying to replicate that spirit of chaos that so arrested him as a child, but with the Cat and his Things as the bullet.

Besides substance, *The Hole Book* may also have provided style. Nel points out that Newell's anapestic verse is replicated in *The Cat in the Hat* (and so many other Seuss books). Ted himself said of what he learned from Newell: "You establish a rhythm, and that tends to make the kids want to go on. If you break the rhythm, the child feels unfulfilled." As Cott wrote, Seuss's anapestic tetrameter verse "embodies movement and swiftness." Once they get the pattern of the verse, early readers can anticipate the rhymes that are coming, teaching them phonemic awareness and use of context. Nel points out that the lengthy list of things the Cat picks up on page 58 (" . . . the cake, and the rake, and the gown, and the milk . . .") serves as a clandestine vocabulary list, something that concluded each Dick and Jane book. *The Cat in the Hat* wasn't so much throwing out the ideas behind Dick and Jane as he was improving upon them.

The sales materials and presentation of *The Cat in the Hat* played up the educational bon-a-fides of the book. The dust jacket of the first edition featured a biography of Ted on the inside cover flap that highlighted his educational background and his one-time wish to be a professor of English literature, calling education his "first love." The penultimate page of early editions features an outline of the Cat's head and more information about the book's soundly comprehensive educational design, highlighting its mix of words that are "familiar" and ones that could be figured out by "using the sense of what they are reading in conjunction with simple phonics." It goes on to say that "the rhythm, rhyme, and strong interest pull" of the book would help kids to read it independently. And if that weren't enough, the back of the dust jacket was adorned with endorsements from education professionals, along the lines of Columbia University professor Dr. Roma Gans's assertion that "*The Cat in the Hat* is a many faceted gem—easy to read for beginning sprouts, rippling with rhythm and humor, and so appealing that it will be read, read—and re-read."

In contrast to his usual eleventh-hour anxiety about a finished manuscript, Ted was very optimistic about the prospects of *The Cat in the Hat*. In a June 11, 1956, letter, he wrote "we've got a possibility of making a tremendous noise in the noisy discussion of Why Johnny Can't Read." He thought this was so, he indicated, by Houghton Mifflin's positive reaction to the book. This would turn out to be ironic. Houghton Mifflin released their edition to schools a few weeks ahead of the March 1 Random House version that went out to bookstores, retailing for an even two dollars.

There are multiple perspectives from which to look at the reception of and reaction to *The Cat in the Hat*. First is sales. Houghton Mifflin's school edition was met with little interest. Dr. Seuss was a known name in educational circles, but not a terribly respected one. His Caldecott Honor Awards in 1948, 1950, and 1951 (for *McElligot's Pool, Bartholomew and the Oobleck*, and *If I Ran the Zoo*) represented a brief flirtation with acceptance by the gatekeepers of children's literature, but his next five books leading up to *The Cat in the Hat* would be ignored. In fact, he'd never come close to the Caldecott again. This may partially explain why education professionals were slow to embrace the book. In Carin T. Ford's biography of Dr. Seuss, Professor Susan Mandel Glazer says educators were lukewarm because the book was a fantasy, a genre that wasn't considered as legitimate as it is now. The same could be said of the fact that the book was humorous.

Teachers may have balked, but parents and kids went gaga. The initial print run of 12,000 sold out immediately, and a second printing followed within a month (dropping five cents in cover price, to boot). Soon the book was selling 12,000 copies a month. The unfortunate William Spaulding, whose idea it all had been, was on the wrong side of a massive hit. Though he'd likely known kids would love the book, what he hadn't anticipated was the role of parents.

Besides their mutual rancor for Dick and Jane, Flesch and Hersey had both encouraged parents to become more involved in their children's literacy development. This tapped into a growing fear of two bogeymen of the time, television and comic books, both of which were seen as direct competitors for books. Comic books were nothing new in the late 1950s, but the fear of them was, with psychiatrist Frederick Werthem's alarmist *Seduction of the Innocent* detailing all the lurid content of comics and their potentially harmful effect on young minds. The book came out in 1954, dovetailing perfectly with Hersey's article, Flesch's book, and the rapid proliferation of televisions in the home. The percentage of US homes with televisions had leapt from 9 percent in 1950 to 72 percent in 1956. This brought consternation from moms and dads who saw their children fall under the spell of the box that provided nearly constant entertainment of questionable value, and could potentially distract or prevent kids from reading. Into this cocktail went the Cold War (the late 1957 launches of *Sputniks I* and *II* stoked the fear that the United States was falling behind educationally) and the fact that in 1957 there were over 11 million five- to seven-year-olds in the United States.

The conditions were thus perfect to sell parents a book that purported to encourage kids to read. As Ted put it later, "Parents understood better than school people the necessity for this kind of reader."

For his part, Ted was not opposed either to comic books or TV. He loved the art form of the comic strip, from which comic books weren't far removed. In his "Mrs. Mulvaney and the Billion Dollar Bunny" speech, he gave comic book writers and artists credit for connecting with young readers. As for television, through his life he consistently praised the potential of the medium, just as he had in "My Hassle with the First Grade Language," for its expansion of both the background experience and vocabularies of its young viewers.

Of course it helped greatly that kids were asking for the book, and this is another aspect of the reaction to *The Cat in the Hat*. As Ted playfully put it, *The Cat in the Hat* became a hit through "playground word of mouth." And though it was too late for Houghton Mifflin's school edition of the book, teachers did eventually come around to the book when they saw how it excited their students. Rita Roth, who was an elementary teacher in the 1960s, wrote of her students, "There was no way I could ignore their enthusiasm as they read and reread *The Cat in the Hat* nor their foot-dragging as they approached the basal reader."

It seems that *The Cat in the Hat* had pleased almost everyone, but perhaps most remarkably it won praise from all sides of the reading wars, including the men who made it a national conversation. In 1959 Rudolf Flesch, likely taken in by Ted's phonics-friendly gift for rhyme, wrote that Seuss books would still be read in one hundred years (a "no duh" prediction now; not so much then) and that the man himself was "a genius pure and simple." John Hersey, who could reasonably be considered a grandfather of the book, said that *The Cat in the Hat* was "a harum-scarum masterpiece" and "a gift to the art of reading." Even May Hill Arbuthnot had praise for the book that took aim at her babies. Recommending it in her *Children's Reading in the Home* (1969) she wrote that

The Cat in the Hat had an ending that "brings every young reader back to a rereading of this completely satisfying nightmare."

The runaway success of *The Cat in the Hat* had many impacts and implications (it turned Dr. Seuss into a genuine superstar, it caused the sales of all of his other books to skyrocket, it made Random House the number one children's book publisher in the United States), but none was more significant than the fact that it revealed a market desperate for more books like it. Ted and Helen (a former educator herself) both recognized this immediately. So did Bennett Cerf's wife, Phyllis.

3

The Birth of
Beginner Books (1958)

The Cat in the Hat wouldn't have existed without William Spaulding, Bennett Cerf, and Ted, but Beginner Books wouldn't have existed without Phyllis Cerf.

Phyllis Cerf was in her early forties in 1957, and had already lived at least three separate lives, including a tumultuous childhood, a stint as a Hollywood ingénue, and a gig writing radio serials. Phyllis was born Helen Brown Nichols on April 1916 in Kansas City, Missouri. When she was ten months old, there was a natural gas explosion on her family's block. Her father, Albert Brown, was killed, and baby Helen was thrown across the house. She bore a small moon-shaped scar on her face for the rest of her life.

Her mother, Verda, received a large settlement from the city and moved Helen to Oklahoma City not long after. Verda wasn't a stable parent, running through a succession of husbands, so at the age of sixteen Helen moved to California to live with her aunt Lela (Verda's sister) and cousin, Ginger Rogers. Yes, *that* Ginger Rogers. In 1932 Ginger had already been a performer on vaudeville and was on the verge of movie stardom. Ginger's given name was Virginia, and family lore said that the nickname came about because Phyllis couldn't say "Virginia" correctly as a child, instead calling her cousin "Badinda," which later morphed into "Ginga."

Once they were living together, Ginger returned the favor by giving her little cousin a new name, Phyllis Fraser, and then helping her get started in acting. Phyllis would appear in over twenty movies in the 1930s, including *Little Men* (1934), *Winds of the Wasteland* (1936), and *Vivacious Lady* (1938).

For a while, Phyllis led the life of a Hollywood actress, palling around with the likes of Judy Garland, Betty Grable, and Anne Shirley. She dated Ben

Alexander, the former child actor famed for his portrayal of Officer Frank Smith on the 1950s version of *Dragnet*. But it wasn't long before Phyllis realized her acting career wasn't going anywhere (the contrast to Ginger's success couldn't have been sharper), and that she didn't especially enjoy the work.

She was both intelligent and ambitious, so she wanted to find something that would challenge and inspire her. She moved to New York in 1939 and landed a job writing daytime radio serials for the advertising agency McCann-Erickson. It just so happened that Ted Geisel, who was then still in the midst of his stint in advertising, was also working at the agency and though he was rarely in the office, he had one drawer reserved there which happened to be located in Phyllis's desk.

Nineteen thirty-nine was the year that Bennett Cerf lured Ted away from Vanguard Press to Random House, and it was the year Phyllis met Bennett Cerf. Harold Ross, editor of the *New Yorker*, was good friends with Phyllis's aunt Lela, and had an on-again-off-again relationship with Ginger Rogers. That summer he invited Lela and Ginger to his house in North Stamford for the weekend, and they brought Phyllis along. Harold got in touch with Bennett, asking him to come up, too, and "take care of that god damn kid cousin." Bennett was reluctant, but worked out a deal with Ross. He'd come along if the *New Yorker* reviewed three upcoming Random House books, and if Harold would play him backgammon for money (Ross was apparently a "dreadful gambler" who always lost).

When Bennett arrived, everyone was swimming at the lake. When he glimpsed Phyllis in her red-and-white-checked bathing suit, he was instantly smitten. "She was absolutely the cutest-looking kid I'd seen in a long, long time," he wrote in his memoir. He went right over and kissed her, but Phyllis was far from pleased. "She smacked me in the face," Bennett recalled. "That's the way we met." He recovered from the rough start and spent most of that weekend talking to Phyllis. The couple, she twenty-three, he forty-one, married a year later.

Bennett gave his wife the nickname that stuck for the rest of her life. Phyllis had quickly established herself in the marriage as highly opinionated and strong willed. This manifested in small ways (decisions over decorating their new townhouse) and big (upon learning that Bennett's father, Gustave, had a girlfriend, Phyllis ordered him to propose to her immediately, and he did). Many years into their marriage, when Phyllis issued a particularly firm command, Bennett off-handedly referred to his wife as "The General." The name stuck, so much so that their friend Frank Sinatra presented Phyllis with a cap that read "Boss" and had five stars emblazoned on it. Phyllis wasn't shy to sport it.

Phyllis Cerf and Frank Sinatra on his yacht circa the late 1960s. Photo by and courtesy Chris Cerf.

Their first son, Christopher, came along in 1941 and motherhood consumed much of the next years of Phyllis's life. But she also published five children's books between 1942 and 1947. The first two were among the first wave of Little Golden Books in 1942, *Mother Goose* (Little Golden Book number 4, illustrated by Miss Elliott) and *This Little Piggy and Other Counting Rhymes* (Little Golden Book number 12, illustrated by Roberta Paflin). The third—*ABC and Counting Book*—was published by Random House in 1946 with illustrations by Jack Sarkin. Though it was primarily an alphabet and numbers book, the text included pages instructing parents on how to help their children learn to write letters and numbers. *The Story of Dimples and Cock Sure*, also published in 1946, had an unusual and innovative concept in which the story—about an elephant and a bird—was presented with text only, and blank

Phyllis, Christopher, and Bennett Cerf as photographed by Philippe Halsman in 1945. Courtesy Chris Cerf and the Philippe Halsman Archive. © Philippe Halsman Archive.

spaces where the pictures should be. The idea was that child readers could create their own illustrations. In these latter two books especially one can see glimpses of Phyllis's future in Beginner Books.

Bennett and Phyllis's second son, Jonathan, was born in 1946, and Phyllis would publish only one more book, *Treasury of Games, Quizzes, and Puzzles* in 1947. As her sons each reached school age, Phyllis took a keen interest in the development of their literacy. "She was very very interested in how kids would learn to read," Chris Cerf recalls. "That partly came, I think, from her raising my brother and me. She was always very interested in our reading progress." Not content to be a stay-at-home mom—Bennett often told her she was too smart to just sit around playing cards with her friends—Phyllis kept busy by writing a celebrity column for *Newsday* (often about her own encounters with famous folks) and a regular household hints feature in *Good Housekeeping* magazine.

She also charmed the authors Bennett brought around. When she met William Faulkner for the first time, Phyllis looked him over and said, "Look at that hole in your sock." The two formed a fast friendship, with the southern gentleman bringing her flowers every time he visited. Phyllis took author photos for dust jackets, and became Bennett's trusted advisor on literary matters. "I began to rely more and more on what she would say about manuscripts,"

Bennett revealed in his memoir, "and when I was in doubt about one that might interest her, I would very anxiously await her approval." One manuscript that he didn't need to wait long on was *The Cat in the Hat*. Phyllis was instantly thrilled, smitten, and inspired by its approach to literacy. Right away she envisioned a whole line of early readers, with *The Cat in the Hat* as a template. She had been itching for a cause of her own, and had always wanted to make a positive difference in the world, and in *The Cat in the Hat* she saw a way to achieve both goals.

Phyllis first took the idea to Louise Bonino, head of Random House's juvenile department. Louise didn't think the idea would work, but Phyllis was not one to take no for an answer. She decided to go directly to the source, and asked Bennett to set up a meeting between her and his star author.

Sometime in early 1957, Phyllis and Ted sat down for lunch at the swanky Manhattan restaurant Quo Vadis. In addition to their shared history at McCann-Erickson, the pair had met socially many times over the years and were friendly and familiar, but this was their first serious discussion about business. Phyllis made her pitch: A new publishing house—she and Bennett had chosen the name Beginner Books—solely devoted to creating early readers. The idea, she assured him, was a guaranteed moneymaker. How much Ted cared about the financial prospects of the line is debatable, but he was definitely intrigued by the creative challenge and the potential educational impact. According to Judith and Neil Morgan, Ted was "convinced he could help other authors find the key that he had discovered with *Cat*."

When the lunch was over, a handshake deal was struck. Phyllis would be the chief executive officer and Ted would be president of Beginner Books. Ted had negotiated for Helen Geisel to be brought in as an equal third partner with the official title of secretary/treasurer. This move, assuming that Helen would take his side, gave Ted a tiebreaker in any matters creative, business, or otherwise, and it would later prove to be significant. Random House would put up $200,000 to start, in exchange for shares for Bennett, his Random House cofounder Donald Klopfer, sales manager Lew Miller, and the company itself. Once the papers were signed, things went into motion pretty much immediately.

But before we get to that, let's consider Helen, because just as Beginner Books wouldn't have existed without Phyllis Cerf, it couldn't have flourished without Helen Palmer Geisel. The two women were largely opposites in personality, but were similar in other ways. Both were strong willed, both stood at 5 foot, 3 inches tall, both authored Little Golden Books in the 1940s, and both lost their fathers at a young age.

Helen Marion Palmer was born to George and Marie Palmer in Brooklyn in 1898. Her only sibling, Robert, was two years older. The family lived in a brownstone in the Bedford-Stuyvesant neighborhood, at 92 Hancock Street right next door to Helen's paternal grandparents. Her father and grandfather (Dr. Adoniram Judson Palmer) were both ophthalmologists, and they shared a practice. Her mother was an active member of both the nearby Central Congregational Church and the Chautaqua Society, which encouraged "intellectual and moral self-improvement and civic involvement."

Helen's childhood was difficult. She contracted polio as a child, but eventually recovered fully, left with—in Helen's own words—"a lopsided smile" as a reminder. George Palmer died suddenly when Helen was only eleven years old. Her grandfather died less than two years later. Neither man had left a will, so the family was forced to move to a small apartment several blocks away until the estate was settled.

Despite these early challenges, Helen excelled in school. She first attended Adelphi College, then transferred to Wellesley as a sophomore, studying literature and graduating in 1920 with honors. She got a position teaching English at Girls High School in Brooklyn, and stayed there three years before enrolling at Oxford University—her mother coming along to live with her for the first year. It was there that Helen met Ted, who was at Oxford in an ill-fated attempt to become a professor of English literature.

The pair ended up in the same literature class together, where one day Helen noticed Ted undertaking a humorous interpretation of Uriel the angel from John Milton's *Paradise Lost*. Ted spent more time drawing than taking substantive notes in class, and as Helen flipped through she glibly suggested he should be pursuing art instead of academia. "What you really want to do is draw," she'd remarked. Ted and Helen became a couple in short order, and it wasn't long before Ted dropped out of Oxford. Helen stayed to finish her master's degree while Ted essentially larked about Europe, primarily Paris and Rome.

With Helen's degree complete, the couple made their way back to the United States, and married in late November 1927. She took a teaching position at a private girls' school—Mrs. Baird's—in Orange, New Jersey, while Ted started to build a career as a cartoonist and ad-man. Around the time of the publication of *And to Think That I Saw It on Mulberry Street*, Helen and Ted learned they would not be able to have children. They fought the disappointment by inventing imaginary offspring, among them Chrysanthemum-Pearl, aged eighty-nine months, and the dedicatee of *The 500 Hats of Bartholomew Cubbins*. They also treated Ted's niece Peggy (daughter of his older sister,

Marnie) as a "surrogate child," lavishing her with attention. They took her to the 1939 World's Fair in New York every day for a whole week.

The couple's move to California during World War II facilitated Helen's entrance into the world of children's literature. In 1944 she published *Walt Disney's Surprise Package* under the name H. Marion Palmer. The book contained adaptations of various projects the studio had in development, many of which—*The Wind in the Willows*, *Peter Pan*, and *Alice's Adventures in Wonderland*—came to fruition over the following decade (a few, like the intriguing fable "The Square World," never did). This began a five-year run of work for Helen at Disney. Her next two books were the direct result of a 1941 visit to Latin America by Walt Disney and sixteen animators. The trip came at the behest of President Franklin Roosevelt with a goal of spreading goodwill and slyly promoting capitalism in countries like Brazil and Argentina where fascism was gaining a foothold. Helen wrote an adaptation of the 1944 film that resulted from the trip, *The Three Caballaros*, as well as the travelogue *Donald Duck Sees South America*. Helen and Ted had visited South America themselves in the mid-1930s.

Helen also wrote adaptations of the 1946 film *Song of the South* (*Uncle Remus Stories*, 1947), and 1949's *So Dear to My Heart*. The latter was published as a Golden Book, one of four stories Helen did for that company in the late 1940s. The others were *Tommy's Wonderful Rides* (illustrated by J. P. Miller), *Bobby and His Airplanes* (illustrated by Tibor Gergley), and *Johnny's Machines* (illustrated by Cornelius DeWitt). By the end of the 1940s Helen had published as many children's books as Ted had, and in half the time.

In the midst of all this Helen helped Ted write *Design for Death* (which won them both an Oscar) and the couple moved to a pink stucco Mediterranean-style home in La Jolla, California, an affluent oceanside community in San Diego. Helen's robust writing career was suddenly cut short in early 1954 by the rapid onset of Guillain-Barre syndrome, which temporarily robbed her of speech and paralyzed her from the neck down. She spent some time in an iron lung, and slowly recovered over the next year, having to relearn how to walk and talk.

By the time of *The Cat in the Hat* and Ted's subsequent meeting with Phyllis Cerf, Helen had shifted focus from her own writing toward providing support for Ted's. According to a 1960 *New Yorker* profile by E. J. Kahn Jr., Helen took care of Ted's finances and correspondence, and served to both reassure him and rein him in. In a 1953 interview, Ted said, "She's a hard task master. Here I sit up all night writing that stuff, and she tears it to pieces the next morning. But she's a great editor and condenser. I couldn't get along without her." Now,

Ted and Helen with a young artist at the La Jolla Museum of Art in 1966. Courtesy and © San Diego History Center.

with Beginner Books, she'd be doing the same for other authors. Helen set up an office in the garage of their home on Mount Soledad in La Jolla as the headquarters of Beginner Books west.

Just as Beginner Books was starting up, in April 1957, Helen suffered a small stroke. When Ted finished his newest book (a little number called *How the Grinch Stole Christmas*) in June, he and Helen took off for a month's vacation in Honolulu. It was ostensibly a time for Helen to relax and recover, but the couple spent much of the time thinking about Beginner Books. Meanwhile Phyllis was doing her homework. She consulted with Dr. Adele Franklin, founder and director of the All-Day Neighborhood Schools program in the New York City Schools. She attended several educational conferences, making connections with teachers and scholars, and she started combing through the

The Villard Mansion, home of Beginner Books from 1958 to 1969. They were located on the top floor, in the dormer you can see sticking up. Courtesy of the Municipal Art Society.

word lists from the seven most commonly used primers, cross-referencing until she had a list of 379 common words to offer to authors.

Phyllis took up residence in the Villard Mansion at Madison Avenue and 51st Street that served as Random House's center of operations. Beginner Books' offices would be on the sixth floor, in what had once been the servants' quarters. She had the walls and stairwells painted blue, and Ted further decorated the place with humorous signs and invented nameplates—the stairs leading up to the office were labeled "Dr. Schmiercase" with an arrow pointing up (Dr. Outgo Schmiercase was the name Beginner Books would use on rejection letters).

4

I Can Read It All by Myself
(1958–1959)

Beginner Books launched in the fall of 1958 with five titles. In the lead-up, Phyllis, Helen, and Ted had lots of big and little decisions to make in designing their line of books. *The Cat in the Hat* served not only as a template philosophically, educationally, and creatively, but also physically. Like *Cat*, the first set of Beginner Books would be about 6 ½ x 9" in size, hardcover with a dust jacket, sixty-two story pages. They'd sell for just under $2. This was not cheap—at the time a Little Golden Book was 25 cents and a Giant Little Golden Book was 50 cents—but the hardcovers were sturdy and kid-proof, signaling something significant and lasting.

The Cat in the Hat also served as a template from a marketing standpoint. The success of the book at bookstores over the school market convinced Ted that the main audience for Beginner Books should be parents. Though they'd have a strong pedagogical design, Beginner Books would not aim to replace basals in the classroom, but instead have the goal of serving as practice and enrichment at home. Phyllis told *Publishers Weekly*, "We want to publish books that take up where textbooks leave off." They also wanted to capture the sense of fun and joy and barely controlled chaos that crackled throughout *The Cat in the Hat*. Phyllis added, "We want to produce books that any child in the first grade not only *can* read but will *want* to read."

Ironically, the new company put forth a daunting set of guidelines for their authors in order to achieve that sense of fun, joy, and chaos. Each story had to have a clear plot with a beginning, middle, and end and a "valid" problem and solution, as well as "dramatic conflict and suspense." The instructions given to new authors stressed that the stories should be funny. "If you can't make them laugh," it reads, "we'll settle for a good warm smile."

The text could not describe anything that wasn't pictured. Illustrators were tasked with telling the complete story with their drawings, and adding depth that wasn't in the text itself. This was to be achieved using one illustration per page, with each pair of pages interlocking design-wise. The illustrations themselves were to be largely black-lined with flat colors, like a cartoon, because Ted felt "that's how kids see things." Many of the author's usual tricks, such as advancing a story through multiple actions on a page or multiple characters speaking per page, were verboten because they were impossible to illustrate effectively.

A humorously illustrated short guide titled "A Few Suggestions for Authors Working on Beginner Books" tells authors to avoid overwriting actions and dialogue and make sure that every sentence advances the story. "Make your reader itch to find out what's going to happen next. Every right-hand page should leave the reader suspended and wanting more." The guide suggested that authors write their manuscripts out as the book itself would be presented, page for page, to help them map it out visually, a nod to Ted's tendency toward storyboarding.

And all of this was to be in the confines of the only barely flexible 379-word vocabulary list, from which authors were instructed to pick somewhere between 150 and 280 words. They were allowed 20 emergency words, with several restrictions. These emergency words couldn't have "ed," "ing," or "er" endings, couldn't be possessives nor contractions. Character names counted as part of the 20. The editorial guidelines suggested that these words be used in "strong context," be verbs or nouns rather than adjectives, be based on phonetic principle (in other words, easily decodable), and if at all possible rhyme with a word on the list.

The author instructions had this to say about working with the vocabulary limitations:

> WARNING: If you pay too much attention to the word list at the start, you're cooked. Read it over once or twice, then put it aside and think about the story you'd like to write . . . AFTER you have your story line is the time to go work with the word list. When you start to tell the story with this handful of small words, it will probably seem completely impossible. But it isn't. So don't get panicked and throw away the story.

Whether or not Ted wrote those words himself, it's clear that it was his own warning from experience.

So remember there are things no illustrator can do.

For example, he <u>cannot</u> illustrate more than one idea at a time. You cannot expect him to draw in one picture a man entering a room, then doing something, then leaving the room.

He can illustrate <u>only</u> the high point of any one action. So keep unnecessary actions out of your story.

Try to avoid unnecessary dialogue.

When you utilize dialogue, make it important and to the point. Someone speaks some words which are indispensable to the story and someone else has a positive reaction that speeds the story on its way.

A sample page from "A Few Suggestions for Authors Working on Beginner Books." Courtesy Michael Frith.

On top of what was expressly dictated to authors and illustrators, Ted also held fast to an instinctual and undefined set of standards. The characters were to be "vivid, believable, and consistent." There was to be no outright or over-bearing moral, though Ted acknowledged that every story had a moral inherently. He was also stridently opposed to anything he considered to be cute, saccharine, or whimsical; "bunny bunny books" he called them after his Utah speech. As the instructions for authors read, "Remember, always, that the six year old is your intellectual equal . . . if you talk-down to him, you lose him as an audience."

So the writers and illustrators for the first four official Beginner Books had their work cut out for them. The group was mostly comprised of up-and-coming writers and artists. Fritz Siebel was new to children's books. Benjamin Elkin and Marion Holland each had a handful of published books, but were both still in the first five years of their careers. Ted called on his old college friend Mike McClintock for a submission, returning the favor of Mike helping *And to Think I Saw It on Mulberry Street* to publication in 1937. Mike had lots of experience as an editor and a writer of nonfiction, but this was his first fiction story. Ted's Fort Fox compatriot P. D. Eastman—who had plenty of experience in animation but none in books—got in on the action as well. Only artist Katherine Evans was a veteran, having illustrated and/or written fifteen books since starting her career in the mid-1940s. Whether this group was picked for their potential malleability, because they had the best submissions, or both, it's difficult to know, but complications arose once the production process began.

The main problem that Beginner Books ran into from the start is while it was a noble intention to "systemize and formulate" what Ted did creatively on *The Cat in the Hat*, only Ted could make a Dr. Seuss book. Trying to copy him in verse or in visuals was a fool's errand. Ted had poured a great measure of himself into the process of creating *The Cat in the Hat*, and had learned a great deal. He thought he could pass that knowledge on to others, but he was a not a born teacher. Instead of guiding through inspiration, he tried to fit others' styles into his own pattern. He also took the work very seriously and didn't believe that just anybody could do it. As the Morgans wrote, "He regarded these books as an art form that grew more complex and intricate as it reached toward younger and younger readers."

So when the initial manuscripts came in and weren't to their liking, Ted and Helen initiated a repeated cycle of editing and revising to make the books meet Ted's exacting, and sometimes esoteric, standards. As the East coast team member, Phyllis was often the face of this process, and often she didn't agree with or fully understand what Ted was asking the authors to do. She had her own high standards, based in the research she'd done about early literacy, but found they often weren't in line with Ted's. She had imagined Beginner Books as a union of her careful research and Ted's "happy genius," but in practice those two things often clashed.

So did Ted and Phyllis's personalities. Both had large egos and both were accustomed to getting their way. Fitting for someone called "The General," Phyllis relished a battle. "She was extraordinarily charming when she wanted to be," Christopher Cerf says, "but also very combative when she wanted to be." Ted was the opposite. He despised confrontation and assiduously avoided it. The more famous he had become, the easier it had become for Ted to get his way, and so daily challenges from the iron-willed Phyllis quickly wore on him. In a 1960 letter to Bennett, Ted described Phyllis as Bennett's "combination U.S. Steel-Corporation-and-wife." It was not at all a recipe for a functional working relationship, and that dysfunction would play itself out in a myriad of ways big and small in the early years of Beginner Books.

The first five Beginner Books—*The Cat in the Hat Comes Back, A Fly Went By, The Big Jump and Other Stories, Sam and the Firefly,* and *A Big Ball of String*—went out into the world in October 1958, but even before they appeared anticipation was high. The runaway success of *The Cat in the Hat* (which by this point had sold 205,000 copies, with orders of 2,500 per week) and Dr. Seuss's growing reputation led critic Clifton Fadiman to prognosticate that Beginner Books might be "the biggest thing that has happened to the American classroom since the advent of William Holmes McGuffey's Readers in 1836."

Each book had a generous initial print run of 60,000, a number that shows the confidence Phyllis, Ted, and Helen had in the demand for early readers. It seems foregone now, but even considering the cachet attached to the Seuss name at the time, it wasn't at all guaranteed that a line of early readers like this would be successful. While there were certainly signs that parents and children were eager for this new category of book, this was uncharted territory.

While Ted had been toiling on *The Cat in the Hat*, Ursula Nordstrom, children's book editor at Harper & Row, was shepherding the creation of a series of accessible, story-based early readers. Popular legend has it that Nordstrom was told by Virginia Haviland, who was then the children's coordinator at the Boston

Public Library, that kids would come up to her saying, "I can read, I can read! What do you have for me?" and that all she could offer were school primers.

Nordstrom didn't have a firm grasp of what it would look like until she received a manuscript by a first-grade teacher named Else Homelund Minarik. Minarik had brought her story "What Will Little Bear Wear?" unsolicited to Harper in September 1956, saying her own first-grade daughter could read the story on her own. Nordstrom asked for more of the gently humorous stories, which she thought would work as an early reader. So she paired Minarik with artist Maurice Sendak, who was still a few years away from becoming a children's literature superstar, to create the first I Can Read! book, *Little Bear*.

Despite having the idea first, Nordstrom was just barely beaten to the punch by Spaulding, Cerf, and Seuss. *The Cat in the Hat* came out in March 1957. *Little Bear* arrived in August of the same year. It was followed by *No Fighting, No Biting!* (also by Minarik and Sendak) and Syd Hoff's *Danny and the Dinosaur*, both released simultaneously with the first wave of Beginner Books.

But there were some fundamental differences between the two lines of books. I Can Read! titles presented themselves as beginner chapter books rather than as child-reader-friendly picture books. There was no formal limitation on vocabulary or sentence structure, which often resulted in the I Can Read! books being written at a higher level than Beginner Books were. Nordstrom encouraged her authors "to write high-quality, imaginative stories" and simplify the language later. Exchanges printed in Leonard Marcus's *Dear Genius* find Nordstrom coaching Syd Hoff not to be "SELFCONSCIOUS" about his language but at the same time encouraging him to simplify his description of Danny's museum trip (no "Roman chariot" or "Egyptian mummies").

So what Phyllis, Ted, and Helen were doing—in a sort of unconscious collaboration with Ursula Nordstrom and her staff—was creating a whole new category of book, not a picture book or chapter book or basal, but something that had elements of all of them. As one early definition put it, early readers were "books with stories or interesting information, with simple sentence structure, reasonably limited vocabulary, and a measure of repetition." That definition would be refined over the next three years, but the template was mostly there in those first five Beginner Books.

Each of those books was emblazoned with a stamp featuring an illustration of a small child dwarfed by a large book labeled "For Beginning Readers," and the soon-to-be-famous motto "I Can Read It All by Myself" circling around it. One of the criticisms of *The Cat in the Hat* came from Heloise P. Mailloux in the *Horn Book*, who wrote that the "For Beginning Readers" stamp would make "self-conscious children" avoid the book. Since that clearly hadn't happened—judging by the book's sales and reception—the stamp lived on. Besides their size, the stamp was really the primary unifying feature of the first Beginner Books, as the company had not yet arrived at the iconic cat logo that would come to define the series.

The back dust jacket of each book featured an image of a chalkboard with the six titles written on it, and a message from Bennett Cerf that read, in part: "What are Beginner Books? They are the answer to millions of parents and educators who have begged for books that beginning readers can really enjoy as well as read by themselves. They are the products of the fertile imaginations and drawing boards of some of our most gifted writers and artists."

Beginner Books were an immediate hit. Newly hired sales manager Robert (Bob) Bernstein arranged for Ted to go on a ten-day signing tour in November 1958. Ted made appearances in bookstores from Boston to Chicago and in between to promote both Beginner Books and the newly released *How the Grinch Stole Christmas*. Random House created buttons featuring the Cat in the Hat as promotional giveaways. The idea of doing a signing tour upon a book's release is fairly common practice now, but at the time was considered to be an innovation. Bob had spent the previous ten years at Simon and Schuster, and brought with him the ambition to push Dr. Seuss and Beginner Books into the sales stratosphere. It worked.

Clifton Fadiman had predicted that Beginner Books' impact would be felt most in the classroom, but in truth it was in libraries and homes where the book truly caught on. Libraries bought them because they gave librarians an answer to the child who told them, "I just learned to read. What do you have for me?" And their primary audience was parents. As Ted expected, parents bought them for their kindergarten, first, and second graders to practice on. What he hadn't expected was that parents would buy them in anticipation of their two-, three-, or four-year-old starting to read.

Sales boomed. Phyllis described the company instantly being deluged by "a flood of income." Beginner Books was turning a profit within four months, and sales continued to grow to the point that Bennett Cerf (only somewhat hyperbolically) called the young company "the most profitable single publishing entity ever created," and added that it was "becoming embarrassing" to Random House.

Though he and Random House were both profiting by being the lender and distributor for Beginner Books, in early 1959 Bennett began working to acquire Beginner Books and bring it fully under the Random House umbrella. The publisher was planning to go public later that year, and Bennett knew that Beginner Books' profitability would sweeten that deal.

It would also sweeten the financial reward for Ted, Helen, and Phyllis. Ted and Helen, who owned twenty-two of the one hundred Beginner Book shares (worth approximately $660 when the company began), would receive shares of Random House stock (worth approximately $800,000) in exchange. It was such a windfall that the Geisels' attorney advised against the deal, citing "unwelcome tax consequences." Phyllis didn't want to sell either, to which Bennett responded, "You're going to get the money anyway." But for Phyllis it wasn't about the money as much as it was about her pride in and ownership of what she'd created.

But Bennett was determined and dogged, and the deal eventually went through. In terms of operations, Phyllis, Ted, and Helen all remained in their original positions, but Helen's title changed to vice president. When she heard this news, Helen wrote to Donald Klopfer: "That's so wonderful! I never did anything so effortlessly. Working on Beginner Books is really such fun, and has become so routine, that I automatically get up in the morning, go into my 'cat house,' and there I stay. Now, to be a V.P. on top of all this, is indeed a great glory."

Phyllis was not so pleased. "Phyllis is still yapping that we cheated her," Bennett said in a 1968 interview. And indeed, the deal to sell Beginner Books to Random House would be yet another source of tension and division between the original three partners.

Lost in the shuffle were William Spaulding and Houghton Mifflin. Their deal with Random House to publish school editions continued with *The Cat in the Hat Comes Back* (and 1958's non-Beginner Book *Yertle the Turtle and Other Stories*) but ended with Random House buying their rights. Spaulding and the company had gotten very little of the accolades or credit for their role in bringing *The Cat in the Hat* to life, and they hadn't made anywhere near the money Random House had from the book.

Meanwhile, Phyllis, Ted, and Helen were already deep into work on the next set of Beginner Books. The second wave of the line featured six new titles, all released simultaneously in the fall of 1959. There was no Dr. Seuss book in the bunch, and none of them save Mike McClintock and Fritz Siebel's *Stop That Ball!* have the timeless quality of the best children's books. Two of the wave were nonfiction titles (*You Will Go to the Moon*; *The Whales Go By*) with an inherently shorter shelf life, another—*Cowboy Andy*—was a product of the cowboy craze of the 1950s that was rapidly giving away to a preoccupation with space exploration.

The books, like their predecessors, also caused their share of creative acrimony between Phyllis and the Geisels. *You Will Go to the Moon* created perhaps the most friction between the editorial team. Helen and Ted were disappointed in the book's first draft, with the former writing Phyllis, "Before any illustrator can breathe life into this story with pictures, the authors have first got to breathe some life into it with words." She called the main character "lunk-headed" and the moon "dusty" and "disappointing." Phyllis dug in, going as far as to verify the Freemans' factual accuracy with Harold Urey, winner of the 1934 Nobel Prize in chemistry. This ended with a rare loss for Helen and Ted, with Bennett, who was friends with authors Ira and Mae Freeman, dictating that the couple be allowed to write the book their way. He advised that in the future Beginner Books steer clear of established Random House authors. Thus *You Will Go to the Moon* would be both the first and last book the Freemans would do for Beginner Books.

BEGINNER BOOK SPOTLIGHT

P. D. Eastman: Part 1

Philip Dey Eastman was born on November 25, 1909, in Amherst, Massachusetts, a college town about one hundred miles west of Boston. He was the middle child of Clarence Willis Eastman, head of the German department at Amherst College, and Ann Hull Dey, a native of Iowa City, where her father—Peter Anthony Dey—had been the chief engineer on the construction of the Rock Island line, and had served as the city's mayor, the state's railroad commissioner, and president of the First National Bank.

Phil showed an interest in drawing from a young age. When he was thirteen, his father took a sabbatical leave, and the family traveled to Europe for nearly a year. Most of their time was spent in Switzerland, where Phil kept a detailed journal/sketchbook and studied art at Institute Minerva in Zurich. This experience both helped him grow and become serious as an artist. He served on the art board for the yearbook during his senior year at Phillips Academy Andover—a boarding school in Andover, Massachusetts, twenty-five miles north of Boston that counts Humphrey Bogart and George H. W. Bush among its alumni—in 1928.

By nature reserved and confident, Phil returned home to get a liberal arts education at Amherst College. He majored in language, was once again on the yearbook, and also served as editor-in-chief of the college's humor magazine, *Lord Jeff* (which was in existence from 1920 to 1934). Here he picked up the nickname "Pee Dee," after his first two initials, though he wouldn't use that professionally until many years later.

After graduating in 1933 Phil enrolled in the National Academy of Design in New York where he studied for three years. It was there that he filled out an admission test to work at Disney, and was hired. He headed to Los Angeles in 1936.

Phil would spend five years working uncredited as a story sketch artist for theatrical shorts (featuring Donald Duck and the like), and the Nutcracker Suite section of 1940's *Fantasia* (specifically the dancing mushrooms). It's also likely that he did work on *Pinocchio* (1940), *Dumbo* (1941), and *Bambi* (1942), all of which were in production during Phil's time at Disney.

While working at Disney he met Mary Louise Whitham, a Glendale, California resident and graduate of UCLA. She was one of the studio's four-color model supervisors responsible for determining the colors of "characters and other moving elements" in the films. The two began seeing each other, and fell in love. But all was not well at work. The harsh working conditions required to finish Disney's first feature-length film, *Snow White and the Seven Dwarves*, had created tensions between the staff and management. Those tensions were exacerbated by a growing unease among the creative staff about intellectual property rights and on-screen credits.

Head animator Art Babbitt led the charge to unionize, teaming with labor organizer Herbert Sorrell to have the Disney staff join the Screen Cartoonist's Guild (Local 852). Disney was in the middle of expanding to a forty-one-acre plot in Burbank, and had several big features in production. So even despite the success of *Snow White*, they were in financial straits. Walt Disney himself made a desperate appeal to his staff not to unionize and put "family" first, but the speech had the opposite effect, and a vote to strike came the next day.

Negotiations fell apart, ending with the firing of Babbitt and other head animators. The strike would stretch from late May to the end of July, getting uglier before it got better. Walt Disney took out an ad in *Variety* blaming the strike on communist agitation. But with Walt away in South America (the same trip that would inspire Helen Geisel's Donald Duck book and *The Three Caballaros*), a deal was reached, and the strikers returned with pay raises.

Phil had left Disney before the strike, but he walked the picket line in solidarity with Mary and his fellow animators. He and Mary did take a break from the picket line to get married in June. Mary was not rehired by Disney follow-ing the strike, a clear result of lingering resentment from management. Indeed, all of the most vocal and passionate organizers ended up leaving Disney.

Phil joined the Local 839 Union of Motion Picture Screen Cartoonists and worked for Schlesinger Productions, creators of Looney Tunes and Merry Melodies. Mary focused on raising a family. The couple's first son, Peter Anthony Eastman, was born in 1942, the same year that Phil moved from Schlesinger to the Army Signal Corps, reporting to Captain Ted Geisel. Besides his work on Private Snafu shorts and educational films, Phil also helped out with the story for the 1943 Daffy Duck short, "Scrap Happy Daffy," in which the energetic duck stresses the importance of donating to scrap drives using a dizzying rhyme ("tires, chains, water mains, skates, plates, fur-nace grates"). He also fights a Nazi goat.

Phil's time at Fort Fox provided a natural transition to a new animation studio called Industrial Film and Poster Service. The company, started by for-mer Disney animators John Hubley, Zack Schwartz, David Hilberman, and Stephen Bosustow in the wake of the strike, worked on Private Snafu films as well as other government-contract educational films such as "Lend Lease" and "A Few Quick Facts" (both 1944). Phil was one of four writers on the stu-dio's "Brotherhood of Man," a film commissioned by the United Auto Workers in part to try to quell racial tensions among auto workers in Detroit. The eleven-minute short, based on a pamphlet called "Races of Mankind" by Ruth Benedict and Gene Weltfish, argued from a scientific and historical perspec-tive that all people have more commonalities than they do differences. It also made a case for "equal opportunity for everyone from the very beginning . . . equal chance for health and medical care, and a good education. An equal chance for a job." The film was well received, and Industrial Film and Poster Service took on a new name to go with its higher profile, United Productions of America (UPA).

One of UPA's primary missions was to bring animation into the modern age. Abstract Expressionism—exemplified by artists such as Jackson Pollock, Mark Rothko, and Agnes Martin—had risen to prominence in the 1940s New York art scene, and its ripple effects extended into the design world as well. Magazines and advertisements began to get bolder in their use of type, color, and white space. Cartoonists such as the New Yorker's Saul Steinberg embraced an expressive, minimalist approach to his drawings. UPA's team, including Phil, believed animation should follow suit lest it get left behind. It didn't hurt that a flat, modernist style was cheaper and was the complete opposite of Disney's complex realism.

Phil would have a productive seven-year stint at UPA, doing story work on fifteen different shorts between 1947 and 1952. The most prominent of these led him to cross paths with Ted Geisel for a second time. Looking for story ideas for animated shorts, Phil thought of his former commanding officer. The two met for lunch, and after hearing Phil's pitch for UPA as a new kind of animation studio interested in more than cats fighting mice, Ted offered "Gerald McBoing Boing," a Dr. Seuss story that was released on ten-inch 78 rpm record in 1950. UPA bought the animation rights for $500.

The tale of a boy that speaks only in sound effects initially proved difficult for the UPA writers to adapt, so Phil and his frequent writing partner, Bill Scott, took over. The duo—"a study in contrast," with Phil being "grave, taciturn, dignified" and Bill usually "bumptious" and "bouncy"—unlocked the adaptation by making only two changes to Ted's original. They added one of the most affecting scenes—where Gerald is rebuffed by his shaving father—and one in which Gerald performs a western serial at the radio station.

The short was a smash, winning the 1950 Academy Award for Best Animated Short Film, the first non-Disney short to win that honor. It was the crown in a year which saw eight "Jolly Frolics" written by Phil, including the second and third Mr. Magoo cartoons. Phil didn't design or create the character, but was vital in his development. In fact, he'd write Magoo's fourth through seventh appearances as well.

But then things went awry. Back in 1947, one of Phil's cowriters on *The Brotherhood of Man*, Ring Lardner Jr., was named by William R. Wilkerson as one of ten communist sympathizers in Hollywood. The list would become known as the "Hollywood Ten" and would set off a years-long investigation by the House Un-American Activities Committee (HUAC) into a communist influence in the film industry. Fanned on by the likes of a vindictive Walt Disney and actor Ronald Reagan, and by the refusal of many of the accused to testify before the committee, the investigation would ruin careers.

In the fall of 1951, Disney production designer Bernyce Polifka Fleury testified to the HUAC that several Disney employees involved in the strike were communists, including Phil. This struck UPA hard, as founders Hubley and Hilberman were both named as well. UPA had little choice but to let Phil go, along with Bill Scott, who said in a 1977 interview, "Phil Eastman was fired, and to keep it from looking political, they fired me too."

The pair continued to do freelance work, a lot of it under the radar, but eventually Scott went on to team up with Jay Ward to create *The Rocky and Bullwinkle Show* (with Bill doing the famous voices of Bullwinkle, Mr. Peabody, and Dudley Do-Right), while Phil and Mary made the drastic choice

Phil Eastman and son Peter (Tony) Eastman circa the early 1950s.

to move their family (which now included a second son, Alan, born in 1947), back east, to Westport, Connecticut.

In March 1953 Phil, having been under subpoena for over a year, testified before the HUAC. He refused to allow his testimony to be broadcast, and he refused to answer the committee's questions, saying it was his right "under that portion of the Constitution which guarantees me freedom of speech and the freedom to associate with whom I please, and also the freedom of conscience." He made no effort to hide his disdain for the HUAC and its purpose. He wrapped up by stating:

My last and final ground for declining to answer is because 161 years ago a woman named Mary Bradbury in Southboro, Mass.—Mary Bradbury happens to be my great, great, great, great, great, great grandmother, and she was convicted of consorting with the devil, despite the fact that 117 of her neighbors testified that she was a good and pious woman. Because I believe she would not have been convicted of witchcraft had she had the privilege of the fifth amendment available to her, to the privilege against self-incrimination, I not only do stand on my privilege, but I am proud to stand on it.

Through the ordeal, Phil found friends (such as Abe Liss and Shamus Culhane) who would give him work on print and TV ads and educational films, including some, ironically, for government entities. Culhane recalled, "We hired him to write 80 spots for the Air Force. He worked for months in a back room in the studio and nobody on our staff ever informed."

With the Hollywood red scare winding down in the late 1950s, Phil was able to return to animation for a brief stint with Terrytoons, the home of *Heckle and Jeckle* and *Mighty Mouse*, where his former UPA colleague Gene Dietch was now creative director. At Terrytoons Phil wrote "Gaston's Easal Life" (1958) and helped develop the Tom Terrific shorts that aired during *Captain Kangaroo*.

It was around this time that Phil crossed paths with Ted Geisel for a third time, with his old commanding officer calling him asking him if he'd like to try his hand at a Beginner Book.

5

The Golden Age (1960–1962)

The six Beginner Books that debuted in 1960 were the first to feature the line's new logo and slogan. Creative art director Robert Lopshire—a Beginner Book creator himself—had the idea to use the Cat in the Hat as the mascot, and so the 1959 set of books had featured the Cat snapping his fingers in a yellow or white circle along with the text, "You can read this by yourself." The 1960 books refined this into the famous hands-folded cat and a return to the earlier motto, "I Can Read It All by Myself," curled around his head. The 1960 books were also the first to feature the same cat on the spine, giving Beginner Books a uniform look, and making them instantly recognizable on shelves.

While the 1959 Beginner Books sold well in the short term (the mid-1959 to mid-1960 fiscal year saw the company with well over a million dollars in sales volume), none of them proved to be long-term favorites, and all eventually fell out of print. In contrast, the books that were published between 1960 to 1963 included five stone cold classics of children's literature—*Green Eggs and Ham*, *Are You My Mother?*, *Put Me in the Zoo*, *Dr. Seuss's ABC*, and *Go, Dog. Go!*— and several more that would sell very well and remain in print for decades.

The amount of quality early readers that Beginner Books produced from 1960 to 1964 is unparalleled, and it's not hyperbole to label these years the publisher's golden age. What's even more impressive about Beginner Books' success during these years is that it happened among rapidly increasing competition and rising tensions between the company's three founders.

In her history of children's literature, Ruth Hill Vigeurs wrote that *The Cat and the Hat* and *Little Bear* were so well received that "the floodgates opened" on early reading books. With the children of the baby boom reaching school (and reading) age, and the National Defense Education Act of 1958 (a Cold

War initiative investing in schools and libraries with the hopes of bolstering the future workforce), the timing was exactly right. Other publishers had taken notice of the massive successes of Beginner Books and I Can Read!, and all scrambled to create their own lines of early readers. By 1961 there was Read Alone (Knopf), My Easy-to-Read True Books (Grossett), Beginning to Read (Follet), and A Book to Begin On / Read It Myself (Holt).

But Harper & Row's I Can Read! remained Beginner Books' primary challenger, as the two lines competed for sales (Beginner Books regularly won this battle), accolades (Harper's *A Kiss for Little Bear* received a Caldecott Honor in 1962; Beginner Books would never be recognized by the awards), and talent (Beginner Book creators Robert Lopshire, Joan Heilbroner, Fritz Siebel, Mike McClintock, and Alice Low all did I Can Read! books).

Not only were Beginner Books well on their way to becoming fixtures of schools and libraries, in 1961 the company struck a deal to go directly into homes. Grolier Publishing had been in operation since 1895, known primarily as a publisher of encyclopedias (Encyclopedia Americana; Book of Knowledge) but in the early 1960s were looking for new ways to expand their direct sales business model to other types of books. Like everyone in publishing, they'd noticed Beginner Books' astonishing success, and got in touch with Random House cofounder Donald Klopfer, who handled the business and book production side of things (complimenting Bennett's talent for management and public relations).

Grolier's pitch was to create a Beginning Readers' Program in which parents would subscribe to a monthly Beginner Book. Customers would be hooked in by an offer of three Beginner Books for $1.49 (plus "mailing costs") and from there receive one book per month at $1.49 (discounted from the $1.95 retail price). To make up for the lower price, the book club editions had cheaper bindings, covers, and paper, and were issued without dust jackets.

Grolier initially planned to include Harper & Row I Can Read! books in the program too, but when Phyllis got wind of this, she told Klopfer to insist Grolier offer Beginner Books only. Klopfer was highly dubious that Grolier would agree to drop Harper, but to his great surprise, they did (Harper instead struck a deal with Weekly Reader).

For their part, Helen and Ted were wary of this untested model of selling children's books. Helen called it "a high dive into cold water." Bob Bernstein reassured the couple, and the Grolier program quickly proved to be popular, as parents responded in droves to ads in coupon mailers, ladies' magazines, and newspapers.

Grolier's Beginning Readers' Program would become the longest-running children's book club of its kind, bringing Beginner Books into more homes and reaching more children than its founders could have possibly imagined. Its success meant massive royalties for the company and for its individual creators. One of the innovations of Beginner Books was the way it monetarily awarded both author and illustrator equally. Ted remembered well the anger and indignation he felt at being denied profits from his best-selling *Boners* and *More Boners* books in the early 1930s. So instead of the typical work-for-hire contracts, Beginner Book illustrators—like authors—were given royalties based on sales. To Ted and Phyllis this was only fair, since Beginner Books' pictures were as important to the storytelling as their words were. With the addition of royalties from Grolier deal, illustrators would be even more generously rewarded for their work on Beginner Books.

The book club struck a nerve with parents because it presented itself as educationally enriching, with ads promising that "each book makes reading more fun, and easier than ever, because it is written in 200 basic words your child has already learned, or can quickly pick up." This wasn't just marketing. Phyllis especially took great pride in the pedagogical bonafides of the series. An eight-page document from 1963 outlines the educational aims of Beginner Books, as well as the research behind it:

> At the heart of the Beginner Book philosophy is the growing belief, professed by such experts as Professor Patrick Suppes at Stanford and Professor B. F. Skinner at Harvard, that the speed and efficiency of the "learning process" is closely connected with the degree to which the child's learning is rewarded (or, in technical terms, reinforced) . . . enjoyment of the material that is suddenly within reach due to his new-found reading ability.

From the start Beginner Books used the approval of educators and reading specialists in the promotion of the books, but in the early 1960s began to use them in their design as well. Jeanne Chall, at that time a professor at City College of New York's educational clinic, began to serve as an advisor to the series. Chall was well known in literacy circles as the co-originator of the Dale-Chall readability formula, a numerical system of determining the difficulty of a text (this formula built off of the Flesch-Kincaid readability test, though it used a list of words difficult for fourth graders rather than basing it on word length). In the late 1960s, while still serving as advisor to Beginner Books (and having moved on to a position at Harvard's graduate school of education and founding their reading laboratory), she'd publish *Learning to*

Read: The Great Debate, an exhaustively researched study which many consider the final word on the reading wars.

Chall offered a signed endorsement of the first Beginner Book of the 1960s, *One Fish, Two Fish, Red Fish, Blue Fish*, praising the way Ted had rhymed difficult words with known ones to help build vocabulary. She also embraced the overall mission of Beginner Books as motivational: "The short, hilariously illustrated sequences invite the beginning reader and the kindergartner to observe, to count, compare, imagine, think, question, and above all—to want to read."

With Chall on board and feedback from parents showing that parents were buying the books for three- and four-year-old children who weren't close to reading yet, the early 1960s saw Beginner Books attempt to reduce word counts further to become even more new-reader-friendly. *Put Me in the Zoo* and *Are You My Mother?* each had 100 unique words, compared to *The Cat in the Hat's* 236. *Ten Apples Up on Top!* and *Go, Dog. Go!* each had seventy-five unique words. *Green Eggs and Ham* only had fifty! All were considered to be part of this new approach, and were listed on the back covers of some Beginner Books as "Books for Beginning Beginners."

BEGINNER BOOK SPOTLIGHT

Roy McKie: Part 1

Roy McKie Jr. was born in 1921 in Medford, Massachusetts, a northwest suburb of Boston. His father, Roy Sr., worked as a gateman for the Boston and Maine railroad's north station, and his mother, Marian, taught primary school.

Though neither of his parents showed much interest in art, Roy recalled being very young, lying in bed sick, and being entertained by his father drawing pictures of what he could see out the window. Roy took to drawing himself at a young age, filling any blank space he could find with doodles, and listening to *Amos & Andy* on the radio with paper and pencil in hand, trying to capture the action as it went along.

When the Great Depression hit, Roy Sr. was fortunate enough to hold onto his job at the railroad when so many others were out of work. Though the family—which now included Roy's three younger brothers—struggled financially, they kept a well-tended vegetable garden and raised chickens for the eggs. They were known to share when their neighbors were in need.

In high school Roy entered a contest to illustrate a history of the school. "It was a tough school," he revealed in a 2011 interview. "There weren't many people who were interested in things like art, and I won." This was partly trademark self-deprecation, but also a way of revealing that Roy's interests didn't exactly match up with those of his classmates. Besides his interest in art, he had an insatiable curiosity about life and culture. He loved to read and had a passion for film. He began attending the Massachusetts School of Art on Saturdays, with a friend of his father's paying the ten-dollar yearly tuition because the McKies couldn't afford it otherwise.

After graduating high school Roy went to work, first at a canning factory, then at a furniture factory. He worked off-hours at Howard Johnson as a soda jerk. Knowing he didn't have it in him to be a factory man his whole life, he made the decision to return to art school, enrolling at the Vesper George School of Art, where *Lil' Abner* cartoonist Al Capp was a teacher and where Robert McCloskey (*Make Way for Ducklings*; *Homer Price*) had been a student. His family was dubious about this career path. Roy recalled his grandfather telling his mother, "Marian, I don't know why you let that boy spend so much time drawing pictures. He's never going to earn a living doing that."

At Vesper George, Roy studied the gamut of fine art. Though he was slightly green-red colorblind, it was his ultimate goal to become a painter, "the next Norman Rockwell." He excelled in his studies and was awarded the school's "Prix de Rome," a scholarship to study in Italy. But given Italy's role in World War II, it was impossible for him to take advantage of it. Instead Roy was sent to the Louis Comfort Tiffany Foundation on Long Island.

In 1943, Roy married sweetheart Lois Barwood, known by her childhood nickname Tuddy, whom he'd met when she was attending Wheelock Collge and he Vesper George. The two likely connected over art, as Tuddy was an amateur painter and jewelry maker. Their first child, Todd, would come along a year later. The family lived in a small apartment on Pinckney Street in Boston, and Roy worked at a small advertising agency, where, he recalls, "I did almost nothing."

It wasn't long before he ran into a former classmate who was working for Bruce Anderson Associates, one of the largest studios in Boston. Roy was hired on there, and did posters and booklets for American Airlines. Bruce helped his employee start to hone in on his strengths by telling Roy, "You're never going to be Norman Rockwell, but you just might be a cartoonist." The family moved to a house in the Boston suburb of Lincoln, and a second child, Sara, came along.

Roy's next big leap was to N. W. Ayer Advertising in Philadelphia. Charles Coiner, the agency's art director, personally recruited Roy after seeing the work he'd done at Anderson. So the McKies relocated to Doylestown, Pennsylvania, about forty miles north of Philadelphia, and here Roy's career really took off. He did some work for the army and navy, and most prominently, an ongoing in-house ad for the *Ladies' Home Journal* called "Never Underestimate the Power of a Woman." Started in the early 1940s by fellow Ayer artist Leo Lionni (who would of course go on to have his own storied career in children's books, including *Frederick* and *Swimmy*), the campaign consisted of a one- or two-panel wordless cartoon demonstrating the title phrase. Roy took over in the late 1940s, continuing in minimalist pen-and-ink style Lionni had established, and would work on it for the next fourteen years. One of the advertisements he was particularly proud of featured a fireplace at Christmas with a man's sock hanging next to a woman's nylon stocking. Lionni had gone to work for Time Life, and began throwing more and more freelance work to Roy, not only advertising, but also album covers for Broadway cast recordings and the like.

After a couple of years, the McKies moved again, this time to nearby New Hope. The town was known as a weekend and summer getaway for writers, artists, and jazz musicians, so the McKies joined a circle of creative people. It was here that Roy both wrote and drew his first book, *The Dog: A Cartoon Inquiry Concerning Man's Relationship with His Best Friend* in 1954. The McKies had a little dachshund named Sport who may have served as inspiration. The book sold well, and Roy was extremely proud of the accomplishment.

Around this time Roy came to the attention of Philadelphia-born artist/agent Ted Riley, who represented cartoonists Roy Doty and Jules Fieffer among many others, and who was quickly becoming a power player in the New York publishing scene. With Riley on his side, Roy's profile increased, landing a regular gig in *The Week Magazine*, a Sunday supplement carried in thirty-seven newspapers nationwide. His work more frequently took him to New York, and Roy and Tuddy's relationship deteriorated. As it became clear that the fracture in their marriage wasn't going to be repaired, Roy flirted with the idea of relocating permanently to London. He spent a winter working there in the late 1950s, but soon realized it wasn't going to be financially feasible to stay.

But his short time in London would land Roy a couple of famous acquaintances and a career highlight. While doing some work for the *London Observer*, Roy befriended art and dance critic Nigel Gosling, and subsequently met dancer (and Russian defector) Rudolf Nureyev. Roy was also drawn into the circle of Julie Andrews, who was at that point a famed stage actress but not yet a movie star. Andrews had recently purchased a miniature

Roy McKie. Courtesy June McKie.

gray poodle she named Shy, and the dog quickly became a regular fixture in London society pages. This was in no small part because Shy had a habit of singing along when Julie practiced, howling to the sky while Julie did scales. The stories inspired author Margery Sharp, a prolific writer whose first book for children—*The Rescuers*—had come out in 1959.

She teamed up with Roy to tell the story of Melisande, a canine opera singer who sings her way to the top. After a mock-serious foreword by Sharp, the story is told completely in Roy's pictures. Done with ink and brush, the style is loose and expressive, but immaculately composed. In the process of creating and promoting the book, Roy got to meet Julie multiple times, and the two became very fond of each other.

Melisande was published in 1960. By then Roy had returned to the United States, settling in New York. Through Ted Riley, Roy met Bennett and Phyllis Cerf, and once the couple saw his work, they thought he would be perfect for

Beginner Books. They sent Ted some samples and he was ecstatic. "This guy is terrific," Ted wrote to Phyllis, "sign [McKie] fast." He added, "We hope to build [McKie], not as a one-time illustrator of Beginner Books, but as a permanent institution within our institution."

The Cerfs invited Roy to their country home in upstate New York for the weekend. Ted also happened to be visiting, and the two artists bonded quickly. "We were sketching," Roy said. "He was looking to see what I could and couldn't do." It turned out there was a lot of the former and not much of the latter. Roy would quickly prove to be Ted's ideal of a children's book illustrator. His flat economical style—most indebted to *New Yorker* cartoonist Saul Steinberg—matched how Ted thought children saw the world. "He liked to look at it from a child's point of view," Roy explained. "It didn't matter how many lines there were." Shading, depth, and realism were not important. The simpler the representation, the better.

Roy's visual mind and experience and skill at telling stories without words matched the Beginner Book philosophy of the illustrations doing much of the heavy narrative lifting. And on top of that, Roy was fast and able to quickly intuit what Ted wanted, largely due to the fact that the two men shared a similarly whimsical sense of humor. The weekend produced rough sketches for two separate books (likely *Bennett Cerf's Book of Riddles* and *Ten Apples Up on Top!*).

The book jacket for *Bennett Cerf's Book of Riddles* demonstrates just how excited Phyllis, Ted, and Helen—in a rare instance of harmony between the three—were about their new artist, describing his illustrations as "the envy of his fellow illustrators everywhere for their humor, their strength, and their absolute simplicity."

BEGINNER BOOK SPOTLIGHT

Stan and Jan Berenstain: Part 1

Besides Dr. Seuss himself, no names are more associated with Beginner Books than Stan and Jan Berenstain. Though they were responsible for more Beginner Books than any other author, writing and illustrating twenty books for the line between 1964 and 2000, it's not just about numbers. The characters they created for their Beginner Books—the Berenstain Bears—became an international phenomenon, selling hundreds of millions of books, and inspiring a multimedia empire. Though their success now seems a foregone conclusion, the husband-and-wife team had to fight their way into children's literature history. The primary opponent, at least at first, was Ted. Only their perseverance, dogged work ethic, and uncanny creative synchronicity allowed them to triumph.

Janice Marian Grant and Stanley Melvin Berenstain were born two months and just a few miles apart, Jan arriving in July 1923 in West Philadelphia and Stan in September in Philadelphia proper. Jan's family moved three times before she was in fifth grade, settling finally in the northwest suburb of Rosemont. Stanley's family moved around Philadelphia five times before he was four, ending up at 4239 Frankford above his paternal grandmother Nelly's army and navy store.

Both Stan and Jan found themselves drawn to the newspaper comics at a young age. Stan said for him "comics were the entirety of popular entertainment." Most of all he loved the adventures of the spaceman Buck Rogers, done at that time by writer Philip Nowlan and artist Dick Calkins. Jan was also a big fan of the strip, but also counted Clare Victor Dwiggins's *Nipper*—which ran from 1931 to 1936 and followed the adventures of a "courageous boy character and a tomboyish girl character"—as a special favorite. Both Stan and Jan loved to draw, but their other hobbies went in opposite directions. Stan indulged in indoor pursuits such as reading and building model airplanes, while Jan was more of an outdoor type, playing field hockey and describing her young self as a "tomboy."

In high school—Stan at West Philadelphia High School and Jan at Radnor High School—both found strong mentors who encouraged and fostered Stan and Jan's interest and talent in art. Both of them painted scenery for their school theater productions. Both served on their respective yearbook staffs, Stan as an art director of his, Jan as art editor of hers, where she introduced an *Alice in Wonderland* theme based on her childhood love of Sir John Tenniel's illustrations for Lewis Carroll's books. Stan and Jan each placed a painting in the annual citywide Cultural Olympics, and both knew they'd continue to study art after graduation. Stan was awarded a four-year scholarship to the Philadelphia Museum School of Industrial Art (known as "Industrial"). Jan got a three-fourths scholarship to the suburban Tyler School of Art, but late in the summer she changed her mind and elected instead to go to Industrial. It was closer, it was her dad's alma mater, and she had the promise of a full scholarship in her second year.

And that's how Stan and Jan ended up in Miss Sweeny's first-year drawing class together. As they drew classical casts, Stan noticed that Jan's drawing was the best in the class and struck up a conversation. She asked him to go with her to a recital by the soprano Dorothy Maynor, and they quickly became a pair, often going off together to draw the bears during Tuesday nature drawing field trips at the Philadelphia Zoo.

Once the United States became involved in World War II, Stan enlisted in the army, but was placed in limited-combat training due to amblyopia in his left eye, a condition that severely limited his vision. He was next assigned to the 106th Infantry Division at Camp Atterbury, Indiana, but suffered an intestinal tear during training, and was admitted to Wakeman General Army Hospital for surgery. While he recovered, his unit shipped out without him. Most of them died in the Battle of the Bulge.

At the hospital, a surgeon got wind of Stan's artistic talent, and recruited him as a medical artist focused on diagramming grafts and reconstructive plastic surgery procedures for wounded soldiers. While Stan was away, Jan continued her schooling, eventually getting a degree in art education. She also got a job as a riveter at Brill's trolley car factory, which had the navy contract to make center wing sections for PBY flying boats. Additionally, she painted china at the Artgift company and taught painting and drawing at Industrial. Though there'd been no proposal of marriage, and the couple had to surreptitiously exchange letters because of Jan's mother's disapproval, Stan and Jan comported themselves as though they were engaged. Jan made a ring from scrap metal and sent one to Stan, too.

Stan was discharged from the army in April of 1946, and he and Jan wasted no time, getting married twelve days later. They settled in a run-down apartment above Stan's father's army and navy store on Woodland Avenue in southwestern Philadelphia. Stan finished his education on the G.I. Bill, finishing up at Industrial and also studying painting at the Pennsylvania Academy of Fine Arts. Though he and Jan both had classical art educations and were accomplished painters, the duo was realistic about doing whatever it took to make a living as artists.

Stan had sold four cartoons to Norman Cousins at the *Saturday Evening Review* for a total of $105, and became convinced cartooning was the ticket. But it didn't quite work that way. "Working together, one of us on one side of the drawing table and one on the other, we cranked out twelve to fifteen cartoons a week and sent them to a succession of magazines . . . week after week we'd send them out, and week after week, they'd come back rejected."

Stan boldly decided to go see John Bailey at the *Saturday Evening Post* in person, and Bailey told them that their cartoons—concerning art, history, science, and literature—were not a good fit for the magazine. "It's a family magazine," he said. So Stan and Jan took the advice, working together to create one-panel comics about family life. And that did it. After a year with no sales, they sold 154 cartoons in their second year, including six in a single issue of the *Saturday Evening Post*.

Going back to their mutual childhood love of the comics, Stan and Jan drew inspiration from other cartoonists. They were most influenced by William Steig and Walt Kelly. Steig's "Small Fry" cartoons in the *New Yorker*, which depicted children and childhood in simultaneously nostalgic and unsentimental fashion, served as a model for their own take on kiddom. Stan and Jan loved the newspaper strip *Pogo*, and Walt Kelly's style of drawing characters, action, and movement certainly found its way into their own approach.

Stan and Jan's stature as cartoonists grew in 1948 with a large, busy, and complicated piece called "Recess," which depicted all manner of games and shenanigans on the school blacktop. *Collier's* bought it, and it led to a series of kid-centered scenes like "Kindergarten," "Gymnasium," and "Saturday Matinee." The latter, which appeared on the cover, "drew more fan mail than any other cartoon in the magazine's history." Their income followed suit, so much so that in 1950 the Berenstains were able to leave their rundown apartment for "a modern Frank Lloyd Wrightish" house in the suburb of Elkins Park.

Son Leo had been born in 1948. Another son, Michael, followed in 1951. Being parents gave Stan and Jan even more material to use for their family cartoons, which by this time included a series of semisatirical books on parenthood, relationships, and sex (*Berenstains' Baby Book*; *Marital Blitz, Mr. Dirty vs. Mrs. Clean*; *Have a Baby, My Wife Just Had a Cigar*, and many more), an ongoing comic—"Sister"—in *Collier's*, Hallmark cards, and advertisements for vitamins. In 1956 they started a regular comic feature in the pages of *McCall's* magazine, *It's All in the Family*. Each month there would be seven or more one-panel comics on a specific theme, all featuring the Harvey family (mom, dad, Michael, Janie, Billy).

At home, getting their boys to bed at night, Stan and Jan began inventing stories, and realized that those stories might work as children's books. They created a dummy for an original fairy tale called *The Littlest Window*, a story featuring a set of personified windows in a royal palace who pride themselves on the view they provide to the citizenry. The most modest and neglected window—the title character—is found in the end to provide the only view of the royal nursery. Through their publisher, they set up a meeting with the editor-in-chief of children's books at Macmillan. She promptly informed them that Macmillan didn't publish children's books that looked the way theirs did. "You are cartoonists," she told them. "Your drawings are cartoons."

When Stan pointed out that children enjoy cartoons, the editor-in-chief responded haughtily, "As I'm sure you and Mrs. Berenstain know, children like many things that aren't good for them. . . ." But it wasn't lost on Stan and Jan that Dr. Seuss was a cartoonist, and doing very well, so they decided to try again with an idea involving a family of bears they'd dreamed up.

It took them two months to create a dummy for a new children's book called *Freddy Bear's Spanking*—the story of a young bear who misbehaves and then cleverly negotiates with his parents options that sound like punishment but are really rewards.

While Stan and Jan were working on the book, two major things happened. First, they signed on with an agent, Sterling Lord—whose most prominent clients at the time were Jack Kerouac and Howard Fast—after their cartoon book publishers tired of dealing with Stan as a businessman. Second, the first wave of Beginner Books was released. Stan and Jan, already fans of Dr. Seuss's work, immediately realized their book could be a Beginner Book. Sterling set up a lunch with Phyllis Cerf, who offered a contract on the spot.

That was the easy part.

Two weeks later Stan and Jan found themselves in the eagle's aerie at the Random House mansion, where the Beginner Book offices were still under construction, for a meeting with Phyllis, Helen, and Ted. Stan and Jan immediately noticed that the entire dummy for *Freddy Bear's Spanking* was tacked up on the corkboard walls like an animation storyboard. Things started well. Ted had known their work as magazine cartoonists, and he liked the bears. Helen liked their drawings. But then Ted turned to the story itself. "There's a helluva lot wrong with it," he told them.

He pressed to find out how deeply the Berenstains had thought about their characters. In another instance of Ted approaching Beginner Books as analogous to making films and cartoons, he asked who they'd "cast" as Papa Bear and Small Bear. Stan quickly thought of the 1931 film *The Champ*, and its stars Wallace Beery and Jackie Cooper.

Ted proceeded to dissect the story. He said the middle needed more progression, that there were too many contractions and that the sentences were too long. He found the verse to be overly complicated, with too many female (such as -oo and –ere), internal, and convenience rhymes. However, when Phyllis suggested they just switch to prose, Ted quickly shot the idea down. Despite all of its faults, he thought Stan and Jan's verse had "get up and go."

"We felt overwhelmed, beat up, abused" after the meeting, they reported in their autobiography. But with reflection came some revelation. One was that Ted was largely right about their book's faults. The other was that working with Beginner Books would mean meeting very high expectations. They'd looked at their book as a fun little story, but realized that "Ted took these little seventy-two [*sic*] page, limited vocabulary, easy-to-read books just as seriously as if he were editing the Great American Novel."

Their resolve was tested through revision after revision, with each successive draft becoming less and less of their original vision and more and more Ted's logical insanity. The Berenstains likened the process to being trapped on a merry-go-round, and Ted seemed to sense he was pushing them too far. "Hey," he told them in the midst of another round of changes, "you could probably sell this to Harper just the way it is now." Even their own son didn't like the book. Mike Berenstain says, "They showed me this when I was about 10 years old and I thought it was a terrible-looking book."

Finally things reached a breaking point. In a team review of the sixth draft of *Freddy Bear's Spanking*, everyone seemed to realize the book had gotten away from them. Perhaps it was the scene where Papa uproots a tree and threatens to smack Small Bear with it. Helen told her husband, "You're turning this into a Dr. Seuss book." And Phyllis added, "Let's back off and let Stan and Jan be Stan and Jan."

Though the Berenstains had already learned that what Ted said usually went, here he acquiesced. His two partners singled out a honey-hunting sequence that had survived every draft of *Freddy Bear's Spanking*, and suggested expanding it into a whole book. The result was *The Big Honey Hunt*.

Though the process was difficult for all involved, the end result was positive. Stan and Jan wrote: "We learned a great deal from Ted. We learned about writing verse. He was a wizard at fixing broken meter and finessing rhyme problems. We learned about advancing the story. We learned to think cinematically. We learned about keeping the reader reading." Their agent, Sterling Lord, claims his clients helped teach Ted a valuable lesson. "Ted Geisel taught the Berenstains how to be children's-book authors," he wrote in his autobiography. "They would teach him that not every book should become a Dr. Seuss story."

As Stan and Jan's career at Beginner Books progressed, things would never really get easier with Ted. As Mike Berenstain puts it, "They tore their hair out working with Geisel." But the difficulties were mitigated by a couple of circumstances. One was that they genuinely liked and admired Ted even in spite of his tendency to tear their work apart; they didn't doubt that his main motivation was to make their work better. Stan said later, "It helps that Ted had extraordinary charm. He didn't look like Cary Grant, but he had that charm." Helen also helped make things easier; Stan and Jan loved her. She and Ted had a good cop / bad cop dynamic, but it wasn't a put on. Helen was genuinely gentle, supportive, and helpful, and that balance helped the Berenstains to persevere.

Sketch version of a Berenstain self-portrait that appeared on the dust jacket of *The Bear Scouts* in 1967. Courtesy Berenstain Enterprises, Inc.

Despite their battles and frustrations with Ted, Stan and Jan would go on to be the most reliable and consistently popular of the Beginner Book authors. Their strength and longevity came in large part from their unbreakable partnership. Lord wrote that he believed a single author would never have survived Ted's initial onslaught of criticism, but that the Berenstains, being a team, were able to prop each other up. Lord says Jan was laid-back and positive, the "quiet power in the partnership." Stan was more extroverted and served as the pair's face and voice. Much like Mama and Papa Bear—whom they readily admitted were modeled after themselves—they balanced each other.

6

Phyllis Cerf, Will You Please Go Now! (1963–1964)

Though the company's sales and acclaim continued to rise, all was not well within Beginner Books. The working relationship between Ted and Helen and Phyllis was uneasy at best, and nasty at its worst. In their *Dr. Seuss and Mr. Geisel*, Judith and Neil Morgan report that when the Geisels had Thanksgiving dinner with the Cerfs in 1959 the conversation became mired in a Beginner Book matter. In response, Bennett implored, "Please, at least eat your turkey!" In a 1968 interview, Bennett revealed this was far from the only time something like that happened.

Besides the natural dissonance of Ted and Phyllis's personalities, a lot of the tension stemmed from the way Beginner Books were evolving. As Christopher Cerf says, when Beginner Books operated best in their early days it was because of the combination of Phyllis's extensive research and Ted's creative mojo. "And when things worked, that division of labor was very meaningful," he says.

But very early on Ted had begun to consistently rail against one of the central tenants of Beginner Books, the word list. Ted hated the limitations it placed on him, and began to believe that the support of the illustrations and the rhythm of the text was what was most important to the child comprehending unfamiliar words. He tended to approach his writing and editing instinctually (what Warren T. Greenleaf called a "serious though sketchy theory of reading"), and while this often led Ted correctly, it was imprecise and not based in pedagogy. Phyllis, however, remained fully committed to the list, believing it gave the books a solid research-based educational foundation.

Another battle was over their publishing pace. Ted had lobbied for Beginner Books to reduce their output, feeling that releasing six books per year was not sustainable. Phyllis, however, wanted to keep up with Harper & Row, who were releasing new I Can Read! books at a very healthy clip. Ted eventually won this battle, and after 1961, the line would reduce to four titles per year.

Another significant point of contention came from the choice of writers. In late 1961, Ted had written to Bob Bernstein: "We are having a hell of a bad time this year, as in all years, finding writers to write these books for us." Part of this was the difficulty of finding writers who could handle both the storytelling and vocabulary restrictions and the constant revisions requested by the editorial team (mostly Ted, but sometimes Helen and Phyllis, too). Just as Ted had driven Random House stalwarts Mae and Ira Freeman away from the line, Phyllis often found herself cleaning up messes when it came to creators. Ted made instinctual decisions about who could or could not do a Beginner Book.

"One of the issues for my mom," Christopher Cerf says, "and I think anyone would have had this issue, but she took it more personally than some, was that obviously Ted had his own idea of who could do books at his level of brilliance, and he didn't think that these people were good enough." In at least two cases, Phyllis nabbed big-name authors to do Beginner Books, but when Ted savaged their work, Phyllis was left to break the news that they wouldn't be published.

One of these was novelist Nathaniel Benchley, whose text for *Sam and the Firefly* was handed over to P. D. Eastman (see that book's entry in the Beginner Books Encyclopedia section for more). Another was Truman Capote. Capote was not only a Random House author, he was a personal friend of Bennett and Phyllis. Phyllis asked him to try his hand at a Beginner Book, and the result was *The Pig That Wouldn't Fly*. Little is known about the story besides its title and the fact that Ted was initially very excited by it, so much so that he half-jokingly suggested that they hire Capote to do all of their books. But after a couple revisions in which Capote struggled to write text that could be easily matched with illustrations, Ted declared the project unsalvageable. Phyllis was left to deliver the bad news, but Capote took it in stride, she later recalled.

At the same time Ted was rejecting big names, he was recruiting novice creators that lived close to him—people like Fred and Marjorie Phleger—and this caused Phyllis to bristle. She may have felt this was Ted's attempt to maintain control, but she also disliked that these authors' scripts took more effort to get into publishable shape.

The editorial team had near-daily phone conferences, and more often than not arguments arose, over details big and small ("They'd spend three days talking about the placement of a word on a page," recalls Chris, without hyperbole). Ted's aversion to conflict, and his belief that the calls were a drain on the time and energy he could be using to write and draw, led him to become "tense and withdrawn" regarding Beginner Books. Phyllis, despite her love of battle, came away from many a phone call in tears of frustration.

It got so bad that Helen suggested Ted "retire" from his active editorial role in Beginner Books, a decision that would have had myriad and major implications had he agreed. He didn't, but he did allow Helen to take over the day-to-day dealings with Phyllis. The two female Beginner Book founders got along very well, and Helen didn't always side with Ted (for example, they were united against his hijacking of the Berenstains' style on *Freddy Bear's Spanking*).

But conflicts continued, it seems, because Ted simply couldn't give up control. Helen tried, usually unsuccessfully, to arbitrate conflicts between her husband and Phyllis, and it soon became clear that things weren't going to get better. The trust between partners deteriorated so badly that the Geisels actually canceled a planned vacation (a safari in East Africa) for fear that Phyllis would get the upper hand while they were gone.

Sometime in early 1964, Phyllis Jackson, Ted's agent, issued a warning to Bob Bernstein, who was now overseeing most of the day-to-day operations at the publisher, that he had "better do something" or Ted would leave Random House. This, of course, was an apocalyptic outcome. Phyllis was Bennett's wife, and essentially a co-owner of Random House, but Ted was Dr. Seuss, their star author. Bob didn't know what to do about the ultimatum. He reluctantly went to Bennett, who said, "Do whatever you have to do, but just don't talk to me about it."

Donald Klopfer made a rare appearance in the Beginner Book offices while Ted was there, and assured him that everything would work out, but what happened next is fuzzy. In their book, the Morgans claim that soon after, Phyllis had a tête-à-tête with Bernstein, which led to him finally deciding to remove her. When asked about this in 2018, shortly before his death, Bob disputed that version of the story. He said that he left it to Phyllis, Ted, and Helen to figure out a way to move forward.

That way forward was Helen and Ted essentially muscling Phyllis out of Beginner Books against her will. "If not for Ted, I'd still be doing Beginner Books," she told the Morgans. It was not an ideal solution, especially for Bennett, but Random House made every effort to give Phyllis a soft landing. She remained in her office at the Villard, and retained Elma Merz—who had been the cheerful, patient, and wryly funny face of Beginner Books from the very beginning of the line—as her assistant. And Phyllis was given the freedom to create her own new line of early readers. Step-Up Books were a series of nonfiction titles designed for second and third graders who had graduated from Beginner Books. The line launched in the spring of 1965 with four titles, including Joan Heilbroner's *Meet George Washington* (with illustrations by Victor Mays) and *Animals Do the Strangest Things* (written by Leonora and Arthur Hornblow Jr., with pictures by Michael Frith).

Though not anywhere near as successful as Beginner Books, Step-Up books would sell fairly well, and eventually encompass over forty titles about history, sports, and nature. Phyllis was able to fully explore the pedagogical side of early readers, and had editorial freedom she'd never had before. It's worth noting, though, that her methodology didn't change much. In 1968 Bennett Cerf summarized his wife's approach to Step-Up books: "Phyllis meets people who seem to be interested and bags them. They don't realize that Phyllis will fight with them for three days over a word that she wants taken out. They always end up giving in."

Though she landed on her feet, Phyllis would forever harbor resentment and bitterness over her ouster from the company that had been her idea. Bob Bernstein and Ted bore the brunt of her ire, but she also held anger toward her husband for essentially choosing Ted over her. Christopher Cerf says, "Our discussions would go something like this: She'd say, 'You know, I can't believe your father forced me to do this.' And I'd say, 'I agree with you mom, you were totally wronged.' And she'd say, 'How dare you talk that way about your father.'"

For many of the creators who liked Phyllis and felt loyalty to her, the ouster brought about mixed feelings and uncertainty. Where would Beginner Books go next with only Ted and Helen in the lead?

In the short term, the books continued as they had before. This is largely because Phyllis worked on these books before her departure. In the line's releases in 1963 and 1964 the name of the game was sequels and follow-ups, further indication that Beginner Books were becoming increasingly insular in finding ideas that could meet their standards and authors that could withstand Ted's criticism. There was another Little Black book from Walter Farley and James Schucker, a second Berenstain Bears book, a new book of riddles from Bennett Cerf and Roy McKie, and two more photo-illustrated books from Helen Palmer Geisel and Lynn Fayman. There were new Beginner Books by stalwarts such as Robert Lopshire and P. D. Eastman. Dr. Seuss made a return after a three-year absence with not one but two new books, *Dr. Seuss's*

ABC and *Hop on Pop*, both concerned with the earliest fundamentals of literacy. Nineteen sixty-four saw the first Big Beginner Book in the form of *The Cat in the Hat Beginner Book Dictionary*.

Somewhat surprisingly, outside of Joan Heilbroner and H. B. Vestal each doing one Step-Up Book, Phyllis didn't recruit Beginner Book creators for her new line. She did, however, make an attempt in 1967 to create a competitive line, and borrowed two of Beginner Books' biggest names in the process. Take-Along Books were sets of small hardcovers (4 ½" x 6") packaged in a clear carrying case. Two sets were introduced, one written and drawn by P. D. Eastman, featuring Aaron the Alligator, and the other illustrated by Roy McKie (with stories by Phyllis Hirschfeld). The line didn't last beyond its initial launch, though the Aaron books have since been repackaged and given a second life as Step Into Reading books.

While Phyllis and Ted's partnership was ultimately a doomed proposition, it's important to acknowledge what they were able to accomplish together. The combination of Phyllis's thirst for and belief in research-based educational design with Ted's creative flair—along with their shared ability to find and nurture talent—is what brought so many classic Beginner Books into existence. It's also important to acknowledge that, though their pride and ego and stubbornness got in the way, they both ultimately had the same goal. "They cared so desperately," Bennett Cerf said of Ted and Phyllis. "That's what made them so wonderful."

7

Transition and Tragedy
(1965–1967)

Phyllis Cerf's departure from Beginner Books turned out to be the first of a series of major changes. In 1965 RCA and Random House entered negotiations for the electronics giant to purchase the publisher. RCA had started a computer division and wanted to acquire a publisher that could provide educational content for their programs. Bennett Cerf and Donald Klopfer sold the company they'd started on a $200,000 investment for the equivalent of $44 million in stock (Ted and Helen made "many millions" in stock options from the deal). One of the features of the contract was that Random House retained absolute editorial control and that RCA adhere to a policy of noninterference. Bennett had also been allowed to handpick his successor as president, and he chose Bob Bernstein. "He's the right man for the job," Bennett said. "He's just as strong as I am. In fact, in some ways, he's stronger."

So on January 1, 1966, Bob took over as president, and Bennett became chairman of the board. Around the same time, Jerry Harrison, a marketing expert, took over as head of the children's division. Walter Retan replaced Louise Bonino as juvenile editor.

With Phyllis gone from Beginner Books, there was no clear replacement, leaving her work to be mostly divided among Ted and Helen, who began running the line on their own from La Jolla. Sue Marquand, whose father was Tom Coward of publisher Coward-McCann, worked as an assistant for both Beginner Books and Step-Up Books, but the Geisels mostly dealt with Anne MarcoVecchio, who was Bob Bernstein's assistant.

Helen continued her day-to-day administrative tasks—soliciting new manuscripts, overseeing revisions, and keeping track of the finances—but her health was deteriorating. In 1964, her Guillain-Barre syndrome symptoms started to recur. She often lost her balance and suffered paralysis in her legs. She also struggled with failing vision. Around this time the Geisels hired assistant Julie Olfe to help with day-to-day matters.

Ted and Helen were now solely in charge of the line, but some problems persisted, mainly in finding writers. For various reasons a lot of the early stable of talent had moved on. Though the money from Beginner Books was significant—due in large part to royalties from the Grolier deal—many authors decided the intensity of working with Ted was not worth it. This mindset is best described by Benjamin Elkin, who wrote Ted in 1965 saying, "Because Beginner Books have paid such liberal returns it has been worthwhile to work year after year in hopes of coming up with something that meets the stringent requirements. However, Beginner Books do not offer certain textbook and paperback outlets that my other books have provided, and they involve as much effort as three other books."

Ted did nothing to ameliorate this, continuing to approach his editorial work with rigid perfectionism. As a result, readers were robbed of some intriguing-sounding Beginner Books. Around the time he agreed to illustrate 1966's *Don and Donna Go to Bat*, artist B. Tobey submitted a dummy called *The Magic Horn* for consideration as a Beginner Book. Ted wrote back that it wasn't "quite right" for the line. "Next time we get together," he added somewhat callously, "I would be delighted to go over it with you and point out what makes it wrong from our point of view." *The Magic Horn* never saw the light of day, as a Beginner Book or otherwise.

Other established Beginner Book authors—such as P. D. Eastman and the Berenstains—at various times found their work similarly rejected by Ted. He wasn't afraid to jeopardize an established working relationship. To him, it was all about the quality of the work and its viability as an early reader.

As such, Ted's circle of trusted creators tightened. He clearly preferred to work with those he could keep close at hand. He hired his Dartmouth classmate Al Perkins—who had editorial and screenwriting experience, but had never created a children's book before—and found his old friend to be "energetic and talented" and worthy not only of writing Beginner Books, but also helping out with editorial matters. Ted also brought his alter ego, Theo LeSieg, out of semi-retirement, and gave his neighbor Fred Phelger a second go-round at Beginner Books after a seven-year gap. Only the stalwart Berenstains would continue their work uninterrupted through the Beginner Book "regime change."

The word list, which had been a huge part of Phyllis's influence on the line, went largely by the wayside. By 1967, Ted was telling *Time* magazine that, thanks to television, kids had larger vocabularies than the children of ten years earlier. He also said word lists were "hogwash." Ted later told Digby Diehl:

> They were a throwback to John Dewey. I've decided that, on the high school and college levels, he did some rather important things. But when he got down to teaching reading, he caused the mess which was examined in the book, *Why Johnny Can't Read*. Dewey and his other so-called scientists had the strange belief that they could turn the teaching of reading into a science. By the end of first grade, a child should know so many hundreds of words, and so on. But they forgot the fact that most people who learn to read learn with love and affection and patience—through teachers. During the same period, they also threw the phonics system out of schools. But now what has happened—and I think the Beginner Book series has helped considerably—is that the pendulum is swinging, and they're teaching both by sight and by the phonics system again.

Not that Beginner Books suddenly became novelistic; if anything they continued to skew even younger than they had in the early days. Rather than rely on research and pedagogy, Ted focused on ensuring readability through the story, design, and layout of the books. As for the text, he made it sound easy: "For Beginner Books all I do is to strike out the complex sentence structure, throw out the unnecessary long words, and simplify."

The Beginner Books released in the three years following Phyllis's departure are short on long-lasting masterworks, but high in quality. They include two strong Theo LeSieg books (*I Wish That I Had Duck Feet* and *Come Over to My House*), two entertaining Berenstain romps (*The Bear Scouts* and *The Bears' Picnic*), a Dr. Seuss classic (*Fox in Socks*), and the debut of two new Beginner Book talents (Eric Gurney and Al Perkins, on *The King, the Mice, and the Cheese* and *The Digging-est Dog*, respectively). These years also saw characters from other storybooks—Babar and Doctor Dolittle—in Beginner Books for the first time, paving the way twenty years later for licensed characters to appear in the line.

Beginner Books continued to sell tremendously well. By 1965 they had earned over $8 million in the United States and another million in Great Britain via publisher Billy Collins. And it would get better. In 1965 the Elementary and Secondary Education Act, a lynchpin of President Lyndon B. Johnson's war on poverty, became law. Title II of the act provided school libraries with generous funds to buy materials. As a result, children's book sales soared.

Meanwhile, the Grolier deal continued to pay off handsomely. At the end of 1964 they had their highest quarter to date, selling 2.5 million books, netting $280,000 in royalties (the equivalent of over $2 million today). In 1965, the Beginning Readers' Club had 500,000 subscribers. That same year, a commercial for the program aired during NBC's *Today Show*, with host Hugh Downs showing viewers *The Cat in the Hat Dictionary* and *Green Eggs and Ham*, and asking them to "See for yourself how these delightful Beginner Books fascinate and encourage your young reader."

In the three years since recurrence of her Guillain-Barre, Helen's health had continued to worsen. In addition to the intermittent paralysis in her legs, her eyesight was deteriorating. She suspected this to be related to post-polio syndrome, which is progressive and affects approximately 64 percent of polio patients.

She soldiered on—continuing to solicit Beginner Book manuscripts; work closely with authors; and cheer, coach, and cajole Ted. But she became depressed about the fact that her health problems could not be cured, only managed. Ted felt helpless, and was perhaps not constitutionally able to reverse roles and become a caretaker for his wife. Donald Pease wrote, "Although terrified of losing her, Geisel believed that to survive he needed to distance himself from her." This also happened to coincide with Ted falling in love with Audrey Diamond, who along with her husband, Grey, were close friends of the Geisels. Ted made minimal effort to hide his feelings for Audrey. Besides dedicating *Fox in Socks* to her, he'd dedicated *The Cat in the Hat Songbook* to her daughters, Lark and Lea.

By outside appearances, things were okay. Helen was known at Random House to be always composed and well dressed in a "perfect little pink suit and mink stole" and to be unfailingly kind. She and Ted continued to present themselves as a carefree couple, taking a 1967 vacation to the Colorado Rockies, and going sailing with their neighbors. But behind the scenes, Helen's health and depression were worsening.

On the morning of October 23, 1967, the housekeeper discovered Helen unresponsive in bed. Ted was still asleep in his own bedroom, having worked late the night before. Helen had taken approximately three hundred sodium phenobarbital pills and died in her sleep. She left behind a note, saying in part that she felt herself spiraling into "a black hole from which there is no escape, no brightness." She obliquely referenced Ted's affair with Audrey, writing that she felt like a failure: "I am too old and enmeshed in everything you do and are, that I cannot conceive of life without you."

A memorial service took place at the La Jolla Museum of Contemporary Art, a fitting venue since Helen had devoted so much time and energy to the place, serving as vice president of the board. Eventually, the museum's art reference library would be dubbed the Helen Palmer Geisel Library.

Friends and colleagues were affected deeply. Bennett Cerf said, "Helen was one of the most wonderful women I've met in my whole life . . . We regarded Helen—as a worker, a creator—[as] the most unselfish person we've ever known." Many cited how vital she was in helping Ted Geisel become "Dr. Seuss." Ted himself acknowledged Helen as his other half in creative matters: "Helen was an editor and a partner," he said. She kept a sharp eye on his character and plot development, and even made sure his verse meter scanned. Though invisible, she was everywhere in his work. Ted even admitted of his books, "Her words are in some of them."

Mike Berenstain says, "Right through until her death she was immensely involved and influential in everything he did, and that was something my parents talked about. They loved Helen." In terms of working with Beginner Book authors, she was the sweet to Ted's bitter, the good cop to his bad cop, which was a genuine extension of their personalities. Her opinions on character, plot, and theme development were often just as strong, or stronger, than Ted's, but she was able to convey them to authors in a gentle and encouraging way, as opposed to Ted's blustery dismissals. As Mike put it, "They were a great partnership that ended tragically."

Though Helen's role in shaping Ted's work is an important part of her legacy, it has unfortunately been portrayed as her only legacy. You could see it in the newspaper notices about her death. The *Los Angeles Times* titled theirs "Helen Palmer; Author's Wife." The Associated Press article had a better headline—"Helen Palmer, Children's Author, Dies"—but the piece itself mentioned three Dr. Seuss books by name and none of Helen's. Neil and Judith Morgan's biography presented a multidimensional portrait of Helen, but drew criticism for presenting her death only through the perspective of what it meant to Ted's career. They included one quote that cast Helen as a detriment to Ted's creativity, and another that labeled her suicide as "her last and greatest gift to him." They also reveled in how Ted's head-spinning remarriage—to Audrey Diamond only eight months after Helen's death—lightened him and extended his life.

This was sexist and deeply unjust. Helen graduated from Wellesley with honors, and held a master's degree from Oxford. She had an Academy Award for cowriting *Design for Death*. It's no exaggeration to say Beginner Books wouldn't have survived its first years without her, nor is it overstating to say that her talent in working with authors and illustrators was a huge reason the books of the line's first decade turned out as good as they did. The works she produced as a writer—her three Golden Books, *A Fish Out of Water*, her three photo-illustrated Beginner Books with Lynn Fayman—were the work of someone who had a gift of writing for children honestly and authentically. As Al Perkins wrote upon Helen's death, he hoped she would be mourned and remembered "as a brilliant writer, editor, and critic in her own right."

BEGINNER BOOK SPOTLIGHT

Al Perkins

Albert Rogers Perkins was born in New York City in 1904, the only child of Charles Albert Perkins and Miriam Rogers Perkins. Albert was named for his paternal grandfather, who for sixteen years was principal of Phillips Exeter Academy, the same school P. D. Eastman attended. Charles Perkins, a lawyer, spent thirteen years in the New York County district attorney's office, where he worked primarily on indicting and prosecuting gang and underworld leaders. Miriam Perkins did not work professionally, but was civic-minded and highly educated, having graduated from Smith College in 1890 and continued on to graduate work at Yale, Cornell, Munich, and Heidelberg.

Al attended Dartmouth, his grandfather and father's alma mater, and there he met Ted Geisel. The two became roommates and worked together at the *Jack-O-Lantern*. Later Ted would recall of Al: "All I remember about you in college is that you never studied. You just drew pictures of owls in your notebooks, and made up stories about them." In reality Ted and Al were much closer than that. Ted even once called Al "the funniest fellow I have ever met."

After graduating cum laude in 1925—he must have done *some* studying—Al went to work for publisher D. Appleton & Company, and married Myrell Armstrong, an artist whose father was playwright Paul Armstrong. The couple settled in Greenwich Village, and often met up with Ted and Helen at a speakeasy called the Dizzy Club, where Al and Ted's shared love of drinking and practical jokes often got the men in trouble.

By the early 1930s Myrell and Al had a son, John, and daughter, Nancy. Al had moved on from D. Appleton to become a reporter for the International News Service and the *New York Journal-American*. From there he briefly served as managing editor for *Outdoor Life* magazine, and then spent three years writing and editing for the popular radio news program *The March of Time*.

In 1937, Al moved the family from New York to Beverly Hills, California, where he successfully transitioned from radio to film, landing writing work for Republic Productions and Universal Pictures (including Deanna Durbin's screen debut, *Three Smart Girls*, in 1936, and the dog film *The Mighty Treve*, in 1937). In 1937 he accepted a position as a story editor with Walt Disney Studios, where he worked—just as P. D. Eastman had—on *Snow White and the Seven Dwarves*, *Fantasia*, and *Alice in Wonderland*. He also cowrote the screenplay for *The Reluctant Dragon*, a 1941 adaptation of the Kenneth Grahame story. Walt Disney reportedly regularly referred to Al as "that big guy who can't draw."

It was during this time that Ted came out and briefly lived with Al and Myrell while he and Helen were beginning their protracted transition from living in New York to living in Southern California. Meanwhile, Al and his family would essentially swap places with the Geisels. In 1941 they returned to New York City, where Al became a script editor for CBS (at that time primarily a radio network). In 1943 he and Myrell divorced, and Al made yet another career change. He began a tenure as the director of film, radio, and television for *Look* magazine, and also began teaching courses in radio and television writing at New York University.

While at an educational conference, he met Jane Tiffany Wagner, who was teaching similar classes at Columbia. The Iowa-by-way-of-Michigan native was also serving as the director of Women's War Activities at NBC, where she was instrumental in the production of a four-week series, *Now Is the Time*, celebrating the role of women in the military. Jane, like Al's mother, was highly educated (she had her master's degree from Columbia University), and, like Al himself, had been professionally restless (she'd worked as a home economist for at least four different companies by 1942). Jane had two children—Diana and Sally—from an earlier marriage to Willard Dean.

Jane and Al married in July 1944, and the new family settled in Mamaroneck, New York, a small village in Westchester County. Miriam Perkins died in 1945, leaving Al a sizable inheritance. Their home and estate in Suffern was sold as a private girls' school. The family maid and butler, a couple named Gladys and Fred, came to live with Al and Jane and the girls.

Al left *Look* in 1946 to help start up a new magazine, *Sport*, with Sumner Blossom. The magazine was an innovative precursor to *Sports Illustrated*, featuring interviews and full-color photos. Though not particularly a sports nut himself, Al loved the work and got to meet many of the big sports stars of the day, including Babe Ruth, Ben Hogan, and Bob Cousy. Al stayed at *Sport* for five years before a group of investors bought the magazine out

Al and Jane Perkins on their wedding day. Courtesy Sally Allen.

and fired its staff, a twist of fate that left Al heartbroken. He moved on to a position at the *American*, where he was a managing editor for another seven years.

In 1957, Al and Jane both essentially retired. They first moved to Bermuda, where Al joined a local authors' group and wrote articles for the *Bermudian* magazine on topics such as horse races at the Bermuda Jockey Club and local reaction to seaplane take-offs and landings from the US Naval Station in Southampton. In the early 1960s the couple moved even farther east, to the archipelago of Madeira (off the coast of Portugal). There, Al began writing for the Goodyear travel magazine *Orbit*. The magazine sent him to write human interest stories about the far-flung places where they had offices, allowing Al and Jane to travel all over the world.

A few years passed this way, but now creeping into their sixties the couple realized it was time to settle down somewhere with more support and services, particularly as it related to their health. They chose to head back to the

Al at the La Jolla Tennis Club. Courtesy Sally Allen.

States, to La Jolla. Around this time Al had been batting around some ideas for children's books, and he got in touch with Ted and told him as much. Ted was encouraging, so Al wrote out a draft for a baseball story while on a flight from Honolulu to LA. It was the story that would become *Don and Donna Go to Bat*, Beginner Book B-42, released in 1966.

Ted and Helen were both excited about Al's work. They asked him to send in another script on a "wackier theme," but were confident enough in his potential to ask Random House to send a $500 advance against a future book. Helen wrote Bob Bernstein's with a vivid metaphor, saying Al would be an excellent Beginner Book author "if we have enough pins with which to spray his anatomy to keep him at work."

In short order, Al became one of Ted's most trusted writers, with two more Beginner Books following in 1967, and three more (plus a Bright and Early Book) in 1968. He quickly proved his strength as a writer was anchoring his stories with an emotional core, something that Beginner Books hadn't

ALBERT R. PERKINS

1904 - 1975

IN MEMORIUM

WITH FULL APPRECIATION OF HIS ABUNDANT TALENTS,

WITH HIGH RESPECT FOR THE GENIUS OF HIS CREATIONS,

WITH TOTAL GRATITUDE FOR THE RARE PRIVILEGE OF KNOWING HIM,

AND WITH DEEP AFFECTION FOR THE FRIEND WE LOVED;

THE MEMBERS OF "KELLOGG'S GANG" OF OLD TENNIS ENTHUSIASTS

DEDICATE THESE SENTIMENTS TO THE MEMORY OF OUR BELOVED

"TINY" PERKINS.

"HE ENRICHED OUR LIVES"

"Kellogg's Gang"

IN MEMORIUM - ALBERT ("TINY") PERKINS

I said above that there was one, I'd mention separately,
whose birthday was in August; but whose spirit now runs free;
May I say to those who joined this group
Too late to know this man:
You missed a gift both rich and rare,
Few men are given to know and share.
When one speaks of Al, one does not preach;
He mentions simply talents beyond man's normal reach.
I need not remind you of other birthdays;
Those over which Al presided;
With that singular eloquence and humorous wit,
As he gently kept prodding while doing his bit.
So I think with heads bowed we should give a few thoughts
To those things so peculiarly his;
And maybe, just maybe, he'll see what we're doing,
And like it--wherever he is.

A eulogy from the other members of Kellogg's Gang. Courtesy Sally Allen.

THE CITY OF

SAN DIEGO

SAN DIEGO PUBLIC LIBRARY • 820 E STREET • SAN DIEGO, CALIFORNIA 92101

February 12, 1975

Mrs. A. R. Perkins
8205 Camino del Oro
La Jolla
California   92037

Dear Mrs. Perkins,

It was with a real sense of loss that I heard
of your husband's death.

His books have brightened our shelves for years,
and the librarians in our twenty-five branches
will miss his work.

We have such pleasant memories of his cheerful
chalk-talks at our branches, and always
appreciated his kindness in giving his time
to the children of San Diego.

We shall all miss him.

Sincerely yours,

Jean Kockinos

(Mrs.) Jean Kockinos
Coordinator of Library Services to Children

JK:ln

MEMBER

A letter Jane Perkins received from the San Diego Public Library's children's department following his death. Courtesy Sally Allen.

previously been known for. Al also began taking on some editorial duties and would end up writing more Beginner Books / Bright and Early Books than anyone besides Stan and Jan Berenstain and Ted himself. Al often drew pictures to go along with his manuscripts, quirky renderings that helped him visualize the story's action and momentum. His stepdaughter Sally Allen says, "He would have liked to have been able to illustrate one of his own books. Had he been younger and been able to carry on with some books, he might have done that."

In La Jolla Al and Jane settled into an idyllic retirement. Al played tennis weekly with a group of older guys at the La Jolla Tennis Club. They called themselves Kellogg's Gang, after owner F. W. Kellogg, and the group gave Al the ironic-but-affectionate nickname "Tiny."

Outgoing, quick-to-laugh, and a natural-born storyteller, he served as master of ceremonies at birthday parties and other events. "He had a way with words," Sally recalls. As his writing career took hold, Al often made appearances at local schools doing chalk talks. He received mountains of fan mail and always wrote back.

In the early 1970s, Al's son John, a veteran of the Korean War who suffered from undiagnosed PTSD, died. Al took it extremely hard and fell into a deep depression. On February 10, 1975, Al's lifeless body was found on a La Jolla beach. Speculation was that he walked out into the Pacific to drown himself, but no one really knows what happened.

Though his end was a tragic one, Al left behind a legacy both in how he lived life and in the books he created. "He was a wonderful man," Sally says. "He filled a room with a soft personality. He was a good listener. He was a good storyteller, and he had a great sense of humor. And he was adventuresome, obviously. My kids just adored him."

8

Ted Takes Over (1968–1974)

Ted said of the immediate aftermath of Helen's death: "I didn't know whether to kill myself, burn the house down, or just go away and get lost." He was no stranger to losing someone close to him. A younger sister—Henrietta—succumbed to pneumonia when Ted was four. When he was in his mid-twenties, his mother died of a brain tumor. And his estranged older sister, Marnie, passed away in 1945, an occurrence that shook him so deeply that he avoided the topic for the rest of his life. It seems the only way he knew how to cope was to move forward with blinders on.

The effects of Helen's death on Beginner Books wouldn't be felt immediately. The release of new Beginner Books and the launch of Bright and Early Books in 1968 had already been in motion. But with Ted as the sole remaining founder, the line's future became a big question mark. Fearing the loss of a very lucrative line of books, Bob Bernstein decided to try to shore things up by moving staff around.

Once again, Phyllis ended up with the short end of the stick. Step-Up Books were essentially dissolved, and Phyllis begrudgingly moved on to other projects, most prominently the popular series of "Miss Craig" exercise books by Marjorie Craig. Elma Merz (now using her married name, Elma Otto) was reassigned to assist with Beginner Books. And Anne Johnson (the former Anne MarcoVecchio, who married Hank Johnson in 1965) was made vice president of Beginner Books, working with contract artists and writers. Ted remained president.

Also moving over from Step-Up Books was editor and artist Michael K. Frith, who took the position of editor-in-chief. Born in 1941, and raised in Salt Kettle, Bermuda, Michael grew up between worlds. Bermuda is both isolated and—during Michael's childhood when commercial air travel was not common—remote. Yet by virtue of serving as US military bases during World War II and as a popular tourist destination, the world came to the island. Michael's family was in the hospitality business, and this brought interesting and influential people into his orbit, such as James Linen (publisher of *Time*) and playwright and ambassador Clare Booth Luce.

This dichotomy also manifested in Michael's artistic influences. As a child, he immersed himself in the work of authors such as Robert Louis Stevenson, Charles Dickens, and Hillaire Belloc, as well as the Oz books by L. Frank Baum and Ruth Plumly Thompson. Illustrators like John R. Neill, Howard Pyle, and N. C. Wyeth captured his imagination. But at the same time he was also enamored with comic books he'd buy each week from the local magazine shop. He recalls, "The guys out there on the navy base and air force base, they were kids themselves, just teenagers, and they'd subscribe to comic books then they'd sell them to the used magazine store and I'd be there to pick them up." He loved Disney comics as a kid, but as he got older he gravitated toward the crime, fantasy, and science fiction books put out by EC Comics, as well as the irreverent, satirical humor of *MAD*.

These were just some of the influences that fed young Michael's imagination and his own drawings and stories. And that, in turn, led to unexpected opportunities. "I was very lucky in that [Bermuda] is a small place and I loved to draw pictures. I would turn up somewhere and people would say, 'Hey, how'd you like to try this?'" At age eleven, he started creating posters and doing caricatures in the local newspaper, the *Mid-Ocean News*. He also wrote and illustrated for a tourist magazine, and fell in the orbit of celebrated British magician Robert Harbin. Harbin was ostensibly retired, but couldn't rest. With Michael assisting, he worked up a touring show. The pair then started a kids' show on local station ZBM, with Michael serving as an on-air sidekick. When Harbin left, Michael took over as host.

In boarding school Michael found his way onto the newspaper and yearbook staffs, as well as into the drama club. He did well in school, but didn't have any ambitions of going to college. "I was already doing what I loved to do," he says. But the headmaster, in his late eighties and a venerated figure at the school, called Michael down during his final year and said, "I have applied for you at Harvard and Yale. Which one do you want to go to?" Michael knew the famous humor magazine, the *Lampoon*, was at Harvard, so that's where he chose to go.

He tried out for the *Lampoon*, made it on staff, and would eventually end up serving as president. It was at the *Lampoon* that Michael became friends with Christopher Cerf, Bennett and Phyllis's son. The two became fast friends. Because going back home to Bermuda for vacations wasn't always feasible, he often relied on his classmates' families to host him. The Cerfs were one of those families. Through the *Lampoon*, Michael and Chris worked together to publish a James Bond parody novel, I*N FL*M*NG's *Alligator*, in 1962 before they'd even graduated.

During Michael's junior year, Bennett and Phyllis asked him to think about moving to New York and working on Beginner Books. Though he also had a job offer from Marshall Field IV—whose son Marshall Field V was another friend and classmate—the idea of working with Dr. Seuss was too enticing. "I said, 'Well, that sounds like the next natural door to step through,'" Michael recalls.

He soon found, however, that he wouldn't be working with Ted. Michael's arrival at Random House in 1963 happened to coincide with Phyllis's removal from Beginner Books. Instead of working on Beginner Books with Ted, he would help Phyllis design, edit, and launch Step-Up Books. Phyllis's anger at Ted was still fresh. Michael was given strict orders as it pertained to Dr. Seuss: "If you happen to run into Ted or Helen in the elevator," he was told, "don't acknowledge or speak to them."

For the next four years Michael worked with Phyllis, Elma, and his own assistant, Théon Banos, on Step-Up Books. He did both editing and art design, and illustrated a series of Step-Ups by Leonora and Arthur Hornblow starting with 1964's *Animals Do the Strangest Things* (followed by *Birds Do the Strangest Things*, *Fish Do the Strangest Things*, *Reptiles Do the Strangest Things*, and *Prehistoric Monsters Did the Strangest Things*). Working on Step-Up Books was Michael's introduction to creating books that were tailored toward specific readability levels (in this case, third grade). "I loved it," he says now. "Having to work with those restrictions of Dale-Chall and Spache [word lists] imposed a very very clarified version of what you could put down on paper and make understandable for the readership."

This made him an ideal fit to move over to Beginner Books. It was also, of course, a round-the-way fulfillment of the initial promise of getting to work directly with Ted. The pair turned out to be a perfect match, and Michael would be instrumental in keeping Beginner Books and Bright and Early Books moving through the end of the 1960s into the 1970s.

Around this same time, the steadily growing Random House had outgrown the Villard Mansion. In 1969 the whole operation, Beginner Books included, moved to a forty-four-story office building at Fiftieth Street and Third Avenue. Random House occupied fourteen floors. Michael was given one of the biggest offices at Random House, ostensibly because he shared it with Ted. But in reality Ted was very rarely there. The walls of the spacious office were covered floor to ceiling with corkboard just like Ted's office in La Jolla. This allowed

Michael Frith circa 1970 in his Beginner Book office at the new Random House headquarters on Third Avenue. Proofs for *Bears in the Night*, *I Can Write!*, *The B Book*, and *The Lorax* line the upper walls. Lower are layouts for the first Sesame Street book Michael worked on. Courtesy Michael Frith.

Michael and Ted to tack up storyboards for Beginner and Bright and Early Books, obsessing over layouts until they felt everything was perfect.

THE BEGINNING OF BRIGHT AND EARLY

Extra easy, breezy and gay, BRIGHT AND EARLY BOOKS make learning to read really child's play for 2-to-6-year-olds.
—September 1969 newspaper ad

The year 1968 saw the debut of a new subset of Beginner Books. They were that same familiar size, and had the same authors and illustrators, and the Cat in the Hat was there on the spine, but on the cover the Cat was striking a new pose, standing off to the right, holding a sign that read "Bright and Early Books for Beginning Beginners."

There's evidence that Ted, Helen, and Phyllis had considered splitting Beginner Books into two lines as early as 1960, as the trio had very quickly discovered both a need and demand for books that were simpler than the first- and second-grade levels. This information came in letters from parents who were sharing Beginner Books with their three-, four-, and five-year-olds, as well as from experts like author and professor David H. Russell. In a 1961 article in *Elementary English* he wrote that early readers had made independent reading possible at an earlier age, but that "the books still do not provide for the children at the beginning of the process of learning to read."

They tackled this by attempting books with fewer words and a more limited vocabulary; *Go, Dog. Go!*, *Green Eggs and Ham*, and *Ten Apples Up on Top!* all had vocabularies of fewer than one hundred words. As these books were being prepared, Harper & Row announced in *Publishers Weekly* that they were starting a new offshoot line called "Early I Can Read!"

Instead of risking looking like imitators, Ted, Helen, and Phyllis continued to put out books for early readers (*Dr. Seuss's ABC*, *Hop on Pop*) without branching off, and contented themselves by creating an ordered reading list arranged by the level of difficulty. This list appeared on the back dust jacket of many early 1960s editions of Beginner Books, as well as in advertisements. However, the idea of beginning Beginner Books got lost in the shuffle of Phyllis's ouster, and the books became less strictly leveled once she left. But Ted and Helen hadn't forgotten, and they finally revived the idea.

What made a book a Bright and Early Book? The word count was reduced severely, in many cases fewer than five words per page. The vocabulary was simple. And on top of that, nearly every word was accompanied by a picture. They were written exclusively in verse. The illustrations were, at least at first, simplified. The books were half as long (thirty-two pages to Beginner Books' sixty-four). And the subject matter was nearly always about something immediate and familiar to children: body parts, vehicles, animal noises, homes, and so on. Save a few instances, the books didn't tell stories as much as riff on concepts. In this way they were very much in the mold of *One Fish, Two Fish, Red Fish, Blue Fish* and *Hop on Pop*.

Bright and Early Books would end up being a significant factor in the gradual decline in the number of new Beginner Books. With the focus split, over the years Bright and Early Books started to outpopulate its parent line. Additionally, the distinction between the two types of books blurred. This may have been due to where Ted's interest lay, or the fact that sales were better, but likely both. In an interview Ted summarized the evolution of the books: "I realized there was a level below Beginner Books, so we began making things simpler and simpler; and then we set up Bright and Early Books for younger and younger readers." Then, he joked, "At the moment I'm working on something I call Prenatal Books."

When one compares the list of Beginner Books (including Bright and Early Books and Big Beginner Books) released in the 1970s to the list of those released in the 1960s, a couple of things stand out. One is that the 1970s list is about twenty books shorter than the 1960s list. The other is how few unique names there are on the list of 1970s authors. Beginner Books of the 1960s were the work of sixteen different authors. The 1970s Beginner Books are the work of only five, with Ted himself responsible for over half of the thirty-four titles released in the decade. The Berenstains made up the majority of the rest.

With both Phyllis and Helen gone, Ted was Beginner Books and Beginner Books was Ted.

In many ways this was what Ted had always wanted: Near-complete control over the quality of the line that bore his trademark Cat. For the first ten years of Beginner Books he felt he had compromised repeatedly, though this was mostly because he imposed his own perfectionism on others, and his excellent track record had given him reason to justify that approach. "He believed very strongly that Ted knew better," Michael Frith says. "He could be very very hard on the various writers and illustrators because no matter what they did it was never as good as he thought it could be."

Ted's assistant, Julie Olfe, said that Ted had difficulty expressing the vision in his head to other writers. When he tried, it often came out as blunt and brutal criticism. Helen had served as a translator of what was in Ted's head, and genteel bearer of bad news. In her absence, Michael took on that same role.

Another motivation for Ted to do the Beginner Books himself was that he could get credit for work he was doing anyway. He often felt that the amount of rewriting required on some manuscripts was more work than had he just written it himself. In the late 1960s he sent a memo regarding a failed collaborative project called *The Sea Encyclopedia*, writing, "Dr. Seuss doesn't want to write any more Beginner Books for other authors to sign." This was likely exaggeration when it came to the books of the 1950s and 1960s, but by the 1970s Ted assuming authorship of the books nearly became the fact of the matter.

According to Michael, the predominate method of working during this time was to develop a manuscript through lively back and forth between him and Ted. This mirrored the way Ted had worked on *Jack-O-Lantern* stories at Dartmouth with his classmate Norman Maclean, each taking turns writing lines. Michael and Ted swapped doodles, sketches, and bits of verse piece by piece, pinning them up to their respective cork-lined offices until they had a complete storyboard of the book, even down to the arrangement of the text on the page. It was a monumental effort to produce something that appeared to be effortless.

When Michael and Ted were finished with this manic process, a dummy version of the book—with all of the text and illustrations in place—would go to the illustrator to carry out. Though this was the process primarily on the Theo LeSieg books, it would also apply to books by other authors. Meaning, that often the name on the cover was not the book's only author. "I don't want to take credit away from anybody," Michael says. "Everybody contributed, but it was such a specific discipline that it would go through a lot before it came out the other end of our little Beginner Book meat grinder."

The philosophy that Ted and Michael—both artists and designers before they were anything else—operated under was that a Beginner Book's visual presentation in both design and illustration were as much part of telling the story as the words, if not more. They oriented everything—the direction of the action, the color, the text itself—to flow left to right and push the reader through the book.

Michael says,

> It was always about the marriage of the text and the pictures in such a way that as you progress through the book you progressed in your learning. That simple, but not so simple in the execution. We were both happily fanatical about layout, and about the structure of how the picture and text complemented each other on the page. And we had a lot of fun. It was terrific fun. The back and forth with the composition on these books—it was just a joy.

That joy that Michael and Ted found in working with each other was one of the defining qualities of this era of Beginner Books. In the second half of the 1960s running Beginner Books had been an increasingly cheerless enterprise for Ted—"Having sweat instead of fun" as he once put it in a letter to an illustrator. But Michael helped turn that around, at least for a while. Elma told the Morgans that pairing Ted and Michael was an adroit move. "Ted always needed someone in New York to understand his artistic mind and playfulness," she said.

Though Ted was the same age as Michael's father (a thirty-six-year age difference), the two had similar senses of playfulness and fun. Though he had the big office in New York, Michael more often visited Ted in La Jolla than Ted came east. Sometimes, when they were stuck and in need of inspiration, Ted would raid his hat closet, in which he kept a prodigious collection of different types of headgear. He'd bring back a hat for each of them, Michael says, and they'd sit there, "two grown men in stupid hats trying to come up with the right word for a book that had only 50 words in it at most."

Ted began to refer to the duo as the Walrus (himself) and the Carpenter (Michael), after Lewis Carroll's famous poem "Jabberwocky." He enjoyed pulling lighthearted pranks on his partner, such proposing a fifty-word Beginner Book manuscript written completely in Navajo, or fabricating a fan letter from a toothless woman named Cassandra Fang in "Upper Plate, Neb." Together they created naughty poetry using the codes on their color charts (such as Ted's "Oh, to be under a Number 3 sky / In the shade of a Number 12 tree! In the Number 9 grass / I would gleefully lie / With my Number 4 lass under me.").

It was in these playful conditions that Ted produced some of his most enduring Beginner Book classics, the majority of them under the Bright and Early banner. Michael asserts, "I think Bright and Early Books excited him because we weren't really bound by the formula. They were really reading readiness books . . . and the assumption was that these were books that were being read to rather than read by. So that kind of loosened the verbiage up a bit, which of course for Ted was always a joy. That was like giving him candy." In this way, simple concepts such as "up" and "go" were expanded into the joyful *Great Day for Up!* (1974) and the cathartic *Marvin K. Mooney Will You Please Go Now!* (1971). And even without a vocabulary list limitation, books like *There's a Wocket in My Pocket!* (1974) and *Mr. Brown Can Moo! Can You?* (1970) are extremely deliberate in what they teach children about sounds and words.

BEGINNER BOOK SPOTLIGHT

P. D. Eastman: Part 2

After completing work on 1964's *The Cat in the Hat Beginner Book Dictionary*, his seventh Beginner Book in as many years, Phil Eastman took a break from the line. He did the four Aaron the Alligator books for Phyllis Cerf's Take-Along Book line, and then pitched a story about a crow and an elephant, which Ted and Helen asked him to heavily revise. In 1968, his eighth Beginner Book, *The Best Nest*, hit the shelves.

Also in 1968, Phil helped launch another Random House early reader line, Early Bird Books. Advertised as "stories for 2 to 6 year olds about the things they like to listen to again and again," the series sounded conspicuously like the just-launched Bright and Early Books. The distinction, according to the publisher, was that Early Bird Books were meant as read alouds while very early readers might actually tackle Bright and Early Books on their own. Phil's book for the line was *Flap Your Wings*, the tale of two birds who raise an alligator as their own. Early Bird Books didn't catch on and the line disappeared unceremoniously the following year (*Flap Your Wings* would be reconfigured as a Beginner Book in 2000).

Phil's final Beginner Book, *I'll Teach My Dog 100 Words*, written by Michael Frith specifically for P. D. to illustrate, appeared in 1973.

Big Dog . . . Little Dog: A Bedtime Story, also published in 1973, was an inaugural title in another new book format, Picturebacks. Unlike Take-Along and Early Bird Books, this one would prove to be very successful, most notably launching the Berenstain Bears phenomenon. Phil would do one more title in the line, 1974's *The Alphabet Book*. Five years later, *What Time Is It?*, an interactive time-telling book featuring Fred and Ted from *Big Dog . . . Little Dog*, would prove to be Phil's final published work.

In 1980, Phil was diagnosed with Parkinson's Disease. Phil passed away in January of 1986, having turned seventy-six a couple of months earlier. Fittingly, that same year Ted had released *You're Only Old Once*, and had used Phil as the model for his bald, mustachioed main character. "That's Ted's tribute to his old friend," Michael Frith says. Though the story—about an elderly man surveying and surviving an array of odd medical tests and procedures— was inspired by Ted's own health troubles, he had been able to commiserate with Phil. For Christmas 1981, he sent a note to Phil and Mary featuring the Cat holding a long sprig of mistletoe. He wrote: "Here with some mistletoe for the Eastmans! And to hell with old Mr. Parkinson. Having just emerged from the hospital after a heart attack, I say to hell with all such nonsense!"

In the 1960s as Phil was occupied with Beginner Books, Mary Eastman had begun a career in photography. She started out in Westport taking photos of friends' and acquaintances' children, and the *Bridgeport Post* noticed Mary's talent, writing, "Her work with children achieves a naturalness and spontaneity that is far different from the usual still posed studio pictures." She combined this with a yen for travel, and ended up documenting the life and culture of women in Tunisian villages as it was before Western influence took over. As a woman, Mary was given access to weddings and family events that men would not have been allowed to witness. Mary considered this her greatest accomplishment. The photos were displayed at the Silvermine Gallery in New Canaan, Connecticut, and in 2003 Mary gifted a large collection of the photos to the El Kef Foundation in El Kef, Tunisia.

Through the 1960s, 1970s, and 1980s she provided photographs for several books including *Dark and Bloodied Ground* (1973) and *Haunted New England*

(1982) by Mary Bolte, *Frost, You Say?: A Yankee Monologue* (1973) by Marshall J. Dodge III, and *Look What I Found: The Young Conservationist's Guide to the Care and Feeding of Small Wildlife* (1983) by Marshal T. Case. Mary outlived Phil by many years, passing away in Hanover, New Hampshire, in 2013.

As of 2014, Phil's books had sold 31 million copies. The sales and popularity were nice, but Phil himself was more gratified that his books had served their mission. "I have had letters from parents and teachers telling me about children with reading problems, who had the first experience with books I have done," he told an interviewer in 1965. "This is most satisfying to me."

⑨

The End of the Line?
(1975–1987)

In 1974, Ted Geisel turned seventy years old. Though he had no notions of retirement, things around him were beginning to change rapidly. In 1971, Bennett Cerf had passed away unexpectedly from a hemorrhage when a blood clot developed following surgery. Though by the time of his death he was no longer president or owner of Random House, his loss was strongly felt. His cofounder, Donald Klopfer, retired in 1975.

Ted's already tiny creative stable was also shrinking. In 1973 the Berenstains had helped launch Random House's new Pictureback series, and with publication of the millions-selling *The Berenstain Bears' New Baby*, were moving toward independence. The year 1973 also marked P. D. Eastman's final original work for Beginner Books. Al Perkins had died tragically in 1975. Michael Frith, meanwhile, had been increasingly called to non-Beginner Book work, and would leave the company for greener pastures in 1975.

When I say "greener" I mean green like Kermit the Frog. Circa 1969 Michael was living in Brooklyn, and his neighbor was Neil Smith, who was directing a preview special for a new children's program going by the name *Sesame Street*. When Michael learned more about the show, he says, "Its goals seemed remarkably parallel to the longtime curriculum for our Beginner Book series, and I wondered if there might be some synergy there." Though Neil didn't expect the new show to last more than a season, Michael was more optimistic, proposing that Children's Television Workshop and Random House team up to make *Sesame Street* books.

After working its way up the chain of command, the idea became reality, with Random House publishing higher-end Sesame Street Books and

Little Golden Books doing mass-market ones. This led to *The Sesame Street Storybook* (1971) and *The Perils of Penelope* (1973), both featuring illustrations by Michael. Just when the first set of books was ready to go to print, Michael was informed that they needed to be approved by Jim Henson. So he headed to Henson headquarters on 67th Street, where Jim delightedly looked over his Muppets in illustrated form.

Jim started calling Michael for freelance design help, first on the 1972 TV special *The Muppet Musicians of Bremen*, and then on the Sesame Street character Mr. Snuffleupagus (who up to that point had been invisible). Eventually Jim offered Michael a job. Michael still enjoyed what he was doing at Random House, and turned Jim down. But Jim was, to use Michael's word, "relentless."

After seeing the new Muppets he'd designed (such as Dr. Teeth) brought to life in the 1975 special *The Muppet Show: Sex and Violence*, Michael could resist no longer. At the end of the year, he left Random House to become the art director at Henson Associates. He'd stay at the company for twenty years, serving at various times as executive vice president, creative and executive producer, and director of creative services. In his tenure there, he designed for the likes of the Muppet movies, *Emmet Otter's Jug Band Christmas*, *The Muppet Show*, *Muppet Babies*, and *Fraggle Rock*.

In 1996, Michael left Henson Associates. In the two subsequent decades, he has continued to find ways to both honor the memory and continue the missions of his two most prominent collaborators. Not only has he pursued the commonalities between Ted Geisel and Jim Henson—innovation, creative problem-solving, instruction through laughter and joy—but he has done work that has furthered their humanistic views.

He was able to literally combine the work of the two men when he served as executive producer of the Henson production *The Wubbulous World of Dr. Seuss*, which aired for two seasons on Nickelodeon. He also teamed with his wife—Muppet performer Kathryn Mullen—as well as Norman Stiles and Christopher Cerf to create the PBS show *Between the Lions*, which focused on developing the literacy of its young viewers. In the early 2000s he and Kathryn joined with Johnie McGlade to create the charity No Strings International, dedicated to using puppetry to create educational videos promoting safety and peace for children in developing countries.

With Michael gone, Ted's response was not to reach out, but to do more by himself. The pace of Beginner Books and Bright and Earlies slowed from four per year to two per year, but Ted was very nearly doing it all by himself. Of the ten books released between 1975 and 1979, Ted had a direct hand in eight of them. He both wrote and illustrated four of those eight (*Oh, the Thinks You*

Michael Frith with the father of the pride in *Between the Lions*. He was called Theo in honor of Ted. Photograph by John E. Barrett. Courtesy John E. Barrett and Sirius Thinking, Ltd.

Can Think!, *The Cat's Quizzer*, *I Can Read with My Eyes Shut!*, and *Oh Say Can You Say?*). This marathon output, along with the final two Theo LeSieg books in 1980 and 1981, represent Ted's final creative gasp on Beginner Books.

Beginner Books' long-term health was in doubt, and Walter Retan, now head of the Random House juvenile department, recognized this. He told the Morgans that Ted's complete creative takeover of the line had dire consequences: "He didn't mean to," Walter said, "but he almost choked off that series." Not only was there a dearth of authors and illustrators to turn to to continue the line, Ted was unlikely to find new ones on his own. He was uninterested in keeping up with children's literature, and always had been (the Beginner Book creators that came from the "inside" had been found by Phyllis). And though his reliance on creators from animation, advertising, and cartooning had served Beginner Books well, Ted no longer had those contacts.

Beginner Books—and by extension the Grolier Beginning Readers' Club— were still phenomenally successful. While the rest of the book industry was starting to experience a sharp comedown from the highs of the 1960s, in 1976 Random posted their highest sales ever—$114 million. Bob Bernstein attributed a large part of that to the strength of their juvenile department, which he says was "minting money." It wasn't just in the United States. After a slow start Collins, who had the UK rights, began to experience great success with Beginner Books, and even started up their own book club with Grolier, reaching not only Great Britain but also New Zealand and Australia. Random House could not afford for Beginner Books to go under.

Ted, likely seeing the writing on the wall and also likely somewhat relieved, agreed to cede more editorial control to Retan and Random House. Though he would still have a hand in Beginner Books through the mid-1980s, his time as "president, policymaker, and editor"—as he described his role to Digby Diehl in 1972—ended with the 1970s.

Nineteen eighty didn't just mark the   turn of a new decade, but also another overhaul at Random House. In February, RCA sold Random House to Donald and Si Newsome, the brothers who owned Conde Nast—the company that published *Vogue*, *Glamour*, and *House & Garden*, as well as several newspapers—for $70 million.

This led to a shuffle of personnel. Jerry Harrison was moved from marketing to become the head of the juvenile department (Walter Retan had left the company in 1978 to become a vice president at Western Publishing). New art director Cathy Goldsmith was immediately assigned to work with Ted, both on Beginner Books and his big books. Janet Schulman took over as editor-in-chief of juveniles. Janet had started out in 1959 at Macmillan, working in marketing and introducing a children's paperback program. She was fired in 1974 as part of a 185-person layoff known as the Macmillan Massacre, corporate retaliation against a movement that was organizing to exploit the publisher's discriminatory practices toward its female employees. Known for being "fierce" and "fearless," Janet landed at Random House, first in the library department, then in marketing. As head of juveniles she would usher in some of the most drastic changes the department had ever seen, changes that would affect Beginner Books in the biggest of ways.

After the baby-boom-and-Title-II-driven highs of the 1960s, the children's book industry as a whole had entered a slump in the early to mid-1970s. Beginner Books remained largely immune, but the cost-cutting showed in lots of little ways. Dust jackets had been phased out in the mid-1970s. Similarly, starting with *Wacky Wednesday* in 1974, Beginner Books had dropped to roughly half of their previous length of sixty-two pages. The books were not only shorter in length, but smaller in size, a half inch shorter on each side. The illustrated endpapers gave way to a generic two-color pattern of the Beginner Book logo.

Janet made an effort to breathe new life into Beginner Books. In the entirety of the 1970s, Ted had only brought one new writer to Beginner Books (Graham Tether, who wrote 1979's *The Hair Book*). In the early 1980s Janet hired Marc Brown and Marilyn Sadler to do Beginner Books, and they'd do two books each for the line. Janet also brought back old friends Robert Lopshire and Walter Farley to do new Beginner Books. This was all part of a concerted effort to keep the line going.

But it wouldn't last.

In 1984, Janet had introduced Step Into Reading, a series of leveled early readers available only in paperback. Janet described her thinking: "Beginning reader books are very valuable, but only for a short time. Kids at that stage should be able to devour these books like popcorn, so I wanted to make them very inexpensive."

Step Into Reading kicked off with six books, all featuring original material and characters (among them *Tom the TV Cat*, by Beginner Book alumni Joan Heilbroner) save the Sesame Street tie-in *Big Bird's Copycat Day*. Besides their price and format, the Step Into Reading books were the first commercial books to be labeled with grade level suggestions. Beginner Books had tried to do this same thing by touting word counts and reading orders and through the addition of Bright and Early Books, but Step Into Reading took that idea to its logical conclusion, and made it feel like an innovation. Much as Beginner Books had once been, Step Into Reading books were an instant hit, and other publishers followed suit with their own leveled readers.

If this all sounds like it had the effect of making new Beginner Books seem obsolete, well, that's how Random House appears to have viewed it as well. It didn't help matters that this all coincided with Ted's declining health (he'd been diagnosed with tongue cancer in 1982 and would deal with operations, recurrences, and complications until his death in 1991). *I Am Not Going to Get Up Today!*, published on the thirtieth anniversary of the first Beginner Book, would be Ted's last for the line. It would also be the final original title in the line for seven years.

BEGINNER BOOK SPOTLIGHT

Roy McKie: Part 2

Roy finalized his divorce in the early 1960s and was deep into his work on Beginner Books when he attended a 1963 art opening for the New York

Society of Illustrators. There he saw a woman he couldn't take his eyes off of. He approached her as she was examining one of the pieces, tapped her on the shoulder, and said, "Before I go, I just have to tell you how nice you look." She was June Reynard, a Society of Illustrators member and Pennsylvania native living and working in New York as a freelance illustrator, working in fashion (having the Christian Dior account with Berkshire International), story illustration, and oil portraits. Roy asked her out to dinner, and she found him "charming and irresistible" with a wry sense of humor and a whimsical nature. The two were mostly inseparable from that point forward. They were married the next year.

June and Roy shared a studio in New York. They each had their own room, but June's looked into Roy's, and she witnessed firsthand as he brought many Beginner Books to life. "I would every so often look up, and it nearly cracked me up, because he would act out all of the facial expressions that he would draw, and even sometimes his body movements would suggest certain things that he was trying to draw." The spontaneity of his final drawings was the result of lots of preparation. He'd make sketch after sketch to work out a composition, and then once he felt ready, rather than lightboxing or inking over, would work directly with ink and brush on paper. The sketches went into the trash, and both June and his son Todd would regularly rescue his discarded drawings from the waste bin.

Despite his love of painting, Roy was less patient about adding color to his drawings. June would sometimes help by tracing his drawings and then doing a rough color version. Then she'd use the printer's chart that listed the percentages of black, white, and gray and the colors to which they corresponded. Roy would use those percentages to paint the blue plates of his original drawings. His first wife, Tuddy, had done this in earlier days as well.

June was a witness to the care and attention to detail that Roy and Ted put into Beginner Books. She accompanied Roy on a trip to La Jolla to meet with Ted and Helen. As the two couples sat together in Ted's studio, Roy and Ted worked over an illustration for a Beginner Book that featured a dog crying. June was astonished to find the discussion centering on whether it was better to have the dog shedding two or three tears ("Talk about detail," she says). "Suddenly Helen looked at me, as though she'd just discovered me there, and she said, 'Dear, would you like to go out?' And I said, 'Woof! Woof!'" Ironically, the much-discussed illustration was never used.

Marrying June and working on Beginner Books gave Roy a second career and life. By all accounts, Roy loved working with Ted, and the two got along famously. "He was the center of my life for a long time," Roy recalled.

"I believed in him completely." Roy always credited Phyllis Cerf for the fact that Beginner Books allowed their illustrators to earn royalties (rather than the industry standard work-for-hire flat fee). This combined with the fact that Beginner Books sold very well provided Roy with a better income than he'd ever had. Roy and June got an apartment in Greenwich Village, traveled extensively, and enjoyed activities such as reading, going to see foreign films and theater productions, visiting art galleries, and ice skating.

Though Roy would illustrate more Beginner Books than any other artist outside of Stan and Jan Berenstain, in his most productive time at the company (1960 to 1975) he continued to illustrate other books, including *The Thinking Man's Dog* by Ted Patrick (1964), *Aesop Up-to-Date* by Robert Zimler (1964), and a series of personality books based on each of the zodiac signs (1972). In the late 1970s, Roy began working with Workman Publishing, illustrating joke and riddle books, and teaming with National Lampoon cofounder Henry Beard for a series of best-selling "dictionaries" focused on various leisure activities (*Fishing, Sailing, Golfing*, etc.).

June believes Roy's work stands out because of his facility with pantomime, of telling stories without words, a skill honed in his years doing "Never Underestimate the Power of a Woman." June says, "The beauty part of Roy's work was that he didn't do the usual thing, in other words, read something and illustrate it. He would come at it from a different way." He brought his own sense of humor and his own ideas, so that his drawings embellished and furthered the story. A small example of this comes in *Ten Apples Up on Top!* in the two-page spread of the lion, tiger, and dog being chased by the mob of bears and birds. Roy has the youngest bear throwing his tennis racket at the trio.

Roy was a pure artist, always doodling while he was on the phone, and drawing for himself when he didn't have an assignment. In his retirement he enjoyed the fact that his artistic legacy would live in his books. At age ninety-one, he told an interviewer, "I often go into bookstores around here. An author told me, 'Go in and take them out. Make sure they're at eye level.' It's fun getting away with it." When he died in 2015 he still had twenty-three books in print, most of them Beginner Books. "It's nice to have a book," he said. "It doesn't change. People will find [books] 100 years from now. Books won't go away, I think."

10

A Legacy Line (1988–2019)

In the late 1980s children's books sales began to skyrocket again, thanks in great part to a new baby boom. The year 1989 saw 4 million babies born, the same as were born in 1953. Children's book sales followed, with both hardcovers and paperbacks showing huge jumps in the first half of 1989. New Beginner Books and Bright and Early Books wouldn't be a part of that. Besides reissues of *The Cat's Quizzer* and *My Amazing Book of Autographs* in 1990, there were no books released between 1988 and 1992. Step Into Reading books had fully overtaken their predecessor.

Part of this was due to Ted's death. He succumbed to cancer in September 1991. Audrey Geisel and Random House were left to shepherd his massive literary legacy. In the years immediately following his death this meant very little activity besides selling his books. Beginner Books became a line that was operating on the strength of its catalog of perennial best-sellers. *I Am Not Going to Get Up Today!* very well could have been the last new Beginner Book, and in many ways that would have been fitting. Ted himself wrote the book, and it came out a tidy thirty years after the first book in the series. And with Ted gone, there was no guiding force behind the line anymore.

And it would have been the end of Beginner Books if not for the ongoing strength of Grolier's Beginning Readers' Program. Even in the lull of the late 1980s and early 1990s, the club was a big moneymaker, providing huge checks for Random House every time the deal was renewed. Grolier understandably wanted new material, and for a while, this was filled by repurposing Step Into Reading into Beginner Books and Bright and Early formats. Between approximately 1987 and 2006 this would be done with a mix of original titles (*Sleepy Dog* by Harriet Ziefert and Norman Gorbaty and *6 Sticks* by Molly Coxe), familiar storybook characters (Marc Brown's Arthur and Richard Scarry's Busytown), and licensed properties (Thomas and Friends and Babe the Pig).

Shortly before Ted's death, Random House had gone through another major upheaval. In late 1989, Si Newsome informed Bob Bernstein that it was time for him to retire. Bob was sixty-six years old and wasn't thinking about hanging it up just yet. "I loved my job and was in good health," he wrote in his memoir, "and I knew that many of the top executives at the company were happy and fulfilled in their work as well." A *New York Times* story about his departure called the forced retirement "inexplicable" and said that it had pierced "the Random House mystique."

Bob Bernstein's ouster was a reflection of changing times. The 1970s and 1980s had seen publishing become increasingly corporatized, with larger houses swallowing up smaller ones. At one time, Bob reflected, "the books the houses published reflected their owners' individual interests, and these owners knew the authors personally." Despite Random House's own massive growth during his tenure, Bob had tried to continue the same relationship-focused way of operating that Bennett Cerf and Donald Klopfer had established.

The new president, Alberto Vitale, had been head of Bantam Books but had arrived at that through finance and accounting. As such, his focus would be on the bottom line. The difference would have immediate effects at Random House, with Vitale making his presence felt through list cuts and firings. He described his philosophy in a 2012 interview, "You cannot do earthshaking things in publishing, you have to set the tone of how you want to go with an eye on costs and one eye on profits. But we never saved money when it came to buying a book . . . you never knew that a best-seller was going to be a best-seller until you published it."

The profitable children's department was left mostly alone. In 1994, Janet Schulman stepped down as head of juveniles. Her replacement was Kate Klimo, an Iowa-born Sarah Lawrence College graduate with experience at Platt & Munk, E. P. Dutton (for whom she created a mass-market imprint called Gingerbread House), and Simon and Schuster (where she helped start the Little Simon imprint). She'd been working in Random House's children's department since 1984.

It was primarily Kate and art director Cathy Goldsmith (who Kate dubbed, "The Keeper of the Seussian Flame" by virtue of Cathy's now decade-plus working relationship with Ted) who would bring Beginner Books back. The first sign of new life came in 1993 with the release of the *Beginning Readers'*

Yearbook 1994, a giveaway through the Grolier Beginning Readers' Program. The book had poems, stories, and nonfiction pieces centered on the four seasons. There was a brief biography of Dr. Seuss, a profile of the Clintons ("Meet the First Family"), and suggestions for craft projects. A couple of Step Into Reading books were excerpted (*Cave Boy* and *Toad on the Road*) as were *The Cat's Quizzer* and *Fox in Socks*. Many Beginner Book characters—including P. J. Funnybunny and the Berenstain Bears—made appearances. In all it seems to have been an effort to honor the past and present of the Beginner Book line, and thus serves as a microcosm for the line in the 1990s and into the 2000s.

The first original Beginner Book / Bright and Early Book, Susan Schade and Jon Buller's *Snug House, Bug House!*, appeared in 1995. And starting in 1996 there would be four new Beginner Books each year for the rest of the 1990s. These were a mix of licensed titles, old favorites returning with new books (Robert Lopshire's *New Tricks I Can Do!*; Stan and Jan Berenstain's *The A Book*; Marilyn Sadler and Roger Bollen's *Hunny Bunny Funnybunny*), established children's authors (Laura Numeroff), and brand-new creators (Angelo DeCesare, Timothy Roland, Eric Seltzer).

This new crop of writers and artists were almost all born in the 1950s and thus were the first generation of Beginner Book authors and illustrators young enough to have read Beginner Books as children. Having the iconic Cat in the Hat on the spine and cover of their stories was a source of great pride. And yet, they didn't do imitations. Most of them submitted their dummies and story ideas not knowing that they'd end up as Beginner Books. While in one way this gave the stories a purity, it also meant that it was essentially the editing team (Kate, Mallory Loehr, Alice Jonaitis, Cathy Goldsmith) that determined what made a Beginner Book. This was tricky. Kate says,

> We know that the most successful Beginner Books didn't have a huge vocabulary, recycled the same words over and over again, were lively, they moved. There was movement from the first page to the last page. If you look at something like *Green Eggs and Ham* that thing carries the reader forward. In the abstract we can tell ourselves what a good Beginner Book consisted of, but could we get it out of an author? Not anywhere near as easily.

One problem was that lower page counts prevented the repetition and riffing that characterized the early books. To compensate Kate tried to lure the very best children's book creators to the line, people like Lane Smith, Peter Brown, and David Small, offering them what she calls "really ungodly" amounts of money to try their hand at a Beginner Book. Most turned her down because, Kate reasons, "They understood that they didn't naturally have the knack or that what they would do wouldn't hold up. It wouldn't add to the glory."

In a strange way, this set of circumstances created a consistency between the Beginner Books of the 1990s and those of the 1960s and 1970s. The books were almost always created by individuals who were already established in the line or who were completely new to children's books.

Of the eighteen Beginner Books released in the 1990s, eight were licensed titles. *What Do Smurfs Do All Day?* (1983) had been a dip of the toe into licensing, but this was a jump right into the pool. Kate Klimo labeled licensed Beginner Books as an "inevitable" development. She says, "The licensors we worked with often made it a stipulation of the deal that there would be Beginner Books showcasing their brands in the august company of the one and only Dr. Seuss."

It was also a function of the new ownership at Random House. In 1998 the Newsomes sold Random House to Bertelsmann, a Germany-based multimedia conglomerate that already owned Bantam and Doubleday, and also had controlling interest in RCA Records and America Online. They shelled out over $1 billion for Random House, and they were laser focused on profits. Also, the increasing focus on sales inevitably meant moving away from the development of original ideas in favor of already established authors and properties. This meant, among other things, licensing of TV and film.

Sesame Street Beginner Books made some degree of sense, given the shared history and philosophy of the two entities. So there was *Can You Tell Me How to Get to Sesame Street?* and *It's Not Easy Being Big!* in 1997 and 1998, respectively. Another Jim Henson–related property, *Bear in the Big Blue House*, which ran on the Disney Channel from 1997 to 2006, had a tie-in book as well. There were also books based on the films *The Land before Time* and *Babe*. And in 1995 there was a book about the toddler favorite *Thomas and Friends*, with a title, *Stop, Train, Stop!*, nodding to the Beginner Book classic *Go, Dog. Go!*

Beginner Books would also become involved in the inevitable monetization of Ted's legacy. In 1995—the year that also saw the release of *Daisy-Head Mayzie*, the first of several posthumous publications—Random House put out a series of eight "Dr. Seuss Beginner Fun Workbooks." These leveled educational supplements repurposed art and text from various Beginner Books into activities to practice math and early literacy concepts. The titles sound almost like parodies: *I Am Not Going to Read Any Words Today!*; *I Can Add Upside Down!*, and so on.

BEGINNER BOOK SPOTLIGHT

Stan and Jan Berenstain: Part 2

After their extremely difficult start at Beginner Books, Stan and Jan Berenstain settled into a productive rhythm. They worked together symbiotically, in what their son Mike describes as "a constantly shifting ad hoc collaboration." As a rule the couple worked out a story together, then Jan laid out the illustrations in pencil. Stan inked over them, and then Jan added color, though in later years Stan took on more of the coloring chores. Although things never quite got easier with Ted, they were able to address his requested revisions quickly, if not always happily.

Even as they provided Random House with at least one Beginner or Bright and Early Book per year, Stan and Jan continued to do the monthly install-ment of "It's All in the Family." Their first attempt at a non-Beginner Book children's book was 1973's *The Berenstain Bears' Nursery Tales*, part of Random House's new Pictureback series of paperbacks. Featuring retellings of "The Three Bears," "The Little Red Hen," and "The Gingerbread Man" using the familiar Mama, Papa, and Small Bear characters, the book did not sell well initially. But the next year Stan and Jan released *The Berenstain Bears' New Baby*, introducing a little sister, Sister Bear, to the Bear family. It was a huge hit, as was its 1978 sequel, *The Berenstain Bears Go to School*.

This led the couple to pitch a new series they called "First Time Books," designed to depict and explain common experiences families go through such as seeing the doctor, going to camp, and getting a bad report card. The first book, *The Berenstain Bears and the Sitter*, was released in 1981, and ignited a genuine phenomenon. Not only did it result in scores more books, there were cartoons, Happy Meal toys, and every other imaginable Berenstain Bears product.

In 1976 Stan and Jan moved from Elkins Park to Solebury township, where they settled in a redwood and fieldstone contemporary home on top of a hill. As before, their studio was in their home, and that was where they spent the majority of their time.

Though it was their creativity, drive, and work ethic that ultimately made the Berenstain Bears the phenomenon they became ("They made workaholics look like amateurs," says their son, Mike Berenstain), Stan and Jan generously credited their first mentor. "We doubt that the Bears would have happened except for Ted," they wrote in their autobiography. Though they often chafed and despaired under his exacting editorship, the couple followed Ted's lead. Sterling Lord wrote, "The Berenstains adopted many of the standards that Ted

Geisel had imposed on them . . . and became just as demanding of themselves and their publisher as he had been with them." The Berenstains themselves said upon Ted's death, "Hardly a day passes that one or the other of us doesn't draw upon his wit, wisdom, and joie de vivre."

Once First Time Books took off, Stan and Jan moved away from Beginner Books, producing only four more after 1980, including two reworkings of books from the 1960s and early 1970s. They loved their editors at the publisher, Janet Schulman and Kate Klimo, as well as art director Cathy Goldsmith, but their relationship with Random House deteriorated in the 1990s. This started, not surprisingly, with dwindling sales. In 1992 the books sold 2 million per year. Ten years later that number was down to about 300,000. Sterling Lord blamed a shift away from original content toward TV and movie tie-ins. Then, ironically, when the Bears got a new PBS show in 2002, the publisher didn't capitalize on it.

It reached the point where the publisher was rejecting new manuscripts from Stan and Jan. So in 2004 when Random House declined *The Berenstain Bears Save Christmas*, Sterling sold it to HarperCollins instead. Thus ended a forty-year relationship between publisher and authors. Stan wrote a furious eight-page letter to Random House, detailing all of the reasons why they were leaving. *That Stump Must Go!*, published in 2000, would stand as their final Beginner Book.

Not long after their departure from Random House, Stan was diagnosed with cancer. He died the next year at the age of eighty-two. Though Jan was without her partner of over sixty years, Stan's death didn't dim her work ethic or commitment to her bears. She teamed with Mike, and the mother-son duo produced dozens of books together. Jan died of a stroke in 2012. "Every day she was very productive," Mike said. "She was working on two books and had been doing illustrations until the day she passed away."

The 2000s and 2010s have been a time of major change at Random House, the Beginner Book team has remained fairly consistent. In 2002, Random House CEO Alberto Vitale was replaced with Peter Olson. That same year, Craig Virden, who had led the children's division for five years, was replaced by Chip Gibson.

A decade later there was another sea change. Most significantly, Random House merged with Penguin Books, creating a gargantuan conglomerate called Penguin Random House. Peter Olson was replaced as CEO by Markus

Dohle. The former head of Scholastic, Barbara Marcus, took over the children's division. Kate Klimo also retired that year, but the team that had surrounded her for many years stayed put. Alice Jonaitis remained as editor in charge of Beginner Books and other lines. Cathy Goldsmith continued on as art director. Mallory Loehr became senior vice president of the children's division. This team has had the responsibility of keeping Beginner Books relevant in a new century. This has meant shepherding new Beginner and Bright and Early Books into existence while at the same time keeping the line's storied legacy alive.

In terms of new books, Random House has had a tendency to rely on creators with a past connection to the line. Of the fifteen original titles released in the past twenty years, only five featured authors and illustrators were completely new to Beginner Books. The other ten were by creators who had already worked on Beginner Books (such as Graham Tether, Joan Heilbroner, Marilyn Sadler) or had a familial connection to a past author (Tony Eastman and Christopher Cerf).

Some "new" Beginner Books released in the 2000s were actually older works remade to fit in the line, titles like *Flap Your Wings, Big Dog . . . Little Dog*, *The Alphabet Book* (all by P. D. Eastman), as well as Richard Scarry's *Chuckle with Huckle*. Additionally, licensed material continues to make up a significant portion of Beginner Book releases. There have been five additional *Thomas and Friends* books, as well as books featuring characters from the 2005–2008 animated show *Harry and His Bucket of Dinosaurs* (itself based on a book series by Ian Whybrow and Adrian Reynolds), the Dreamworks film *Trolls* (*Too Many Cupcakes!*), and DC Comics superheroes (*Catch That Crook!*).

While the number of new Beginner Books has steadily diminished decade to decade since the 1990s, Random House has put a larger focus on the line's long list of classic titles, mostly through repurposing, repackaging, and reillustrating.

One of the most inventive ways the publisher repurposed the older books was in a 2004 to 2006 subseries called Bright and Early Playtime Books. This featured *Go, Dog. Go!*, *The Best Nest*, *A Wocket in My Pocket*, *Sam and the Firefly*, and *A Fly Went By* reworked into interactive pull-the-flap books. Less ingenious are the abridged (and in some cases revised) board book versions, as well as a recent series of books that takes Ted's illustrations from a variety of books and arranges them by theme, adding new rhyming text to go along. These include *Dr. Seuss's 123*, *Dr. Seuss's Book of Animals*, and *Dr. Seuss's Book of Colors*.

Random House has also reissued classic Beginner Books in a six-books-in-one format. The first of these, *The Big Green Book of Beginner Books*, was released in 1997 and featured six different Theo LeSieg books. Over the ensuing ten years it has been followed by several color-coded compilations. The red, blue, orange, and aqua collections all feature random story selections that mix the well known and the obscure. The purple book focuses on P. D. Eastman characters. Other collections feature the Berenstains and the body part stories. These big books are widely available at department stores.

A somewhat controversial practice Random House has employed increasingly in the past two decades is having older Beginner Books, particularly ones written by Theo LeSieg, redone with new illustrations.

Kate Klimo says that if a book's sales numbers were lagging, commissioning new illustrations was the publisher's way of giving the book a new life. In 1993 Kate hired Roy McKie to do new pictures for one of the first wave of Beginner Books, Marion Holland's *A Big Ball of String*. The original had been illustrated by Marion herself with charming, but dated, colored-pencil pictures. It would turn out to be ironic that Roy was asked to do the first reillustration in the modern era, because largely it would be his work that was replaced from that point forward.

In 1999 Beginner Books redid *Bennett Cerf's Book of Riddles* and *More Riddles* as a single book with new illustrations by Debbie Palen. From 1999 to 2002, *The Eye Book*, *The Nose Book*, and *The Tooth Book* were all given new pictures by Joe Mathieu. Kate says Joe was chosen because his style is "modern but hearkening back in the right spirit." In each case, Joe mostly preserved Roy's original composition and design choices. *The Hair Book* got new pictures from Australian artist Andrew Joyner in 2018.

Refreshing an older book with new illustrations is a common practice in children's literature, but it feels a bit different with Beginner Books. Perhaps that's because the art in these books take on so much of the storytelling load, and the books are heavily characterized by their design. As such, reillustration hasn't been a particularly popular practice. Burgin Streetman, who writes the blog *Vintage Children's Books My Kid Loves*, has decried the idea of replacing older illustrations, "What I don't understand is why [Random House] feels it must constantly muck with a good thing," she writes. Roy's wife, June, is no fan of it either, calling it "dirty pool" to take royalties away from an artist or an artist's family who might rely on that ongoing source of income.

There are cases where the new pictures were warranted. *A Big Ball of String*, *Bennett Cerf's Book of Riddles*, *More Riddles*, *Hooper Humperdink? Not Him!*, and *The Hair Book* all featured stereotypical depictions of Native Americans, something that was rectified in the new versions. Similarly, 1980's *Maybe You Should*

Fly a Jet! Maybe You Should Be a Vet! was a survey of potential professions acted out by an entirely white cast of characters. Random House reissued the book in January 2020 with new pictures by Kelly Kennedy. The press materials for the rerelease note that the book now contains "a multicultural cast in nontraditional gender roles." Similarly, the 1971 reissue of Ira and Mae Freeman's *You Will Go to the Moon* features new pictures that not only feature more accurate space vehicles, but astronauts that are diverse in both gender and race.

Finally, the 2000s saw the first significant Beginner Book offshoot since Bright and Early Books. Though technically its own line, The Cat in the Hat Learning Library takes much of its DNA from Beginner Books. Before his death, Ted had been in discussions with NASA about creating a series of nonfiction Beginner Books on astronomy. Kate Klimo says they continued to pursue the idea, but when their contact at NASA left, the line moved toward a more general science focus. Debuting in 1998 with *Fine Feathered Friends: All about Birds*, the line has since grown over thirty books strong. In each book, the Cat serves as a guide to the topic. In the mid-2000s, PBS approached Kate about developing the line into a TV show. In 2010, *The Cat in the Hat Knows a Lot about That*, featuring Martin Short as the voice of the Cat, debuted on PBS. The show has introduced a whole new generation of preschoolers to Dr. Seuss and the Cat, and proved to be a big sales boost for the whole Beginner Book line.

Meanwhile, Grolier's Beginning Readers' Program lives on, though under a different name and different ownership. The original club lasted well over three decades, even after Hachette purchased Grolier in 1988. In 2000 Scholastic bought the company as part of its acquisition of all of its competitors, including Troll and Baby's First Book Club. The latter was run by a Norwegian company, Sandvik, that got its start giving a free child development guide to new mothers. Sandvik now operates out of Grolier's headquarters in Danbury, Connecticut, and runs Early Moments, a collection of book clubs. One of these is Dr. Seuss and His Friends, and it's almost identical to the Beginning Readers' Program. This all but ensures that new generations of children will continue to have some of the first reading experiences with Beginner Books, and that the classic titles in the line will continue to be discovered and rediscovered.

In multiple interviews later in his life, Ted singled out Beginner Books as his most significant and satisfying achievement. "I feel my greatest accomplishment," he once said, "was . . . encouraging students to approach reading as a pleasure, not a chore."

Ted and Phyllis didn't see eye-to-eye on much, but they agreed on their shared legacy. Phyllis continued to live a full and colorful life following her stint in publishing. In 1975 she married Robert Wagner, the former mayor of New York City. One of her great causes in her later years was fundraising for the restoration of Central Park, which she championed through cofounding the Women's Committee of the Central Park Conservancy. One of her big ideas was the highly successful Adopt-a-Bench program. After Wagner died in 1991, Phyllis returned to work in advertising, organizing lavish parties to attract clients. "My mother was an incredibly gifted hostess, wonderful at putting people together," her son Jonathan said upon her death in 2006. "But the thing that always made her proudest was those books that helped so many children learn to read."

The year 2018 marked the sixtieth anniversary of Beginner Books. Children who learned to read on the first wave of Beginner Books are now grandparents. And it's wholly conceivable that their grandchildren's own grandchildren will still be reading them in 2078. It's easy to believe teachers of the future will still recommend their first graders practice their newly hatched reading skills with *Are You My Mother?*, that parents will cuddle with their toddlers while reading *Green Eggs and Ham* and *Mr. Brown Can Moo*, that budding young artists will be stunned into reverence by the popping colors in *Put Me in the Zoo* and the busy two-page spreads of *Go, Dog. Go!*, and that young lovers of slapstick comedy will double over in laughter at Papa Bear's pratfalls.

As popular and successful as Beginner Books have been from the very start, this is still an unlikely achievement. For one, it's rare for any book to be in print beyond a generation, let alone several from a single line. It's also unlikely because they've survived and thrived in very harsh, critical conditions.

Certainly within the context of Ted's body of work Beginner Books have been dismissed as lesser works, not as significant or pure in intent. In a 1965 article that appeared in the journal *Elementary English*, John P. Bailey Jr. wrote:

> It is beyond the scope of this article to discuss, praise, or criticize the concepts of the Beginner Books as they were envisioned by the founders, or even as they have developed. However, I feel strongly that this marks the beginning of a rather crass marketing approach to Dr. Seuss's output. The engaging fun of the previous periods is lost in a marked forcing of ideas, a driving which seems out of character, and a perfection which is both unrealistic and unimaginative.

Similarly, Barbara Bader, in her survey of American picture books, wrote that Ted's books after *The Cat in the Hat* are "more frantic, more forced" and went on to add, "it is fair to say that they add very little to what he has done before." A 1964 *Business Week* article claimed, "Some librarians and store buyers say the Beginner Books trade on Dr. Seuss' reputation and are not all up to his quality."

Critics were often harsh on Beginner Books, as when the *Southern Literary Journal* wrote that *Oh, The Thinks You Can Think!* was "the latest of Dr. Seuss's mediocre nonsense rhymes which in no way measure up to his earlier stories." *Kirkus Reviews* tended to be especially catty, assessing Beginner Books with glib dismissals such as calling *Tubby and the Poo-Bah* "a CRASH!ing bore" or this thirty-three-word review of *There's a Wocket in My Pocket!*: " . . . and a findow in my window and a nook gase in my book case . . . and a jertain in the curtain . . . and a noth [*sic*] grush on my tooth brush . . . and a pain in my. . . ."

The gatekeepers of children's literature—librarians and elementary school teachers—had been trained to regard kid's books as a deadly serious business. They had little patience for Ted's attempts to insert a sense of anarchy and nonsense into their affairs. His background in advertising didn't help either. As Michael Frith put it when talking about the parade of bad Beginner Book reviews in *School Library Journal*: "These were a generation of people who would have known Ted from Standard Oil ads and such. They brought all of their preconceptions to his work. We forget that he was not always seen by the establishment as the breakthrough artist we now understand him to have been."

As such, Beginner Books didn't win awards that librarians voted on. No Beginner Book ever came close to an award. This was especially stark in contrast to the accolades given to Harper & Row's I Can Read! books. In addition to *A Kiss for Little Bear*'s Caldecott Honor, Arnold Lobel's Frog and Toad books grabbed Caldecott and Newbery Honors, respectively, in 1971 and 1973.

Of course, time changes things. By the time of his death, Ted was already being lionized, with celebration and appreciation coming from nearly every corner of the children's literature universe. The exaltation has only, of course, grown in the subsequent years. And his legacy simply can't be extricated from his work—as writer, artist, and editor—on Beginner and Bright and Early Books. These books make up more than half of his celebrated oeuvre. In fact, his best-selling and most known books are Beginner Books.

Beginner Books now consistently appear on lists of the best children's books of all time. *Time* magazine's 2015 list and New York Public Library's 2013 list each included three of them. Lists from *Amazon*, *Medium*, and *Reader's Digest* have all included *Green Eggs and Ham*, with *Are You My*

Mother? joining it on two of them. But perhaps the most significant of all was a 2007 survey of teachers conducted by the National Education Association, in which five Beginner Books made the list of 100. The support of educators and librarians, once so elusive, is now a given.

The early reader itself has only grown stronger and more proliferate as the years have passed, to the point that there's scarcely a major children's book publisher that doesn't have a line of books for beginners. And while the concept of leveling—as introduced by Janet Schulman and Step Into Reading—is a newer innovation, for the most part these lines stick to the formula created by combining Ted and Helen's eye for talent and Phyllis's pedagogical research. As Shannon Maughan put it in a 2000 *Publishers Weekly* article, "When it comes to developing a beginning/early reader series, the majority of publishing houses rely on a combination of editorial vision and educational expertise."

Library children's departments have entire sections devoted to early readers, and elementary classrooms across the country have bins full of them. Hit series like Tedd Arnold's Fly Guy, Eric Litwin and James Dean's Pete the Cat, and Mo Willems's Elephant and Piggie have returned these types of books to the spotlight in a big way. The children's literature world now acknowledges their popularity and their necessity, but has been slow to recognize early readers as an art form on par with a picture book or novel.

That began to change in 2004 with an annual award established by the Association for Library Service to Children (ALSC). And they named it after Ted. The Theodor Seuss Geisel Award is an honor that does for early readers what the Caldecott and Newbery do for their respective disciplines, namely recognize the outstanding accomplishments in the field. The Geisel award is given to "author(s) and illustrator(s) of a beginning reader book who demonstrate great creativity and imagination in his/her/their literary and artistic achievements to engage children in reading."

The first award was given in 2006 to *Henry and Mudge and the Great Grandpas* by Cynthia Rylant and Suçie Stevenson. A look at the list of winners and honor books since then shows that writers and artists who have made their names in other disciplines are increasingly trying their hand at early readers, people like Kate DiCamillo, Grace Lin, Kevin Henkes, and Jon Klassen.

As for what qualifies as an early reader, the criteria sound exactly like what Ted, Helen, and Phyllis set out back in 1958 and refined over the years. Here's what Robin Smith, a teacher and reviewer who served on both Caldecott and Geisel award committees, wrote in the *Horn Book* blog:

The font is usually clear and readable, so the eye easily knows where to go next. The vocabulary is generally limited to words that are sight words or can be decoded easily using the rules of phonics. Sentences tend to be simple and do not extend over a page turn. The book should appeal to new readers who are about five to eight years old (as opposed to many easy-to-read books with themes that appeal to toddlers and babies). The illustrations are critical in books for new readers and need to directly reflect the text, helping give clues about harder words and tell the story.

In the same article, Smith also acknowledged the high level of difficulty involved in writing an "excellent" book for new readers. Of course this is something the Beginner Book founders knew sixty years ago.

One hopes that the arrival at respectability won't lead to a lessening of the originality and anarchy that made Beginner Books work in the first place. One hopes that the publishers, authors, and illustrators of early readers will continue to remember that the ultimate legacy of Beginner Books is that it introduced humor, joy, and absurdity into the process of learning to read. This was best summarized on the sixteenth page of the very first Beginner Book, in a bit of wisdom voiced by the Cat himself:

It is fun to have fun
But you have to know how.

Part 2

The Beginner Books Encyclopedia

This encyclopedia is arranged chronologically by decade. Please refer to the index to find a specific title or author.

Most Beginner Books are coded with the letter B and the number indicating the order in which they were published. Bright and Early Books are coded similarly, starting with a "BE" designation followed by a number.

The 1950s

THE CAT IN THE HAT COMES BACK (1958), B-2

Dr. Seuss

The Cat in the Hat Comes Back finds mother once again leaving Sally and her brother home alone, this time charging them with shoveling snow. Once again the Cat shows up, snowshoes on his feet. Sally has learned from last time, and takes the role of the fish, warning, "That cat is a bad one . . . He plays lots of bad tricks." The Cat comes in, draws a bath, and tucks into a cake with pink frosting. When the narrator tries to throw him out, he discovers a pink ring left in the tub. The stain proves to be surprisingly transferrable, but also indestructible, at least until Little Cats A through Z (each of whom resides in the hat of the letter cat that precedes it, like Russian nesting dolls) get involved. In the process, the children's shoveling chore is also magically accomplished before the cat goes on his way again.

The Cat in the Hat Comes Back came to fruition quicker than its predecessor, but it was no less of a creative challenge. Ted seems to have borrowed the idea from his own 1951 *Redbook* story, "The Strange Shirt Spot" (reprinted in *The Bippolo Seed and Other Lost Stories*), in which a boy tries to rid himself of a persistent green spot, transferring it from item to item—including, as in *The Cat in the Hat Comes Back*, a bathtub and a dress.

The Little Cats and the magical Voom, however, are brand-new inventions. Author, psychologist, and Harvard professor Stephen Pinker says *The Cat in the Hat Comes Back* was his first book, and that the alphabet cats in the Cat's hat were a revelation. "That image forced me to think about nested sets, infinitesimals, Zeno's paradox, and other concepts that I studied much later in mathematics." Voom seems to be a nod to Ted's time as an ad-man. As Philip Nel pointed out, "The locutions of advertising recur in Seuss's books, sometimes in parody and other times in earnest." Voom even has its own readymade slogan: "Why Voom cleans up anything / Clean as can be."

There's also a sophisticated lesson in the vagaries of English spelling conventions on pages 22 and 23, in which Ted rhymes the words use, whose, news, and shoes. Each makes the same sound using a different combination of letters, preparing readers to be aware of the irregularities and to be flexible in their sound reading.

Some responded to *The Cat in the Hat Comes Back* with the usual criticism that dogs a sequel, namely that it was a rehash of the original. But others saw it as a perfecting of the formula. Warren T. Greenleaf wrote that the book was a shining model of Seuss's theory of "logical insanity": "A simple, straightforward situation unfolds, step by rational step, into a cumulative uproar that is then suddenly, easily, and satisfyingly resolved."

The happy ending is one thing that sets *The Cat in the Hat Comes Back* apart philosophically from its predecessor, which had wrapped up with an unanswered question. This approach would inform Ted's view of Beginner Books moving forward. Logical insanity was not just slapstick and chaos for the sake of it. By depicting fictional situations spinning hilariously out of control, a story can not only induce laughter, but provide a much-needed sense of order to a disordered world. As Ted put it, "If you can see things out of whack, then you can see how things can be in whack."

A FLY WENT BY (1958), B-3

Mike McClintock and Fritz Siebel

A Fly Went By takes Ted's "logical insanity" plot formula and reverses it. Using the cumulative structure of the nursery rhyme "The House That Jack Built" and the nonsense rhyme "There Was an Old Lady Who Swallowed a Fly" (which had been popularized as "I Know an Old Lady" in 1953 by Burl Ives), the story starts with the insanity—a succession of animals chasing after one another—already fully underway. The main character, a young boy, spends most of the book figuring out the sequence of events that led to the trouble. This structure allows for a natural repetition, with each line ("The fly ran away in fear of the frog. The frog ran away in fear of the dog.") building on the previous.

Another unconventional aspect of the book is that it was a complete reversal of the usual picture book hierarchy in which art embellishes text. *A Fly Went By*'s entire story is told in its illustrations, with the words providing the embellishment. In fact, it could have easily been a wordless book, and in this way it's an ideal of the Beginner Book approach.

Junior Reviewers was ecstatic about *A Fly Went By*'s inventiveness, writing, "Here is stunning proof that beginning-to-read books can also be minor masterpieces. If all beginning-to-read books were so well-done, children could learn to read with enthusiastic rapidity."

Author Marshall "Mike" McClintock (1906–1967) had a long history with Ted Geisel. The two men had attended Dartmouth together, with Mike just one year behind Ted. The story goes that in early 1937, at the end of an exhaustive and fruitless search for a publisher for his first children's book *And to Think That I Saw It on Mulberry Street*, Ted ran into Mike on the streets of New York City. When Mike inquired what he was carrying, Ted replied, "A book that no one will publish. I'm lugging it home to burn." After nearly ten years in publishing, Mike had just started work at Vanguard Press as a sales manager and juvenile editor. It just so happened that he was looking for manuscripts.

And that was how Ted's career as a children's book author had begun. Vanguard published *Mulberry Street* (the main character of which was named after Mike's son Marco; the book was dedicated to Mike's then-wife, Helene) and *The 500 Hats of Bartholomew Cubbins* before Ted made the leap to Random House in 1939.

By 1958 Mike had held editorial positions at several different publishers and had authored over twenty books, mostly nonfiction, under several different nom de plumes (including Gregory Duncan, Douglas Marshall, and William Starret). Whether he approached Ted with the manuscript for *A Fly Went By* or whether Ted solicited it (either is plausible), the book represented a huge change in fortune for Mike's writing career. Titles like *The Story of War Weapons* (Harper, 1945) and *How to Build and Operate a Model Railroad* (Dell, 1955) didn't sell poorly, but they were no Beginner Books. *A Fly Went By* would sell well over a million copies during Mike's lifetime alone. Not that the book wasn't worthy, but Ted publishing *A Fly Went By* could definitely be seen as him paying Mike back for his kindness two decades before.

Illustrator Frederick "Fritz" Siebel (1913–1991) was born in Vienna, Austria, to Czechoslovakian parents. His father was a lawyer and his mother a homemaker, and the family maintained dual citizenship (they co-owned a hops farm in Czechoslovakia where Fritz often spent his summers). He attended the Kunstgewerbeschule—the School of Applied Arts—in Vienna, where he studied illustration and stage design. He served in the Czech army from 1934 to 1936 and then immigrated to the United States, landing in New York City.

Fritz, who spoke German, Czech, French, and English, formed a studio with a group of fellow European émigré artists and found work illustrating movie posters for Paramount Pictures. One of Fritz's most famous images was a brush drawing of Veronica Lake on a poster for the 1941 Preston Sturges comedy *Sullivan's Travels*.

In 1942 Fritz placed fifth in a poster contest sponsored by Eleanor Roosevelt. His entry resulted in an iconic World War II image entitled "Someone Talked!" featuring a man drowning while pointing accusingly at the viewer. From there Fritz, who was funny, gregarious, dynamic, and dedicated, steadily built a freelance career. He did illustration work for magazines (*Holiday, Collier's, Saturday Evening Post*) and advertising agencies, showcasing a facility for tailoring his style to whatever best suited the work, from realistic painting to animation-inspired cartooning to modernist minimalism. In 1939 he married Winifred Vaughan. The couple settled in Ossining, New York, and had two children, John and Katherine.

Fritz had worked on several big accounts, including Schlitz Beer, Shell Oil, and Ford Motor Company, but his most memorable achievement came in 1957 when he was tasked by Tatum-Laird, a Chicago advertising firm, with creating the label for a new cleaning product by Proctor and Gamble. The company requested that the label's mascot "emanate an aura of power, security, safety, and low-key virility," while also seeming nonthreatening. Fritz, through much trial and error, came up with Mr. Clean, the bald-pated, white-shirted, hoop-earringed, muscle-bound hero that would grace the labels of what quickly became the best-selling household cleaner on the market. Another illustrator, Richard Black (creator of Smokey the Bear), is often credited for Mr. Clean, but Siebel's family maintains that Fritz was the true originator. His daughter Barbara Thomas says that she and her siblings all recall seeing sketches for the character in their father's studio when they were children.

By this time the family had relocated to Solebury, Pennsylvania, and added three more children—Heddi, Barbara, and Margaret. There they bought a one-hundred-acre farm, renovated the old granite house, and started a dairy farm with fifty head of cattle. One of those cows likely served as the model for the one in *A Fly Went By*.

Fritz's first children's book seems to have had a liberating effect on him. The pictures are done in a much looser, free-wheeling style than the controlled, painterly approach Fritz typically used in his magazine and ad work. In *A Fly Went By*, Fritz's lines are so kinetic, you can almost see his pencil moving. And yet the framing and storytelling are immaculate.

For more on Mike and Fritz, see the entry for *Stop That Ball!*

Fritz Siebel circa the late 1950s when he was working on *A Fly Went By*. Courtesy Barbara Thomas.

THE BIG JUMP AND OTHER STORIES (1958), B-4

Benjamin Elkin and Katherine Evans

The Big Jump and Other Stories contains three tales that feature the same characters and build on one another subtly, but can also be read individually or out of order. The first story, "The Big Jump" introduces us to a kingdom where the king has decreed he is the only one who can own a dog, at least until a young boy named Ben (with some help from one of the dogs) ingeniously accomplishes a feat the king has set out for him. In the next story, "Something New," the kingdom is troubled by a "bad King" from another land who will take the kingdom's gold if they don't give him something that has never been seen. Once again, Ben comes up with a clever solution to the conundrum. Finally, in "The Wish Sack" Ben is given a magical bag that grants its owner's desires. When the bad king gets ahold of it, Ben must outwit him to get it back.

The Big Jump is—in both content and presentation—the most traditional children's book of the first five Beginner Books. Being concerned with kingdoms and magic place it in the realm of fairy tales, the illustrations are not done in the cartoony style of the other Beginner Books. Its episodic "chapter" structure, told in straightforward prose, puts it more in line with an I Can Read! book.

The three fables avoid stating their morals overtly, instead presenting daunting problems met with unexpected solutions. The fact that it's the boy who comes up with those solutions provides the child reader with a sense of empowerment, and allows them to see themselves as similarly capable, intelligent, and resourceful. In fact, the solution to the second story actually came from a child. Author Benjamin Elkin (1911–1995) was also Dr. Elkin, longtime beloved principal of Philip Rogers School, a K–8 school in the West Rogers Park neighborhood of Chicago. He often greeted his students with a riddle: "Find something in this world that no one has ever seen before, since the very world began." One child answered promptly, "a new chick just hatched."

Benjamin Elkin was born in Baltimore, Maryland, one of nine children in his family. His father was a rabbi and an authority on Hebraic law. His mother was an immigrant from Lithuania, and made news in 1946 for graduating high school at the age of sixty. Benjamin was a born storyteller, and from a young age would regale his siblings and their friends with invented tales. He went to college at the Lewis Institute in Boston. He eventually relocated to Chicago where he taught high school and attended both the Chicago Teachers College (now Chicago State University) and Northwestern to acquire his master's degree and PhD in philosophy. After a stint during World War II teaching military administration, he settled in at Phillip Rogers School in 1947.

Benjamin claimed to have written his first children's book while in the army. With more spare time than he knew what to do with, he came up with a story titled "A Day at Daddy's Camp." The manuscript went unpublished, but it awoke in Benjamin a desire to write. His career started in earnest in 1954 with Viking's publication of *The Loudest Noise in the World*. His second book, *Gillespie and the Guards* (1956), won a Caldecott Honor. In total he would publish nearly twenty books, almost all of them adapted or original folktales, more often than not featuring plucky protagonists in medieval settings ("fantasy in a humorous vein" is how Elkin described his own work).

Even as his writing career took off, Benjamin remained in his job as principal of Rogers School. The school's former students recall him as firm without getting loud, often smiling, and kind. Jerry Paul Becker, a self-described "bad boy" who was often sent to Dr. Elkin's office, labels the principal as "a

Benjamin Elkin, pictured here in 1974. Courtesy the International Portrait Gallery.

wonderful guy." Another student, Elliot Korr, recalls Dr. Elkin entering his classroom and asking excitedly, "Who would like to be decapitated?" When all the hands went up, it opened the opportunity for teaching both caution and the importance of looking up words you don't know.

What nearly all of his former students recall most vividly, though, is that whenever Dr. Elkin had a new book out, he'd gather students in the school assembly hall and read it aloud to them. As they filed out from the assembly, he'd play marching music.

Benjamin never married, nor had any children of his own, but he kept plenty busy. In addition to his full-time principalship and writing, he lectured in education at Roosevelt College and indulged in a variety of eclectic hobbies. He was an avid cyclist (having covered most of New England, the Carolinas, and Pennsylvania on his bike), a magician, a square dance caller, and an amateur composer of advertising jingles (he claimed to have won thirteen wristwatches in jingle-writing contests).

Five of Benjamin's books, including *The Big Jump and Other Stories*, would be with Katherine Floyd Evans (1899–1964) as the illustrator. Benjamin and Katherine first worked together on 1957's *Six Foolish Fishermen* for Children's Press. The *Kirkus* review of the book mentioned that "This is just the sort of nonsense small children love . . . many first and second graders could read and understand it independently," making it clear why its creators would be perfect for a Beginner Book.

Katherine Floyd was born in Sedalia, Missouri, and studied at the Provincetown Art Colony (in Massachusetts) and the École de Beaux Arts (in Paris). Settling in Evanston, Illinois, she continued her education at the Chicago School of Design and the Art Institute. She married Clinton B. Evans in 1926, and the couple had a son and a daughter. Her children's book career began in 1946, and the next year she illustrated Charles Tazewell's *The Littlest Angel*, a popular Christmas story. She'd go on to publish over seventy books, many of which she wrote herself. She was a world traveler, known for her intelligence and fearlessness. She was also quite active in her local art community as a member of the Writers Round Table of Chicago, the Chicago Book Clinic, and the National Women's Book Association. She also founded the Evanston Art Center. She died of a heart attack at her summer home in Wisconsin in 1964.

Though it hasn't remained in print, nor has it endured as a classic of children's literature, *The Big Jump* has some high-profile fans. Author and illustrator Jon Klassen—clearly a big Beginner Book fan—recorded video of himself reading his favorite story in the book, "The Wish Sack" while lying in bed, as part of the MyMusicRX fundraiser Bedstock 2015. Two-time Newbery honoree Gary D. Schmidt also celebrates the book, saying that as a child he was an extremely reluctant reader and considered a "lost cause" until one particular teacher took him under her wing. One of the books she introduced him to was *The Big Jump*, which Gary calls the first book he "really, really loved."

A BIG BALL OF STRING (1958), B-5

Marion Holland

A Big Ball of String uses verse to tell the story of a mischievous, inventive boy who appears to share some DNA, visually, with Hank Ketchem's Dennis the

Menace (who had debuted in the funny papers in 1951). Told in the first person, the book begins with the boy's pursuit of enough string to make a large ball. He eventually finds it at the city dump. Next, he makes several unsuccessful attempts to fly a balloon ("POP") and rig up his own caravan ("KERPLOP"). The second half of the book finds him confined to his bed "with a cold in his head" but ingeniously using his string to accomplish tasks and play games such as retrieving darts, pulleying a box of books, turning on the lamp, and playing with his cat. The overarching joke of this section, of course, is that he really isn't staying in his bed or resting at all.

The book employs repetition to great effect in its second half, building up the list of things the boy can do with his string, and the chorus "I can do anything!" The illustrations are done in black, red, and blue colored pencil with a thin line and a light touch. A highlight of looking at the pictures is spotting the cat that curiously follows the boy's escapades from page to page. It's also worth noting the books that are in the protagonist's collection, among them Little Lulu and Popeye comic books, *Babar* (which was published by Random House), *Mike Mulligan and His Steam Shovel, Mr. Popper's Penguins*, and, naturally, *The Cat in the Hat*.

Marion Hall Holland (1908–1989) both wrote and illustrated *A Big Ball of String*. A native of Washington, DC, Marion had two sisters; their father was a veterinarian and their mother, a teacher. An honor student at Swarthmore College, Marion studied law for a year at Columbia University before returning to Washington and focusing on motherhood and writing children's books. She got her start when working as an illustrator for magazines such as *Story Parade*. In the midst of one assignment, she griped about the choice the author had made and the editor replied, "If you think it's so easy to write a children's story, why don't you run home and write one?"

Marion was by that point a mother of five children (one by her first marriage, four from her second), so she had no shortage of inspiration. She wrote a story and submitted it to the sassy editor, who agreed to publish it. By the time Marion landed *A Big Ball of String* with Beginner Books, she had written and illustrated four books for children—*Billy Had a System* (1952), *Billy's Clubhouse* (1955), *No Children, No Pets* (1956), and *A Tree for Teddy* (1957)—for Alfred A. Knopf. After *A Big Ball of String* she published one more title for Random House, *No Room for a Dog* (1959), part of the Gateway Books series for second- and third-grade readers. She'd publish a total of ten books in her career.

Marion became well known in the DC area for her "chalk talks," during which she'd delight children by telling a story and illustrating it on a giant pad

Marion Holland with her daughter Barbara—who went on to become an accomplished author herself—in 1937. Courtesy Emily Brewton Schilling.

of paper as she went along ("she draws fast and talks faster" is how the bio on the dust-jacket flap of *A Big Ball of String* put it). She gave chalk talks at libraries, the annual Washington Post Children's Book Fair, and local schools, including Chevy Chase Elementary School, which was across the street from her house in Chevy Chase, Maryland.

Marion had a "sharp, pithy verbal style" tossing off opinions such as, "Any fool can be a Yankees fan. It takes real talent to be a Senators fan." In her later years her writing often appeared in the *Washington Post*. Not only did she contribute reminiscences of her youth, she became known for her regular correspondence with columnist William Raspberry (who referred to her in print as "my friend in Chevy Chase"), and often wrote letters to the editors pointing out mistakes in their grammar.

With the money she made from *A Big Ball of String* (which sold over a million copies), Marion was able to buy land and build a cabin near Bluemont, Virginia. She and the family prized the home in the mountains, which provided a needed refuge from the sweltering, humid summers in town. When

Marion Holland in 1985. Courtesy Emily Brewton Schilling.

she died in 1989, Marion's cabin went to her oldest daughter, the writer Barbara Holland, who lived there from 1990 until her death in 2010.

A Big Ball of String was reissued in 1993, although Marion's illustrations were replaced with new ones by Roy McKie. Done with a light pencil line and watercolors, Roy's new illustrations are compositionally similar to the originals, but add a sense of energy and chaos that's not present in the original.

SAM AND THE FIREFLY (1958), B-6

P. D. Eastman

Sam and the Firefly is the story of Sam, an owl in search of a friend to play with. When he meets Gus the firefly and teaches him to skywrite using the trail from his light, it awakens the lightning bug's mean streak. Gus uses his new knowledge to cause chaos in traffic, in the sky, and in town. When he cheekily changes the hot dog stand's sign to read "Cold Dogs" the stand's owner captures Gus. Then it's up to Sam to rescue his wayward friend (and stop a train wreck).

Sam and the Firefly was originally the brainchild of author Nathaniel Benchley. Though known primarily as an adult novelist in the 1950s, Nathaniel was working on his first children's novel—*Sinbad the Sailor*—with Random House when Beginner Books started up. Phyllis asked him to try his hand at an early reader, and he came up with the idea of a firefly who uses his light to play tricks. Ted and Helen liked the concept, but not the execution, and ultimately decided Nathaniel wasn't going to be able to write the story to their satisfaction. P. D. Eastman, who was already slated to be the illustrator, took over the whole production. Nathaniel would receive royalties on the book, however, and go on to have a productive career as an early reader author with Beginner Books' competition, writing more than ten I Can Read! books for Harper & Row, including several with illustrator Arnold Lobel.

P. D. Eastman proved to be more than up to the task of taking on both words and pictures. His text has a rhythmic feel despite being prose: "He saw the light hop. / He saw the light jump. It went here, it went there. It went on. It went off." It's also funny, as in Gus's recrimination to his friend: "'Oh, go on home!' said the firefly. 'You old GOOSE! You old HEN! What do you know about fun?'"

The axing of Nathaniel Benchley wasn't the only bit of drama surrounding *Sam and the Firefly*. Judith and Neil Morgan reported that Ted and Helen didn't like the book's illustrations, so much so that they didn't want the book to be published. Brian Jay Jones's *Becoming Dr. Seuss* claims Ted was angry because Phil hadn't used the word "owl" even though he had one for a main character. Phyllis, meanwhile, loved the book, and defended it fiercely.

In the end Random House cofounder Donald Klopfer had to get involved, imploring Ted and Helen to honor the contract with Phil. They reluctantly agreed. The irony is that the book would go on to be one of the line's most enduring classics, and would give Beginner Books one of their prolific and beloved creators.

School Library Journal wrote that *Sam and the Firefly* "provides interest, suspense and word repetition." They also deemed the pictures to be "excellent." *Sam and the Firefly*'s illustrations are highly unique and memorable, largely because of the dominance of the deep blue of night. Phil achieved this effect by drawing and painting directly on Bourges 50 percent process blue acetate sheets. Black colored pencil defines characters and shapes while painted white and yellow provide details and highlights (and, of coruse, Gus's bright skywriting). Author and illustrator Jon Klassen is a big P. D. Eastman fan, citing *Sam and the Firefly* as his favorite, "mostly for the color of nighttime and how soft his illustrations are in it . . . If I ever make a night time book, it will rip this book off hard."

In a letter to Ted and Helen, Phil wrote to thank them for the opportunity to create the book, saying in essence that it helped him find his calling at nearly fifty years old:

> Doing *Sam* made it a very important year for me, because thanks to you, I was able to break into a field which, everybody tells me, is extremely difficult to enter. I am grateful to you for this more than I can tell you. I hope I can make it pay off because I enjoy doing this more than anything I have ever done. I feel for the first time in my life I am doing something useful in a field where I have a contribution to make.

YOU WILL GO TO THE MOON (1959), B-7

Mae and Ira Freeman and Robert Patterson

You Will Go to the Moon is a combination of science fact and informed speculation. Narrated in the rare second person ("This is how you will go to the moon"), the book details a young boy's rocket journey with a surprising amount of plausibility considering how little was known about space travel at the time. The boy goes first to a space station, and then on to the moon itself, where he rides in a "moon car" and sees the "moon house" he'll live in. The book couldn't have been more topical and timely, with the launch of *Sputnik* just two years earlier, and Project Mercury taking its first flight almost simultaneously with the release of the book.

The idea of creating a nonfiction early reader harkened back to when Ted was mulling over William Spaulding's challenge to write a limited-vocabulary book. One of his first ideas was a book about Mount Everest. He'd quickly given up on the notion once he realized how much terminology he'd need to use to do the topic justice.

You Will Go to the Moon has the same challenge. It very simply and clearly explains concepts like gravity and centrifugal force, but never actually uses those words. Nor will you find "astronauts" (they're called "rocket men" instead) or "craters" (they're called "dish holes"). A two-page addendum at the end of the story titled "The Science of Your Moon Trip" attempts to address these omissions by serving as sort of a reverse glossary. It discusses the concepts above, as well as others such as reaction, scattering of light, weight-lessness, and inertia, along with page numbers where they appear. While this is a somewhat clever solution, it's difficult to see how it was expected to be used. Elizabeth Guilfoile, in her *Books for Beginning Readers*, speculates that it was more for the adults reading along with the children than for the children themselves, and yet the brief intro is addressed to the child reader. It seems like it would have been better to just use the words with a lot of contextual and picture support, especially the decodable ones.

Part of the reason the book wasn't done this way was that the lexicon of space travel was just starting to come into common usage. Indeed, the main change in the 1971 revision is that it removes the two-page section at the end and instead uses the words astronaut, gravity, dock, and crater in text.

Chicago-born and Easton, Connecticut-based artist Robert Patterson (1898–1981) was a versatile draftsman and painter who had built an impressive career in advertising and magazine illustration stretching back to the 1920s, with work in *Judge*, *Life*, and *Vogue* among many others. So it's no surprise the pictures in *You Will Go to the Moon* have a 1950s advertising sort of style with a wider color palate than the Beginner Books before it. Patterson was tasked with imagining much of the equipment, including the rocket, space suits, moon rovers, and space station, so they tend to look more in line with science fiction depictions of the time than the reality that was soon to come. The scene with the rocket launch on pages twelve and thirteen is the most dynamic and exciting of the bunch, and one wonders why that wasn't chosen as the book's cover, instead of the non sequitur image of the boy watching with a telescope out his window as the rocket takes off, when in the story he's actually on the rocket. And if you lost the dust jacket all you had was the boy looking at the moon with no window or rocket at all.

New Jersey-based husband and wife team Mae and Ira Freeman were Random House regulars, having authored ten nonfiction children's titles for the publisher stretching back to the early 1940s. Mae (1907–1985) had the writing background. Ira (1905–1987) held a PhD from the University of Chicago, was an associate professor in physics at Rutgers University, and had gained some renown as a lecturer and writer who could communicate science concepts and findings to a wide audience. Together they produced books such as *Fun with Chemistry* (1944), *Fun with Geometry* (1946), and *Fun with Astronomy* (1953), and were thus a natural fit for a Beginner Book about the moon. They'd go on to publish nearly fifty books in total, some together and some separately, almost all with Random House.

Despite its shortcomings, *You Will Go to the Moon* inspired lots of young space nuts, with bloggers fondly recalling the way the story lit their young imaginations. The illustrations especially made a large impact, with readers recalling them as "mesmerizing," and saying, "images from this book have been in my head for 50 years." In 1997 Canadian cult band Moxy Fruvous released a humorous a capella song inspired by the book, titled, "You Will Go to the Moon."

In 1971 the book was reissued with revised text and brand-new illustrations. Thanks to the *Apollo* missions and the first moon landing in 1969, knowledge of space travel and the moon itself had expanded exponentially. So besides the expanded vocabulary and the removal of the now-false line "No one has been there yet," the new version features more accurate illustrations. Whereas Robert Patterson's originals were based on informed speculation, the new pictures were able to portray a moon shot realistically thanks to the *Apollo* landings. The new artist was Lee J. Ames, perhaps best known for his *Draw 50* . . . series of instructional books. Though there was still speculation involved, the rockets, space suits, and the moon itself are much more realistic than they were in the earlier version.

COWBOY ANDY (1959), B-8

Edna Walker Chandler and E. Raymond Kinstler

If *You Will Go to the Moon* represented the very beginnings of a national craze, *Cowboy Andy* represented the tail end of one. The United States' obsession with cowboys and the Wild West had its roots in the 1930s, but really took off in the early 1950s with the Disney-produced *Davy Crockett* television show. At that time Sacramento, California-based Edna Walker Chandler (1908–1982) was an elementary school teacher and a mother of five children. This put her in the position of recognizing the need for high-interest books written expressly for remedial readers, especially boys. She drew upon her upbringing in Kansas to create the Cowboy Sam series, which was published by the Beckley-Cardy Company starting in 1951. Though too wordy to be true early readers, the books used controlled vocabulary and were leveled for classroom use. They'd prove popular, and Edna would produce sixteen books in the series, most with artist Jack Merryweather.

Cowboy Andy is essentially a reworking of the second and third entries in the series, *Cowboy Sam and Freddy* and *Cowboy Sam and the Rodeo* (both 1951), detailing the adventures that Cowboy Sam's young nephew has while visiting his uncle, including learning to ride, rope, brand, and compete in a rodeo. While some of the characters and plot outlines come from those earlier books, there are many original elements in *Cowboy Andy*, including a new main character, new illustrations, and the story's main source of conflict. The latter is the most striking element, with the ranch cook expressing a catty disdain for the "town boy," motivating Andy to prove the man wrong.

Though Edna is credited on the cover as the author, the title page reads "Based on a story by Edna Walker Chandler," which would indicate that someone else adapted the original books into this new story. There's no way to know for sure, but given her past writing experience it's most likely that Helen Geisel did the adaptation.

The new illustrations were done by Everett Raymond Kinstler (1926–2019). Born in New York City, Everett dropped out of high school at age fifteen and began illustrating comic books and pulp magazines. After a stint in the army during World War II and an abandoned attempt at art school, he continued in the comics and pulps working across genres. Westerns were one of his specialties, including pulp titles such as *Ranch Romances* and a mid-1950s Wyatt Earp comic published by Atlas (the future Marvel Comics). His pen-and-ink illustrations for *Cowboy Andy* have that comic book feel, with dynamic perspective and composition.

The book seems to consciously eschew the stereotypical western conventions. There are no cattle rustlers or savages or quick-draw duels. In our first two glimpses of Andy he's carrying his plastic six-shooters and watching a gun-toting cowboy on TV. But when Andy informs Sam that he brought his guns, the cowboy responds, "There are no guns on my ranch . . . we are cowboys, not bad men." Then they get in Sam's car to drive to the ranch.

Cowboy Andy would be the only Beginner Book for both creators. Edna would go on to author dozens more books throughout the 1960s and 1970s for various publishers. In 1963, Everett Kinstler would transition out of illustration work and into full-time portraiture, where he became world renowned. During his lifetime, he captured the likenesses of Ruth Bader Ginsburg, Katherine Hepburn, Tennessee Williams, and eight US presidents, among many others.

THE WHALES GO BY (1959), B-9

Fred Phelger and Paul Galdone

The Whales Go By is a nonfiction prose story told in first-person narration by a female gray whale as she makes her annual migration south, from the Bering Sea to a lagoon off the coast of Mexico in the Pacific. Along the way she sees all sorts of sights, gets beached and separated from her pod, eludes a killer whale, and becomes a mother.

The second nonfiction Beginner Book fares better than *You Will Go to the Moon* for a few reasons. For one, it was based on fully established fact with no speculation. For another, its concepts were naturally easier to describe without getting bogged down in terminology. At the same time *The Whales Go By* also doesn't shy away from difficult-but-vital vocabulary words such as "porpoise" and "lagoon." And though Ira and Mae Freeman were certainly qualified to write their book, Dr. Fred Phelger (1909–1993) was a Harvard-educated expert in ocean life, serving as a professor of oceanography at the Scripps Institution of Oceanography.

Fred was born in Kansas City in 1909, the only child of Fred and Norabelle Phelger. The family moved to Los Angeles when Fred was young, and his father owned a gas station. Fred attended LA public schools, and then enrolled at UCLA, where he majored in drama. In the school's theater department he met Marjorie Temple, and the two became an item. As his undergrad years went on his interests moved from drama to science, specifically geology. After graduation Fred and Marjorie headed to Pasadena, where Fred earned his master's degree at the California Institute of Technology, focusing on Ordovician fossils.

Marjorie and Fred were married in 1933, and next moved across the county to Cambridge for Fred to work on his PhD in geology at Harvard. His dissertation was on trilobites, but his time at Harvard also led him to the study of microscopic Protozoa called foraminifera. Foraminifera ecology and paleoecology would become Fred's lifelong specialty. Upon completing his doctorate, Fred began teaching at Amherst College. He and Marjorie would have two children, Charles and Audrey.

In 1949 Fred became a visiting professor at Scripps in La Jolla, and the family moved there when his position at Scripps was made permanent. Marjorie became very involved in the La Jolla community (more on that in the entry for *You Will Live under the Sea*) and it wasn't long before the Phelgers met and became friends with Ted and Helen Geisel. The Phelger children were regularly welcomed into Ted's studio, and he gave their dog her name, Countess Theodora Strugo von Strugovich.

Once Beginner Books started, Ted reportedly pestered his friend into trying his hand at writing one about the ocean. Fred was hesitant, but eventually gave in, resulting in not one, but two manuscripts being accepted (the other was *Ann Can Fly*, B-12, also published in 1959). Fred had spent the preceding six years researching and writing a book, *Ecology and Distribution* of *Recent Foraminifera* (Johns Hopkins University Press), which was to be published in 1960. His two Beginner Books beat it to print by half a year, and their sales predictably and humorously dwarfed those of his carefully researched professional work.

Paul Galdone (1907–1986) was already an established children's illustrator when the assignment to do *The Whales Go By* came along. The New York resident (who'd emigrated from Budapest when he was in high school) started out in the art department at Doubleday, eventually designing book jackets before transitioning to interior illustrations, including Ruthven Todd's Space Cat books and two separate series by Eve Titus (Anatole and Basil of Baker Street). Though his work featured highly anthropomorphized and urbanized animals, Galdone had a deep love for biology and nature ("I love the outdoors. I love everything about nature. Look at these trees. Trees give you such permanence," Galdone told an interviewer).

His colorful paintings for *The Whales Go By* are a departure from black-and-white inkwash illustrations in his earlier work and point toward his later work adapting fairy tales and fables. Because the story calls for it, his animals are more realistic, too, with only a hint of cartoony expression in their eyes and mouths. The book relies heavily on Galdone's imagery to provide drama and a sense of the magnitude of the whales' journey.

STOP THAT BALL! (1959), B-10

Mike McClintock and Fritz Siebel

Stop That Ball! is a logical insanity plot in which a runaway red ball travels all over town, eluding a young boy and his dog through a construction site, a burning house, a baseball game, and a military ceremony. The ball eventually makes its way home again, only to fly off at the end, starting the ordeal over again.

This was the second Beginner Book collaboration between Mike McClintock and Fritz Siebel. Like *A Fly Went By*, the story concept is all about momentum. The tale is told in peppy verse, using repetition ("Could this go on all day and night? / It could, you know, and it just might.") and onomatopoeia ("Then WHACK! He hit a long home run . . ."). Also as with the pair's previous book, Siebel's dynamic, black pencil pictures tell a complete story on their own. The situations (a building under construction, a hill that's being demolished, a baseball game) through which the ball continues its journey are consistently humorous. Of special interest is the beret-sporting neighbor girl, who is not mentioned at all in the text, but who appears regularly and plays a crucial role. When the ball returns home the boy finds it has already been tied to its string again by "someone—I do not know just who"). The sharp-eyed reader will have solved this mystery.

It would be McClintock and Siebel's last Beginner Book, but not their last book together. That would be *David and the Giant*—a retelling of the religious tale David and Goliath—published in 1960 by Harper & Row as an I Can Read! book. That's right, one of Beginner Books' best early teams went over to the competition. According to Fritz's widow, Gretchen Siebel, it was a simple matter of economics. After *Stop That Ball!* they didn't have another contract with Beginner Books, so when Harper & Row came calling offering a higher royalty rate, they jumped. "[Mike and Fritz] were very happy with the change," she reports.

McClintock would do one more I Can Read! book, 1961's *What Have I Got?* with artist Leonard Kessler. The same year he cowrote a reference book—*Toys in America*—with his second wife, Inez (nee Bertail), which would be his final book. He and Inez had two children, Michael and Claudia, in the 1940s, but their marriage would eventually end in divorce. In his final years Mike married writer and editor May Garelick, who worked at William R. Scott and published several books herself, including 1961's *Where Does the Butterfly Go When It Rains?* with illustrations by Leonard Wiesgard. Mike passed away suddenly in 1967.

In a letter regarding a memorial for Mike, Ted wrote that while they had once been close, "two very unpleasant explosions" blew them apart. He indicated that one of those explosions had to do with making toys out of Seuss characters, but left the other a mystery. Judging by letters from the time, it's clear that the way Mike handled his move to Harper & Row was that other explosion. The entire Beginner Book team was upset that he, in the midst of dragging his feet on a manuscript he owed the publisher, had announced *What Have I Got?* in the February 15, 1960, issue of *Publishers Weekly*. What's more, the new book was the first in a subseries Harper was calling "Early I Can Read!," aimed at younger beginners.

It was something Beginner Books themselves had been planning, and suspicions ran high that Mike had leaked the idea to the competition. While they later found Harper's offshoot line had been in the works for a while, the damage as it pertained to Ted's relationship with Mike was already done. It was a shame, since the old classmates had been so mutually beneficial to each other's careers.

Fritz, meanwhile, would briefly become one of Harper & Row's star artists, illustrating Else Homelund Minarik's *Cat and Dog* (1960), Crosby Newell Bonsall's *Tell Me Some More . . .* (1961), and Joan Nodset's *Who Took the Farmer's Hat?* (1963). His biggest accomplishment at Harper & Row, though, was the design of one of their most enduring characters, Amelia Bedelia. The daffy, literal-minded maid created by Peggy Parish first appeared in 1963, and Fritz illustrated the first three books (the last one being *Amelia Bedelia and the Surprise Shower* in 1966). Amelia Bedelia would go on to the children's literature hall of fame, but by the time of her emergence, Fritz had undergone some major life changes. His first marriage ended in 1957, and he returned to New York, marrying again in 1959 and having three more children.

He'd also move on from book illustration. In the early 1960s he'd begun doing design work for clients such as Allerest and Seagram, rising to a position as president of the graphics division at Seagram. In 1969 he formed his own company—known in its final iteration as the Siebel Marketing Group—and had a long career in package design and sales promotion before retiring. He died in 1991 at the age of seventy-eight.

BENNETT CERF'S BOOK OF LAUGHS (1959), B-11

Bennett Cerf and Carl Rose

Bennett Cerf's Book of Laughs is a collection of loosely connected episodes featuring a precocious and incorrigible boy named Marvin. Like Amelia Bedelia (whose debut was still four years away) Marvin is continually misunderstanding what people are asking him or telling him, and most of his misunderstandings are due to the nuances of language. For example, Marvin falls in a lake and a man saves him, then asks, "How did you come to fall in?" Marvin replies, "I didn't come to fall in. I came to fish." In episodes like this one Marvin's confusion seems genuine. In others, he seems to be consciously misconstruing out of mischievousness, such as when a salesman finds Marvin sitting on the stairs and asks if his mother is at home. Marvin replies yes, and the salesman rings the doorbell repeatedly with no answer. The salesman asks Marvin why his mother isn't coming to the door, and Marvin replies, "This is not my house."

The situations in the book are largely realistic and the wordplay not hit-you-over-the-head obvious, thus avoiding the sort of puns that elicit eye rolls and groans. *Kirkus* wrote of the book, "the humor may be of the smart aleky kind that children adore and adults abhor, but they all go through it and there are too few books intended to make young readers laugh."

Bennett Cerf (1898–1971) had been publishing books of jokes, puns, and humorous anecdotes since 1944's best-selling *Try and Stop Me*, and had been exercising his funny bone weekly on the CBS game show *What's My Line?* since 1951. So doing a humor book for children was a natural fit. Ted the editor didn't give his boss any slack. Though Bennett typically worked very quickly on his joke books with very little revision required (or requested), Ted sent the *Book of Laughs* manuscript back several times asking for changes.

Book of Laughs was illustrated by celebrated New York cartoonist Carl Rose (1903–1971), who also did the drawings for Bennett's first book and its 1948 sequel *Shake Well before Using*. Rose was one of the first *New Yorker* cartoonists, placing a drawing in the magazine during its first year (a man jumping off of a bridge with a stone tied around his neck and a cab in free fall next to him, the driver asking, "Taxi, sir?"). He'd go on to publish six hundred cartoons in the *New Yorker* during his lifetime, all the way up to the year of his death. He was also responsible for one of the magazine's most famous cartoons, a 1928 depiction of an affluent mother and daughter at the dinner table with the caption, "'It's broccoli, dear.' 'I say it's spinach, and I say the hell with it.'" The exchange entered the popular vernacular in the 1930s, even going so far as to inspire an Irving Berlin song in the 1932 musical *Face the Music* ("I Say It's Spinach (And the Hell with It)"). The caption as printed was actually written by E. B. White, revised from Rose's original, in which the daughter finds out there's no pudding for dessert and remarks, "Well, the hell with the spinach."

Rose was prolific, and socially and politically minded, his editorial cartoons appearing in *New York World*, *Late PM*, *Collier's Today*, and the *Boston Herald*. Besides the *New Yorker*, his gag cartoons appeared in *Popular Science* and *Atlantic Monthly*. His feature in the latter, "Accent on Living," was in every issue of the magazine for twenty consecutive years. Carl's style tightened over the years into the precise pen-and-ink line work of his drawings in *Book of Laughs*. These would prove to be the blueprint for the type of artwork Ted wanted to see in Beginner Books, and from this point forward he'd regularly seek out cartoonists as illustrators.

ANN CAN FLY (1959), B-12

Fred Phelger and Robert Lopshire

Ann Can Fly, the last in the second wave of Beginner Books, was, at its core, another nonfiction title. A pilot himself, author Fred Phelger used the experience of taking his daughter Audrey—whose middle name was Anne—from

San Diego to camp in Colorado as the basis for the story of Ann and her father's two-day flight. The book covers the basics of small plane operation, from navigation to reading gauges to checking the weather conditions along the route to making multiple stops along the way. The route is accurate, with the father and daughter stopping in Lake Mead in Nevada to refuel, and flying over (and marveling at) the Grand Canyon.

Its adherence to realism makes the story feel somewhat prosaic. Even when the pair gets caught in a rainstorm there's no real sense of danger or fear. Ann and her father remain extremely even keeled, and Ann only gets overly, and understandably, excited when she's allowed to take the controls as they fly over her campsite.

Unlike the other nonfiction books in this wave of Beginner Books, there's no terminology to either try to incorporate or to explain without using the actual words, mostly because the book avoids getting technical. Through Ann's father, Fred explains everything that's happening in a straightforward and matter-of-fact way.

Illustrator and Random House creative art director Robert Lopshire (1927–2002) took on the challenging task of creating the book's pictures. He was uniquely qualified. For one, he had spent over a decade as a freelance illustrator, working in a variety of styles. But perhaps more importantly, he was an aviation nut, an avid builder and flier of model planes (and real ones; he got his pilot's license at age fifteen). He was a contributor to *Model Airplane News*, and would later author two informational books on model and remote-control airplanes. *Ann Can Fly* was Bob's first book, and those who know his later children's illustration work would be hard-pressed to recognize his style. Instead of the controlled-line cartooning he'd become known for, Bob employed a realistic 1950s advertising style.

The 1960s

ONE FISH, TWO FISH, RED FISH, BLUE FISH (1960), B-13

Dr. Seuss

One Fish, Two Fish, Red Fish, Blue Fish marked Dr. Seuss's return to Beginner Books after sitting out the 1959 offerings. The book—a tour through a menagerie of invented creatures—is best described by Ellen Lewis Buell in her *New York Times* review: "a collection of daffy verses about the daffiest of subjects and situations." Rather than tell a story, the book's main goal is to play into a child's natural tendency to play with language by rhyming nonsense words off of a base word. So the creatures we meet are the likes of the Yink who likes to wink and drink pink ink and the seven hump Wump who belongs to Mr. Gump. In *Books for Beginning Readers*, Elizabeth Guilfoile labeled *One Fish . . .* an exercise in introducing readers to phonic families. Likewise, Buell points out how several of the creatures have their name written on them to help readers with "quick recognition and word-association."

Along with the simultaneously released *Green Eggs and Ham*, *One Fish . . .* shows the results of Ted's immersion in matters of early literacy. Whether Ted consciously realized he was introducing phonics or whether he was just indulging his natural senses of rhythm and rhyme and fun with sounds is debatable (the line "So . . . if you wish to wish a wish, you may swish for fish with my Ish wish dish" would seem to indicate the latter). He said of the book that it was "actually a pre-beginner book, or, as the educators say, a reading-readiness book . . . based on an educational theory I have, but one I unfortunately can't define." The essence of that theory was he had provided enough picture support that, after perhaps one reading by an adult or older child, a nonreading child might read it on his or her own. Ted told of a professor who concluded that the book might lead to children learning to read too young!

It was the first result of Ted pushing Beginner Books to be simpler and more fundamental, though *One Fish . . .* was not an easy book to create, perhaps partially because of the way it evolved from his original idea. There's evidence that the book started with a more conventional narrative about a boy and a girl trying to choose a pet. It's likely that the posthumously discovered manuscript for *The Pet Shop* (published as *What Pet Should I Get?* in 2015) was an early version of *One Fish . . .* , as it features the same boy and girl protagonists. Even in its new iteration, Ted had severe doubts. Helen told Phyllis regarding the book, "Now, if I can just keep Ted from fussing with it and telling me that it is no good."

THE KING'S WISH (1960), B-14

Benjamin Elkin and Leonard Shortall

The King's Wish contains all the hallmarks of Benjamin Elkin's work. It's set in medieval times, it has the feeling of a folktale, and it features characters solving problems with clever thinking. In format and style, Benjamin Elkin's second Beginner Book is very similar to his first; both contain three stories following the same characters. But, unlike the ones in *The Big Jump*, the stories in *The King's Wish* don't quite stand alone. Instead they work together to form a larger adventure narrative told in three parts. In the first story the King of Tam's sons offer to safeguard the kingdom while he goes out to fish and relax, but the king gives them a test to prove they are ready. In the second story, the king aids a trapped squirrel and then gets the favor repaid when he becomes ensnared himself. The final story finds the king returning home only to discover the kingdom is on fire.

Elkin once again seems unfazed by the vocabulary limitations, with his prose flowing naturally. The only seeming concession is that the king is nameless, as are his sons, who are instead given numbers. Though this would be Elkin's last Beginner Book, his philosophy of writing for children was uncannily in line with Ted's. He saw children as the "most difficult, most challenging" audience a writer could have, so he put great care into crafting stories for them. He didn't believe in writing down or giving young readers a story with an obvious moral, but instead honoring their perceptiveness and imagination:

"[Children] have two great qualities," he told an interviewer in 1962, "they see sham in a minute, and they have soaring minds."

As principal he advocated for readers being allowed to choose what they wanted to read based on interest, rather than be forced along as a class on a leveled reader. As a result, he witnessed reading performance accelerate. He felt students having choices of early readers like Beginner Books were a large part of the reason this was possible.

Benjamin Elkin retired from Rogers School in 1972, eventually heading to Coronado, California. He would publish ten more books after *The King's Wish*, including *Al and the Magic Lamp* (Harper & Row, 1963) and *The Wisest Man in the World* (Parents' Magazine Press, 1968), which was illustrated by Anita Lobel.

The King's Wish has illustrations that are a bit more modern than Katherine Evans's were on *The Big Jump*, but still more traditional than the cartoony Beginner Book house style. They're done in black pencil with heavy shading, and a striking forest-green-and-carmine-red color palate. The illustrator was Leonard W. Shortall (1916–1989), a prolific artist with a decades-long career in children's books. He grew up in Seattle, Washington, and attended the University of Washington, initially intending to become a doctor. On the bio on the dust jacket of *The King's Wish*, he said, "I made so many anatomical drawings I decided to be an artist." So he enrolled at the Cornish School of Allied Arts (now known as Cornish College of the Arts).

Leonard married Bette Adams, and the young couple moved to New York circa 1940, where Leonard got a job as a window dresser. He eventually began landing work in advertising and in magazines such as *Redbook* and *Women's Day*, and transitioned to children's books in the late 1940s, first doing pictures for Jarrod Beim's *Andy and the School Bus* in 1947. For the next thirty-seven years, Leonard would publish at least one book per year, and often many more than that. He most famously illustrated the first nine books in Donald J. Sobol's Encyclopedia Brown series. In all he'd illustrate over one hundred books, seventeen of which he wrote himself. In the last five years of his life, he worked on an animated film, and illustrated Disney storybooks uncredited.

He and Bette had lived with their three children, Stephen, Thomas, and Kathy, in Valhalla, New York, and Waccabuc, New York, until the early 1950s when Leonard divorced Bette and left the family. He headed to Westport, Connecticut, where fellow and future Beginner Book creators Nancy and Eric Gurney and Phil Eastman also resided. In the late 1950s and early 1960s the affluent, idyllic town became known as a haven for artists, writers, and actors (some of its many famous residents include Annie Liebowitz, Hardie

Gramatky, Shirley Jackson, Ruth Krauss and Crockett Johnson, and Paul Newman). In 1961, Eric, Phil, and Leonard (along with *Saturday Evening Post* cover artist Amos Sewell) all served as judges for a poster contest advertising the Burr Farms Elementary School's annual book fair.

When a second marriage ended in divorce as well, Leonard left for New York City, living there for many years. He eventually settled for good in Southport, Connecticut, just four miles east of Westport.

BENNETT CERF'S BOOK OF RIDDLES (1960), B-15

Bennett Cerf and Roy McKie

Bennett Cerf's second Beginner Book is a collection more accurately described as "jokes" than "riddles." As with *Bennett Cerf's Book of Laughs*, the humor comes from multiple meanings of words ("What did the big firecracker say to the little firecracker?" "My pop is bigger than your pop."), the difference between literal and figurative statements ("When is a cook bad?" "When he beats the eggs."), or subverting the expected ("Name five things that have milk in them." "Butter. Cheese. Ice Cream. And two cows."). Cerf once again does an admirable job of making his humor age appropriate, providing many perennial schoolyard favorites. The book takes a simple Q-and-A format, with the set-up on the left-hand page and the punchline on the page turn.

In an interview late in his life, Bennett explained his facility for writing joke books:

> I believe that joke books have a certain rhythm. I can't explain it, but I know how to do it. It's like Gershwin was born knowing how to write songs, and other people are born knowing how to write books. I have a certain skill at assembling these books that makes them easy to read. I don't understand what it is myself, but I do know how to do it. My joke books are quite different from other joke books, and there's a very good reason why they sell ten times as many I think. I've always said that I've learned how to exploit a very small talent to the absolute ultimate degree.

Book of Riddles was technically the first Bennett Cerf book to be published by Random House, since *Bennett Cerf's Book of Laughs* was published before the publisher bought Beginner Books. To that point, Bennett had sought out other publishers for his work, finding it "impolitic for a publisher to publish his own book." The book was also the debut of the artist who would become one of Beginner Books most ubiquitous names, Roy McKie. Here, his simple, expressive, and innately funny illustrations punch up Cerf's punchlines. Cerf and McKie would team up for two additional books, *More Riddles* (1961) and *Bennett Cerf's Book of Animal Riddles* (1964).

GREEN EGGS AND HAM (1960), B-16

Dr. Seuss

The Cat in the Hat is the book that started Beginner Books, but *Green Eggs and Ham* is the one that defined them. It's not only the best-selling Beginner Book, it's the best-selling Dr. Seuss book, even outpacing the *Cat*, and very nearly the best-selling children's book of all time (it came in at number four on *Publishers Weekly*'s 2001 list). Legend has it that the book grew out of a bet between Bennett Cerf and Ted, with the former challenging the latter to create a book using only fifty words. The two men shook hands on a $50 wager, and Ted went to work.

Like many of Ted's books, the story itself arose from a sketching session. Sam-I-Am, an uncategorizable creature who looks like he could be the Cat's distant cousin, came first. Then came the unnamed long-eared, gray-hatted, unnamed grouch. Once Ted put these two into a conflict, his story began. As he had with *The Cat in the Hat*, Ted took the word count limitation deadly seriously, keeping a chart that tracked which words he'd used and how many times he'd used them. He also kept a running word count at the bottom of his multiple drafts.

That the book itself shows no evidence of the intense work behind it, nor indeed even of its severely limited vocabulary, is a testament to Ted's skill. It also proves the appeal of the story itself, both in presentation and content. The story is progressive much in the way that *A Fly Went By* was, with each new way that our protagonist won't eat green eggs and ham getting added to the previous ones, building a large, increasingly absurd list that leaves the reader almost breathless by the end. The couplets are written in short sentences, providing the reader a constant sense of momentum, while the various modes of transportation (car to train to boat) provide their own push forward.

In an early draft of the book, the phrase was written as "ham and eggs" ("I do not like them in a tree / On a tree / Green ham and eggs"). Animator Chuck Jones—who worked with Ted at Fort Fox as well as on adaptations of *How the Grinch Stole Christmas*, *Horton Hears a Who*, and *The Cat in the Hat*—pointed out the significance of Ted's ultimate decision to invert the common phrase into "eggs and ham." When presented in that unconventional order it not only grabs the attention, but has the same metric emphasis as "Sam I Am."

Another element that added to the book's appeal for both children and adults is Sam-I-Am's gentle but insistent antagonism. To watch him continue to pursue the grouch is both highly entertaining and safely rebellious. Nearly all adults have dealt with a child who simply will not let up. And all children, who often have to be persistent to be heard and acknowledged, enjoy seeing a younger person best an older one. And then there's the unexpected ending, where the grump not only tries the green eggs and ham, but actually likes them. Many took the moral of the story to be that you should never say you don't like something without trying it, but Ted hated that. To him it was a funny way to end the story, and nothing else.

Not only did Ted use only fifty words, forty-nine of them were a single syllable (the one exception was the compound "anywhere"). Any word likely to be unfamiliar is supported by a picture (fox, train, dark, boat) and a rhyme, or bound to be grasped quickly it is repeated so often, usually in the same order. This led the book's dust jacket to proclaim that the book would "stimulate the URGE TO READ in children even as young as the tender age of four."

Ted typically presented a new book to the Random House team in person, reading and acting it out along with the illustrations. This usually took place in the offices, but in the case of *Green Eggs and Ham* the unveiling happened at a dinner party at the Cerfs' 62nd Street apartment. The Morgans reported that "when Ted read *Green Eggs* aloud that evening the room erupted with huzzahs and demands that he read it again." Bennett, accustomed to being astonished by Ted's work, was "dazed" by *Green Eggs and Ham*, and made a great ceremony of handing over the $50. When Ted would tell the story later, likely because it made a great punchline, he often claimed Bennett had never paid up on the bet.

Near the end of his life, Ted would say that *Green Eggs and Ham* was the only book of his own that still made him laugh. Its reach was vast and its influence lasting. Once *Green Eggs and Ham* was released, nearly every banquet Ted attended featured green eggs and ham on the menu. In 1985 he was presented with an honorary degree at Princeton. After being introduced, he walked to the podium to give his remarks, and the entire room full of serious academics jumped to their feet and proceeded to recite *Green Eggs and Ham* word for word. In 1991 the Reverend Jesse Jackson gave a reading of *Green Eggs and Ham* on *Saturday Night Live*, using the tone of a preacher reading a Bible verse. The audience ate it up.

PUT ME IN THE ZOO (1960), B-17

Robert Lopshire

Like *Green Eggs and Ham*, *Put Me in the Zoo* was the happy result of an artistic challenge in the guise of a friendly wager. During a conversation with Robert Lopshire, Ted Geisel proclaimed Dick, Jane, and Spot to be a "horrible concept," and asserted that nothing interesting or worthwhile could be done with them. Bob took up the gauntlet, betting his boss he could create a compelling Beginner Book about a boy, a girl, and their dog.

And that's just what he did. His story centered on Spot, who performs extraordinary tricks for the two children (who aren't named in the book, probably to avoid a lawsuit). And though Bob ostensibly won the bet, calling Spot a dog seems a stretch, as he has characteristics of several different animals: He's the size of a bear, his tail is cat-like, the legs and feet almost those of a kangaroo; only his face is vaguely dog-like. The Dick and Jane stories would also never include a fantasy element like spots that can expand, shrink, change color, or fill the sky.

Dick, Jane, and Spot may have been the impetus for the book, but major elements of the story appear to have origins in Bob's childhood. Robert Martin Lopshire was born Robert S. Walker in 1927 in Sarasota, Florida, a small city on Florida's southwestern coast. His father was born Conrad Davidson in Spokane, Washington, but had taken on the name "Robert E. Walker" because he was in hiding after going AWOL from the marines. He married Jesse Martin not knowing she was still married, having abandoned her first husband and a daughter. Unsurprisingly, Robert and Jesse's relationship barely lasted past the birth of their only son.

Young Robert lived with his mother and took on her last name, but Jesse was no more interested in motherhood than she had been before. Family legend has it she left three-year-old Robert on the doorstep of Roy and Dorothy Lopshire with nothing but a teddy bear and a toy drum.

Early in *Put Me in the Zoo*, Spot approaches two zookeepers and says, "Will you keep me in the zoo? I want to stay in here with you." They respond by unceremoniously carrying him out, saying, "We do not want you in the zoo." Knowing, then, that Bob was given up by his parents lends a deep emotional resonance to Spot's rejection from the very place he feels he belongs.

Of course, in the book's resolution Spot finds a place to belong. And so did Robert. His new parents had moved to Sarasota from Indiana in 1925. Roy was a realtor, working at the agency of John Paul Cobb, brother of hall-of-fame Detroit

Robert Lopshire at age four, not long after
being adopted. Courtesy the Lopshire family.

Tigers player Ty Cobb. Dorothy stayed at home. They adopted young Robert and
encouraged his interests, including drawing, model building, and aviation.

After graduating from Sarasota High School, Bob enlisted in the US Navy
Coast Guard and was sent into battle in the Pacific Theater in the final year
of World War II, serving aboard assault landing ships, then on air sea rescue boats in 1945 and 1946. He also worked as a combat photographer. After
his service, he married his high school sweetheart, Jane Haller Ingalls, and
enrolled at the Vesper George School of Art (the very same school Roy McKie
had attended just a few years earlier) and the School of Practical Art (now the
Art Institute of Boston).

Wrapping up his education in 1948, he embarked on an eleven-year career
as a freelance illustrator and designer that took him from Philadelphia (where
he met and became friends with Roy), back to Boston, and then to New York.
In 1959 he was working in the art department at Random House, and he and
Jane had four children, two sons and two daughters. The family lived primarily in Flemington, New Jersey.

His position at Random House led to his first children's book illustration
work, *Ann Can Fly*. On the strength of his work on that book, Ted offered him
the role of creative director of Beginner Books. Bob accepted, and worked at

Robert Lopshire, sometime in the 1960s. Courtesy
the Lopshire family.

home primarily, with occasional trips to New York to meet with Phyllis, either
at the Random House offices or at the Cerf home in Mount Kisco.

In *Put Me in the Zoo*, Spot settles in at a circus. This was another way that
Bob drew from his own experience. In 1927, the same year Bob was born, his
birth city of Sarasota became the winter home of the Ringling Brothers and
Barnum & Bailey Circus. This meant that many of the show's performers settled in Sarasota year-round. The city had regular circus performances, and
Cecil B. DeMille's 1952 film *The Greatest Show on Earth* was largely filmed
there. Bob's wife, Jane, was the granddaughter of Clyde Ingalls, who was the
assistant manager and chief lecturer of the circus (he also had a stormy marriage to famed aerialist Lillian Leitzal).

The art in the book is a striking mix of smooth ink outlines, flat color (on
Spot's spots), and colored pencil. Bob's years of freelancing had made him into
an extremely versatile illustrator. The rounded cartoon style of the drawings
is a far cry from the realistic approach he used on *Ann Can Fly*. That said, the
pictures in both books share an impeccable sense of composition, with every
visual element carefully placed on the page or pages. This attention to careful
visual arrangement is likely a function of Bob's background as a photographer. Unlike Ted's work, there's no sense of chaos at all.

The fact that Bob's first attempt at writing had to be done within a one-hundred-word vocabulary limit doesn't seem to have fazed him at all. He did, however, need some help with writing in rhyme. In a note written later in his life, he credited Jane as being a "big help on the verse" of *Put Me in the Zoo*. Her help was very worthwhile indeed, resulting in rhyming couplets that flow easily and naturally throughout. The book uses repetition surreptitiously, mostly in Spot's repeated claims, "I can take them . . ." and "I can put them . . ." Elizabeth Guilfoile's analysis in *Books for Beginning Readers* uses *Put Me in the Zoo* as an example of the way limited vocabulary alone doesn't guarantee readability. She writes, "Its use of the first person, its verse form, and its exclamatory style result in phraseology that the small reader cannot anticipate." She does, however, praise the "extravagant humor" of the pictures. This—along with the fact that the book became one of Beginner Books most memorable, successful, and lasting classics—show that a sense of fun and wonder was at least as important as pedagogical design of the books.

Bob would always credit Ted for his second career as a children's book author. His appreciation can be seen doubly in *Put Me in the Zoo*. For one, the book is dedicated to the Beginner Book founders, but there's a subtler tribute on the book's final two pages. If one lingers long enough on the crowd scene where Spot performs at the circus, you'll spot the familiar red-and-white stripes of the Cat's hat.

ARE YOU MY MOTHER? (1960), B-18

P. D. Eastman

P. D. Eastman's second Beginner Book is a straightforward tale of a just-hatched baby bird in search of his mother, who has chosen the very worst moment to leave her nest in search of food. The baby bird's search is a comedy of errors, all of it stemming from the fact that he has no sense of self-image to allow him to be able to recognize what his mother looks like. He mistakes a kitten, a chicken, a dog, a cow, a boat, an airplane, and an excavator for his mother before returning home for a joyful meeting with his real mom.

Besides the inherent cuteness of the premise and Phil's accompanying pictures, the story is most effective with children because of its use of dramatic irony, something that Phil was well used to employing during his time working on Mr. Magoo cartoons. That is, young people are allowed to delight in the fact that they know something the baby bird doesn't, and that delight builds in each successive misunderstanding. This culminates in his encounter with the excavator, though, which he names after the sound it makes: "Oh, you are not my mother," said the baby bird. "You are a Snort!"

There's also a bit of drama, with the big noisy excavator picking up the baby and seeming for all the world to wish him harm, and then there's the surprise and relief and comfort of realizing the Snort is being helpful and returning the hatchling to his nest for a happy ending. "The happiest ending of all time," according to *Charlie Joe Jackson's Guide to Not Reading* author Tommy Greenwald.

The story is told in prose with only one hundred distinct words. There's some repetition, especially in the first half, but for the most part its readability leans on story momentum and picture support. Elizabeth Guilfoile wrote about the book for her *Books for Beginning Readers*, praising its "brief, direct sentences with normal word order" and its "logical and satisfying conclusion" while admonishing "the fact that as nature lore it is arrant nonsense."

Phil illustrated the story with a sketchy black pencil line much looser than the one he used in *Sam and the Firefly* (and his later Beginner Books). Phil used blue, red, yellow, and black as his only colors, with a muted bronze-tinged brown created by mixing these. That color dominates the pictures, which are enlivened by small areas of red and yellow until the Snort arrives and the palate reverses. Backgrounds are nearly nonexistent, allowing the reader's focus to remain on the baby bird's quest and nothing else.

As in *Sam and the Firefly*, Phil's characters are designed like cartoons, but they're grounded in a setting that reflects reality. In *Are You My Mother?* this manifests in the vehicles (the abandoned car, the airplane, the boat, and the Snort) but also in the nest and tree. His daughter-in-law Susan Eastman says this is a result of his classical art training. "He had the ability to take an object and capture its essence, drawing it as a simplified version of a real object, unlike the busy, cartoony images that many children's books feature." This ability would form the foundation of his style.

Alison Bechdel used the title of the book for her own 2012 graphic novel. Ken Parielle wrote in the *Comics Journal*, "Like Eastman's child's picture book, Bechdel's adult graphic novel hinges on the primal human struggle with interdependency and the psychic distress it inevitably breeds." The National Education Association in 2007 named Phil's book one of its "Teachers' Top 100 Books for Children." And in 2012, it was listed as one of the "Top 100 Picture Books" of all time in *School Library Journal*.

TEN APPLES UP ON TOP! (1961), B-19

Theo LeSieg and Roy McKie

Ten Apples Up on Top! follows a lion, a tiger, and a dog through an escalating game of one-upsmanship. It starts with a couple of apples balanced on their heads and ends with an angry mob and an apple cart explosion.

The book was illustrated by Roy McKie. It was his second Beginner Book and the first for a seemingly new author, Theo LeSieg. The dust-jacket flap described LeSieg as living on a mountain in Southern California, "where he was suddenly discovered by his neighbor, Dr. Seuss." It goes on to describe how they had led "oddly" parallel lives, both studying at Oxford, both working for the same advertising agency, and both serving in the same division in the army. This was all very tongue-in-cheek, because in reality, Theo LeSieg was really the debut of a new nom de plume for Ted. Or was it a nom de plume for Dr. Seuss?

Ted had a history of employing pseudonyms even before he took on the name Dr. Seuss, signing his high school and college work in a variety of ways, including Quincy Quilp, Dr. Xavier Ruppzknoff, Thomas Mott Osborne, and L. Burbank. The LeSieg name—an inversion of "Geisel" that turns the German into French—in particular was one Ted has used on some of his high school cartoons. The idea originally came from his father, who wrote the name on betting slips to avoid embarrassment. Though it may not have been the intention from the start, the LeSieg name would come to signify a book written by Ted but illustrated by someone else. This was done, in part, to avoid muddying up the Dr. Seuss brand. Only books completely created by Ted would get to use that name.

Ted would later say that many of the LeSieg books were born out of necessity:

> As editor in chief of Beginner Books, one of my problems has always been the appalling scarcity of authors capable of and willing to endure the pains of writing books using only a mere hand full of words. Consequently, when a hoped-for author fails to produce, I am frequently faced with an incomplete line of books for autumn publication. Thereupon, I look in my trunk. In my trunk are many Dr. Seuss manuscripts that for one reason or another I do not wish to illustrate myself.

He was careful to point out that he didn't regard these stories as inferior or less-than his Dr. Seuss work, only that he felt his style of illustration would not suit it. Elsewhere he expanded on this explanation, saying that most of these stories called for human main characters, rather than animals ("I've always been more comfortable with animals," he told Sybil Steinberg at *Publishers*

Weekly in 1978). And while that plays out for the most part in the LeSieg books that came later, it doesn't quite explain *Ten Apples Up on Top!*, which features animals exclusively.

It's not too much of a leap, then, to conclude that Theo LeSieg arose partly from Ted's pure joy and excitement at having "discovered" Roy McKie. The flap basically says as much, "To whet LeSieg's interest, Seuss promised that Roy McKie would draw the pictures. When McKie was promised, LeSieg went right to work; for Roy McKie's illustrations, with their humor, strength, and absolute simplicity, are the envy of fellow artists everywhere."

Roy's work on the book lives up to the raves. Employing his trademark dry brush inkwork and a simple color palate of red and tones of yellow, Roy's pictures are full of energy and motion. As with Fritz Siebel's work on *A Fly Went By* and *Stop That Ball!*, a reader can "read" the pictures and still understand the whole story. This was the ideal of the Beginner Book model.

It was also ideal in that the whole point of the book is fun and chaos. One might make an argument that it teaches (or reinforces) children's counting abilities, or that it offers a moral "cooperation over conflict," in that the angry mob, comprised of gulls and bears, comes around to the fun of the game in the end. But it's entertainment before it's anything else. John Gough, writing about the LeSieg books in *Children's Literature Association Quarterly*, likened its slapstick to a Mack Sennett silent movie (Sennett was most known for his hit series of Keystone Cops films). Or, as writer Bruce Handy, who marks the book as the first one he read by himself, writes: *Ten Apples Up on Top!* "blends imagination, humor, rhyme, rigor, silliness, aggression, and chaos theory . . ."

The lack of Dr. Seuss's name on the cover didn't hurt the book's sales, which by now are well over a million copies. All of Geisel's royalties for *Ten Apples Up on Top!* were pledged to the charitable Dr. Seuss Foundation, which had formed in 1958 in order to address causes close to Ted and Helen's hearts, including education, research, and income inequality.

GO, DOG. GO! (1961), B-20

P. D. Eastman

Had P. D. Eastman retired after 1960, his Beginner Book legacy would have been set, but the very next year after *Are You My Mother?*, he produced what is arguably an even more enduring classic, *Go, Dog. Go!* This seventy-seven-distinct-words, plotless tale of a diverse group of dogs making their way to a "big dog party" has remained in print for over fifty years and regularly finds itself on lists of the best children's books, including a recent list of "25 Baby Books Every Nursery Should Have" by the *Onion AV Club*. Just what is it about the book that has made it so beloved?

The key ingredient is fun. *Go, Dog. Go!*—a title, by the way, that seems to be yet another Beginner Book tweak of Dick and Jane sentence constructions—is all about enjoyment. There are concepts introduced ("pronouns, prepositions, conjunctions, and adjectives" is how Phil described its contents), but no moral or lesson. Instead the reader revels in scenes of dogs in labyrinths, on roller coasters, playing tennis on top of a zeppelin, and riding a Ferris wheel, all culminating in the epic jubilee on the top of a tree.

Though only separated by a year, there's a drastic difference between the illustrations for *Go, Dog. Go!* and *Are You My Mother?* Whereas the latter book is minimalist, with mostly muted color, *Go, Dog. Go!* is packed with detail in bright primary colors (though both books feature plenty of open white space). Think of the four-page sequence where twenty dogs share a giant bed or the epic two-page spread depicting the dog party, which one could pore over for several minutes finding new details. *Are You My Mother?* is a lullaby; *Go, Dog. Go!* is a rave-up.

Many who haven't read the book in years would likely tell you it rhymes, but it doesn't. It's also, of all the Beginner Books not by Dr. Seuss or Theo LeSieg, most likely to be mistaken as such, mostly because it bears Ted's influence in structure and in its sense of manic energy. But where Ted conveyed energy with verse, *Go, Dog. Go!* is told in short declarative sentences and occasional bursts of dialogue. The most memorable of these dialogues is undoubtedly the recurring interaction between the yellow-and-black hound and the pink poodle. The poodle asks, "Do you like my hat?" and the hound says no, and the poodle leaves annoyed. These are spaced out in a way to lend the book a rhythm and predictability. They also lend an extra payoff—after the dog party—to the book's conclusion, when she finally wears a hat he likes (the hats themselves get more and more ostentatious, so he obviously has outré tastes), and they drive off together into the sunset just like in a cartoon.

This recurring interaction has been the source of some scrutiny. Philip Nel sees it as evidence of sexism, with the female dog being forced to cater to the man's tastes to win him over. Kate Coombs, author of books such as *The Runaway Princess* and *The Tooth Fairy Wars*, has a different view, likening the recurring joke to a routine George Burns and Gracie Allen might have concocted, with the poodle playing the clown to the hound's straight man. Actress and author Jamie Lee Curtis labeled the exchange "one of the funniest non

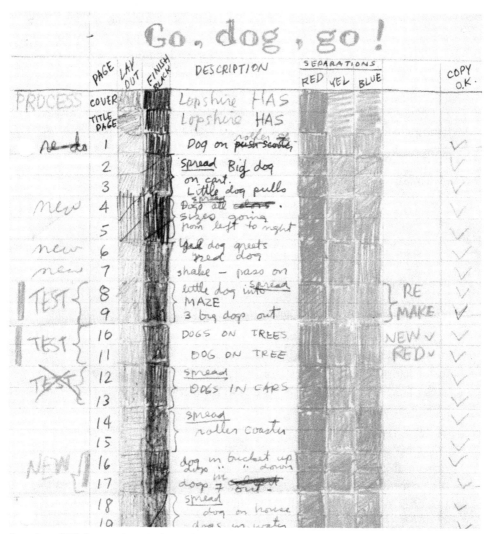

A portion of P. D. Eastman's meticulous color separation chart for *Go, Dog. Go!* Courtesy Tony Eastman.

sequiturs in all literature," adding that it "made me laugh then and makes me laugh now as I am writing this."

Shakespeare scholar Stephen Booth, a professor at the University of California–Berkeley, often used *Go, Dog. Go!* to introduce his students to great literature, walking them through the book the same way he wants them to eventually approach reading Shakespeare. Actor and author Michael Ellis-Tolaydo wrote about Booth's approach in an essay called "*Go, Dog. Go!* A Lesson on the Pleasures of Language," detailing how Booth "argues what is good about *Go, Dog. Go!* is the same as what's good about *King Lear* and *Romeo and Juliet*."

Authors Lisa Yee and Jon Scieszka have both cited the book as a favorite. Scieszka, author of the Time Warp Trio series and many other funny books, writes that *Go, Dog. Go!* is "a story clear as a spring day, funny as a dressed-up monkey, wise as the most gnarly Zen koan." He goes on: "*Go, Dog. Go!* made me want to be a reader, to read aloud those truths that were right there to see, and to knowingly revisit the question of the hat. *Go, Dog. Go!* made me start thinking about being a writer—to build a world as funny and as purpose-driven as a bunch of dogs in cars speeding toward a party in a tree."

LITTLE BLACK, A PONY (1961), B-21

Walter Farley and James W. Schucker

Just as Ira and Mae Freeman were successful and established Random House authors given the chance to do a Beginner Book, so was Walter L. Farley (1922–1989). At the age of seventeen he'd sold his first novel, *The Black Stallion*, to Random House for $1,000. It was a hit upon its publication in 1941, and its success inspired fourteen best-selling sequels over the next twenty years. Farley had grown up in New York City and developed a fascination with horses at a very young age, largely due to the fact that his uncle was a horse trainer and ran a riding academy.

"My great love was, and still is, horses," he said in an interview not long before his death. "I wanted a pony as much as a boy or girl could possibly want anything, but I never owned one." When his family moved to Flushing, Walter spent as much time as he could at the stables that once populated the area near the 1939 World's Fair site, and this was where he would eventually set much of the action for his Black Stallion books. He began writing at the age of eleven, and never stopped.

After a stint in the army during World War II, Walter worked briefly as an advertising copywriter, enrolled at Columbia University, and married Rosemary Lutz. The couple had four children—Pamela, Alice, Steven, and Timothy—and bought a farm near Earlville, Pennsylvania, where Walter finally achieved his dream to own his own horses. He wrote steadily through all of this, producing a new book nearly every year.

Little Black, A Pony, was Walter's first true foray into writing for very young readers (in 1955 Josette Frank had adapted *The Black Stallion* as a picture book called *Big Black Horse*). The story, told in first-person prose, follows a boy who abandons his pony, Little Black, in favor of riding the majestic Big Red. The pony is sad, but determined to not be left behind. He keeps trying to do things only the big horse can until the boy finds himself fallen through a frozen lake, and only the smaller, lighter Little Black can help.

The book was noticeably wordier than most Beginner Books, clearly meant for a child with a good set of reading skills already acquired, or as a read-aloud book. But it still works within vocabulary limits, and Farley handles this well, even managing to squeeze a surprising amount of pathos out of the relatively few words he has. Not only do we feel Little Black's sadness, but also the boy's deep love for his pony and his conflicted feelings about being on the verge of outgrowing his friend.

That sense of pathos is aided greatly by the expressive painted illustrations that could almost be mistaken for photos if not for their reddish-brown-and-green spot coloring. Artist James W. Schucker (1902–1988) and Walter Farley were already familiar with each other by the time of *Little Black, A Pony*. James had illustrated the 1955 edition of *Big Black Horse*, as well as Walter's 1958 *Black Stallion* prequel *The Horse-Tamer*. James was a native of Mount Carmel, Illinois, a small town in the southeastern portion of the state. He developed a love of drawing and painting very early on, and after graduating high school attended the Carnegie Institute of Technology in Pittsburgh. He continued his studies at both the Art Institute of Chicago and the Grand Central School of Art in New York City.

James landed a position at the Grauman Studio in Chicago before moving on to the J. Walter Thompson agency, one of the world's largest advertising firms, and relocating to New York City. Working his way up to art director at Thompson, he illustrated ads for hundreds of large companies, including Coca-Cola and Maxwell House, and in the late 1930s settled for good in Quakertown, Pennsylvania, to better facilitate a career in freelance illustration. By this time he had married high school classmate Vona Cleveland, and the two had a daughter, Sarah (called Sally).

From 1942 to 1946, James served as a captain in the army. After the war he picked back up where he left off, doing covers and illustrations for the *Saturday Evening Post* and *Reader's Digest*, among many others. In the mid-1950s he was illustrating children's books, providing pictures for the likes of *Big Treasure Book of Clowns* (1953) and *The Wonder Book of Trucks* (1954) before teaming up with Farley.

In 2006, *Little Black, A Pony* was translated into Navajo and re-illustrated by Baje Whitethorne Sr. to depict a Navajo boy as the main character. Beginner Books did not have a hand in its creation or publication, which was done to honor the fact that the Black Stallion books were extremely popular with young Navajo readers, and to give young readers a chance to see themselves represented in a similar story.

LOOK OUT FOR PIRATES! (1961), B-22

Iris Vinton and H. B. Vestal

Look Out for Pirates! follows Captain Jim and his men in their efforts to protect a chest full of gold from a band of pirates. It involves a shipwreck, a deep-sea dive, an encounter with a shark, swarming wasps, and a stolen ship. Captain Jim triumphs, naturally, leaving the pirates stranded on a tropical island: "Find work and fun there on the land," he advises them. "Your pirate days are over." The story is a work of historical fiction, a first and a last for Beginner Books. The book's dust jacket claims: "This is a real story based on the salvaging of a British merchant ship near Hong Kong in 1912." Given the often-tongue-in-cheek nature of the flap descriptions, one would be forgiven for being dubious. But the book's creators both had a strong pedigree in the historical fiction genre.

Writer Iris Vinton (1905–1988) was born in West Point, Mississippi. She moved to New York in the 1930s and published several short plays. She married Louis German, and began publishing novels in the '40s, most notably *Flying Ebony* (1947), which featured illustrations by Marc Simont and was made into a Disney TV movie called *The Mooncussers* in the early 1960s. During this time she also served as one of several ghostwriters on the Nancy Drew books (which were always credited to the fictional Carolyn Keene).

In the 1950s Iris turned her attention to writing biographies of notable American figures such as Stephen Decatur, John Paul Jones, and Robert E. Lee. She also began a two-decade stint as the director of publications for the Boys' Clubs of America. One of the initiatives she helped foster there was a program to "stimulate interest in books and reading," admitting that most of the boys in their club were not avid or habitual readers, but believing, as she wrote in a 1953 article for *The Reading Teacher*, that adult guidance and "skillful promotion of interest" was the key to changing that. Part of that promotion was the availability of the right kinds of books in both topic and level.

Look Out for Pirates! definitely seems to be a culmination of that belief, perhaps almost transparently so. The flap boasts, "Slow readers will want to read faster to find out how it all turns out." It may have been insensitively stated, but it wasn't wrong. Todd R. Nelson, a writer and educator, counts *Look Out for Pirates!* as his "Ur text," the first book to put him "in hot pursuit of reading" when he was in first grade. When he revisited the book as an adult, he says, "I was under the sway once more of Iris Vinton's simple prose and repetitive lexicon, and the tantalizing choice: pirate or heroic merchant mariner."

The book was illustrated by Herman Beeson Vestal (1916–2007), who had the exact right pedigree to do a historical book set mostly at sea. Born in Manhattan, H. B. was raised primarily by his mother, as his father lived and worked as an importer in Canada. H. B. joined the merchant marines after graduating high school in 1933, and sailed all over the world, visiting India, Haiti, and Columbia among many other places. In World War II he enlisted in the Coast Guard and served in active duty overseas, and that was where he nurtured his love for drawing and painting. After his service, he enrolled at the Art Students League in New York, and was soon a professional artist. Like E. Raymond Kinstler (of *Cowboy Andy* fame), H. B. found steady work illustrating pulp magazines published by Fiction House such as *Action Stories*, *All-American Football, Lariat,* and *Adventure House*. His detailed pen-and-ink drawings adorned stories with titles like "Slave of the Jackal Princess" and "Mr. Quarterback!" Once in awhile he landed a painted cover.

In the 1950s he did lots of work for a magazine called *Everywoman*, and by the end of the decade he'd begun to illustrate books for young readers, including a trio of volumes about the American Revolutionary War and an adaptation of *Moby Dick*. So a historical adventure tale set at sea was a perfect fit for a versatile artist who was also a former sailor. H. B.'s pictures in *Look Out for Pirates!* are not as heavily rendered or chiaroscuro as his pulp and magazine work, but his knack for detail shines through, especially in his depictions of the ships, the flora on the island, and the pirates (on whom you might even spot a tattoo or two). The color palate is shades of yellow, green, and blue, and is perhaps most striking in the all-green underwater diving scenes.

Speaking of those, the appearance of the shark, while providing a nicely tense moment of action, is also a place where the vocabulary limitation caused a hiccup. Rather than calling the shark by its name in the story, Vinton instead labels it a "big fish." This is curious, since sharks are one of the first animals children learn to name, and H. B.'s picture leaves no doubt as to what it is. It's even stranger for the fact that the word "wasps" appears multiple times later in the story, and is arguably a less familiar word. Most young readers would be looking for the word "bees" instead.

Both Iris and H. B. continued to work in children's books into the 1960s, but by the 1970s had moved on to other pursuits. Iris retired from her position in the boys' clubs in the mid-1970s, but stayed active as a member of Pen and Brush and the Women's National Book Association. H. B. retired to his father's home state of North Carolina and turned his focus toward painting, especially watercolors.

A FISH OUT OF WATER (1961), B-23

Helen Palmer and P. D. Eastman

A Fish out of Water is the story of a boy who buys a goldfish and promptly ignores the pet shop owner's warning not to feed it too much. The fish, called Otto, proceeds to grow steadily until he is literally as big as a whale. The book was a first in many ways. It was the first Beginner Book Phil Eastman drew without having written the story. It was the first Beginner Book that Helen Geisel wrote (at least that she got credit for; see the entry on *Cowboy Andy*). And it was the first Beginner Book to adapt an existing Dr. Seuss story (*The Cat in the Hat Comes Back* had used elements from an earlier Seuss work, but was a wholly new tale).

During the 1950s, Ted published over twenty short stories in the pages of *Redbook* magazine. The first one, appearing in June 1950, was "Gustav, the Goldfish." Helen appears to have had the idea of making it into a Beginner Book, but Ted doesn't appear to have been interested in doing the adaptation himself. Instead, Helen took on the task of expanding the story into an early reader.

Helen kept the bones of the plot intact. The two stories progress in very much a similar way with the fish moving from a vase to a pot to a bathtub as he grows, leading to a cascade of water down the stairs to the basement ("like Ni-ag-ara Falls," Ted's version says). In "Gustav" the story ends there, with the pet shop owner making a house call and mysteriously shrinking the fish after "an hour and a quarter." In *A Fish out of Water* there are calls to the police and the fire department before Otto ends up in the local municipal swimming pool and is there operated on by the pet shop owner.

There were other changes, such as the fish's name (though he remains of German origin) and the pet shop owner's name (from Mr. VanBuss to the on-the-nose Mr. Carp). And Helen wisely decided to forgo verse and instead present the story in prose, save only Mr. Carp's warning. In "Gustav," Mr. VanBuss says,

> "Take care! When you feed this small cuss / Just feed him a spot. If you feed
> him a lot, / Then something might happen! It's hard to say what."

Mr. Carp cautions,

> "When you feed a fish / never feed him a lot. / So much and no more! / Never
> more than a spot, / or something may happen! You never know what."

This warning is the heart of the tale, as it leads to the story's problem and lesson. And that lesson is an unusual one, perhaps it's not even so much a lesson
as it is a truth: People can be warned about something, but will more often
only learn their lesson by making the mistake themselves. In Helen's version, Mr. Carp even says as much: "So you fed him too much!" he says when
the boy calls. "I knew you would. I always say 'don't' but you boys always do."
Indeed, the store owner's warning gets a similar tweaking at the finale of both
versions of the story. Here's how *A Fish out of Water* ends: "Now I feed Otto /
so much and no more / Never more than a spot / or something may happen.
/ And now I know what!" The exclamation point makes it seem as though the
boy feels more proud than regretful.

Phil's illustrations, decorated with shades of orange, brown, and pale green,
are in his trademark soft black pencil line. In most of the colored areas the
pencil line is visible. He gives Otto a look of perpetual surprise, eyes wide, tiny
mouth open, as if even he can't believe and/or comprehend what's happening to him. Speaking of not comprehending, both versions of the story don't
bother to explain what exactly the store owner does to fix the fish. Partly this
is because it doesn't really matter, although the fact that it's left a mystery will
inevitably bother some readers, it will also give them a chance to engage their
imaginations to decide what it is they think Mr. Carp did.

There's evidence that Helen held herself to the same high standards that
Ted demanded of other Beginner Book authors. In a 1961 letter she wrote that
the final draft of the book was "the 9,373rd version."

As was typical during this era of Beginner Books, the dust jacket has fun with
the biographical info. Helen's asserts that she is "married to an eccentric writer,
Theo LeSieg" and that she "raises eucalyptus citadora, swims fearlessly into caves
full of lurking moray eels and devotes the rest of her time to local civic projects." As for Phil, his status as a beloved Beginner Book author was cemented:
"It would take a thousand pages to quote all the warm, glowing tributes written
by teachers, librarians, children and literary critics about P. D. Eastman and his
first three Beginner Books. So let's just say this: Everybody loved P. D. Eastman's
first book *Sam and the Firefly*. They loved him more when he did *Are You My
Mother?* Then more and more because of his third book, *Go, Dog. Go!*"

MORE RIDDLES (1961), B-24; *BENNETT CERF'S BOOK OF ANIMAL RIDDLES* (1964), B-34

Bennett Cerf and Roy McKie

Bennett Cerf and Roy McKie teamed up again in 1961 for a sequel to *Bennett Cerf's Book of Riddles*. Once again there's wordplay ("What kind of coat should be put on when it is wet?" "A coat of paint."), unexpected twists ("What is white, has one horn, and gives milk?" "A milk truck."), groaners ("What is the best thing to put into a pie?" "Your teeth."), and absurdity ("What sings, has four legs, is yellow, and weighs 1,000 pounds?" "Two five-hundred pound canaries.").

Roy's illustrations are done in bold, flat primary colors, and feature cameos by a couple of other Beginner Book characters. The tiger on page 22 looks an awful lot like the one in *Ten Apples Up on Top!* And the child playing in the snow on page 54 is a dead ringer for the ones in *Snow* (which would come out the following year).

Nineteen sixty-four saw the release of the duo's final collaboration, *Animal Riddles*. Bennett's jokes are as inspired as ever (Q: "Ten cats were in a boat. One jumped out. How many were left?" A: "None were left. All the rest were copycats."), so the only real change is in Roy's art. The flat, limited color and controlled brush lines of the first two books have evolved into something wilder and looser, akin to his work in 1963's *Summer*. The color work here is more purposefully slapdash, almost like a kid gleefully coloring outside the lines.

The original *Book of Riddles* and *More Riddles* were reissued in 1999 as a single book called *Riddles and More Riddles*. Roy's illustrations were replaced with new ones by Cleveland-based artist Debbie Palen. Debbie's illustrations are lively and fun, but to fit all of the riddles into a shorter book, the answers are on the same page instead of the front-and-back structure of the originals. As a result the pictures often give away the punchline, though one might argue that's a more early-reader-friendly way to do it, since using context is an important skill.

ROBERT THE ROSE HORSE (1962), B-25

Joan Heilbroner and P. D. Eastman

Robert the Rose Horse is a prose story concerning a young colt who discovers, on his birthday of all days, that he is violently allergic to roses. The doctor recommends Robert leave the country and head for the big city. There, his allergy continues to trouble him until he becomes a police horse and finds himself in a situation where he can use it to his advantage.

The book is a model early reader: engaging, funny, and natural. The text uses repetition judiciously, with Robert's sneezes always starting ("His nose began to itch. And his eyes began to itch . . .") and ending ("and the _____ fell down flat!") the same way. There's also a bit of fun wordplay here and there, such as this exchange:

> "Say AH," said the doctor.
> "AH," said Robert.
> "AHA!" said the doctor.

Author Joan Heilbroner (1922–2020) had a natural facility for writing humor for children, but becoming an author wasn't a lifelong ambition. As the dust-jacket flap for *Robert the Rose Horse* explained, she came from a family of writers. Her husband, Robert, was an economic historian with a long list of published works. Her sister, Barbara, and brother-in-law, Peter Cary (to whom the book is partially dedicated), both wrote and worked as editors at *Reader's Digest*.

Joan Knapp was born into a wealthy family in Garden City, New York. Her father, Robert, was a partner in a real estate firm called Webb and Knapp; her grandfather was a former county judge who served as New York tax commissioner and United States commissioner. Joan's mother, formerly Jessie Allen, was the daughter of a physician who ran a sanitarium in upstate New York. Jessie was "very good-looking," highly educated, and an avid reader, but also, according to Joan, "a terrifying lady" who was "stern and unpleasant." Joan adored her only sibling, Barbara, who was ten years her senior.

Robert Knapp died suddenly just a month after Joan's second birthday, and this threw the family into turmoil, though they remained financially stable thanks to her father's advance planning. "We had an elegant apartment and lots of servants," Joan recalls. In school, Joan excelled at spelling and enjoyed learning to read, but she wasn't a particularly bookish child. Her true passion was the piano.

Each morning she would wake up at 6 o'clock to practice for hours. When the Great Depression hit, the family lost their financial cushion, and were forced into a more modest lifestyle until the markets recovered. The family left their fancy apartment and servants for Manhattan, where Jessie Knapp opened a dress shop, and Joan continued with her schooling. She attended the private all-girls Brearly School, and then went on to her mother's alma

Joan Heilbroner with sons David (on her lap) and Peter circa 1962. Courtesy Peter Heilbroner.

mater, Smith College. A couple of years into college, she decided to follow her musical dreams, and was accepted into the Oberlin Conservatory of Music in Ohio. Once there, however, she learned, "I wasn't as good as I thought I was."

She left Oberlin and headed northeast to Cleveland, where she finished her degree at Case Western Reserve University. She returned to New York, and met Robert Heilbroner, an economist, historian, and writer. The two married in 1952 and had two sons, Peter and David. When the boys were young, Joan created a witty and funny story about their attempts to buy her a birthday present with very limited funds. Happy with how it turned out, she wrote out two more story ideas, one based on the Manhattan apartment building where the family lived on East 74th Street between Park and Lexington, and the other on a "charming" New York police horse she'd encountered during Fidel Castro's 1960 visit to the city to address to the United Nations General Assembly.

By that time, Robert Heilbroner had published two books with Harper & Row. Through his connections there, Joan was able to get her manuscript for *The Happy Birthday Present* in front of Ursula Nordstrom, who accepted it as an I Can Read! book and assigned artist Mary Chalmers to do the illustrations. Emboldened by her success, Joan submitted her manuscript about the horse to Nordstrom. Nordstrom rejected *Robert the Rose Horse*, but Joan decided to use another connection to get it in front of another early reader publisher,

The photo P. D. Eastman took of the police horse for future reference. Courtesy Tony Eastman.

Random House and Beginner Books. Joan and Robert were friends with Bob and Helen Bernstein, and in fact it had been Bob—when he was still at Simon and Schuster—who had helped Robert publish his most successful and lasting work, 1952's *The Worldly Philosophers: The Lives, Times, and Ideas of the Great Economic Thinkers*. With Bob now at Random House, Joan was able to get the manuscript for *Robert the Rose Horse* to Phyllis Cerf, who agreed to publish it.

P. D. Eastman was assigned to illustrate *Robert the Rose Horse*, and by lucky coincidence, Phil had been in that exact same crowd outside the UN as Joan had been, and had snapped some pictures of that exact same police horse to use for reference in case, he thought, "I ever have to illustrate a book about horses." Phil's pictures in the book are on the whole his most detailed since *Sam and the Firefly* and the "big dog party" in *Go, Dog. Go!* with lots of city and crowd and action scenes. The story's settings allow him to show some great versatility, ranging from an-all animal birthday party on the farm all the way to a run-down neighborhood in the big city. He also manages to work in a depiction of the actual building where Troop B of the mounted police were stabled, located at 55th Street and 10th Avenue (it's on page 43 of the book).

School Library Journal wrote that *Robert the Rose Horse* was "an amusing story" with "illustrations [that] add greatly to the humor." Librarian Betty Ainslie wrote in the *Chicago Daily Herald* that "The illustrations are a comic joy, and this is a book young boys and girls will love." True to that, while the book never quite ascended to the status of a classic, it remains in print fifty-five years later.

The Happy Birthday Present was released in February 1962. *Robert the Rose Horse* followed three months later. While those two books were in production, Ursula Nordstrom had accepted Joan's third manuscript, the one about the apartment building. Aliki—at the very beginning of what would be a long, distinguished career in children's books—was tasked with providing the pictures. *This Is the House Where Jack Lives* would be published in November 1962 ("The picture in the book looks exactly like the building where we lived," Joan says), and in the space of three months Joan had gone from unpublished to a three-time author at the two most prominent and successful children's book publishers.

For more on Joan, see the entry for *A Pet Like Sneakers* (2013).

I WAS KISSED BY A SEAL AT THE ZOO (1962), B-26

Helen Palmer and Lynn Fayman

I Was Kissed by a Seal at the Zoo arose from a friendship between Helen Geisel and photographer Lynn Fayman, a fellow La Jolla resident. The two got to know each other at the La Jolla Art Center. First established in a house in 1941, the gallery served as a cultural nexus point for the city's art community, "attracting artists and teachers from around the country and fostering an atmosphere of cooperation and friendly competition." Lynn was highly active in the center, serving as board president and helping to oversee its eventual transformation into the La Jolla Museum of Contemporary Art. Later, Helen would join him as vice president of the board.

How exactly the idea to do a photo-illustrated Beginner Book came about is unknown, but it certainly was a unique proposition. Ruth Alexander Nichols used photographs as illustrations in books such as *Nancy* (1933) and *Betty and Dolly* (1935). Celebrated animal photographer Ylla (born Camilla Koffler) had some success in the 1940s and early 1950s using her photos to tell fictional stories (she did four of these with Margaret Wise Brown, including

The Sleepy Little Lion and *O Said the Squirrel*), and Albert Lamorisse's picture book version of his film *The Red Balloon* was a big hit upon its release in 1957. But overall, photos in fiction books were something novel.

There's indication that *I Was Kissed by a Seal at the Zoo* underwent some creative growing pains. Phyllis Cerf told Neil and Judith Morgan that "There was one book with a photographer at the San Diego Zoo who was a friend of theirs [and] we were all in despair . . . It was [finally my idea] that [made] it a best-seller." This implies that the project was started without a clear idea of what the premise of the book was going to be. Phyllis's idea, then, turned out to be a good one.

Rather than depict a typical visit to the zoo, *I Was Kissed by a Seal at the Zoo* uses photographs of real children interacting with the animals to create a story of wish fulfillment. The kids in the book are allowed to ride turtles, feed grapes to a chimpanzee, play with a lion cub, and wrangle a baby elephant. The book blurs the lines between fiction and nonfiction in that the boys and girls in the story did do the things depicted—there's no trickery going on—but they were allowed to do them under exceptional circumstances.

Helen and Lynn gathered a group of schoolchildren from the Francis Parker School, a private K–9 (at that time) day school and took them to the San Diego Zoo, making special arrangements with the zoo staff to allow the children to go "behind the scenes" with the animals. The flap states that Lynn took over two thousand shots, wearing out multiple cameras and pairs of shoes in the process. He also brought along his own children. The girl with the camel on page 32 was his daughter Kate. The one with the gazelle was another daughter, Laura Lou. His two youngest sons, Corey and Bruce, are seen walking together through the trees and feeding the goats on pages 16 through 21. The book's cover "star" was Jeff Clark, a neighbor and Francis Parker student.

The photos in *I Was Kissed by a Seal at the Zoo* are fairly straightforward, but in many cases the backgrounds have been replaced by a flat color field in pink, sea green, light blue, or yellow. This livens things up, and gives a bit of a hint as to the sensibility of the man who "illustrated" the book.

Lynn Gray Fayman (1904–1968) was born and raised in Kansas City, Missouri. One of four boys, he attended Kansas State University, majoring in landscape architecture. Upon graduation, he headed to Europe to further study his craft. When he returned stateside, he spent a handful of years in Chicago and then returned to Kansas City, working all the while as a land-scape architect. There he married Ruth Glover (nee Johnson), a modern dancer and dance instructor he'd met while doing stage lighting on the side.

Lynn adopted her two teenage children from her previous marriage, David and Faith. In 1942 Ruth and Lynn headed for Los Angeles, where he found work as a stage lighting engineer. An amateur interest in photography had been growing steadily, and so he enrolled at the Art Center School in LA. Here he studied photography with Edward Kaminski and found himself taken with the Bauhaus movement of experimental photography.

After finishing his coursework, Lynn got a job as a photographer at Ryan Aeronautical in San Diego. He set up a studio in the seaside Bird Rock neighborhood of La Jolla in the late 1940s, and began experimenting with a new kind of Kodak film called Ektachrome, which was easier to develop than their famous Kodachrome. Using this new process, he became fascinated by the possibilities of creating abstract forms using only color and light. He developed a process wherein he refracted, diffracted, or reflected light to create color slides that had the "illusion of solidity and form although no visible objects were photographed." He thought of them as paintings made of light.

Lynn continued to experiment, next with another Kodak process, Flexichrome, which essentially allowed the photographer to paint color dyes onto a black-and-white negative. His unusual work began to catch on, first in Photographic Society of America group shows (where in 1955 he won the top prize in color film) and then in spotlight shows at galleries and museums across the country. He also began to create short films, starting with *Color in Motion* in 1951, which set "undulating color forms" to music ("Greensleeves" in the first section). Its follow-up, *Color in Motion II*, was shown at the 1954 Cannes Film Festival.

Lynn's involvement in and effect on the arts scene of La Jolla in the 1950s cannot be overstated. In addition to his tireless work for the museum, he cofounded the Allied Arts Council, regularly opened his studio for exhibitions and film screenings, and documented the local scene and community extensively in photos of artists and their work. He also was a generous patron of his fellow artists.

In 1955, Ruth passed away at the age of fifty-three after a prolonged illness. Two years later Lynn married Danah Colby, a New York native and a freelance writer for the *San Diego Union*. Danah, sixteen years Lynn's junior, had been widowed in 1954 and was mother to four children (Kate, Ann, Laura Lou, and Fred). She and Lynn would add sons Corey and Bruce to the family.

For more on Lynn and his creative partnership with Helen, see the entries for *Do You Know What I'm Going to Do Next Saturday?* (1963) and *Why I Built the Boogle House* (1964).

Lynn Fayman. Courtesy Corey Lynn Fayman.

SNOW (1962), B-27

P. D. Eastman and Roy McKie

P. D. Eastman, it seems, spent the early 1960s vying for the title of hardest-working Beginner Book creator. He'd had a hand in five of the ten Beginner Books released in 1961 and 1962. Roy McKie was his closest competition, illustrating three of those ten. The prolific duo teamed up for the first and only time on *Snow*. The story features a boy, a girl, and their dog (Dick, Jane, and Spot again?) romping through several winter activities, including skiing, sledding, snowball fighting, and snowman building.

According to the book's flap, the book's idea originated with Roy. Bringing Phil on to do the text and story was a natural, as the two men were friends and had once been neighbors in Westport, Connecticut (where Roy rented a house for a year or so following his divorce). When he conceived the book, however, Roy was living in Castine, Maine. So the flap lightheartedly indicates that Roy brought the pictures from snowy Maine, and Phil brought the words on a snowplow from Connecticut. In place of author photos, Roy also drew himself and Phil as snowmen.

Perhaps because it was his idea, and because he loved winter sports himself, Roy would later in his life cite *Snow* as his favorite of all of his books, which he called a result of his "old-fashioned" way of approaching the story, in that it depicts very wholesome fun with no sense of conflict or danger, even when the boy hits the girl right in the face with a snowball (something that it is very difficult to smile through). Presented in flat primary colors, there's a palpable sense of joy in the drawings throughout the book, and one can see how much fun Roy had depicting the dog. Rarely is he the center of the action, but he's up to one thing or another in nearly every picture.

Phil's verse is done in a series of four-line rhymes: "We go up hill. / The snow is deep. / We can't go fast. / The hill is steep." Like Dr. Seuss, he wisely breaks or extends the pattern a small number of times, once to create a short breather (adding a rhyme to the lines above: "We think our dog has gone to sleep") and then the second time to convey and generate excitement: "Now make another / Ball of snow. / Push it! Push it! / See it go. / What a snow ball! / See it grow! / See it grow / And grow and grow!"

The verse and vocabulary list limited Phil's use of terminology, so though the activities are depicted, the book doesn't include the words "ski" or "sled" or "snow angel." It does, curiously, include the word "appetite," sure to not be in the reading vocabulary of most first graders.

THE BIG HONEY HUNT (1962), B-28

Stanley and Janice Berenstain

Once they made it past the marathon of revisions on *Freddy Bear's Spanking*, the creation of *The Big Honey Hunt* was comparatively easy for Stan and Jan Berenstain. The story arose from a section of *Freddy Bear* in which one of the alternate punishments Freddy suggests is that all of his honey be taken away and that he be "forced" to go on an adventure to get more.

In the expanded version, the story is sparked by the Bear family running out of honey. Mama asks Papa to head to the Honey Store, which is no more than six feet from the bottom step of their tree house. But hard-headed Papa insists that the best honey comes directly from trees, and sets out on a quest to show Small Bear how to find it. This leads to a series of mistakes and pratfalls, all predicated on Papa's soaring overconfidence. In the end, he proudly buys honey at the store, claiming it to be the very best kind of honey.

The Berenstains bravely decided to write this new book in rhyme, perhaps because that was one of the few things Ted had praised about Freddy Bear. The tale is told in four-line rhyme, with occasional interruptions (in some cases to rhyme the same word: "Well it looks just so. And it feels just so. Looks so. Feels so. So it's SO!" or "And so / you see this tree must be / Must, must, must be / A honey tree!"). Like many other Beginner Books (*Put Me in the Zoo*, *Green Eggs and Ham*), there's no narrator, but instead the story is told completely through dialogue, the words usually placed above or next to the speaker. All that's missing are balloons around the words.

Those familiar with the later style of Berenstain Bears books will be taken aback by the look of *The Big Honey Hunt* (and the first handful of Berenstain Beginner Books). Much in the way the early Snoopy and Charlie Brown don't quite resemble their later iconic looks, the familiar Bear family are not quite themselves yet. The basics are there: Mama and Papa Bear wear their signature outfits, but they have fuzzy hair and ears, they aren't nearly as smooth and rounded as they would become. The overall style of the book is much looser and a bit cruder than the Berenstains' later work. Stan and Jan themselves looked back on the book's artwork with some sense of bafflement, saying it didn't even meet their standards of the time. "It's almost as if we had forgotten how to draw," they wrote. They added that the pictures were done with "wild abandon," and lamented the "worm-thin" tree house and the fact that "on some pages Papa Bear looked like a haystack wearing overalls."

None of that stopped the book from becoming a hit, with great sales and a write-up in the *New York Times* (by children's author Irma Simonton Black), celebrating its "fast action and humor." In fact, *The Big Honey Hunt* sold so well that it sabotaged the next book the Berenstains planned to release. See the entry for *The Bike Lesson* (1964) for that story.

HOP ON POP (1963), B-29

Dr. Seuss

Ted returned to his role as a Beginner Book author/illustrator for the first time in three years with not one but two new books, *Hop on Pop* and *Dr.*

Seuss's ABC. Both reflect his growing interest in the foundations of reading; namely, phonics and letter sounds.

Hop on Pop, subtitled "The Simplest Seuss for Youngest Use," was similar to *One Fish, Two Fish, Red Fish, Blue Fish,* in that it was less a story than a collection of absurd comedy sketches built around word families. But *Hop on Pop* makes its purpose more explicit. The book emphasizes rhyming words by placing them first and in capital letters: "ALL TALL / We all are tall. / ALL SMALL / We all are small. / ALL BALL / We all play ball. / BALL WALL / Up on a wall. ALL FALL / Fall off the wall." The book's endpapers feature some yellow Seuss creatures capering among the sixteen sets of words that appear in the book. From an early literacy standpoint, word families help young readers quickly build their reading vocabulary by explicitly showing them how to use a word they know to read other words that are phonetically similar. This is likely why Ted didn't use any rhyming words that follow a different spelling pattern.

In *Learning to Read: The Great Debate,* Jeanne Chall singled out both *Green Eggs and Ham* and *Hop on Pop* as exemplars of writing for emerging readers. She called *Hop on Pop* "a veritable phonic or linguistic reader that controls words on a common phonic-element or spelling-pattern principle." In a *New York Times* book review, E. L. Buell wrote, "As for Dr. Seuss, that wizard is bent on removing reading frustrations before they start . . . the illustrations are as funny as ever; they also provide clues for figuring out the meaning of words." Indeed, the National Education Association included the book on its 2012 list of Top 100 Books for Teachers.

Though he was thinking of the youngest readers Ted had some fun with the manuscript he submitted to Bennett Cerf. In the conclusion of the book he included the line "My father can read big words, too. Like Con Tra Cep Tive, Kan Ga Roo" and waited anxiously for Bennett to discover the line and be forced to say "no" to his star author.

Even without adult material, *Hop on Pop* stirred up controversy in 2013 when a patron of the Toronto Public Library submitted an official complaint alleging that the book "encourages children to use violence against their fathers" (unconsciously echoing Homer Simpson's line *The Simpsons* season 12 episode "HOMR": "[I read] everything from *Hop on Pop* to *Death Be Not Proud.* It's so tragic the way they hopped on pop."). The patron requested that the library withdraw the book, apologize, and pay damages to the patrons of the library. The librarians refused, lauding *Hop on Pop* as "a humorous and well-loved children's book designed to engage children while teaching them reading skills." They also pointed out that the book actually advocates against violence ("Stop! Do not hop on pop.").

DR. SEUSS'S ABC (1963), B-30

Dr. Seuss

One of Ted's first attempts at writing for children was in 1932, when he created an alphabet book with a fantastic creature for each letter. C was for the green-striped chomondelet, W for a long-necked whizzleworp, and so forth. That book was never published, but thirty-one years later he revived the idea as a Beginner Book, abandoning most of the menagerie in favor of a series of unconnected, alliterative riffs.

Alphabet books have a long history in both reading instruction and children's literature. Hornbooks typically displayed upper and lowercase letters. In the seventeenth century battledores—thin trifolded cardboard—added pictures of animals to accompany the letters, helping children to associate a sound with the letter. When primers came along, they often used this same approach. In the 1840s Edward Lear released "A Nonsense Alphabet," with a poem and illustration for each letter ("J was a jackdaw / Who hopped up and down / In the principal street / Of a neighboring town") in the 1880s, Kate Greenaway published *A Apple Pie*, in which the title item is followed through the alphabet. Greenaway took the unusual approach of personifying the letters and using verbs instead of nouns for many of them ("Q quartered it"; "R ran for it.").

Closer to Ted's time, in 1962 in fact, Maurice Sendak had released an alphabet book called *Alligators All Around* as part of his Nutshell Library. The book featured two-word alliterative sentences with the alligators as the implied subject (e.g., "Having headaches").

Ted used a combination of all of these approaches, starting with the letter as Greenaway did, writing in verse like Lear, and using Sendak's alliteration. The end result is a series of brightly colored vignettes introducing each letter, á la "Big S, little s / Silly Sammy Slick sipped six sodas and got sick sick sick." By constructing it this way, Ted teaches capital and lowercase letters and beginning sounds. The rub of the book, though, is that a child just learning the alphabet and its sounds would not be able to read words like "quacker-oo" or "Yorgenson" or "Warren" independently. This means the book is most effective as a teaching tool when it is read aloud to children. For kids who can read it on their own it instead serves as a fun review and reinforcement of what they already know.

As with *Hop on Pop*, Ted slipped a joke into his initial manuscript for Bennett to catch. On the page for X he wrote "Big X / Little x / X . . . x . . . X / Someday, kiddies, you will learn about sex." Kidding aside, his actual approach to X is a clever and refreshing one. Rather than rely on the worn-out "x-ray" or "xylophone" (which doesn't make an "x" sound), he instead appropriately uses words where the "x" sound is in the middle ("Nixie") or the end of the word ("fox," "ax").

Finally, though the book's cover depicts an imaginary set of Seussian animals, all but two of the animals featured in the book are real, with only the Fiffer-Feffer-Feff and the Zizzer-Zazzer-Zuzz left as any trace of Ted's original idea.

DO YOU KNOW WHAT I'M GOING TO DO NEXT SATURDAY? (1963), B-31

Helen Palmer and Lynn Fayman

Following the success of *I Was Kissed by a Seal at the Zoo*, Helen Geisel and Lynn Fayman got together again, this time creating *Do You Know What I'm Going to Do Next Saturday?* The book is similar to its predecessor in that it portrays fantasy situations using real photos. Playing off of a child's propensity for exaggeration, flights of fancy, and boasting, the story features a boy detailing all the fantastic things he's going to do next Saturday. This includes winning a five-to-one tennis game, taking rides in a jet and helicopter, and leading a military parade. There are also plenty of stops for meals and snacks, including ice cream sundaes, watermelon, and "TEN MILES OF SPAGHETTI."

This is all, of course, accompanied by actual photos of the boy doing these activities, and in many cases the pictures exaggerate even more than the words. When the boy says he's going to eat a "big, big breakfast" the photo shows him in front of a spread including a pile of sausages, several stacks of pancakes, and a large bowl of fruit. Later, when the boy has to stop mid-morning to "eat a little something," the photo shows him making himself four milkshakes.

Lynn's style is similar to the earlier book, black-and-white photos with a canary yellow backdrop (in some cases replacing the original photo background). Where the book deviates from *I Was Kissed by a Seal at the Zoo* is in the composition of the photos. Lynn clearly had more freedom to set up and create, which results in the extreme perspectives and action shots of the boy diving and climbing and doing the training course with the marines.

The blond, freckled star of the book was Rawli Davis, who remembers at age ten being called to the front office of Ellen Browning Scripps Elementary. Since visits to the principal were nothing new for Rawli, he was sure he'd gotten in trouble somehow. Instead he found himself being interviewed by Helen and Lynn for the lead role in their new book. Though Rawli can't remember anything the authors asked him, he must have given the right answers. Helen and Lynn had been looking for a very particular type of kid, and Rawli fit the bill.

The photo shoots for the book took place over a series of Saturdays in the summer of 1962. Rawli had to endure a salon visit before every shoot to make sure his hair remained consistent throughout. He also had to wear the same outfit every time. Sometimes the photo sessions would take place at the Fayman residence. The little boy to whom Rawli is telling his whopper is Corey Lynn Fayman, who also appeared in *I Was Kissed by a Seal at the Zoo*. Corey remembers being unhappy to have been drafted into the shoot. His little brother, Bruce, had been sent off to take a nap. "I was upset that we got separated. I wanted to be with my brother and take a nap." So he pretended that he was sleepy, allowing for that iconic final page, with Corey slumped over while Rawli continues to boast.

The tennis scene was shot at the La Jolla Beach and Tennis Club, and the volleyball game took place at La Jolla shores. The segments featuring the marines were taken at the Marine Corps Recruit Depot and Camp Matthews (which was decommissioned in 1964 and sold to the University of California–San Diego). The spaghetti scenes were shot at a pizza parlor called Pernicano's, and featured restaurant owner George Pernicano, who was also one of the original minority owners of the San Diego Chargers. Rawli also got to visit Helen and Ted's home a handful of times.

Rawli reports that there were several photo sessions that didn't end up in the book, including ones at the San Diego County Fair in Del Mar, the model train exhibit in Balboa Park, and Torrey Pines. There was also an attempt to get some photos of Rawli surfing, but the waves didn't cooperate that day.

Rawli says in some cases Lynn gave him very clear directions, but in others allowed him to improvise, but always praised him for figuring out what to do. For the most part Rawli found the experience to be fun, but there were some that were more difficult than others, such as having to "lead" the military parade, which had to be done guerilla style because it was an actual parade, not one the book's authors had arranged.

Once the book came out Rawli's life didn't change all that much. Unlike what his character in the book might have done, he didn't go around bragging about being the star of his own book. He recalls some casting agents visiting his house and being kindly turned away by his parents. He ended up pursuing a career as a design engineer, working in the aerospace industry, a career he says he never would have imagined for himself when he was a kid. He's also an avid golfer, surfer, and softball player.

A success at the time—the *New York Times* listed it as one of the best juvenile books of 1963—*Do You Know What I'm Going to Do Next Saturday?* has turned out to be one of the most controversial and misunderstood Beginner Books. This is mostly due to the advent of the Internet and blog culture, wherein writers either rediscovering or first encountering the book were amused and shocked by some of its elements. In 2002 an AOL user who apparently didn't know the difference between a book being out of print and a book being pulled from circulation, created a webpage dedicated to *Do You Know . . .* , titling it "The Banned Book of Dr. Seuss!" and then presenting the text of the book out of context. This had the effect of making lines like "Next Saturday I'll blow my head off!" (accompanied in the book by a photo of Rawli playing the tuba) or "Did you ever beat more than one kid at a time?" (with a photo of Rawli playing tennis against multiple children) seem ominous. The site also mentioned the pages (38–41) where Rawli brandishes a handgun and rifle, something that in a modern context of school shootings is admittedly jarring.

The webpage circulated widely enough that the leading fact-checking website Snopes.com created an entry about the controversy, declaring, "*Do You Know What I'm Going to Do Next Saturday?* was never 'banned,' and nothing about it was really the least bit unwholesome." It's also worth noting that reviews at the time were positive, along the lines of the *Chicago Tribune*'s write-up: "Boys are certain to identify happily with the ambitious dreamer and enjoy watching his exploits in Lynn Fayman's lively photographs."

SUMMER (1963), B-32

Alice Low and Roy McKie

An unofficial companion to *Snow*, *Summer* follows a boy, a girl, and their dog (Dick, Jane, and Spot again?) as they caper through various June, July, and August activities. These include the fun (riding bikes, watching fireworks, swimming), the delicious (eating watermelon, ice cream, toasted marshmallows), and the unbearable (being stuck in traffic in a car without air conditioning; getting attacked by bugs and birds at a picnic).

The story is told in jaunty four-line verse, with the children narrating. The vocabulary limitations are present, with the pictures doing the heavy lifting in lieu of big words like watermelon, Ferris wheel, and marshmallows (though the latter word appears on a package). The only awkward word list moment comes when the kids make a "sand house" in text, while the picture clearly shows a sandcastle.

Summer marks the debut of a more liberated Roy McKie. Though the pictures are still impeccably drafted and composed, Roy's dry brush technique is more free and loose than in his previous Beginner Book work. The color is also quite different. Not only does he make use of a larger palate, he experiments for the first time in his Beginner Book work with using color—rather than ink lines—to define background details. The overall effect matches the book's subject matter well, capturing the warmth and vividness of summer days.

It's worth noting here that the appearance of watercolor in Beginner Books—as opposed to a solid flat color—was actually a sophisticated trick of the printing process. First the illustrator would create line drawings. These would be printed on watercolor paper in a pale "non-photo" blue that wouldn't show up in reproduction. Next, instead of painting in the actual colors, the artists used a color chart that showed various tones of magenta, cyan, yellow, and black in percentages of gray. When photographed together with the original black line drawing "plate" (and often a black half-tone plate, too) the printed effect—if everything went well—was a full-color watercolor painting. In nod to this complex process, P. D. Eastman wrote a brief note that he pinned to the wall of his office at Random House (a space he'd inherited from Edward Gorey, and would pass on to Michael Frith). The note read, "McKie now has the non-photographic blues."

Writer Alice Low (1926–2012) was born Alice Bernstein, in New York. Her father worked in textiles and her mother wrote children's books with illustrator Rosalie Slocum under the name Ann Todd. Alice, who early on took a great interest in painting and ceramics, graduated Smith College with a degree in studio art in 1947. Around this time she met Martin Low, a fighter pilot who had been at both Pearl Harbor and the invasion of Normandy. They married in 1949, and would have three children, Andrew, Katherine, and David. The family settled in Briarcliff, New York, in Westchester County.

Post-college, Alice found her interests starting to fall in line with her mother's, and she began writing poems and songs. Alice's cousin on her father's side was Random House sales manager (and future president) Bob Bernstein. In the early 1950s, when Bob was still in sales at Simon and Schuster he had encouraged his cousin to send a song she'd written to Little Golden Records. The song was never recorded, but its lyrics became the 1954 Little Golden Book *Open Up My Suitcase*. The next year she published another Little Golden Book, *Out of My Window*, but she didn't immediately jump into a career in children's literature. Instead, feeling she needed an academic background for her writing career, she enrolled in creative writing courses at Columbia University.

By the early 1960s she was contributing stories to magazines such as *Seventeen*, and was writing book reviews for the *New York Times*. Bob was now at Random House, but it's purely a coincidence that Alice happened to place material in two Captain Kangaroo anthologies at the publisher, as well as her third children's book, *Grandmas and Grandpas* (1962).

Next came *Summer*, and creating a Beginner Book dovetailed nicely with Alice's passion for early literacy and keen interest in education. As such, Alice took the job very seriously. Andy recalls, "She wrote the allowed words on file cards and taped them to the sliding doors of the clothes closet in her and dad's bedroom. She would prowl back and forth looking for possible rhymes and for words she could use to advance the story." He says she wrote and rewrote each page, asking her family which version was better. "Although the final product is relatively short," Andy says, "she surely spent more time per word on this book than any other in her career!"

At least one situation in the book was taken directly from life. Andy remembers, "The scene where the family is stuck in the hot car was absolutely based on one of our family trips to Martha's Vineyard, when we were caught in a huge traffic jam of cars approaching the ferry at Woods Hole."

While steadily publishing books through the second half of the 1960s and the early 1970s (including one more with Roy McKie—*A Day of Your Own*), Alice would work on educational filmstrips for Warren Schloat Productions, teach creative writing at the Birch Wathen School, and return to Random House to help with the Grolier Beginning Reading Program. She finished out her career as an editor for Scholastic's Children's Choice Book Club.

Her publication pace slowed from 1974 on, but she managed to release a new book every two or three years, including work with such high-profile illustrators as Tomie De Paola, Gahan Wilson, Aliki, and Marc Brown. In 1978 she became one of the select few to author both a Beginner Book and an I Can Read! book. *The Witch Who Was Afraid of Witches*, illustrated in its original edition by Karen Gundersheimer, turned out to be a big hit. It inspired a

Alice Low. Courtesy Andy Low and Kathy Low.

short film by Sesame Street animator Eli Noyes in 1979, and a musical play in the early 1990s, for which Alice herself wrote the book and lyrics.

At home equally in telling both realistic stories (*Kallie's Corner*; *All around the Farm*) and fantastic ones (*The Charge of the Mouse Brigade*; *The Macmillan Book of Greek Gods and Heroes*), Alice also compiled several anthologies, such as *Spooky Stories for a Dark and Stormy Night* (Hyperion, 1994) and *Stories to Tell a Five-Year-Old* (Little, Brown, 1996). In the 1990s she was invited to become of a member of the Century Association, an exclusive organization for artists and writers. In her later years, Alice served as a volunteer at the Metropolitan Museum of Art, sang in a local chorus, traveled, and played tennis. Ever creative, she often marked family member's milestones (birthdays, anniversaries, weddings) by writing personalized poems.

LITTLE BLACK GOES TO THE CIRCUS! (1963), B-33

Walter Farley and James Schucker

Walter Farley and James Schucker's second book about Little Black is sillier and stranger than its predecessor. When the boy and Little Black happen upon Bruno's Circus setting up, the pony tries and fails at a trick, and all of the performers laugh at him. Stubborn as ever, Little Black becomes determined to show them he can perform in the circus. The premise is very much Beginner Book material, but James Schucker's realistic illustrations—which had been such a perfect complement for the action and emotionality of *Little Black, A Pony*—lend an unintended sense of menace to the circus folk and an air of danger to Little Black's multiple falls.

Where James wasn't an ill fit was in his depiction of the circus, something he'd had a lot of practice with in *The Big Book of the Real Circus* (published by Grosset & Dunlap in 1958). His illustrations here are painted with inkwash and then filled in with flat, full color (unlike the limited spot coloring in the first book).

Little Black Goes to the Circus! also has noticeably fewer words than its predecessor, and though Walter ably avoids tricky circus terminology such as "trapeze," "balance," or "ringmaster" he uses the phonetically irregular words such as "plank" and "Bruno" that would require modeling for a beginning reader.

Why put Little Black in a circus? Well, besides Schucker's facility with that milieu, Walter Farley and his family had since the 1940s summered in a beach home in Venice, Florida, just a short drive from Sarasota and the summer home of the Ringling Brothers and Barnum & Bailey Circus (and the hometown of Robert Lopshire).

Walter and James would collaborate on one more Little Black book, 1968's *The Little Black Pony Races*. Though it was published by Random House, it was curiously not a Beginner Book. By that time, Ted was solely in charge of the line, and perhaps he rejected it, or perhaps Farley decided to not work within the confines of limited vocabulary.

James Schucker died in 1988. In the last two decades of his life he'd turned from commercial illustration to doing murals and portraits. He gained much local esteem in both disciplines, and his work can still be seen in schools, offices, hospitals, and banks throughout Bucks County. James also held weekly painting classes in the barn that he used as a studio. A look at the way James masterfully depicts the boy's facial expressions in *Little Black, A Pony* and it's no surprise he found success in portraiture.

WHY I BUILT THE BOOGLE HOUSE (1964), B-35

Helen Palmer and Lynn Fayman

Helen Geisel and Lynn Fayman's final collaboration is a logical insanity story about a boy who has to keep adapting a house for new and larger pets. The house starts as a small home for a turtle, but when the reptile escapes, the boy adopts a duck and needs to expand the house. Things continue like this through a succession of pets, and expansions. When keeping his final pet, a horse, turns out to be a violation of city code, the boy decides to repurpose his house for a Boogle. "I don't quite know what a Boogle is," he admits. "But one of these days I hope I'll find one."

The boy in this book was "played" by Lynn's grandson, David Lyerly (his mother, Faith, was Lynn's adopted daughter from his first marriage), who was ten years old at the time. David was a natural performer, and jumped at the chance to be the star of his grandfather's newest book. His twin brother Chris makes a cameo on page 17 as the boy who swaps his kitten. David passed away in 2010, but Chris recalls the joy David got from participating in the project. "He talked excitedly every evening about what he'd done that day," Chris says. "He was really into it."

Lynn's black-and-white photographs are once again accompanied by fields of color (blue and gold in this book), but unlike *I Was Kissed . . .* and *Do You Know . . .* the photos are, in all but one case, presented with their full original backgrounds, and the color only serves to accent the photos. The photos themselves are sharp and well composed. One gets the feeling that, due to the nature of the book's story, Lynn had more control over the shots. In the previous two books, he was documenting various situations as they occurred in a variety of locations. In *Why I Built . . .* he was able to direct the action, albeit with such unpredictable actors as animals. He also had control of the environment, shooting mostly around his home, and building the Boogle House itself in an open area on the northeast side of his property.

The fact of Lynn having more control over the shoot shows not only in the composition of the photos, but in their details as well. The house the boy builds is a progressive construction. It's never rebuilt, only expanded, so that when it becomes the Boogle House in the end, one can still spot the original tiny turtle house at the very top of the construct. It was this element of the story that captured the attention of children's book reviewer David Elzey when he was young. "What *Why I Built the Boogle House* has going for it is the unbridled enthusiasm this boy has in building homes for these animals," Elzey writes. "That and a seemingly endless supply of lumber and access to hand tools. I'm not even going to pretend that this book didn't somehow inspire me to want to do the same thing."

Another blogger, Burgin Streetman, points out the way Helen, after writing in a sort of anonymous voice in her first run as a children's author, had developed a clearly identifiable style over her four Beginner Books. "Ms. Palmer's incantation is a delight," Streetman writes, "and once you've gotten into reading her stuff, you can instantly tell if a book is hers." This was likely a function of all four books being told in first person from the perspective of a child, allowing the sentence structure and vocabulary to feel naturally simple. As with most Beginner Books, repetition is key, but Helen does more than just use the same line or lines over and over again throughout a book. Instead, she uses a trick of introducing a phrase and then building onto it in the next sentence with added information.

Streetman points to the lines in *Why I Built* . . . "So, I swapped him. I swapped the rabbit for a dog" as an example. It shows up tentatively in *A Fish Out of Water* ("I grabbed him. I grabbed him by the tail.") and then ramps up in *I Was Kissed* . . . ("Penguins look like little men, little men in black and white coats" or "I would give him a push—a hard push.") But by *Do You Know* . . . she's perfected it: "I'll make him take a walk. I'll make Sam walk about a hundred miles."

Another way Helen captured the child's voice was through short (sometimes fragmented) sentences. This shows up in *A Fish Out of Water* ("I ran with him. Up to the tub!"), *Why I Built* . . . ("I took it away. I dumped it. No more houses!"), and *Do You Know* . . . ("No, sir! No, sir! Not next Saturday.") This is something she'd been experimenting with since her first Golden Books. While the style is wordier and more narrative, there are moments in *Tommy's Wonderful Rides* (1948) that read like they could have come from a Beginner Book: "And how he ran! . . . Faster . . . faster . . . nearer and nearer . . .". If *Why I Built the Boogle House* hadn't been Helen's final book one wonders how she might have continued to refine and develop this ingenious approach toward writing for early readers.

Lynn Fayman would also retire from the literary world after *Why I Built*. . . . He stayed busily involved in the La Jolla Museum of Art (the museum named its main gallery after him in 1966) and his art career would continue to flourish, his work becoming known through one-man shows at museums and galleries held all over the country. In 1964, perhaps inspired by his work on Beginner Books, he began moving away from color and toward black-and-white experimentation, playing with the development process to strip away details to get at the sculptural essence of the subject.

In June of 1968 Lynn was returning from the family's summer home in Meeker, Colorado, when he suffered a fatal heart attack aboard the plane. He was sixty-four years old. His son Corey was only ten years old at the time. He says, "For the short time I got to be with him, he was an awesome dad, full of life, generous and loving. I have only good memories." His wife, Danah, widowed for a second time, carried on their shared love of the arts. She helped found the San Diego Foundation for the Performing Arts in the early 1980s to facilitate the formation of local dance companies and bring nationally touring dance companies to the city at a time when San Diego was typically bypassed in favor of LA. She served as public relations director for the San Diego Museum of Contemporary Art, and later as board president. She also advanced Lynn's spirit of philanthropy, donating generously to San Diego artists and art organizations.

Lynn was honored in 1969 with a retrospective of his work at his beloved La Jolla Museum of Art, "The Photographic Art of Lynn Fayman" and nearly all of his work and archives are housed at the Museum of Photographic Arts in San Diego. One gets the idea that Lynn would have continued to experiment and push the boundaries of his medium: "As an extension of man's physical eye to his inner eye," he wrote, "photo/imagery offers unlimited opportunity for expression."

THE BIKE LESSON (1964), B-36

Stan and Jan Berenstain

For their second Beginner Book, Ted advised Stan and Jan Berenstain to move away from bears. "Worst thing you could possibly do," he told them. "A series would be a millstone around your necks." On the train ride home Stan found himself looking at an ad for Kool cigarettes featuring an ice-skating penguin. Riffing on a Popeye cartoon where Olive Oyl sleepwalks through the city while narrowly missing various dangers, Stan and Jan came up with the idea of a penguin trying to document what happens at the South Pole, but just barely missing huge event after huge event. They titled it *Nothing Ever Happens at the South Pole*.

When they met with Ted, Helen, and Phyllis to present the book, Ted said prememptively, "Berenstains, let me run something past you. An interesting thing has happened. The salesmen have *The Big Honey Hunt* out on the road. And it's going over big. The buyers love it. We've already upped the first printing. So let me ask you. What would you think about doing another bear book next? There's no reason why there couldn't be a whole bear series."

Dejected and exasperated, Stan and Jan agreed to put the *South Pole* on ice (where it stayed until the book was finished by Jan and released in 2012, though not as a Beginner Book), and the couple went back to where they'd wanted to start, with Papa Bear teaching Small Bear how to ride a bike.

This particular idea had its genesis in Stan's attempts to teach his sons how to ride their bikes. He and Jan chronicled that experience in a January 1959 entry of the comic feature "It's All in the Family" where the dad takes on teaching young Janie to ride a bike. He balances, rides into the water, and gets menaced by a small dog, only to find his daughter riding off on her own at the end.

In the Bear version, Papa Bear, once again eager to show off his wisdom and experience, brings Small Bear a new red bike, but won't let him ride it. Of course, Papa's "lessons" end in disaster. Here the Berenstains upped the slapstick quotient, having Papa fall off the bike, ride over a cliff, run smack into a tree branch, and cause a multicar pile-up by riding on the left-hand side of the road. Unlike in *The Big Honey Hunt*, Papa seems a bit humbled by his mishaps, and accedes the bike to Small Bear in the end. Mama greets them bemusedly as Small Bear states (not incorrectly) that Papa "had some very good lessons for me."

Style-wise, in both words and pictures, the book is very much of a piece with *The Big Honey Hunt*. Papa still has a Brillo pad for a head, and his fingernails and toenails are long, pointy, and curved (Ted hated that particular aspect of the character and ordered the Berenstains to cut them, but they held firm, citing a letter from a fan that called the nails "awesome"). Though still loose, the brush work is more intricate, and the backgrounds and landscape are more fully realized. The story is once again told in dialogue, using four-line verse.

Doubling down on his newfound belief that Beginner Books had its first series on its hands, Ted decided to place a white box on the book's cover proclaiming "Another Adventure of the Berenstain Bears." Stan and Jan were surprised, having never thought to name their bears after themselves. Ted said that he'd gotten the idea from the old vaudeville troupes such as Murgatroyd's Mules and Dugan's Dogs.

Ted made one other decision on that cover that would have a long-lasting impact on the Berenstains' career. He credited them as Stan and Jan, rather than as Stanley and Janice, the names they'd used for publishing since the early 1950s. He reasoned that it was what they called each other, and it rhymed, so why not? The shortened versions stuck, so much so that even the

Dell paperback reissues of their 1950s and early 1960s cartoons were changed
to reflect the new names.

HOW TO MAKE FLIBBERS, ETC. (1964), B-37

Robert Lopshire

Despite the success of *Put Me in the Zoo*, Robert Lopshire didn't plunge
headfirst into authorhood. It would be three years until *How to Make
Flibbers, Etc.* Part of this delay was the fact he had left Random House to
work in advertising and consulting, but mostly it was down to Bob's fastidi-
ous nature. "It takes me a year to write a book and illustrate it," Bob revealed
to Gale. "Mainly because I am never satisfied with the product unless I can
nit pick it to death."

Robert Lopshire's third Beginner Book is the product of his inventive
imagination and his facility with building and construction. It's a collection of
thirty rainy-day make-it-yourself projects using household items. Each activity takes up two pages and is explained in five or six illustrated steps. In many
ways *How to Make Flibbers, Etc.* can be seen as a precursor to the interactive
Beginner Books that followed, such as *My Book about Me*, *My Amazing Book
of Autographs*, and *I Can Write!*

Some are typical kid craft fare, such as bird feeders, tops, and a cup-and-
string "phone," but others are less conventional, such as a party hat made of
a cup and straws, or an air freshener made of an orange and cloves. Besides
doing the projects yourself, the fun of the book comes in the Seussian names
given to many of the projects (Zum Zum Fiddle, Yakky Pup, Moogle Mask).
Most of the projects end with a humorous statement or directive, such as "You
can even talk with your dog . . . if he knows how to talk" (Phony Phone) and
"Maybe you can make a chain half a mile long!" (Link Link Chain).

Though his work had a light and airy feeling, Bob was by nature serious,
introverted, and stoic. His sense of humor was dry, not madcap or whimsical.
"He was not someone you would imagine wrote children's books," his daughter Terry, a nurse and freelance photographer, says. He wasn't an affectionate
father, but he cared deeply about giving his children a well-rounded experience of life, and he held them to high standards. He sent them on trips to
Europe, taught them woodworking and archery. "If you had an interest, he
would encourage it," Terry says, recalling how he put a darkroom in the house
when she expressed an interest in photography.

He treated his child readers much the same as he treated his own sons and daughters. In a *Contemporary Authors* profile, he described his work as "stimulating young minds to think and go further than the immediate limits of their own small world." He disliked the idea of the author as a celebrity or self-promotor. "A book, article, drawing, or painting should stand on its own for what it is," he said, "not as something sold by media or appearance hype."

He'd go on, "My audience is children—I write and draw for them, not the critics or any possible awards." He disliked that awards such as the Caldecott were voted on by adults and not the children themselves. "Personally, the best award I've ever received was the news that one of my books was the most often stolen from a large metropolitan library system." He added, with his dry sense of humor, "Of course, it would now seem only fitting that I do a book about why one should not go about stealing books from libraries!" He respected his young readers so much that, according to Terry, every single child that wrote a letter to him received an individualized answer.

How to Make Flibbers, Etc. was rereleased as *The Beginner Book of Things to Make*, with a new cover, in 1977.

THE CAT IN THE HAT BEGINNER BOOK DICTIONARY (1964)

The Cat Himself (Ted Geisel)

P. D. Eastman

The Cat in the Hat Beginner Book Dictionary was a new take on the old idea of a children's picture dictionary. Ted clearly thought he could improve upon the concept. He acknowledged in the book's introduction that the dictionary had a serious purpose, "but the Editors of Beginner Books, who put this dictionary together, decided they could be serious . . . and still avoid being stuffy."

The book contains 1,350 words, predominantly nouns and verbs, though there are adjectives and prepositions included here and there, each with an accompanying illustration by P. D. Eastman. It was another example of Ted's focus moving toward very early literacy, as well as him playing both sides of the reading wars. If books like *Dr. Seuss's ABC* and *Hop on Pop* were Ted acknowledging the importance of alphabet knowledge and phonemic awareness, the dictionary recognizes the necessity of young readers building a sight word vocabulary.

The Cat in the Hat Beginner Book Dictionary was the first oversized Beginner Book, featuring larger dimensions (approximately 8 ½ x 11) and longer page count (133 pages). It was used as a centerpiece of Grolier's Beginning Readers' Program, given away free to parents who enrolled their child in the club. In the advertisements it was described as an "exciting new 'storybook' dictionary." And indeed, the book was unlike any dictionary that had come before it.

Certainly there are some unconventional word choices—difficult to illustrate concepts like "happen," "true," and "remember" that many other children's dictionaries would likely shy away from. There are also unique and absurd combinations such as "There is a reindeer in our refrigerator" or "Bears in chairs." Only a few times does Ted indulge his penchant for nonsense—once in the name of an Inuit boy and his town (Oobooglunk who lives near Nubbglubb) and again in a fictional lake in Minnesota called Lake Minnihaweetonka—but these are jokes within the definitions of other words. The most egregious from a pedagogical standpoint is the final page, where we see a "nest full of zyxuzpf birds" along with an illustration of twenty-six trademark Eastman birds, colored green. When all of the other words in the book are real, it's strange that the two creators chose to end the book this way. If it were clear that the birds were not real creatures, the child would be in on the joke, but as presented it looks like this is a specific type or species of bird, so the trick is on the reader.

But the innovation of *The Cat in the Hat Beginner Book Dictionary* was not so much in word choice as it was in presentation. In a 1965 interview Phil explained: "I think the real purpose of the book is to get children used to a dictionary, and to prepare them for later use of more advanced dictionaries. We don't expect them to really look words up in this book, but rather to enjoy the book for its own sake."

So Phil's illustrations feature a recurring cast of characters including Aaron the Alligator, a young bespectacled girl named Abigail, her aunt Ada, a baby, a hound dog, a bear family, and a set of round-headed quadruplets named James, Jack, Jerry, and Joe. There are also jokes that carry through, such as the small chick who introduces various members of her chicken family, or the multiple times Aaron crashes his airplane.

Fans of P. D. Eastman will enjoy seeing some of his other characters, including Otto the goldfish from *A Fish out of Water* (page 49) and Robert from *Robert the Rose Horse* (page 84). Aaron the alligator was also soon to spin off into his own books for Phyllis Cerf's post–Beginner Book series, Take-Along Books, and the covers of all four of those books appear under the entry for "season" on page 98.

The breezy and fun nature of the book belies the circumstances of its creation, which were drawn out and contentious. It took about two years from start to finish. It began as *The Dr. Seuss Dictionary* with Ted working on it solo. Once Phil was brought in as illustrator, the two started working in collaboration, but it was a difficult process. In a late-1960s memo Ted wrote of the *Dictionary*: "In the course of doing it my love of writing for children was sort of trampled to death." The trouble seems to have been down to his working relationship with Phil on the book, which Ted described as a "war." Though Phil was grateful for the opportunity and the guidance provided to him by both Ted and Helen, he was also self-assured and steadfast in his opinions. And Ted, as we know, was an intense perfectionist. There had been small battles fought in their work on Phil's other Beginner Books up to that point (Ted, in a fit of angry hyperbole, wrote in the same memo that Phil had "fought every one of the thousand ideas that have made him a wealthy retired useless country squire."), but those problems were magnified when the two worked together.

Indeed, after *The Cat in the Hat Beginner Book Dictionary*, though they remained personally friendly, Ted and Phil would not work directly together again. Phil did the aforementioned Take-Along Books with Phyllis, and it would be four years before he put out another Beginner Book.

Not long after its release, *The Cat in the Hat Dictionary* was issued in both English-Spanish (translated by Robert Nardelli) and English-French (translated by Odette Filloux). In 2007, it was revised, with the help of Phil's son Tony (Peter) Eastman, to remove depictions of guns and stereotypical Native Americans.

FOX IN SOCKS (1965), B-38

Dr. Seuss

In direct opposition to the previous two Dr. Seuss Beginner Books, both of which skewed younger and easier, *Fox in Socks* is not for the novice reader. As the book states on its cover, "This is a book you READ ALOUD to find out just how smart your tongue is." The first edition read "A Tongue Twister for Super Children." It's not for the reader who's still learning, it's for the reader who's ready to show off her skills.

A review of the book in the *Tennessean* stated, "Parents are forewarned that if they expect to read it to somebody, they had better take a couple of trial runs first." Even Ted admitted that his friend, and future wife, Audrey

Diamond (to whom he partially dedicated the book) was "the only adult who could read them aloud." He also dedicated the book to his neighbor Mitzi Long, and claimed both women were from the "Mt. Soledad Lingual Laboratories," seeming to indicate that they had served as test subjects for the rhymes in the book.

As was becoming the norm for Dr. Seuss Beginner Books, there was no clear storyline to the book. It's framed, however, similarly to *Green Eggs and Ham*, with the be-socked Fox playing the persistently insistent Sam-I-Am role to Knox, a character that looks like he could be the brother or cousin of the grouch in *Green Eggs*. Instead of trying green eggs and ham, however, the Fox is trying to get Knox to say the tongue twisters in the book. In this way Knox serves as a stand-in for the reader. In *Green Eggs and Ham*, the persistence of Sam-I-Am prevails, but in *Fox in Socks*, Knox's frustration boils over and he leaves the Fox trapped in a bottle and speechless.

In 1992, the *Oxford Companion to the English Language* used fourteen lines from the epic tweetle beetle battle section to discuss "compounds in context," writing of the Fox's piling up of nouns ("tweetle beetle puddle paddle battle," etc.): "In the flow of a narrative, new information is placed in focus in various ways. One such device is primary stress, already significant in compounds. It becomes particularly noticeable when texts containing patterns of compounding are read aloud."

THE KING, THE MICE, AND THE CHEESE (1965), B-39

Nancy and Eric Gurney

The first Canadian-born Beginner Book authors, Nancy and Eric Gurney, made their debut with an original folktale, *The King, the Mice, and the Cheese*. It's a circular story about how solutions can often be worse than the problems they're intended to fix, and in this way is somewhat similar to the song "There Was an Old Lady Who Swallowed a Fly," though with a thankfully happier ending. A cheese-loving king, distraught over thieving mice in his castle, brings in cats to get rid of the pests. But soon the cats outstay their welcome, so the king brings in some dogs. And the pattern continues, next with lions and finally with elephants. You might just guess how everything ends up.

Eric Gurney (1910–1992) was born and raised in Winnipeg, and in 1930 headed to Toronto where he attended Ontario College of Art nights and weekends while also working in the display department at Eaton's department store. It was around this time that he met Nancy (Jack) Gurney (1915–1973), who had been born in Montreal, lived in Scotland until she was eight years old, and spent the rest of her childhood and young adult life in Toronto.

The couple married in 1938, and the same year moved to the United States after Eric was one of thirteen applicants chosen out of one thousand to become a Disney animator. This means Eric worked at Disney at the same time as both Al Perkins and P. D. Eastman. In ten years at Disney, Eric would work on the "Peter and the Wolf" and "Casey at the Bat" segments in 1946's *Make Mine Music*, but the bulk of his contribution would be on cartoons starring Mickey Mouse's loyal pup Pluto. Eric had a hand in twenty Pluto cartoons released between 1941 and 1950. Nancy, meanwhile, got her degree at UCLA.

In 1948, Eric left Disney to go freelance, and the family (which now included son Lance and daughter Laurie) relocated to Westport, Connecticut, which was coincidentally where P. D. Eastman would end up as well. Here the family would grow by two more, daughters Lassie and Lorna. Eric found work in cartoons (doing Woody Woodpecker shorts at Walter Lantz) and in print, contributing to *Life*, *Reader's Digest*, *Saturday Evening Post*, as well as various advertising campaigns such as the Ethyl corporation's "Road Birds." His years in animation had made him an expert at comic body language and story-telling, which he conveyed using clean, skilled brush work. In 1962, Eric was given the Silver Plaque for Best Advertising and Illustration from the National Cartoonists Society.

His first book appeared in 1960, Steve Baker's *How to Live with a Neurotic Dog*, with Eric's illustrations informed greatly by his years of experience writing and animating Pluto, as well as his own love of dogs. In 1962 he both wrote and drew a companion volume, *How to Live with a Calculating Cat*. He combined the two in 1963's *Gilbert*, the story of a dog raised as a cat. It's no surprise that the Gurney family had their own "modest menag-erie" that in the mid-1960s included "one dachshund, one German Shepard, two Siamese cats, one non-Siamese cat" and a parrot, according to the *King* dust-jacket flap.

So Eric and Nancy were naturals for a book full of animals. Up to this point, Eric's book illustrations had been limited to black and white, and he didn't fully abandon that in *The King, the Mice, and the Cheese*. Some pages feature full color, others have spot coloring, and still others feature color back-grounds with black-and-white figures. Throughout the coloring is flat, bright, and widely varied (pink, blue, green, purple, orange, yellow).

The story itself, told in prose, makes very little concession to the early reader in terms of sentence structure or vocabulary. There is some repetition;

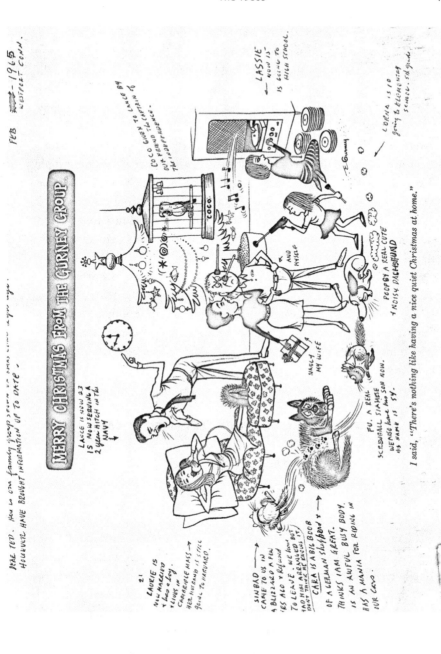

A Gurney family Christmas card from the mid-1960s introduces all the members of the family, both human and animal. Courtesy the Random House Records in the Rare Book and Manuscript Library at Columbia University and the Gurney family.

the bit about the cats, dogs, and lions all being very happy to live with the king is nearly word-for-word each time. But opportunities to make things more predictable, such as when the king continually asking his wise men for solutions, are missed. The book also contains some formal language sure to trip up a beginning reader, phrases such as "cat-chasing dogs" and "most unhappy" and "we surely can."

None of this is to say that the book is poorly written—the opposite is true—it just draws a sharp contrast to what the Beginner Books philosophy had been up to this point. Because of the timing, it's difficult to know whether Phyllis Cerf would have allowed the book to go out like this or not. The book, as with all Beginner Books, did see intense revision. In response to the author questionnaire inquiry about what gave them the most trouble in creating the book, Eric wrote: "The EDITING DID. However it was the FINEST + MOST CONSTRUCTIVE EDITING I have ever had done to any of my projects."

Random House was ecstatic about the book, with Bob Bernstein writing to Eric, "The whole thing is hilarious and it is going to be one of those books that parents will love to read to their children because they will enjoy it themselves."

For more on Eric Gurney, see the entries on *The Digging-est Dog* and *Hand, Hand, Fingers, Thumb*.

I WISH THAT I HAD DUCK FEET (1965), B-40

Theo LeSieg and B. Tobey

Four years after his Beginner Book debut in *Ten Apples Up on Top!*, Theo LeSieg made a triumphant return with *I Wish That I Had Duck Feet*. It's no coincidence that Phyllis's departure from Beginner Books coincided with the return of Ted's alter ego. In Ted's mind, the only way to guarantee the quality of Beginner Books was to write them himself.

The book tells the story of a young boy who imagines himself with various animal appendages (in addition to the duck feet: a deer's antlers, a whale's spout, a tiger's tail, and an elephant's trunk), but deciding that each scenario has too large of a downside. After running through the idea of having all five, he decides, "I think that I just wish to be like ME." Ted disliked morals, so as tempting as it is to call this a paean to self-acceptance, we'll avoid that and instead call it a collection of humorous musings from an inventive kid.

Just as the first Theo LeSieg book, *Ten Apples Up on Top!*, had introduced Roy McKie into the world of Beginner Books, the second brought on B.

Tobey (1906–1989), who would go on to illustrate two more books in the line. Though by 1965 he'd been drawing cartoons for the *New Yorker* for over thirty years, *I Wish That I Had Duck Feet* would be Tobey's first work in children's book illustration.

Barney Tobey was born and raised in Manhattan. His mother and father, Anna and Nathan, were Jewish immigrants from Russia. Nathan sold paper and twine, first from a pushcart, and then eventually from his own store. Barney, third of four children, attended public schools, ending up at Evander Childs High School on Gun Hill Road, where he had a comic, "Ambitious Ambrose," in the school newspaper. His proud father would put the drawings up on the walls of his store.

Barney won a scholarship at the New York School of Fine and Applied Arts, but had only attended for one year before landing a job in the art department at an ad agency called Batten, Barton, Durstine & Osborn. He'd stay there for the next six years while also taking night classes at the Art Students League in Manhattan.

In 1928 he married high school classmate Beatrice Szanton, a fellow artist and an actress who had performed on Broadway while still in high school, and who briefly went to Hollywood to seek fame and fortune. In the late 1920s, Barney took the plunge into freelancing, doing theater posters and book covers. He was also working on one-panel gag cartoons, three of which he sent to the *New Yorker*. They were accepted, and his first cartoon appeared in the magazine's August 3, 1929, issue.

Eventually the *New Yorker* would sign Barney to a contract, and over the next six decades he'd help define the magazine's cartoon humor: wry, apolitical, cerebral. John Russell, chief art critic of the *New York Times*, would later say of Barney's work: "With some cartoonists, the caption helps the drawing along. With others the drawing raises hopes which the caption doesn't fulfill. With Tobey, the two are in a perfect equilibrium."

Beatrice, who also studied at the Art Students League, later joined Barney at the *New Yorker*, with her paintings gracing eleven covers between 1959 and 1969. The couple would have two children, David and Natasha.

Outside of a 1941 NBC radio advertising pamphlet parodying *Alice in Wonderland* (*Alice in Sponsor-land*, it was called) and Addison Webb's 1943 *A Soldier's Diary*, Barney didn't go for interior book illustration until Beginner Books came calling. His work on *I Wish I Had Duck Feet* is done in the loose, assured pen-and-ink line of a veteran cartoonist, with bright watercolor finishes. Presented this way, and not in the black, white, and gray of his typical work, Barney's illustrations look not dissimilar to Roy McKie's. And Ted and

Barney Tobey as photographed by Leonard Nones for the flap of the 1985 retrospective *B. Tobey of the New Yorker*. Courtesy David Tobey and Leonard Nones.

Helen were nearly as excited to "discover" Barney as they had been Roy. "Ted is simply delighted with them," Helen wrote of his *Duck Feet* illustrations. "They're so simple, and yet he's got a great deal of character in all of them! Hurrah!"

Indeed, Barney adds some great details, like the endpapers featuring the boy imagining the book's animals in the clouds and the wordless final page with all of the beastly accoutrements in the garbage.

For more on Barney's work, see the entries for *Don and Donna Go to Bat* (1966) and *Chitty Chitty Bang Bang* (1968).

THE BEARS' PICNIC (1966), B-41

Stan and Jan Berenstain

There was an uncharacteristic two-year gap between *The Bike Lesson* and the next Berenstain Bears adventure, but it wasn't because the prolific Stan and

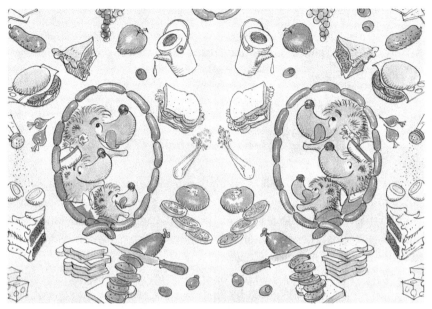

The original endpaper spread for *The Bears' Picnic* which was nixed by Ted for looking too much like a deli. Courtesy Berenstain Enterprises, Inc.

Jan were taking it easy. Originally their third Beginner Book was to be *The Little Stump*, a story of Papa Bear's quixotic quest to remove a stump from his lawn. According to Mike Berenstain, Ted liked the story idea and encouraged Stan and Jan along. But, in a repeat of what had happened with *Freddy Bear's Spanking*, Ted requested revision after revision until finally declaring the story unworkable. All told, Stan and Jan had spent well over a year on the book (for the rest of the story of *The Little Stump*, see the entry for *That Stump Must Go!*).

To smooth things over and work out a new book idea, Ted invited the Berenstains to La Jolla. "It was a big deal," recalls Mike Berenstain, who was around thirteen years old at the time. "I don't think they'd ever flown before. It was early in the era of transcontinental travel." Anne MarcoVecchio wrote to the Geisels that "The Berenstains are headed West full of enthusiasm and anxiety."

Working with Ted in California they decided to revert to an earlier idea in which Papa leads the family on a quest for the perfect picnic spot. The book very much follows the formula of the first two Berenstain Books, with the well-intentioned but overconfident Papa Bear making one bad decision after another. This time, poor Mama Bear gets dragged along, enduring having trash dumped on her head, a mosquito attack, and a thunderstorm.

Though things went more smoothly with Ted and *The Bears' Picnic*, there was one last hiccup. As the Berenstains recalled in their autobiography, *Down a Sunny Dirt Road*: "We had a wonderful time drawing every imaginable kind of picnic food for *The Bears' Picnic*'s endpapers: sliced olives with pimento, a wedge of Swiss cheese, pickles, liverwurst, three kinds of pie, and chocolate cake to die for. Ted's response: 'Looks like a damn delicatessen. Do something else.'"

DON AND DONNA GO TO BAT (1966), B-42

Al Perkins and B. Tobey

Don and Donna Go to Bat tells the story of twins who are nearly identical, even down to having the same number of freckles on their face ("23 to be exact"). Don is a baseball nut who teaches his sister how to play the game, then goes off to join a team. When he falls ill the morning of a big game, he sends Donna to deliver his equipment to the team. A case of mistaken identity leads to her playing in the game, and what's more, bringing home the winning run.

Continuing the trend started by *The King, the Mice, and the Cheese*, *Don and Donna Go to Bat* strays from the restricted word lists, featuring such first-grade mouthfuls as "perhaps," "frightened," and "somehow." There's not much repetition either, though Al does use short, declarative sentences.

As for the illustrations, Barney Tobey was on board for his second Beginner Book. In a contrast to *I Wish That I Had Duck Feet*, his work here is largely figural, with the backgrounds on most pages either sparse or nonexistent. Barney was also allowed in three separate places to break one of the Beginner Book cardinal rules by putting more than one illustration on a single page.

Beginner Books as a rule did not feature female lead characters. If there was a girl in the story, she was often paired with a boy in a bystander role (as in *The Cat in the Hat, Snow, Put Me in the Zoo*). So *Don and Donna Go to Bat* immediately stands out as the first Beginner Book that features a female playing a central role in the story. Unfortunately, this bit of progress is impeded by a muddled message about female empowerment.

The *Amazon* reviews of the book illustrate this. One labels the book as "early politically correct propaganda" because it shows Donna being just as good as the boys at baseball. And yet another review calls it "super sexist" because Donna isn't allowed to join the team and is instead made their equipment manager ("a secretarial role," as the reviewer calls it). Because both observations contain some merit, neither is wholly true. The book contains messages of both feminism and patriarchal reinforcement, but attributing this to either political correctness or overt sexism is off base.

Al Perkins and Babe Ruth, year unknown, but likely from Al's days as editor of *SPORT Magazine*. Courtesy Sally Allen.

On the feminist side, Donna is clearly the story's main character. The book spends more time on her than on her brother, and she's the one who makes a (figurative) journey. When Don is teaching her baseball early in the book, the one aspect of the game she fears and struggles with is batting, so her game-winning hit at the end of the book represents her ability to overcome. The book also establishes that her physical skills are equal to Don's ("Donna already could run as fast as her brother."). So boys reaching for a good baseball yarn were actually being treated to a message of equality. As the original 1966 *Kirkus* review of the book states with unintentional humor, "The baseball tie-up is good bait for the sport enthusiast / reluctant reader, but boys may be put off by Donna's success."

That said, the book's ending is problematic. Donna never states outright that she wants to be on the team (though she does cry when Don leaves her to go join them for the first time), but relegating her to caring for equipment and keeping score reinforces the idea that the woman's role is to provide support to the endeavors of the men. And this is not just a modern interpretation. A 1974 newspaper article by Linda Delvental Greenberg of the Monitor News Service decried the book's ending, saying that Donna "is made housekeeper for the boys . . . and this resolution is described as wholly satisfying to all concerned!"

Don and Donna Go to Bat began to be removed from libraries in the late 1970s and was taken off the recommended list of titles for school and libraries. Random House has allowed the book to fall and stay out of print, and as yet it has not been included in the color-coded compilations of Beginner Books.

YOU WILL LIVE UNDER THE SEA (1966), B-43

Marjorie and Fred Phelger and Ward Brackett

Looking out on the Pacific Ocean every day as he worked, it followed naturally that Ted would want to create a Beginner Book about the water. *The Sea Encyclopedia* was a grand idea Ted had to create an early-reader-friendly guide to life under the water. It's perhaps most significant in that it showed Ted's desire to recruit his Fort Fox and *How the Grinch Stole Christmas* cartoon collaborator Chuck Jones as a Beginner Book creator. In fact it almost seems that he wanted Chuck to run the show, coordinating contributions from Al Perkins and Fred and Marjorie Phelger, and bringing in any talent Chuck saw fit. While Chuck's zany, distinctive style would have been perfect for a Beginner Book, and while Ted had had luck recruiting writers and illustrators from animation, this particular idea seemed destined to fall flat. For one, Chuck had no experience with creating books, let alone editing them. He was also firmly ensconced in his work at MGM. And finally, a nonfiction book about marine biology didn't seem to be the best fit for his talents. Unsurprisingly, the project was deep sixed.

But Ted didn't give up on an ocean-themed Beginner Book. Next, author Joanne Oppenheim was tasked with developing the concept. She offered three ideas: a documentary underwater tour, a story of a boy of the future living under water, and a present-day boy looking around under the sea but with a fantasy twist.

For unknown reasons, Joanne wasn't contracted to do the book, but her first two ideas were essentially combined into the concept for *You Will Live under the Sea*. To carry it out, Ted called on his La Jolla friends Fred and Marjorie Phelger. It had been seven years since Fred Phelger's last Beginner Books (*Ann Can Fly* and *The Whales Go By*), though he was among the group of early Beginner Book creators who crossed the aisle to also do work with Harper & Row (his *Red Tag Comes Back*, featuring illustrations by Arnold Lobel, was a 1961 I Can Read! book). Fred, as a marine biologist, was uniquely qualified to tackle the subject.

In Fred and Marjorie's hands *You Will Live under the Sea* became a work of speculative nonfiction akin to 1959's *You Will Live on the Moon*, even down to its second-person, future-tense narration. The story drew inspiration from the 1965 launch of the US Navy's SEALAB II in the Scripps Submarine Canyon on the coast of La Jolla. SEALAB II was a 9-feet-tall and 57-feet-long cylinder with capacity for ten inhabitants. It was submerged 205 feet below the surface, with the goal of testing the effects of long-term saturation diving and deep-sea diving. Aquanauts—as the inhabitants were called—manned the station in fifteen-day shifts. The project took place on the doorstep (figuratively) of the Scripps Institution of Oceanography, where Fred Phelger had been a professor since 1949. Many Scripps scientists worked on SEALAB.

You Will Live under the Sea imagined an ideal outcome and extension of the SEALAB project, one in which permanent underwater stations serve as habitats for kelp farmers, fish ranchers (called "fishboys," like "cowboys"), and miners. The book is seen through the eyes of an approximately twelve-year-old boy who takes a two-day trip to try out for the Sea Snoopers Club, which seems like a cross between Boy Scouts and Young Astronauts. His tryout involves catching and identifying a live fish in a bag, riding a sea turtle for five minutes, and catching a live lobster for dinner.

Former astronaut Scott Carpenter—the second man in orbit—played a big part in the SEALAB II, spending thirty days underwater. *Amazon* reviewer "Monty Karlow" astutely points out that the Snooper-in-Chief who guides the boy through his tryout bears a "striking resemblance" to Carpenter.

The Phelgers used the book to show off some of the wonders of the ocean, including an underwater volcano, massive canyons, and a battle between a giant squid and a whale. The prose in the story hews fairly closely to the early-reader ideal, despite the complex subject matter. That said, once again there's evidence of Ted's easing up on vocabulary lists: When the boy is catching and identifying fish, the narrator says, "That won't be easy if you catch a humu humu nuku nuku apu aa!" That's the Hawaiian name for the trigger fish. The Phelgers also have some Seussian fun with names, such as the Kelly Kelp Farm and the Finnigan Fish Ranch.

Marjorie Phelger (1907–1986) had grown up in the LA suburb of Glendale, California. She met Fred studying drama at UCLA, and while he left the theater in favor of marine biology and geology, Marjorie stuck with it. When Fred was at Harvard, she completed a master's degree in theater arts at nearby Smith College. When the couple relocated to La Jolla, Marjorie taught drama at Bishop's School, an independent day school. Later she was the head of public relations at La Valencia Hotel, a Mediterranean-style hotel that often served as a destination for vacationing celebrities such as Clark Gable and Tennessee Williams.

Eventually Marjorie began writing, doing columns for the *San Diego Union* and *La Jolla Light*. The book jacket for *You Will Live under the Sea* reveals that Marjorie helped Fred write his first two Beginner Books, though they were credited only to him. In 1963 Harper & Row published her first book, a YA survival novel called *Pilot Down Presumed Dead*. The book did well, but it, along with *You Will Live under the Sea* and *Off to the Races*, would make up the total of Marjorie's bibliography. In her spare time she was a founding member of La Jolla Playhouse, a professional not-for-profit theater on the UCSD campus that is still in operation today.

The illustrations in *You Will Live under the Sea* are unlike any Beginner Book before or after, a mix of watercolor, thick pencil, and textured collage. They don't attempt full-on realism, but nor are they cartoony. Sketch lines are clearly visible on the human figures, which are also periodically colored flat in green, yellow, or blue. The ocean features and creatures are just short of abstract. Illustrator Ward G. Brackett (1914–2006) was a seasoned commercial illustrator who had found inspiration in modernism.

Ward was born the third of four children to Guy and Mary Brackett in Milwaukee, Wisconsin. Guy worked as a commercial photographer, and Ward inherited his father's visual sense, enrolling in the Layton School of Art after high school. He stayed for just a couple years before landing steady work at the Chicago studio of Haddon Sundblom, the illustrator who created both the Quaker Oats mascot and the iconic Coca-Cola Santa Claus. Ward worked with Sundblom for four years and then moved on to Grauman Brothers Advertising. It was in Chicago that he met fellow artist Dolli Tingle, a native of the city and graduate of the Chicago Academy of Fine Arts. The two would marry in 1940 and move together to New York City, where Ward found work at the Charles E. Cooper Studio. After World War II—during which he created visual aids and training posters—he started freelancing, and his work appeared in magazines such as *Good Housekeeping, Redbook, Esquire*, and *Reader's Digest*, illustrating short stories and ad campaigns for the likes of TWA and Sanforized.

In 1947 Dolli and Ward settled in Westport, Connecticut—joining Beginner Book creators P. D. Eastman, Leonard Shortall, and Eric Gurney—and had their only child, a son called Gordon. In 1953, Ward joined a USO group that toured Japan and Korea creating portraits of soldiers. Ward worked steadily throughout the 1950s in a style that was well executed but very slick and typical of the times. In the early 1960s, though, things started to change.

In a 1962 article in the *Bridgeport Post* he said, "I've completely altered my approach. I'm being more and more influenced by the fine arts." He went on to say that he saw a trend of "farther out" progressive work being more and more celebrated in the commercial arts. His own art certainly began to reflect that freedom to experiment, which is why *You Will Live under the Sea* is such a visually striking book.

It wasn't Ward's first book. That would be 1964's *How Far Is Far*, a Parents Magazine Press book by Alvin Tresselt, of which *Kirkus* wrote, "The illustrations are superb and combine a number of techniques: blotted, dripped color; cut paper; pressed on prints; and other techniques." He'd only do one more children's book after *You Will Live under the Sea*, 1967's *One Way Is Down: A Book about Gravity.*

Concurrent with his book illustration, Ward had joined Dolli in creating artwork for commemorative stamps. He'd create in the neighborhood of ten stamps, ranging from the fiftieth anniversary of the Girl Scouts in 1962 to a 1980 W. C. Fields edition (Dolli specialized in Christmas designs). Ward returned to art school mid-career, studying with Reuben Tam at the Brooklyn Academy, and as he eased toward retirement began painting with oils almost exclusively. In 1985, Ward published *When You Paint*, an instruction book focusing on technique and philosophy of painting. He and Dolli kept a summer studio in Sarasota, Florida, where fellow Beginner Book creators Robert Lopshire and Walter Farley also made their homes.

Ward passed away in December 2006 at the age of ninety-two.

COME OVER TO MY HOUSE (1966), B-44

Theo LeSieg and Richard Erdoes

As with *You Will Live under the Sea, Come Over to My House* began as a concept in search of a writer. Letters from 1965 indicate that more than one author—including Little Golden Book writer Carl Memling—had attempted and failed to crack a story celebrating different types of homes around the globe. Eventually it fell to Ted, who expanded the idea outward to a celebration of cultural diversity and difference.

Random House vice president Ray Freiman was ecstatic about the manuscript Ted produced. "It is one of the most beautiful stories I have ever read," he wrote. "It is truly lovely." Ted uses human activities—eating, playing, sleeping, bathing, and building homes—to highlight differences but also recognize the power of friendship to overcome, especially between children. "But wherever you go," the text says early on, "you will hear someone say, 'Come over to my house. Come over and play!'"

If it all sounds a bit sappy and idealized, it's not. The story is told in jaunty verse that remains light and fun throughout (e.g., "I eat with chopsticks and you can learn how. But, boy, you are terribly sloppy right now."). All too often children's books, especially from this era, treat other ways of dressing and living as objects of novelty or ridicule. But *Come Over to My House* is striking in its lack of judgment, even when it comes to economic status: "Some houses are rich, full of silver and gold. / And some are quite poor, sort of empty and old." And the message (as it were) is not just one of tolerance, but of exploration and adventure. As social psychologist Karen E. Dill-Shakelford wrote, this particular book serves a purpose to "help replace potential fear of the unknown with a sense of excitement and a zest for adventure and travel."

Ted knew immediately that he couldn't illustrate the story himself. "Seuss can't draw the pictures," he wrote Ray. "They call for more realism than he can muster." In the same letter he outlined the "very rare" illustrator they'd need to find:

He must like to do research. Checking up on architecture, races, costumes, and scenery around the world must not be a chore to him. He will have to love research. This book goes everywhere. He will have to simplify his research into bold, colorful pictures that don't get bogged down in details. He must know how to give strong impressions, without drawing all the diddly-diddly.

He must, also, love kids and be able to present them as individuals with personalities, shadings of reactions to any given situation, and not as run-of-the-mill namby-pambies with frozen smiles and sweet-phony stances. He must create real characters in exciting action.

He must love drawing animals.

This illustrator will not be a comic, but he will have a sense of humor. This book needs someone new with imagination and guts and a desire to work hard.

The artist they found, Richard Erdoes (1912–2008), lived up to nearly all of that, turning in pictures that were bright, lively, and joyful, but also well researched. Richard was an ideal choice to create pictures for a book about cultural diversity, travel, and embracing differences. Born in Frankfurt, Germany, Richard never knew his father—a Hungarian Jewish opera singer who died a few weeks before his son's birth. Richard and his mother went to live with his aunt, an actress named Leopoldine Sangora. The trio spent much of Richard's childhood traveling from show to show in Germany and Austria.

As an art student in Berlin in the early 1930s, Richard got involved with an underground newspaper and drew cartoons critical of Adolf Hitler. This drew the attention of the Nazi regime, and Richard fled to Vienna, where he continued his art education at the Kunstgewerbeschule, which is now the University of Applied Arts (the very same school where Fritz Siebel had studied). He continued to draw cartoons railing against Hitler and the Nazis, which again forced him to run, this time to Paris. Here he attended the Academie de la Grande Chaumiere. He'd make one more stop, in London. There he married artist Elsie Schulhof, and then the couple were off to the United States and New York City with five dollars to their name.

It was the early 1940s, and Richard set about building a career as a commercial artist. Soon he was getting work in magazines such as *Sports Illustrated*, *Saturday Evening Post*, and *Harper's*. He developed a modern, flat style that had a lot in common with the look of the UPA cartoon shorts. In 1953, *Life* and *American Heritage* magazines sent Richard to paint and photograph the landscape and people of the Southwest Plains, and this quite literally changed the direction of his life. He had grown up with a fascination with the American West from books he read as a child, but seeing it in person awoke a deep connection and a deep concern. He later revealed, "I was struck by the shock and outrage of first-hand experience of conditions on American Indian reservations." Though it would take a while to come to fruition, Richard would go on to become one of the foremost documentarians of American Indian life, and a fierce supporter of American Indian civil rights.

Richard's first book illustration work showed up in the mid-1950s in Helen Hoke's collection of gags, *Jokes Jokes Jokes*. In 1962 he wrote and drew *A Picture History of Ancient Rome* (Macmillan). That was followed by illustrations for James Joyce's short story *The Cat and the Devil* (Dodd, Mead, 1964), and a self-authored picture book called *The Green Tree House* (Dodd, Mead, 1965). *Come Over to My House* was the first of his books to display his zest for the international, and he'd pursue that in 1967's *Policemen around the World*, the first of three richly illustrated and deeply researched books from

McGraw-Hill looking at occupations in different countries and cultures (the other two books focused on salespeople and musicians, respectively).

But it was American Indian life and legend that truly and fully captured Richard's imagination from 1967 on. That year he published a book on the Pueblo, and another *Life* assignment took him to Pine Ridge, an Oglala Lakota reservation in South Dakota. He became friends with Lakota holy man John Fire Lame Deer, and did a series of interviews which led to Lame Deer's 1971 biography. Nearly twenty books on American Indian history, culture, and legend would follow, many in close collaboration with such prominent figures as Mary Brave Bird and Leonard Crow Dog. He was also heavily involved in the American Indian Movement, allowing his New York apartment to serve as a "free restaurant, hotel and communications center" for activists.

Richard, whose first wife died shortly after they arrived in the United States, married artist and *Life* art director Jean Morton in 1951. The couple had three children: Rick, Erich, and Jaki. In 1972 he and Jean bought a home in Santa Fe, New Mexico, and began to split their time between the Southwest and their New York City apartment. As he grew older Richard found himself more and more pulled to writing over art. He told *Contemporary Authors Online*, "I found writing so rewarding that ninety per cent of my time is now devoted to it. I do artwork and photography now only on prestige projects which tickle my fancy."

He died in 2008 at the age of ninety-six. Upon his death, the *Lakota Country Times* wrote of Richard, "He influenced the lives of generations of Lakota people and other tribes by describing Native life and their spiritual culture and essentially preserving it for future generations."

Beginner Books considered creating a companion volume to *Come Over to My House* that would have expanded upon the exploration of different places and cultures. *The Cat in the Hat's Wide, Wide World* was envisioned as a "combination atlas and introduction to sociology," as Walter Retan described it to Anne Johnson, detailing the transportation, food, clothing, sports, and pets of the world. Retan hoped this could be accomplished with "humor and—hopefully—a light touch" but the book never came to fruition.

Come Over to My House was reissued in 2016 with new illustrations by Katie Kath.

BABAR LOSES HIS CROWN (1967), B-45

Laurent de Brunhoff

By the mid-1960s, Babar was one of the stars of Random House's juvenile department, with over twenty books to his name. How exactly he ended up in a Beginner Book is unknown, but it stands to reason that combining one of their most popular characters with their most popular line of books was a win-win for the publisher.

Babar Loses His Crown is a fast-paced Hitchcockian chase set off by a pair of swapped identical red bags. One is Babar's, containing his crown. The other belongs to a mustachioed man named "Mustache-man," and holds his flute.

As the Babar family chases Mustache-man, the book provides a tour of Paris, including the Eiffel Tower, the Seine, the Arc de Triomphe, and the Palais Garnier. In a tidy resolution, the reader learns that Mustache-man is a musician in the orchestra pit for the opera Babar and Celeste are attending. "It turns out to be a great night after all," the text tells us, "The crown is on the head of the King . . . and the flute is under the Mustache-man's mustache."

Babar began in Paris, France, as a bedtime story for Cecile de Brunhoff's young sons Laurent and Mathieu when they were five and four years old. Her husband, Jean, was a post-impressionist painter, and for fun he created some illustrations of his wife's elephant characters. He liked the outcome so much that he was inspired to make the whole thing into a picture book. *The Story of Babar* was published in 1931 in France, with an English translation debuting in 1933, and was an immediate hit. Jean would do six more Babar stories before succumbing to tuberculosis at the age of thirty-seven. The final two Babar books released under his name had originally been done for the newspaper, and thirteen-year-old Laurent, who was already developing into a talented artist in his own right—was called upon to add color.

Laurent de Brunhoff (born 1925) finished school, attending both Lycée Pasteur and the Academie de la Grande Chaumiere (where Richard Erdoes had also studied), and in a tribute to his father and his own childhood he decided to continue Babar's adventures. "Babar was a friend to me," he said in a 1961 interview. "I had lived with him for years. It occurred to me that I could follow a tradition that had been cut off too early, and also it was a job to make money."

Laurent's Babar books were written in his native French throughout the 1950s and early 1960s and then subsequently translated and printed in the United States. But right before the publication of *Babar Loses His Crown* he seems to have begun creating books in English for the American market. *Babar Goes to America*, published in 1965, appears, appropriately, to have been the first of these. Despite—or perhaps because of—English not being his first language, Laurent's text in *Babar Loses His Crown* is naturally early-reader friendly. The prose doesn't have any repetition, but the vocabulary and sentence structure are simple and straightforward. The whimsical pictures provide ample support.

Laurent married Marie-Claude Bloch in 1951 and they had two children, Anne and Antoine. The couple officially divorced in 1990, but in the meantime Laurent met a professor from the United States named Phyllis Rose. He moved to Middletown, Connecticut, with her and the couple married after his divorce was finalized. They've since settled in New York City. Since 1985 Phyllis has written the text for all of his books. In 2017, at the age of ninety-two, Laurent released *Babar's Guide to Paris*, declaring it to be his final book. "I had my life with Babar, and he made me happy," he said.

THE BEAR SCOUTS (1967), B-46

Stan and Jan Berenstain

The Berenstains' fourth Beginner Book was yet another variation on their well-established plot wherein Papa Bear overenthusiastically tries to prove his expertise and fails spectacularly. Stan and Jan wrote that this formula allowed them to employ "cartoonist's tools such as shameless slapstick and outrageous jokes." In *The Bear Scouts* Papa Bear accompanies Small Bear and three friends on their Bear Scout campout, eschewing the advice of the Bear Scout Guidebook at every turn. This results in one comic mishap after another, and the final money lines: "Dad has shown us quite a lot about what's smart and what is not."

As with many other Beginner Books of the mid- to late 1960s, the easing up on vocabulary limits and readability formulas is evident in *The Bear Scouts*. While on one hand phrases like "on second thought" and "presto, chango, ala kazoo" are too difficult for an emerging reader, on the other hand, they have the effect of making an engaging read aloud. The memorable verse flows with a natural rhythm, such as "But a bear like me, / A bear who's clever, / Takes the short way. / The long way? Never!"

The Berenstains by this time had become masters of their slapstick formula, but they were feeling a bit hemmed in by it as well. In their autobiography they wrote, "We still wanted to do something that related to our

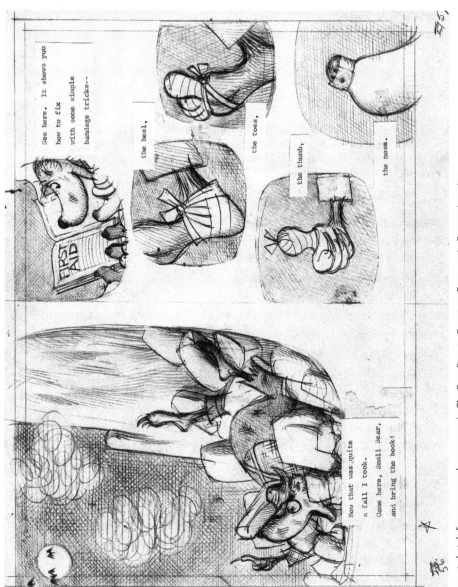

Layout sketch for an unused sequence in *The Bear Scouts.* Courtesy Berenstain Enterprises, Inc.

everyday experience with children." They proposed to Ted a book in which Small Bear and his friends dress up using a trunk of Mama and Papa's clothes. Ted responded, "This is just Norman Rockwell stuff. Kids don't really do that." The Berenstains knew he was wrong, but also knew it wasn't worth arguing.

THE DIGGING-EST DOG (1967), B-47

Al Perkins and Eric Gurney

There are slightly conflicting stories of the origin behind Al Perkins's second Beginner Book, *The Digging-est Dog*. The book's dust-jacket flap claims that the story was based on a dog Al owned in New York in the mid-1930s. When he moved out to the country, the dog didn't know how to dig and had to be taught how to bury his bone. His daughter, Sally Allen, remembers things differently. She recalls that in the mid-1960s, Al and her mother were visiting Sally's family, and they all flew up to northern California together. There they met up with Sally's college friend Robin Sittig, and went together to Robin's aunt's house in Sacramento.

> Her aunt was talking about living in Chicago and how they had a dog and it was in the city and they loved this dog but when they moved out to the country, they felt like they had to teach this dog how to dig because he'd lived on concrete for so long. And so Dad said, "Hey, you've just given me an idea for a book!"

It's possible that both stories are true, and that the aunt's story jogged Al's memory of his own dog. There's also a good chance the details on the flap were fudged. At any rate, the result was the same: Al wrote a manuscript for a fable about adjusting to new surroundings called *The Dog That Couldn't Dig*, and Ted accepted it.

The story concerns Duke, a sad city pet shop dog who is brought to live on the farm of Sammy Brown. He starts to make friends with other dogs, but when they learn he can't dig, they shun him. After some lessons, Duke learns to dig, and becomes so enthusiastic that he digs up the entire countryside, including the garden of Mrs. Thwaites, Highway Eighty-One, and a deep, deep hole he can't get out of without some help.

The tale is told unconventionally, with Duke narrating in first-person verse. What's more, rather than the typical Beginner Book four-line rhyme, Al uses couplets ("I dug up Mister Rodney Thayer, / Sitting in the barber's chair.").

As for illustrations, the book went through a carousel of potential artists. It was initially slated for B. Tobey, but the publisher became excited about Don Madden, a cartoonist just then in the beginning stages of what would be a long career in children's books. Random House liked Madden's initial sketches for the book, finding his colorful, exaggerated style a perfect fit. But for unknown reasons, things fell through. The book was next offered to P. D. Eastman, who turned it down, citing being happiest as both author and illustrator.

The job then fell to Eric Gurney, who despite being a fourth choice was a perfect fit. Who better to tackle a dog book than the man known for his Pluto cartoons and *How to Live with a Neurotic Dog*? Eric's illustrations feature strong character work in pen and ink, accompanied by the same bright color palate he used in *The King, the Mice, and the Cheese*.

The Digging-est Dog has remained popular through the years and is still in print as of this writing. This is due perhaps in part to the fact that despite its comic premise, it also contains genuine pathos. Ted's aversion to bunny-bunny-bunny-bunny books meant Beginner Books were rarely sentimental or emotional, but Duke's story is one of misery ("I was the saddest dog in the world"), joy (when Duke finally learns to dig), remorse, and forgiveness. A 1972 review stated: "This book contains child-appeal ingredients: vibrant colors, animals with exaggerated expressions, much action, conflict, rhyme-all tospy turvy object and animals in an all-right world."

THE TRAVELS OF DOCTOR DOLITTLE (1967), B-48; DOCTOR DOLITTLE AND THE PIRATES (1968), B-49

Al Perkins and Philip Wende

In 1967, 20th Century Fox released *Doctor Dolittle*, a musical featuring Rex Harrison as the well-dressed physician who can talk to the animals. The film was based on Hugh Lofting's 1920–1948 series of books, originally published by J. B. Lippincott. Beginner Books featuring the character were part of a concerted marketing effort that featured not only books, but an inordinately large number of tie-in products created to go with the film (dolls, cereal, sewing sets, inflatable pool toys, etc.).

As it turns out, the film was a financial flop and so was most of its merchandise, but the Beginner Books ended up being a charming introduction to the world of the good doctor. The first book details how Doctor Dolittle learned to talk to the animals, saved a troop of monkeys from disease, escaped an angry tribe, and came to own a rare pushmi-pullyu, an animal with a gazelle-like head at both ends of its body.

Workhorse Al Perkins—no stranger to world travels himself—was called on to do the adaptations, and in *The Travels of Doctor Dolittle* he turned out perhaps the most storybook-like Beginner Book there is. Certainly the book has more words per page than any Beginner Book before it, and few first graders would be able to take it on independently. "Vaccinations"—which the doctor has to give to Chee-Chee's fellow monkeys—is definitely not an early reader word. However, many of Lofting's animal names (Dab-Dab the duck, Gub-Gub the pig) are perfectly suited to an early reader.

Doctor Dolittle and the Pirates—which picks up immediately after the end of the first book—details the doctor and his crew's attempts to escape and outsmart a band of pirates as they sail home to England from Africa. Like the first book, its story elements are drawn from Lofting's *The Story of Doctor Dolittle*. In fact, the two Beginner Books could be viewed as halves of a whole. *Doctor Dolittle and the Pirates* certainly provides a poetic and warm resolution to the events of the two books. After taking over the pirates' ship and leaving them stranded (echoing the earlier Beginner Book *Look Out for Pirates!*), the group gets back on course. The pushmi-pullyu gets up in the crow's nest:

> "I see no danger ahead of us,"
> he said with his front head.
> "And I see no danger behind us,"
> he said with his back head.
> "Then," said Doctor Dolittle, "we shall all get safely home to England."
>
> And that's exactly what they did.

Hugh Lofting illustrated his own books, and newcomer Philip Wende (1939–2011) follows the character designs of the original fairly closely. This is particularly true of the monkeys, the pushmi-pullyu, and Doctor Dolittle himself. At the same time Philip's work shows the influence of New York's Push Pin Studios, particularly cofounder Seymour Chwast, who employed a colorful, open, chunky-style very much associated with the 1960s psychedelia. There's also an element of the "ligne claire" style of cartooning, with a single weight line used throughout and minimal shading.

Philip was born in Ogdensburg, New York, but spent much of his early life in Tennessee and Florida. He attended the University of Tennessee and then went on to the Ringling School of Art in Sarasota, Florida—like

Westport, an accidental mecca for Beginner Book creators. After a brief marriage to Janet Dant, he met and married Beverly Heacock, a painter he'd met at Ringling. The couple had three children, Christopher, Jill, and Seth. Philip's brief career in children's book illustration began in 1967 with two books he both wrote and drew, *Hector the Dog Who Loved Fleas* and *The Rhinoceros Who Loves Trees*. They were published by L. W. Singer, a company that had been owned by Random House since the early 1960s. The Doctor Dolittle books followed closely after.

Philip would illustrate eleven more books between 1968 and 1971 before bowing out of publishing. Why he chose to quit is unknown. Perhaps he burned out after doing the equivalent of four books per year. Or perhaps the business side of things wore him down. A brief, flinty quote given to *Contemporary Authors Online* gives some credence to the latter theory: "Philip Wende says he writes and illustrates books for children, not for 'mothers, fathers, critics, distributors, salesmen, and other persons whose motives are questionable.'"

It's not known what career path Philip pursued after moving on from publishing, but he eventually settled in Georgia, first Atlanta, then about forty miles north in Canton. Most interestingly, he had a brief film career in the mid-1970s, with roles in 1973's *Payday* (starring Rip Torn as a country singer), and *Just an Old Sweet Song* (a 1976 TV movie featuring Cicely Tyson, Robert Hooks, and Melvin Van Peebles). Philip died in 2011 at the age of seventy-two.

THE CAT IN THE HAT SONGBOOK (1967)

Dr. Seuss

One of the biggest curiosities in the Dr. Seuss oeuvre is 1967's *The Cat in the Hat Songbook*, which was the second Big Beginner Book after *The Cat in the Hat Beginner Book Dictionary*. The *Songbook* contains music (for guitar and piano) and lyrics for eighteen songs, each with accompanying illustrations. Though the book bears his name and likeness, none of its songs are about the Cat himself.

Ted wrote all the lyrics, naturally, a process he quite enjoyed. He charged composer Eugene Poddany with putting them to music. Eugene and Ted were fresh off another collaboration, as it was Eugene who had done the music for the *How the Grinch Stole Christmas* TV special, which had premiered on CBS in 1966. It was part of long resume of cartoon composing credits for Poddany, which also included Woody Woodpecker and Looney Tunes shorts.

An LP of the *Songbook*'s songs was released in 1967 on RCA Camden as *Dr. Seuss Presents the Cat in the Hat Songbook*. The songs were performed with male and female choral singers—accompanied often only by an organ—in a sugary style very much typical of the music children's programming and films of the era. A song like "Rainy Day in Utica, N.Y.," the lyrics of which are nothing but a series of variations on the words "drip," "drop," "dibble," and "drop," wouldn't be out of place in a Disney film.

What's interesting is that Ted created several types of children's songs delineated by Iona and Peter Opie in their book *The Lore and Language of School Children*. These include action songs ("The No Laugh Race"), counting rhymes ("Hurry Hurry Hurry" and "I Can Figure Figures"), lullabies ("Lullaby for Mr. Benjamin B. Bickelbaum"), and nonsense rhymes ("Plinker Plunker" and "Somebody Stole My Hoo-To Foo-To Boo-To Bah"). Podanny's music ranges between many different styles: waltzes, marches, rounds, and ballads. One style not represented, however, even right in the midst of a watershed year for the genre, is rock and roll.

Lyrically, the songs are actually less silly than, say, the vignettes in *Fox in Socks* or *Hop on Pop*. Besides the "Hoo-To Foo-To Boo-To Bah," there's little of the expected Seussian word inventions. Instead, the songs have fun with sounds ("Ah-a-a-a-a-a-h . . . choo" is essentially a sneeze set to a melody) and names (Sally Spigel Spungel Sporn has her own song; Uncle Terwilliger gets two).

The Cat in the Hat Songbook did not sell well and quickly followed *The Seven Lady Godivas*—Ted's 1939 attempt at an adult picture book—as the extremely rare Dr. Seuss book allowed to go out of print (though the *Songbook* was returned to print for its fiftieth anniversary). This is not surprising. Songbooks typically sell based on the strength and popularity of the recorded versions or the songwriter. But the recorded versions came out basically simultaneously, and while Ted was well known, he wasn't well known as a songwriter. It's also odd that Ted chose to release the book with a Beginner Book logo, as it didn't fit in the line: there was no story and the lyrics were not early reader friendly.

Proud of the work he'd done and unaccustomed as he was to public indifference to his efforts, Ted was reportedly frustrated and disappointed by the poor reception of his songbook.

OFF TO THE RACES (1968), B-50

Fred and Marjorie Phelger and Leo Summers

After *You Will Live under the Sea*, there's evidence that Fred and Marjorie Phelger worked on a travelogue called *You Will Go to Hawaii*. The project got far enough that Ted placed the book on a list of potential titles for fall 1967. For whatever reason—likely that the story didn't meet Ted and Helen's standards—that book never materialized. Instead, the Phelgers wrote *Off to the Races*.

In 1959, Fred had used his experience of flying his daughter Audrey to camp to create *Ann Can Fly*. Nearly a decade later Fred and Marjorie again drew from Audrey's life to write a Beginner Book. Both of the Phelger children were athletic, with Charles (called Rick) a competitive swimmer and surfer, and Audrey initially pursuing her mother's lifelong interest in horseback riding. Audrey became quite accomplished in barrel racing, dressage, and jumping in her early teens. But when she was around fourteen, she fell off her horse and landed on her head, requiring forty stitches. That marked the end of her horse-riding days.

She next became interested in the quintessential California pastimes of surfing and skateboarding, but again an accident—a broken ankle after a spill from her skateboard—put an end to her persuits. By this time it was the early 1960s and Audrey was in her junior year of high school. She met Scott McElmury, a college student who was involved with the San Diego Youth Hostelers, a cycling club that regularly organized rides and tours of various lengths and difficulties. Cycling at that time was just on the verge of a massive growth in popularity, a boom that at its height in the United States would see more bikes sold per year than automobiles for three straight years.

Scott and Audrey became an item, and much of their time together was spent on bikes. In 1962 they went on a ten-week bicycle tour of Europe, and the couple married soon after returning home. Audrey completed a degree in zoology at the University of San Diego–California while at the same time building herself up as a competitive racer. In 1964 she won the Californian cycling championship. The next year she competed in her first World Road Championship, placing fourteenth. The year after that, she raced again and finished eighth.

After taking 1967 off to have a baby (son Ian), she returned to the World Road Championship in Rome in 1968—the same year *Off to the Races* was published—and improved to a fifth-place finish. With some adjustment, namely a child protagonist, Audrey's accomplishments would seem to have made the perfect Beginner Book tale, but curiously, *Off to the Races* isn't that story.

Instead it follows two brothers, the older one an established racer and the younger a novice, as they compete in a bike rally. There are traces of Audrey's story in the determination of the younger brother to get to the rally on his own after being told by his brother, "You'd slow me up." Becoming a competitive cyclist wasn't an easy road for Audrey. In addition to the staggering amount of work she put into practice and training, she was also met with disdain from men who thought she might slow them up, little knowing that she was more likely to pass them up.

In 1969, Audrey would compete once again in the World Road Championship, that year held in Brno, Czechoslovakia. This time she overcame rain and a nasty fall to win the race, and thus became the first US road cyclist—male or female—to win a world championship. Her win got her featured in a 1969 *Sports Illustrated* article called "What Makes Audrey Pedal? Tiga Muk" (the first part of which would have been a good Beginner Book title). She'd go on to win more national titles and set more records before retiring from cycling in 1974 to focus on coaching. She passed away in 2013 at the age of seventy.

The illustrator of *Off to the Races* was Leo Ramon Summers (1925–1985), a veteran draftsman most well known for his work illustrating hundreds of science fiction pulp magazine stories and covers for titles such as *Amazing Stories*, and *Thrilling Science Fiction*. Leo grew up in Seattle, relocating to New York City circa 1949. There he landed steady work at the pulps, eventually becoming art director at Ziff-Davis Publishing. He went freelance in 1956, adding some advertising and movie posters to his resume. Books came next, with *Off to the Races* joining titles such as *Mystery of the Breton Fort* and *Danny Dunn and the Voice from Space*. He also tried his hand at comic books, most prominently in the Warren horror anthology *Creepy*. Veteran comic book writer and artist Howard Chaykin wrote of Leo's *Creepy* work: "This was no dilettante sniffily slumming in a ghetto. He dove in headfirst, with a style of drawing that was utterly personal, supported by a clear and apparently instinctual grasp of comic-art storytelling."

Leo's Beginner Book work was a departure for him, not only in subject matter, but also in style. Where his pulp and comic book work featured strong pen-and-ink work with dramatic light and dark contrast, and his painted covers (often in oil) were done with rich colors, his work in *Off to the Races* features thin, sketchy lines and splotchy watercolor in pale blues, yellows, and pinks. The one carryover is his clear storytelling.

Off to the Races wasn't destined to be a long-term Beginner Book classic, but it did have an impact. Cycling enthusiast James T. Nunemaker wrote on his blog that the book made a strong impression on him when he was young: "Even though the bikes and outfits look dated and I've never heard of a rally like the one described, the book rings true to me as a cyclist now that I've finally taken the training wheels off and set out on my own two-wheeled adventures."

THE BEST NEST (1968), B-51

P. D. Eastman

Following the massive amount of work that went into 1964's *The Cat in the Hat Beginner Book Dictionary* and the period of Beginner Book ubiquity that preceded it, P. D. Eastman disappeared for a while. He completed four Aaron the Alligator books for Phyllis Cerf's Take-Along series, but was otherwise quiet.

That wasn't intentional. In early 1965 Phil was working on his next book, a story about an elephant and a crow that was tentatively scheduled for a fall 1966 release. But Ted and Helen had concerns, with Helen writing Bob Bernstein in 1965 calling the manuscript "quite unsatisfactory." Phil expanded on this in his own letter to Bob a couple of weeks later, saying: "[Ted and Helen] feel that certain story problems still have to solved. It is, partly, they feel, a matter of construction, and partly a matter of character development." He added that he was working on some ideas to address their concerns.

Apparently it wasn't enough, as the elephant and crow story never became a book. Instead, Phil started over, this time on a tale of two birds in search of a new nest. But it still wasn't clear skies ahead. At some point Ted requested that Phil come to La Jolla to work out the new story's text. Phil refused, and so instead Ted called on Al Perkins to help. It's not known to what extent Al worked on the story's text. It was significant enough for Ted to grant him royalties on the book, but not enough to credit him as a writer or cowriter.

The Best Nest is a classic tale of the pitfalls of wanderlust. When Mrs. Bird reveals to Mr. Bird that she hates their familiar wooden birdhouse, the two set out to find a new home. A series of other options (a hollow tree, a boot, a mailbox) don't work out, but a church bell tower seems to offer the perfect solution, at least until frizzy-haired Mr. Parker comes along to ring the noontime chimes. The ensuing chaos leads Mr. Bird to the assumption that his wife has been gobbled up by a big fat cat, and so he returns, grief stricken, to the old wooden house. There, he finds Mrs. Bird has not only returned there safely, but that she has laid an egg. "I used to hate it," she says. "But a mother bird can change her mind. You see there's no nest like an old nest—for a brand new bird!"

The text is full of memorable phrases, from Mr. Bird's "I love my house, I love my nest" song (feel free to make up your own melody) to the gathering of "soda straws and broom straws" and "horse hair" and "man hair." And Phil's artwork is as skilled as ever, done in his signature black pencil line with strong senses of composition, character expression, and place.

The book is also one of the few Beginner Books to have an established real-life setting, though it takes some careful observation to spot it. When Mr. and Mrs. Bird are in the mailbox, the carrier inserts a letter addressed to Oberlander at R.D. #1, Waldoboro, Maine. Waldoboro is a port town in the southern part of the state where Phil and his wife, Mary, had purchased a cottage in 1967.

Blogger Thomas D. Gutierrez speculates that the Waldoboro Broad Bay Congregational Church was the model for the church in the book. As for why Phil chose the name Oberlander, it's not clear, but Gutierrez found that there were Oberlanders in the old town records, and the cottage was across from the town cemetery, so perhaps Phil lifted the name from a gravestone. Mr. Parker's name isn't a mystery, however. The Eastmans' neighbor in Waldoboro was named Parker Simmonds.

The book's dedication—"To H.P.G."—was a tribute and memorial to Helen Geisel, for whom Phil had a great deal of respect and affection. Helen felt similarly, often addressing letters to Phil as "Feathers" because of his penchant for drawing and telling stories about birds.

THE BEARS' VACATION (1968), B-52

Stan and Jan Berenstain

The Bears' Vacation finds the Bear family heading to the beach on a summer holiday. There, the familiar formula ensues as Papa attempts to educate Small Bear on the rules of swimming, surfing, sailing, and skin diving. As usual, a lot goes wrong.

Mike Berenstain says, "*The Bear's Vacation* certainly was influenced by our own family vacations to the New Jersey beach. The whole setting and the feel of it was influenced by that." Stan and Jan Berenstain drew from their own lives often in their work, be it in *It's All in the Family*, their epic *Collier's* covers, or their cartoon books. The Berenstain Bears Beginner Books were no exception. Stories like *The Bike Lesson* and *The Bears' Vacation* came from their family experiences, but all the Bear books share one main autobiographical thread, in that Papa and Mama were patterned on Stan and Jan themselves.

Jan, like Mama Bear, was calm, soft spoken, and sensible. Stan, like Papa, was "impulsive, antic, and funny," according to Mike. Though Stan and Jan took their personalities and embellished them to comic effect, the Bears are not exact analogs of their creators. Mama, though wise and in control, is often portrayed as exasperated and long-suffering. Mike says his mother was much more likely to be amused by Stan's messes, the way Mama is when she smiles upon Papa's return at the end of *The Big Honey Hunt.*

Stan, meanwhile, wasn't anywhere near as bumbling or clueless as the Papa Bear of the initial Beginner Books. He could be unintentionally funny, but also intentionally as well. His faults sometimes came from having a bit too much confidence.

Mike says, "A lot of us dads have Papa Bear moments. It's not that you're incompetent, or stupid, it's just that you sometimes overestimate your ability to do things. It's an extroverted, optimistic personality type that's very realistic, and I think that's why Papa Bear resonates with a lot of people."

IAN FLEMING'S STORY OF CHITTY CHITTY BANG BANG! THE MAGICAL CAR (1968), B-53

Al Perkins and B. Tobey

Chitty Chitty Bang Bang has a lot in common with the two Beginner Book Doctor Dolittle adaptations. Like those books, it was released in conjunction with a film, in this case, a 1968 United Artists picture starring Dick Van Dyke. As with *Doctor Dolittle*, the movie was a based on a children's novel: James Bond creator Ian Fleming's 1964 *Chitty Chitty Bang Bang: The Magical Car.* And, of course, Al Perkins was responsible for the adaptations.

Also like the Doctor Dolittle books, the Beginner Book of *Chitty Chitty Bang Bang* is—despite being released in conjunction with a film—not based on the movie script (which was cowritten by children's author Roald Dahl) but on the original book. The story concerns Mr. Pott, who finds a car in a junkyard and brings it home. The Pott family, comprised of Mrs. Pott and kids Jeremy and Jemima, head to the beach in their new car, which they've named Chitty Chitty Bang Bang after the sound it makes when starting up. They learn quickly that this is no ordinary car; it can both fly and float and also might be a sentient being. At the beach the Pott family happens into the hideout of the notorious bank robber Joe the Monster, which leads to the children being kidnapped. Chitty Chitty Bang Bang must then rescue the children by pursuing the criminals through the streets of Paris.

Once again Al was able to include the essentials of the story without making it seem like an abridged version. Because of the dense amount of plot, there are more words per page than the typical Beginner Book, but the vocabulary and sentence structure are just right: not so simple as to compromise the story, but not too difficult for newer readers.

Here Al is reunited with his *Don and Donna Go to Bat* collaborator, Barney Tobey. Barney's work on *Chitty Chitty Bang Bang* is another showcase for his mastery of cartooning, but also highlights his skillful color work, an aspect of his talent he rarely got to show off in his black, white, and gray *New Yorker* cartoons. The result is several eye-popping two-page spreads.

It would be Barney's third and final Beginner Book, and indeed his last book of any kind besides the 1985 retrospective *B. Tobey of the New Yorker*. Barney's last original cartoon appeared in the *New Yorker* in 1986, but he remained on staff until his death in 1989. In total he placed over twelve hundred cartoons in the magazine, and drew four covers.

Though the majority of his work had been for adults, Barney's mindset about his work made him perfectly suited for children's books. He once said, "All the people in my cartoons are grown-up children—like me, like us all, though some of us forget it. You can't go wrong if you remember where you came from. I try to draw so my father would want to put it on the wall of his store."

All of the original illustrations for *Chitty Chitty Bang Bang* were donated to the New York Historical Society, who displayed them for public viewing in the summer of 2017.

THE FOOT BOOK (1968), BE-1

Dr. Seuss

THE EYE BOOK (1968), BE-2

Theo LeSieg and Roy McKie

THE EAR BOOK (1968), BE-3

Al Perkins and William O'Brian

Ted kicked off Bright and Early Books with the return of Dr. Seuss, who hadn't done a Beginner Book since 1965's *Fox in Socks*. *The Foot Book* is essentially a 130-word poem about different kinds of feet (sick, clown, pig, fuzzy fur) accompanied by very literal illustrations. There's no plot, lesson, or Seussian inventions, making the book appear light and throwaway. But its simplicity is deceptive. It's almost as if Ted's real challenge in making the book was in restraining himself down to the very basics, knowing he was creating the prototype for his new line. When he created *The Cat in the Hat* he hadn't known he was also making a template for future books, but here he did.

And so *The Foot Book* sports propulsive rhythm ("Up in the air feet, over a chair feet, more and more feet"), a judicious amount of repetition, and illustrations that connect directly to the text while also providing humor and context (such as the "trick feet" juggling multicolored balls). While future Bright and Early Books would eventually stray from these elements, *The Foot Book* was Ted's attempt to create an ideal preschool reader.

The Eye Book does for seeing what *The Foot Book* did for walking, but it's different by nature of its subject. Whereas *The Foot Book* had to be a bit more esoteric, *The Eye Book* is essentially a listing of things we see (such as "Our eyes see flies. / Our eyes see ants. Sometimes they see pink underpants."). Perhaps this is why Ted chose to do *The Eye Book* as a Theo LeSieg, and leave the artwork to the prolific Roy McKie, who himself was returning to Beginner Books after a three-year absence. Roy's drawings are as expressive as ever, but seem a bit perfunctory compared to his usual work. He also replaces his usual ink with a watercolor line that's almost translucent, and he gives his main characters (a nearly bald boy and a rabbit) identical pale pink skin and fur tones. For a book about the wonders of vision, the washed-out look was an odd choice.

For *The Ear Book*, Ted called upon Al Perkins, who created an ode to sounds such as popcorn popping, rain falling, and hands clapping. Using the trusty iambic tetrameter, the verse gives the book much of its momentum, but there are also breaks in the meter for onomatopoeia such as the "drop, drop, drop" of a water faucet.

The book's pictures were by *New Yorker* cartoonist William O'Brian (1909–1985). By the time of *The Ear Book*, the New York native had already been a professional cartoonist for many years. From the late 1940s into the mid-1950s he was a staff cartoonist at the *Los Angeles Times*, producing, among other things, multipanel wordless gags. He started placing cartoons in the *New Yorker* in 1952, serving as one of the magazine's regulars until 1976. He'd also do work for *Playboy*.

His career in books wasn't nearly as robust. His first children's books illustrations were for Mabel Neikirk's *All about Oscar the Trained Seal* in 1943.

Over twenty years later Random House published *No Dessert until You've Finished Your Mashed Potatoes*, an expansion of a series of cartoons he'd done for the *New Yorker* under the theme "The Golden Years." These comics featured kids misunderstanding, misinterpreting, and exaggerating the meanings behind common parental sayings such as "Go to sleep, there's nothing to be afraid of." Bob Bernstein was a fan of the book, and suggested that Bill work up an idea for a Beginner Book. Though nothing materialized from that, the publisher kept his name on file.

This led to his work on *The Ear Book*. Bill's drawings add humor and depth into the story, especially on the line "We hear my sister sing a song," which finds the story's heroes (a boy and his dog) covering their ears in revulsion. Style-wise, Bill's work on *The Ear Book* is markedly simpler than his *New Yorker* cartoons, which sported a slick ink line and a strong command of ink-wash tones to create depth. In *The Ear Book* the ink line is rougher and the coloring bright but flat. The backgrounds are nonexistent. This, along with Roy McKie's work on *The Eye Book* as discussed above, leads one to wonder if the artists were instructed to simplify their style, just as the writers had simplified theirs.

The book was reissued in 2007, with new pictures by editorial cartoonist Henry Payne.

INSIDE OUTSIDE UPSIDE DOWN (1968), BE-4

Stan and Jan Berenstain

Breaking away from the body part theme of the initial three Bright and Early Books was the Berenstains' first for the line. Initially *Inside Outside Upside Down* was intended to be novel in more ways than that. When Ted presented Stan and Jan with the idea for Bright and Early Books, he told them not to use their bears. The Berenstains jumped at the chance to do something different. Using an iambic phrase they liked the sound of, "inside outside upside down," they created a story about a red gorilla (who sat inside a hollow tree), a crow with a beret (who sat outside on one of the tree's limbs), and a sloth in a striped shirt (hanging upside down on another limb). The book followed them on a "topsy turvy trip to town."

When Stan and Jan presented the dummy to Ted, he liked what they'd done and the way it slyly introduced the idea of prepositions. But then he broke the bad news. In a repeat of what had happened with *Nothing Ever Happens at the*

South Pole, he claimed that the salespeople had told him they hoped to see a Bright and Early Berenstain Bear book, likely because their familiarity and proven success would help anchor the new line of books. Their gorilla, crow, and sloth would have to go. The Berenstains didn't take the news well. As they told it: "We arrived home in a deep funk. We remained so for most of the next day. Jan came out of it first. She took a pencil and drawing pad into the yard and sat at our weathered old picnic table. By late afternoon she had penciled a whole new bear version of *Inside Outside Upside Down*."

The book uses sixty-six words and fifteen pictures to tell of Small Bear's own brief journey to town, first going inside a box, then outside on the bed of Papa Bear's truck, then falling off the truck upside down. The words in the story are progressive, building up and then breaking down again until Small Bear summarizes, "Mama! Mama! I went to town. Inside, outside, upside down!" As with the other three Bright and Early Books, the illustrations are stripped to basics. The blank ink line is thicker, the color is flat, backgrounds are minimal, and there's none of the cross-hatching that helped define Stan and Jan's Beginner Book work.

KING MIDAS AND THE GOLDEN TOUCH (1969), B-55

Al Perkins

Illustrator: Harold Berson

Originally told by Ovid in his epic poem *Metamorphoses*, the Greek myth of King Midas was further popularized by *The Scarlet Letter* author Nathanial Hawthorne in 1852 in his *A Wonder-Book for Boys and Girls*. Though the basics are the same in each version—King Midas is granted the ability to turn anything he touches into gold, but quickly discovers the power is a curse—the specifics change quite a bit. In the original, the power is granted to Midas by the god Dionysus, and Midas's final fate is unclear, though it's likely he died of starvation. Hawthorne keeps those essentials, but adds Midas's daughter to the story, and allows him a happy ending in which he can reverse the effects of his touch by submerging his hand into the river Pactolus.

Al's version is similar to Hawthorne's, especially in its use of the king's daughter (Princess Leela) as a turning point in the story. But in the place of Dionysus as the wish granter is a "strange little man" resembling an elf. And instead of the river Pactolus, the key to the king's redemption is a wish that gives him the power to return all of the gold items to normal. Driving this wish, of course, is his realization that he loves Princess Leela more than gold.

By this time, Al's knack for reinterpreting stories efficiently and simply was in full bloom. All the necessary information is there without frills, but the prose manages to still be evocative:

> King Midas jumped up.
> And he wished with all his heart.
> He put out his hand.
> He touched his cold, gold daughter.

The story's pictures were by Harold Berson (1926–1986), who was no stranger to illustrating myths and folktales. Born and raised in Los Angeles, Harold attended UCLA. After graduation, he briefly worked for the Bureau of Public Assistance in LA, but spent the next several years traveling. He studied in Paris, and spent time all around Europe, North Africa, and Turkey. In the mid-1950s he settled in New York, and began illustrating for *Humpty Dumpty's Magazine*. He met fellow artist Paula Winter, and the two married in 1958. That same year Harold started to get regular work illustrating children's books, first in novels and then picture books. By the time he got the assignment for *King Midas* he had done twenty-six books, including *Watermelons, Walnuts, and the Wisdom of Allah, and Other Tales of the Hoca*; *Belling the Cat and Other Stories*; and *Raminagrobis and the Mice*.

Harold's work in *King Midas and the Golden Touch* is done with ink and brush, accented by bright colors. He clearly took great pleasure in the period costumes, as those are the most detailed aspect of the drawings. Especially striking is his depiction of the forlorn king tiny on his throne after he's turned everything around him to gold. Though *King Midas and the Golden Touch* would be his only Beginner Book, Harold went on to produce nearly thirty more books, including many he wrote himself, in the 1970s and 1980s.

King Midas and the Golden Touch went on to have a second life in 1973 as a Scholastic book club selection, with new illustrations by husband and wife team Haig and Regina Sherkerjian. It was also issued with a seven-inch vinyl record (and later as a cassette) read by actor Lewis Arquette (father of actors Patricia, Rosanna, Alexis, and David).

MY BOOK ABOUT ME (1969)

Dr. Seuss

Roy McKie

My Book about Me—a big Beginner Book—was an ingenious way to not only occupy children, but to make them think about themselves and their world. There are over eighty fill-in-the-blank questions, some demographic (address, phone number), some descriptive ("My best friend's name is _____"), some aspirational ("When I grow up, I want to be _____"), some active ("I can stand on my hands for _____seconds").

They're arranged in categories like "About ME and EATING" and "Some Secret Things I Know." There's also one page for the child to draw and name a bird, and another for her to write a story.

One review wrote: "Dr. Seuss doesn't believe in taking chances. Well aware (as are all parents) that a child's universe centers on ME, he has prepared, with Roy McKie, 'My Book About Me.'" The approach of keying into a child's sense of self, and affirming it, was very much in line with children's preschool entertainment and child psychology trends of the time (when *My Book about Me* was released, *Mister Rogers' Neighborhood* had been on the air for three years, *Sesame Street* had just premiered, and Marlo Thomas's *Free to Be You and Me* record was a couple of years away).

In a lot of ways, the book echoes and presages the child-centered themes Ted would use for Bright and Early and Beginner Books in the 1970s. There are categories for body parts (*The Eye Book, The Foot Book*, etc.), noises (*Mr. Brown Can Moo! Can You?*), household items (*In a People House*), autographs (*My Big Book of Autographs*), and jobs (*Maybe You Should Fly a Jet . . .*).

And with its questions about height, weight, address, phone number, and so on, and tracing of hands and feet the book also serves as a snapshot in time. Another review suggested that every grandparent buy a copy for their grandchild, "and after the child has had all the fun of filling out the book, the grandparent can latch onto it as a memento." Ted was quite proud of the book, so much so that it's the first book he didn't illustrate to be credited to Dr. Seuss.

Roy provided hundreds of colorful, animated illustrations for the book, all done in a more controlled style than his free-spirited work on *Summer* and *Animal Riddles*, and more solid than his watercolor work in *The Eye Book*. One could spend a very long time indeed poring over his animals on the "My Favorite Pet" or the activities on "My Favorite Sport."

HAND, HAND, FINGERS, THUMB (1969), BE-5

Al Perkins and Eric Gurney

Hand, Hand, Fingers, Thumb was another entry in the Bright and Early body part books. Ted and Michael Frith worked closely with Al Perkins on the story, asking him for several revisions with the goal of adding excitement to the story. The final version, Michael says, was "basically put together late at night sitting on the floor of his living room in La Jolla." The title phrase, more intriguing and exciting than "The Hand Book," was a refrain in the book. It was inspired by the poet Vachel Lindsey, creator of a rhythmic, onomatopoeic style he called "singing poetry."

The story builds from a lone monkey (technically a chimpanzee) striking a drum with his thumb into millions of monkeys drumming with abandon. The book also has a quick tempo, as drums are not only a plot point, but also provide the verse with its staccato rat-a-tat rhythm ("Rings on fingers / Rings on thumbs / Dum ditty / Dum ditty / Dum Dum Dum"). As the book goes on, monkeys also use their hands to strum guitars and play banjos and fiddles. They also shake hands ("Hello Jack" / "Hello Jake"), blow their noses, and pick fruit.

The book re-teamed Al with his *The Digging-est Dog* illustrator, Eric Gurney. Though Eric's favored subjects were dogs and cats, he shows himself equally adept at apes. As Michael says, "Eric Gurney's gleefully crazed monkeys were icing on the cake." There's little evidence of the oversimplification of style that characterized the first round of Bright and Early Books, though the work is largely figural, with the backgrounds filled by fields of flat bright color.

Hand, Hand, Fingers, Thumb would be Eric's final Beginner Book, though he continued to put out books at a steady pace through the early 1980s, including three more with Random House (*Eric Gurney's Pop-Up Book of Cats, Eric Gurney's Pop-Up Book of Dogs,* and *Someone Is Eating the Sun*). In 1971 he won another Cartoonist of the Year award, this time for his illustration work. Nancy Gurney unfortunately passed away prematurely in 1972 at the age of fifty-eight. Eric married another Nancy, Nancy Prevo, and the couple moved to a twelve-acre plot of land in Tucson, Arizona, where they lived in an adobe hacienda and Eric continued to create. The day before his death of a heart attack at the age of eighty-two, he completed a painting of a cat chasing a dog. "He was very serious about his work, although his work was very humorous," Nancy said of her husband.

BEARS ON WHEELS (1969), BE-6

Stan and Jan Berenstain

Bears on Wheels is not, as the title would seem to indicate, an examination of different types of vehicles. Random House seemingly recognized the potential for confusion, and billed it on the cover as "A Bright and Early Counting Book." But it's not a traditional counting book either. Most counting books progress in order, with only one animal/person/thing being counted. In *Bears on Wheels* there are two things to count: the bears and the number of wheels they're riding on. And the numbers, while generally growing larger as the book moves along, are not presented in a predictable order.

Besides featuring a bear that looks like Small Bear (though not wearing his then-typical red shirt and blue pants), *Bears on Wheels* has very little in common with the Berenstain Bears either in content or form. The drawings are in the same simplified style of *Inside Outside Upside Down*, and the logical insanity of the plot—which features all manners of cycles careening and colliding—is downright Seussian. Papa Bear's exploits were often exaggerated in the Berenstain Beginner Book stories, but you'd never see him riding a unicycle with nine bears balanced on his shoulders.

The 1970s

THE BEARS' CHRISTMAS (1970), B-55

Stan and Jan Berenstain

The first, and surprisingly only, Yule-themed Beginner Book is not really about Christmas at all. The holiday serves as backdrop for Papa Bear to attempt to teach Small Bear various winter sports. The book begins with Small Bear receiving a sled, a pair of ice skates, and a pair of skis for Christmas. Immediately Papa wants to instruct his son on their proper use. So he belly-flops off a hill, falls through the ice, and rolls down the hill in a giant snowball. Back at home, the family enjoys a Christmas dinner and Small Bear enthuses about it being the "best Christmas we've ever had!" with Papa agreeing as he dries off and warms up.

Though it follows the usual formula of Papa Bear "instructing" Small Bear, *The Bears' Christmas* offers some small variations on the theme. For one, Papa is not merely—as in the other books—overconfident in his skills. He claims to have once been known as the "Great Skating Bear." Besides the intriguing glimpse into his past, it also implies that his self-confidence is not baseless, but his hubris in believing that he can still do the same things he did when he was young (and on too-small skates) is his actual downfall.

By this time Stan and Jan were locked in on both words and art. In design, the Bears are very close to their final selves, and the endpaper spread of Papa and Small Bear setting off through the snowy woods is a lovely piece of artwork.

I CAN DRAW IT MYSELF (1970)

Big Beginner Book

Dr. Seuss

The spiritual sequel to *My Book about Me*, *I Can Draw It Myself* was initially issued as a twelve-by-sixteen-inch, landscape-oriented, top comb-bound Big Beginner Book. Through eighteen pages, the child is encouraged to embellish upon or finish the drawings Dr. Seuss has started, and in some cases completely invent their own. The tasks range from adding green hair to Stan Stine's head to completing the back half of a Yill-iga-yakk to designing the whole look of the Blue Hoo-Fish.

The child's guide through the book is the same young version of the Cat in the Hat that was introduced in *I Can Lick 30 Tigers Today*, and his bravado ("The more I keep drawing, / The better I get!") serves as encouragement to the reader/artist.

Ted viewed the book as a "revolt against coloring books." As such, the rhyming instructions and drawings are designed to give the young artist enough direction to get them started, but not so much that they aren't able to let their imagination play. Though not a massive sales hit on the level of *My Book about Me*, *I Can Draw It Myself* has been reissued periodically through the years, the latest edition coming packaged with crayons.

MR. BROWN CAN MOO! CAN YOU? (1970), BE-7

Dr. Seuss

Mr. Brown Can Moo! Can You? is a book that teaches the concept of onomatopoeia, or sounds written as words. It starts with that staple of nearly every child's early learning—animal noises—but quickly expands from there to all sorts of unusual sounds, such as those made by a squeaky shoe ("eek eek"), a hippopotamus chewing gum ("grum grum"), and a goldfish kiss ("pip").

As if presenting the sounds weren't enough, Ted also ingeniously includes noises that rhyme with one another. This allows him to periodically "review" all the sounds that have been made so far, culminating in the final two pages where every single sound is included in a symphony of noise (e.g., "Boom boom / splat splat / tick tick tock / sizzle sizzle / blurp blurp / knock knock knock").

Ted also structures the book to maximize the child's participation. Knowing an early reader is unlikely to be able to read this by themselves but instead will have it read aloud to them, he regularly challenges the child to replicate Mr. Brown's noises. "Maybe YOU can, too. I think you ought to try."

Ted's illustrations are relatively more grounded in reality than his typical work. Mr. Brown is even presented as a real human (as opposed to the Mr. Brown in *Hop on Pop*, though the two characters do wear the same hat). The directive of simplified illustrations that ruled the first six Bright and Early Books doesn't seem to be in effect anymore, as the book's artwork—sporadic backgrounds and fields of bright color—is very much in line with earlier Seuss Beginner Books such as *Green Eggs and Ham* and *Fox in Socks*.

THE NOSE BOOK (1970), BE-8

Al Perkins and Roy McKie

The Nose Book features two Beginner Book stalwarts—Al Perkins and Roy McKie—working together for the first and only time. The book starts by celebrating different shapes, sizes, and colors of noses on various creatures. Then it explores the virtues of noses, with seals using them to play horns and balance balls; and woodpeckers using their beaks to take on trees, roofs, and barber poles. It also details the dangers noses face, such as sniffles, sunburns, and punches. Finally, Al asks a reader to imagine what life would be like with no nose at all: "Then you could never smell a rose / or pie, or chicken a la king. / You'd never smell a single thing." Also, the text points out, noses give us a place for our glasses to rest!

Roy uses a thick ink line and bold multitoned watercolors, reminiscent of the loose style he employed on *Animal Riddles*. In some cases, his work on the book almost reaches toward the abstract.

OLD HAT, NEW HAT (1970), BE-9; *BEARS IN THE NIGHT* (1971), BE-10; *THE B BOOK* (1971), BE-11; *C IS FOR CLOWN* (1972), BE-14

Stan and Jan Berenstain

The Berenstains began the 1970s with a rash of Bright and Early Books, all of which became multimillion best sellers.

In *Old Hat, New Hat* Small Bear goes shopping to replace his hat, an old patched leather number with a wilted flower sticking out. At the haberdashery, he tries on a wide variety of new hats, but finds each one wanting. One's too shiny. Another is too loose. Yet another is too lumpy. Et cetera. In the end, he discovers one hat that's just right: His old hat.

Similar to *Inside Outside Upside Down*, the Berenstains keep the word count very low. In fact, there's no sentence longer than two words. And the couple clearly had fun coming up with the most ostentatious hats they possibly could, something that Ted—with his collection of hats—surely appreciated.

Bears in the Night is a palindromic story that finds septuplet bears sneaking away from home after bedtime to investigate Spook Hill. The text is comprised exclusively of prepositional phrases, a clever way to teach and reinforce position words. The bears go out the window, over the wall, under the bridge, and around the lake. This all leads them to a frightening encounter with an owl and the reversal of the path they took to get there. Upon superficial perusal, the book appears to be about the usual Bear family. The seven bears all have a passing resemblance to Small Bear, their mom is clearly akin to Mama Bear, even their house inside the hollow tree recalls the Bears' home. But there are differences in each of these, some subtle (Mama's blue dress doesn't have its trademark white polka dots) and some not (Small Bear clearly doesn't have six siblings).

A bear (who appears related to the Great Natural Bear in *The Bears' Almanac* and the Great Sleeping Bear in *The Spooky Old Tree*), a baboon (who is also a ballerina), and a blue bull (likely named Babe) are the stars of *The B Book*, a progressive story with a logical insanity plot.

As the three animals bike backward, they bump into a lot of trouble, including black bug's banana boxes and Buster Beagle's banjo-bagpipe-bugle band. Most impressively, the story is made up almost exclusively of words that begin with "b" ("and," "that's," and "what" are the sole exceptions). Even the sound effects—"BAM," "BOOM"—get in on the act.

While this means that there's little chance a young reader could handle the book on their own, it makes for a very fun read aloud. There's also a satisfying punchline at the end, where we find out that all this mayhem is what "broke Baby Bird's balloon."

It wasn't an easy book to make. "There was immense frustration with *The B Book*," Mike Berenstain recalls. "They went through half a dozen versions," he says, before Ted was finally satisfied.

C Is for Clown came next, following the same pattern as its predecessor. In this story Clarence Clown attempts to carry an ever-increasing number

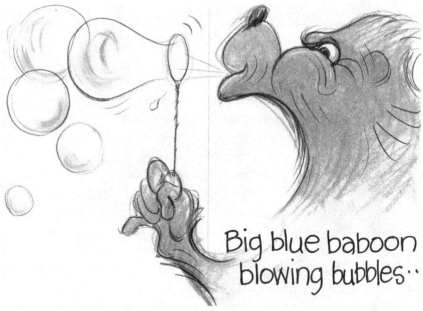

An abandoned concept for *The B Book*. Courtesy Berenstain Enterprises, Inc.

of things that start with "c," including collies, clubs, cows, cakes, and candles. Again every word in the book begins with "c" save "and" and "no," and a bird once again figures in the punchline (tiny Clara Canary proves to be the proverbial straw that breaks the camel's back). The Berenstains may have had a whole new formula on their hands, but multiple attempts at *The A Book* were rejected by Ted until they gave up and moved on (it was eventually published as BE-30 in 1997).

TUBBY AND THE LANTERN (1971), B-56;
TUBBY AND THE POO-BAH (1972), B-57

Al Perkins and Rowland B. Wilson

Al Perkins's final Beginner Books feature a Chinese boy named Ah Mee and his small anthropomorphic elephant Tubby. Considering how much Al traveled, one might surmise that he based these books on a visit to China, but his stepdaughter Sally Allen says that's not the case. She believes the idea for the Tubby books may have come from Random House and given to Al to flesh out.

No matter their origin, the two books are sweet tales of adventure, inge-nuity, and friendship. The first book introduces Ah Mee and Tubby, who live by the Rolling River on the Street of Golden Lanterns. On Ah Mee's birth-day, his friend thoughtfully makes him an ENORMOUS lantern (the word "enormous" is used five times ensuring it gets added to the young reader's vocabulary; it's also fully capitalized each time, directing the inflection for read aloud). When the lantern floats too high and far, the friends must do some quick thinking to escape some pirates and get back home.

In the second book, Tubby unwittingly steals the Poo-Bah's SPLENDIFEROUS boat (the adjective serves in the same role as "enormous" in the first book), landing Ah Mee in jail. Tubby's determination to rescue his friend, and the Poo-Bah's unexpected perceptiveness and kindness, help lead everything to a tidy conclusion.

The Doctor Dolittle and King Midas books demonstrated Al Perkins's facility for telling a plot-driven narrative story within the Beginner Book parameters, and the Tubby books are further proof. An early reader might struggle independently, partly because the text sometimes tells more than is pictured, and also because there's some unusual sentence construction ("Up into the sky it floated"). But for the most part the books manage to feel much more substantial than their limited vocabulary and word count would seem to allow. Also like *Doctor Dolittle and the Pirates* and *King Midas and the Golden Touch*, the books have thoughtful, emotional endings, *Tubby and the Lantern*'s especially: "In their dream they float away again in the most beauti-ful, most ENORMOUS paper lantern in the world. But they always come back . . . safely . . . every morning."

The books' pictures also help lend depth. Done in black oil pencil and vivid watercolors, they feature clear, strong storytelling. The colors especially con-tribute to the mood and atmosphere of individual scenes, such as the orange sunset as the Poo-Bah's men take Ah Mee to the palace, or the blue starry night as Tubby contemplates how to mount a rescue in *Tubby and the Poo-Bah*.

Illustrator Rowland B. Wilson (1930–2005) was born in Dallas, Texas, and spent his childhood Saturdays at the movies. Inspired, he would return home and draw Disney characters at his kitchen table. He majored in fine arts at the University of Texas–Austin, and after graduation made his way to New York to do graduate work at Columbia University. He started a career as a freelance cartoonist, selling work to the likes of the *Saturday Evening Post* and *Collier's*, but was drafted into the army in 1954. He served as a draughtsman in Austria and Germany for three years. Once out of the military, he entered the world of advertising, joining the firm of Young & Rubicam. He also became a regular contributor to both *Esquire* and the *New Yorker* in the late 1950s and early 1960s. His *Esquire* work is where he really developed a signature style: highly detailed, fully colored one-panel gags.

Some of his work is collected in the 1962 book *The Whites of Their Eyes*, which also shows off Rowland's penchant for recreating historical locales. He thought of his gag cartoons as "one-line plays." He explained further, "You set the stage, choose the actors, and portray their business."

In the mid-1960s Rowland moved to Westport, Connecticut (joining a host of other Beginner Book artists), and went freelance, doing a syndicated strip called "Noon" about an out-of-work cowboy in Rowland's native Texas (the strip lasted only six months), and beginning a longstanding relationship with *Playboy*. Rowland claimed to love working for *Playboy* because they were the only magazine that would still print full-color cartoons. He also created a series of well-remembered and well-regarded ads for New England Life Insurance that depicted situations just on the verge of going very wrong.

Since the 1950s he'd had a strong interest in animation, and in the late 1960s Rowland started moving into that field. He moved to London for two years at Dick Williams's animation studio, known for its film credit sequences on the likes of *A Funny Thing Happened on the Way to the Forum*. Upon returning to the states, Rowland designed and storyboarded two sequences for *Schoolhouse Rock*—"Luck Seven Sampson" and "Twelve Toes"—winning a daytime Emmy for his work. It was around this time that he illustrated the two Tubby books—Michael Frith was a longtime admirer of Rowland's work, and had intuited correctly that he would be a good children's book illustrator. Alas, these two would turn out to be Rowland's only work in the field.

In the early 1980s he moved to California and began working for Disney, where he did preproduction work designing characters and settings for films such as *The Little Mermaid*, *The Hunchback of Notre Dame*, and *Tarzan*. While at Disney he mentored a young artist named Tim Burton, discouraging him from becoming a magazine cartoonist, and encouraging him to instead stick with filmmaking.

Married twice, Rowland had four daughters—Megan, Amanda, Reed, and Kendra—all of whom became commercial artists. Upon his death in 2005, colleagues remembered him as a "cartoonist's cartoonist" for his dedication to the craft and the purity of his approach. His second wife, painter Suzanne Lemieux Wilson, posthumously published *Rowland B. Wilson's Trade Secrets*, assembling Rowland's collected wisdom from his five-decade career.

SOME OF US WALK, SOME FLY, SOME SWIM (1971)

Big Beginner Book

Michael Frith

With five "Strangest Things" Step-Up books on his resume, Michael Frith was a natural to create a Beginner Book centering on different kinds of animals. And though he'd been behind the scenes on nearly every Beginner and Bright and Early since 1968, the oversized *Some of Us Walk, Some Fly, Some Swim* was his first time on stage. The book's cover says it features "246 Animals Every Beginner Should Meet" and not only does it fulfill that promise it also provides a name label for each of the 246. This style seems to be inspired by Richard Scarry's *Best Word Book Ever*, which had come out in 1963.

The book is an admirable effort to inject the Beginner Book sense of fun into a nonfiction format by using rhyming verse to present broad strokes ("Up on our heads some of us wear / feelers, feathers, antlers, hair") and pairing that with pictures of specific animals. As such, the book is organized not by species, but by the similarities between different animals, such as size, locomotion, habitat, or how they eat and sleep. Perhaps the most impressive feat—beyond the depth of research required—are the several pages where Michael puts the animal names into verse ("hedgehog, titmouse, Siamese cat / firefly, sailfish, leaf-nosed bat")

"When I did that book there was no nature channel," Michael says. "It wasn't part of everybody's visual vocabulary the way these things are now and they would really be discovering a lot of those animals for the first time." Indeed, even adults are likely to find more than a few animals they've never heard of, such as the klipspringer, jerboa, and the uakari. To wit, Michael recalls: "I gave a copy of the book to a friend of mine—[writer and actor] George Plimpton—I thought it might be a fun book for his kids when they get a little bit older. And after that whenever I'd run into Plimpton he'd say, 'Oh, there you are, I have to tell you how much the twins love that book about the bongo!'"

Due to the subject matter, Michael's illustrations lean toward realism, more in line with his "Strangest Things" books than his more cartoony Beginner Book and Muppet style. That said, one can clearly see the beginnings of Gonzo's chicken troupe in the humorous middle section that measures a giraffe's height, hippopotamus's weight, and whale's length in number of chickens.

I CAN WRITE! A BOOK BY ME, MYSELF (1971)

Big Beginner Book

Theo LeSieg and Roy McKie

I Can Write! belongs in the same interactive category as *My Book about Me* and *I Can Draw!* but with one major difference. Whereas the two earlier books encouraged children to invent and imagine and explore, *I Can Write!* is essentially a more amusing version of a school handwriting book. Rather than filling in blanks, the child is tasked with creating a copy of the text.

It's not difficult to see the educational philosophy behind the book. Reading and writing is a reciprocal process, so having a child write a word they can also read or associate with a picture is a way to help them internalize that word as part of their personal vocabulary. In *I Can Write!* the reader/writer is asked to copy numbers, color words, prepositions (in, on), nouns (fish, men), and verbs (eats, are), all of which are presented in Roy McKie's typically colorful and exuberant illustrations. The story itself finds a school of fish, a cow, and a red-haired girl (making this, significantly, the only book Ted ever published in his lifetime to have a female lead character) navigating silly, nonsensical situations as they count from one to ten.

It's all professionally done, but there's little lasting value after the child has gone through the first time and written the words, unless he or she is inspired by rereading their own writing. But even in that case once it's filled in, there's double text on each page ("Oh boy / Oh boy / What a party / What a party"), which is not representative of an actual reading experience. Having the child fill in blanks by tracing the words may have been a better approach for the child to feel ownership, and for the book to be reread over and over. Perhaps this is why in the Morgans' biography, they give *I Can Write!* as the only one of Ted's books he actively disliked; he later had the book withdrawn from print.

IN A PEOPLE HOUSE (1972), BE-12

Theo LeSieg and Roy McKie

In a People House is essentially a vocabulary book put to verse. In the story, a mouse and a bird go on an anthropological study of a human home. The mouse serves as the well-informed tour guide, presumably because he grew up in a house himself. He lists off all of the names of things you might find in a home, such as "piano, peanuts, popcorn, pails / pencil, paper, hammer, nails." As with Richard Scarry's word books, the text, done in pink, is placed right next to its picture. It would all seem a bit pedestrian if not for Roy McKie's buoyant illustrations and the final punchline, "A People House has people, too!" which delivered as our heroes are chased out of the home.

MARVIN K. MOONEY, WILL YOU PLEASE GO NOW! (1972), BE-13

Dr. Seuss

Marvin K. Mooney, Will You Please Go Now! began its life as a fun little book about the act of going, but a couple of years after its publication would take on a whole other dimension. In the story, an unseen narrator informs young Marvin that it's time to leave, then proceeds to detail all the ways in which it might happen. "You can go by balloon or broomstick OR / You can go by camel in a bureau drawer," reads a typical page.

The concept lends itself to a propulsive forward momentum, and after reading it aloud one feels almost breathless. Fittingly, Ted's illustrations are all motion and action. There's also an irritated insistence in the narrator's voice, as though Marvin has committed an offense (what that might be, and whether Marvin deserves the rancor, is left up to the reader). All of this makes for a book very similar in tone and feel to *Green Eggs and Ham*.

Marvin K. Mooney, Will You Please Go Now!'s second life came in 1974 thanks to nationally syndicated newspaper columnist Art Buchwald. That spring, Buchwald and Ted had run into each other by chance at the San Diego Zoo and struck up an acquaintance. A couple of months later, as a joke, Ted sent a copy of *Marvin K. Mooney, Will You Please Go Now!* to Buchwald, crossing off Marvin's name and replacing it in every instance with the syllabically identical "Richard M. Nixon," the president who was then on the verge of impeachment because of the Watergate scandal.

Buchwald asked for Ted's permission to print the revised text in its entirety in his column. Ted agreed, and on July 30, 1974, the piece went into homes across the nation. A little over a week later—August 8, 1974—Nixon resigned. Though it was clearly coincidence, Ted wrote to Art, "We sure got him, didn't we? We should have collaborated sooner."

It wasn't the first time Beginner Book characters had been used for political ends. During the 1968 presidential campaign (in which Nixon ultimately defeated Hubert Humphrey), Robert Coover published a piece called "The Cat in the Hat for President" in the *New American Review*. Satirizing the US political election process, Coover's piece features the Cat as a candidate and Sam-I-Am as his vice president. Ned and Mr. Brown from *Hop on Pop* and Clark from *One Fish, Two Fish, Red Fish, Blue Fish* all play different roles in the campaign. The piece was published as a book called *A Political Fable* in 1980 and was reissued again in 2017.

THE MANY MICE OF MR. BRICE (1973), BE-15

Theo LeSieg and Roy McKie

Movable books for children—books with not only pop-up elements, but also pull tabs, flaps, and other interactive features—had enjoyed a few bursts of popularity since the late 1800s, notably with Lothar Meggendorfer's work in Germany and the UK, and again in the 1920s and 1930s. The medium enjoyed another surge in the mid-1960s at Random House. A man named Wally Hunt had created a company called Graphics International devoted exclusively to the art of what he called "paper engineering." While creating an interactive movable promotional booklet for a corporate client, he came to Random House for help in producing the physical product.

The process of creating that booklet led Bennett Cerf, Christopher Cerf, Wally, and marketing man Jerry Harrison to come up with the idea of a movable riddle book where an interactive element revealed the punchline. The result was *Bennett Cerf's Silliest Pop-Up Riddles*, published to great success in 1967. This led to a whole line of successful pop-ups such as the *Pop-Up Animal Alphabet Book* and *Pop-Up The Night before Christmas*, with Chris in charge of the series.

Michael Frith immediately saw the medium's potential as a teaching tool, and began the process of creating movable Sesame Street and Electric Company books. This led naturally to a movable Beginner Book with 1973's *The Many Mice of Mr. Brice*. Yet another LeSieg/McKie collaboration, it features the red-bowtied and mustachioed Mr. Brice introducing his menagerie of twenty-six talented mice, each one with a name that starts with a different letter of the alphabet. Roy's artwork is solid as ever, with the added innovation of a textured watercolor look that's a far cry from the flat solid colors of his early Beginner Book work.

Michael Frith recalls, "Ted LOVED the physicality of the medium, and became, typically, completely involved in the mechanics of the paper engineering." Michael believes that Wally Hunt's partner at Graphics International, Ib Penick, did *Mr. Brice*'s features.

And those features are impressive. On one page a turning wheel moves Harriet Mouse around the bedroom, her location revealed by lifting the rug, opening the cupboard, looking under a blanket on the bed, and more. Eddie Mouse drinks a whole bottle of soda pop when you pull the tab. And a mailbox opens when you push the flag up, revealing one of the mice holding a letter. There are also glued-in elements, such as Quackenbush's whiskers, Mary Rose's yarn bows, and a rubber band on Charlie's stringed instrument.

The book was reissued in 1989 as *The Pop-Up Mice of Mr. Brice*, and in 2015 as an abridged board book under the original title with no movable elements.

THE SHAPE OF ME AND OTHER STUFF (1973), BE-16

Dr. Seuss

The Shape of Me and Other Stuff appears to have begun life as a Theo LeSieg manuscript to be assigned to an artist. But then, while reading a magazine on a flight, Ted came across photos of stone-cut silhouettes of a hunter and a whale done by Inuits from northern Quebec. He described them as "about the strongest illustrations I've ever seen." He immediately worked up a silhouette of the Cat, and then realized the style would be perfect for his LeSieg manuscript about shapes.

The book, similar to *In a People House*, reads as a rhyming list of familiar items ("Just think about the shape of beans / and flowers and mice and big machines") with the only Seussian invention coming near the book's conclusion, where we see some unnamed creatures and the long-necked "Blogg."

The result is a Seuss book that looks unlike any other. Though many of the silhouettes are done in black, in other cases Ted makes use of possibilities of flat color, presenting orange on white, white on blue, and indigo on lavender. In terms of overall page composition, though, Ted seems to have struggled. While he was clearly thoughtful about it, and while it was an inspired idea to use silhouettes to dramatize the concept of shape, most of the pages feature their subjects just floating in a void with nothing to ground them, and little to engage the reader fully. It's one of the rare Seuss books that seem visually unfinished, which is perhaps why Ted never tried another book like it.

I'LL TEACH MY DOG 100 WORDS (1973), BE-17

Michael Frith and P. D. Eastman

I'll Teach My Dog 100 Words is a combination vocabulary list, phrase guide, and counting book. In the story, a boy has decided to expand his dog's lexicon by one hundred words. The words and phrases start out as mostly dog-related things ("I'll teach him walk and run, and then catch a ball.") but as the book goes in it expands out to decidedly non-canine concepts ("short and tall") and actions ("Cut the grass! / Shine my shoe! Comb your hair! And clean the zoo!"). The boy details his plan in future tense, imagining not only the words and phrases he'll teach his pup, but also the acclaim it will bring. It all leads to a satisfying punch-line, "My dog will learn those hundred words—and how my friends will cheer! I'll teach my dog those hundred words . . . I think I'll start next year."

Michael Frith (along with Ted) wrote the four-line verse specifically for P. D. Eastman to illustrate, tailoring it to his "charming approach" to drawing dogs. The flap bio had fun with the team-up, stating, "Between them, Mr. Frith and Mr. Eastman have two pairs of glasses, one pair of mustaches and this, their first Bright and Early Book."

While still clearly Phil's style, the book had a different feel from his past Beginner Book work. Part of that is likely due to the fact that Michael had provided an illustrated dummy version of the manuscript for Phil to follow, and that included many more drawings per page than Phil's past work. But the character designs are also simpler than before, and the pencil line thicker. If one looks closely one will notice a striking similarity between Uncle Abner in this book and the man on the bench from whom Mr. and Mrs. Bird retrieve "man hair" in *The Best Nest,* even down to the blue-and-white-striped shirt.

It may have been his first Bright and Early Book, but *I'll Teach My Dog 100 Words* was also the last original work Phil would do for the Beginner Books line.

THE BEARS' ALMANAC (1973)

Big Beginner Book

Stan and Jan Berenstain

Subtitled "A Year in Bear Country," this oversized Beginner Book has fun exploring details about each of the four seasons. Starting with winter, each section includes rhyming signs of the season (for winter, it's "Papa puts on long underwear. / There are snowflakes in the air."), a Richard Scarry–style spread of labeled things you'll commonly see during that time of year, and some information on various holidays. There are also pages full of facts on snow, wind, the sun, lightning and thunder, and the moon (purposefully or not, the latter page includes a throwback to another Beginner Book, stating, "Some day, you may go to the moon.").

The spring section features a brief revisitation of the old Berenstain Beginner Book formula, featuring Papa Bear attempting to instruct Small Bear on how to fly a kite. Of course Papa ends up tangled and tripped while Small Bear gets the knack right away. At the same time, followers of the Berenstain Bears universe will note that this book represents the first major expansion of their world beyond Mama, Papa, and Small Bear. We catch glimpses of Farmer Ben, Granny, and even Sister Bear, a whole year before she was officially born in the pages of *The Berenstain Bears' New Baby*.

MY AMAZING BOOK OF AUTOGRAPHS (1974), B-58

Michael Frith

The fifty-eighth Beginner Book was also an activity book along the lines of *My Book about Me*, *I Can Draw!*, and *I Can Write!* Smaller than the typical Beginner Book (9" x 7"), and printed landscape, it put a wacky spin on the typical autograph book.

Though they've mostly fallen out of favor in current times—at least outside of Disney theme parks—autograph books enjoyed a long run of popularity. They originated in Germany as "friendship books" in the late 1500s, used mostly on college campuses to collect names of other scholars. The concept rebounded about one hundred years later, and German immigrants brought the idea to the United States, where it peaked in popularity during the Civil War. Yearbooks took over as the popular way to exchange signatures, quotes, and poems, and by the mid-twentieth century, autograph books had become a niche hobby, with some collectors gathering celebrity signatures, others just seeing how many of their friends and families they could get to sign their book.

Rather than simply provide space for friends and family to sign, *My Amazing Book of Autographs* asks its owner to seek out very specific types of autographs. These include

—left-handed autographs by left-handed people
—left-handed autographs by right-handed people
—blindfolded autographs
—middle names
—autographs of people in uniforms
—autographs from other lands
—autograph of a man with a beard
—autograph of a girl with green eyes
—autograph written by a foot (a "foot-o-graph").

Accompanying each page are Michael's charming little bunnies (and the occasional Seussian dog) performing all manner of actions. The style is bright and colorful and cartoony, an appealing middle ground between Seuss and McKie.

The book was reissued in 1990 as *Autographs! I Collect Them.*

WACKY WEDNESDAY (1974), B-59

Theo LeSieg and George Booth

Wacky Wednesday is the tale of a boy who wakes to find a shoe stuck to his wall. And then things only get stranger from there. The book didn't invent the "what's wrong with this picture" concept, but it has certainly become an exemplar for it. *Wacky Wednesday* also doubles as a counting book, since the reader has to keep track of an increasing number of oddities on each page. Spotting absurd mistakes—like a turtle in a tree, a child with white hair and beard, or a tree growing out of a chimney—is not only fun and funny, but also provides children with a sense of comfort. Being able to identify what's wrong makes them feel smart and in control.

Wacky Wednesday is atypical for a Beginner Book. The first indication of that is the upside-down Beginner Book logo on the front cover. It was such a departure that an early cover mock-up indicates that Ted considered issuing it under a new pseudonym, *Hjalmar Bonstable Jr.* The book encourages the reader to slow down and linger on the illustrations rather than move forward quickly. Also, rather than using the pictures to support the text, the text supports the pictures.

As such, the book required an artist who could fill the pages with unusual details, and Ted and Michael found one in *New Yorker* cartoonist George Booth (born 1926). Booth grew up on a vegetable farm in northern Missouri.

His parents were William and Irma Booth, both educators. His mother was also a musician and a cartoonist who would give chalk talks to local women's groups. George had loved to draw from a young age, and his mother heartily encouraged it, even bringing him along to her chalk talks to draw while she spoke. Of drawing he says, "It became a part of me."

In grade school George created his own comic strip, called "Cherokee Cherky." By high school he was doing cartoons not only for his school paper but also the local newspapers. He enlisted in the US Marine Corps in 1944, and ended up as a linotype operator at Pearl Harbor until the end of World War II. Based on his interest in cartooning, he was asked to sign up for another hitch to work at the Marine Corps magazine, *Leatherneck*, in Washington, DC. George did just that, becoming art director.

Once out of the service, George bounced between a couple of art schools, Corcoran College of Art and Design and the Chicago Academy of Fine Arts, before being recalled into the marines in 1950 when the Korean War started. He once again worked at *Leatherneck*. In 1952 he headed for New York, getting a place in Cold Spring Harbor, attending both Adelphi College and the School of Visual Arts (he'd finish neither), and starting to sell cartoons to the likes of the *Saturday Evening Post*, *Collier's*, and *Look*. He also had a syndicated strip, *Spot*, for a year in the mid-1950s. But the income was barely enough to live on, so once he got married—to Dione Babcock—he got full-time work as art director at Bill Communications, which published trade magazines such as *Railroad Progress* and *Sales Management*.

He'd stay for nine years, eventually deciding to go freelance again. Since his *Leatherneck* days, it'd been George's goal to get his work in the *New Yorker*. He'd even submitted work there in the 1950s, only to be turned away. It didn't happen immediately, but when the *Saturday Evening Post* folded in 1969, the editor there got George an interview with the *New Yorker*, and this time they bought his work. It was the beginning of a fifty-year (and counting) relationship.

By the time *Wacky Wednesday* came along, George was a cartooning star on the rise, albeit one in his early fifties. His mangy characters (both human and animal) and unkempt, overstuffed settings were typically paired with dialogue taken from a much different social stratus. By the early 1980s George had illustrated a couple of humor books by Henry Morgan, and had published several collections of his cartoons. His work appeared on greeting cards, calendars, bedsheets, towels, stickers, scrapbooks, and more. He tried his hand again at a syndicated strip, this one called *Local Item*, inspired by his high school experience working at the local newspaper. The strip only lasted a year.

For many years *Wacky Wednesday* stood as George's only children's book. It was joined in 1992 by Nancy Van Laan's *Possum Come-A-Knockin'*, and then in the late 2000s George began illustrating kids' books on a regular basis. The latest—*Here, George*—was done in collaboration with early-reader superstar Sandra Boynton and published in 2017 when George was ninety-one years old.

But it's his one-panel *New Yorker* cartoons that will be his lasting legacy. "I never run out of ideas," he told an interviewer. "There are lots of them. But I do feel it's a gift. People laugh at that, but it's true."

As for *Wacky Wednesday*, it has become a fixture of the celebrations that surround Read Across America Day, which happen the week of March 2 (Ted's birthday). Teachers read the book, make some things wacky in their classrooms, and encourage students to dress "wacky" on the Wednesday of that week.

THERE'S A WOCKET IN MY POCKET! (1974), BE-18

Dr. Seuss

Anyone who's been around young children for any length of time has heard them practicing nonsense rhyming. They may not be able to articulate what they're doing, but they know that continually swapping out the initial sound while leaving the rest of the word (the vowel and final sounds) makes for some satisfying verbal gymnastics. This skill, combined with phonics knowledge, can help kids read fast, because they learn to make analogies between known words and unknown words. *There's a Wocket in My Pocket!* helps develop that skill in very early readers by pairing a common household item or location with a rhyming-named creature that resides there. So the sink has a Nink, and the steps have Yeps. The chimney has a Quimney, and there's a Zlock behind the clock.

Following the experimental *The Shape of Me and Other Things*, *There's a Wocket in My Pocket!* finds Ted returning to his strengths. The creature designs are inspired and memorable, and the page layouts are inviting and engaging. The text is simple enough that a pre-reader hearing the book once or twice could easily begin "reading" the names of the creatures herself the next time through. And though it doesn't cement the idea of word families as well as *Hop on Pop*, it does give one page of practice, with "the Tellar and the Nellar and the Gellar and the Dellar and the Bellar and Wellar and the Zellar in the Cellar."

GREAT DAY FOR UP! (1974), BE-19

Dr. Seuss and Quentin Blake

A riff on the prepositional concept of "up" (it uses the word forty-eight times), *Great Day for Up!* approaches the word directionally, of course, but also goes deeper than that. Ted uses the story to tell the world to rise and shine, and in places it reads almost like an inspirational pep talk for the entirety of human and animal existence: "UP! UP! UP! Great day for UP! Wake every person, pig and pup, till EVERYONE on Earth is up!" It might just be too much cheeriness if not for the punchline on the final page, with a boy happily still under the covers declaring, "Except for me / Please go away. / No up. / I'm sleeping in today."

Though books he didn't illustrate were typically attributed to Theo LeSieg, Ted decided to release *Great Day for Up!* under the name Dr. Seuss. Michael Frith says this choice, which would only be made three times in total, was an indication that Ted was exceedingly proud of the final product. The main reason for that on *Great Day for Up!* was its pictures. Michael recalls a letter in which Ted thanked him "effulgently" for suggesting Quentin Blake (born 1933) as an illustrator. "Those drawings were just so full of joy . . . that to Ted was magical . . . right away he understood what a special thing that was."

Quentin Blake was a Beginner Book rarity in that he was not US born or based, and that by 1974 he was already well established as a children's book author and illustrator as opposed to being at the very beginning of such a career. Quentin grew up in Sidcup, a suburb of London. His father was a civil servant and his mother was a homemaker. He'd taken an interest in drawing early on, but found little encouragement from his parents, who wanted him to be a banker or a teacher.

In grammar school, he wrote and drew for the school magazine. His Latin teacher noticed his drawings and arranged for Quentin to meet her husband, *Punch* cartoonist Alfred Jackson. After their talk, Quentin began submitting his own work to *Punch*, and the next year the humor magazine began to accept some of his drawings. After grammar school, Quinten spent two years in the Army Education Corps, then studied English at Downing College at Cambridge University. Though he knew all along he wanted to be an artist and illustrator, he also knew that going to university would give him a chance to study literature.

Likely to appease his parents, Quentin took teacher training and passed his qualifications, though he never sought a teaching position. Instead, he got regular work at *Punch*, and began illustrating stories in the literary magazine *Spectator*. Whereas drawing satirical cartoons of the type that populated *Punch* weren't his interest or forte, the "continuity of narrative" of creating pictures to go with prose definitely was. "I was interested in storytelling and in showing how people react, how they move, and how they're placed in a scene," he says. He likened being an illustrator to being an actor in a member of a repertory company.

So it's no surprise he found himself drawn to children's book illustration. His first work in the genre began to appear in 1961, in books by Evan Hunter (*The Wonderful Button*), Frances Gray Patton (*Good Morning, Miss Dove*), and Rosemary Weir (*Albert the Dragon*). His style was set from early on: a thin ink line that hits the page in an expressive, kinetic, and childlike way. The final product looks spontaneous, as if every element was invented right in the moment. If he added color it was more often than not a slapdash application of watercolor wash. From this point forward Quentin's career was full steam ahead, and he'd do three to five books per year through the next two decades.

In 1968 he did his first self-illustrated picture book, *Patrick*, which was followed in short order by *Jack and Nancy* (1969) and *Angelo* (1970). *Snuff* appeared in 1973, but it was a struggle. "I didn't know how to do it anymore," he said of illustrating his own stories. Interestingly, he credits his *Great Day for Up!* for breaking that block. Working from Ted's roughs, he says, "It was very interesting to look closely at the way he writes a book and the way he works . . . it made me think, 'Oh, it doesn't have to be a story.'" Speaking of the way the book riffed on a concept rather than hinging on a narrative, Quentin realized, "You can form [a book] out of something else." And that got him going again. He'd go on to create over two dozen more of his own stories.

Ever prolific, Quentin's body of work now includes well over three hundred books, as well as murals and design work. His most famous association has been with the work of Roald Dahl. Quentin began doing illustrations for Dahl's books in 1978, and quickly established himself as the definitive interpreter of Dahl's creations. He has done illustrations for every Dahl book published, including the ones released before 1978.

Quentin has garnered praise from nearly every corner of the children's literature world, especially in his home country. From 1999 to 2001 he was named Great Britain's Children's Laureate. In 2002 he won the Hans Christian Anderson Award. In 2012 he was honored with knighthood. Writer Naomi Lewis summed him up best, declaring: "Any book which has Quentin Blake as an illustrator is in luck, for who can match his zany wit and euphoria, his engaging charm, his wild assurance of line?"

HE BEAR SHE BEAR (1974), BE-20

Stan and Jan Berenstain

As with many of the Berenstain books, *He Bear She Bear* had a difficult beginning. Ted didn't like the initial draft of the book in which Small Bear and a
female counterpart (likely Sister Bear, though she'd just that year been introduced as a baby) explore their career possibilities. He complained about the
lack of conflict, and asked, "What exactly does this book do to interest a child
reader? What's its message? Where are the laughs?"

It's not known exactly what that first version of the book contained, but
it's difficult to believe the message wasn't clear all along. After being told by
Mama and Papa Bear that they can be a mother and father, the two cubs begin
to explore all of the other possibilities ("You could / Be a doctor—make folks
well. / Teach kids how to add and spell. / Knit a sock, sew a dress, / paint a
picture—what a mess!").

Despite the book's title, none of these is stereotypically gendered. In fact,
we see a female doctor and police officer, and the girl bear imagines herself as
a construction worker, race car driver, and marine biologist. Beginner Books
had struggled for its entire existence with presenting a balanced depiction of
gender, but especially in the 1970s when Jan Berenstain was the only female
Beginner Book creator. So a book like *He Bear She Bear* should have been welcomed and celebrated by Ted.

The book is meant to be inspiring, not necessarily funny, though Stan and
Jan appear to have added some more outlandish ideas—the spread about being
circus performers comes to mind—to appease Ted. And Ted's request for conflict was never met (many of his own books from this era, such as *The Shape of
Me and Other Stuff* and *Great Day for Up!* were also devoid of conflict).

THE BEAR DETECTIVES (1975), B-60

Stan and Jan Berenstain

In the five years between this and their last Beginner Book (*The Bears'
Christmas*), Stan and Jan Berenstain had expanded their Bears' world by quite a
bit, introducing Sister Bear and some of the residents of Bear Country. They'd
experimented outside of their usual formula with the Bright and Early Books
and Picturebacks. *The Bear Detectives* finds them returning to familiar territory

with all of the changes in tow. In this case we find Papa Bear not so much instructing the Bear detectives (comprised of Brother, Sister, and two bespectacled friends) as competing with them to see who can solve the mystery of Farmer Ben's missing prize pumpkins first. To help he has his "old dog Snuff."

It's most akin to *The Bear Scouts*, with the kids following a guide book and Papa charging ahead brimming with confidence. The kids find all the clues, of course, while Papa falls into a pig pen, gets baled into hay, and wrestles with a scarecrow. In the end they discover that Mr. Ben's wife has turned the prize pumpkins into pies, and then the whole group tucks into a wonderful treat.

The story is written in the familiar four-line rhyme ("O.K., thief! / You've munched your last. / Your pumpkin-stealing / days are past.") and the illustrations are notable for the way they bridge the old style and the new. Stan and Jan's take on their Bears has rounded into final form but the kinetic composition and the heavy cross-hatched finishing are still in line with their early Beginner Books.

BECAUSE A LITTLE BUG WENT KA-CHOO! (1975), B-61

Rosetta Stone

This collaborative effort between Ted Geisel and Michael Frith was based on the proverb "For want of a nail" but also happened to be an effective demonstration of Edward Lorenz's butterfly effect, an aspect of chaos theory that posits a small change (like the flapping of a butterfly's wings in Mexico) in one place can have large consequences elsewhere (such as a hurricane in Texas). In *Because a Little Bug Went Ka-Choo!*, a bug's sneeze causes a seed to bonk a worm who gets so angry he kicks a tree, loosening a coconut that in turn knocks a turtle into the water. And on it goes until the story's conclusion, which features absolute mayhem on the streets of a city several miles away. Many of Ted's stories were centered on chaos theory, logical sequences of events that escalate wildly, but it had rarely been so explicitly laid out.

The progression of the text and the pictures compliment the chaos. For the first half of the book the text is written in prose, but once we meet Farmer Brown and his wife, it switches to verse. This has the effect of increasing the reader's pace and sense of urgency as events get more and more out of hand. Michael recalls, "Ted always said, 'When you write something, do it in verse— you'll sell twice as many copies.' I felt strongly that I wanted that book to have

Michael and Ted by the Geisel's pool in La Jolla, circa 1973. Michael made semi-regular trips to California to work out books such as *Because a Little Bug Went Ka-Choo*. Courtesy Michael Frith.

a build that started with simple rhythm—think Kipling and 'The Sing-Song of Old Man Kangaroo'—and built to rhyme for the climax. Happily, despite the above dictum, my co-writer agreed—it just kind of worked."

Likewise Michael's pictures start simple, with just one character at a time, and grow more and more complex, with the cast increasing exponentially page by page.

Style-wise, the illustrations look like they could have come directly from a Sunday comics page of the 1940s, clean, classic, and eye-catching. This would be Michael's final Beginner Book as an author and illustrator before leaving to work for Henson Associates, and one can almost see the bridging of his two worlds in the pictures. There are clear Seussian touches: The turtle who gets bopped looks like a cousin of Yertle the Turtle. The posing of the human characters have echoes of Ted's work (look at the waiter on the boat *Mary Lou*), as does the ink line, especially in the shading technique. At the same time, Michael's work designing for the Muppets and drawing Sesame Street books had clearly influenced his style. Like the chickens in *My Amazing Book of Autographs*, the one here might be Muppet Gonzo's beloved Camilla. The mouths of many of the characters—ovals in three-quarter and triangles in profile—look like Muppet mouths. And even the Little Bug with his bulbous orange nose seems like an ancestor of the Doozers from *Fraggle Rock*.

Because a Little Bug Went Ka-Choo! encapsulates everything that worked well between Ted and Michael. It's also—with just a handful of exceptions—the last Beginner Book to represent the classic style and construction. Because the authorship of the story was so collaborative, the duo decided to release it not as a LeSieg story, but instead under a joint pseudonym. Michael says, "I suggested 'Rosetta Stone'; the reference was relatively obscure then, so it seemed like both a pleasant little amusement and a nice nod, for those who got it, to the goals of Beginner Books, breaking down the mysteries of written language. Ted went for it immediately."

OH, THE THINKS YOU CAN THINK! (1975), B-62; THE CAT'S QUIZZER (1976), BIG BEGINNER BOOK

Dr. Seuss

Ted had a difficult time reconciling his roles as both instructor and entertainer. Despite evidence to the contrary, he told Digby Diehl in 1972 that he would never presume to teach reading, but that Beginner Books were only about generating excitement for reading. In reality, it was both, and in the final act of his career, starting with the mid- to late 1970s, he seemed to accept that his work was going to be looked at for the messages it gave to children (and their parents) about language and life.

As such, his stories in both Beginner Books and his big books began to reflect Ted's philosophies and accrued wisdom. One of his central concerns was certainly the fostering of imagination and creativity of thought, ideas that are exemplified in *Oh, the Thinks You Can Think!* and *The Cat's Quizzer*.

Of the two, the former is arguably more fun and light-hearted. It's a plotless tribute to absurdity and imagination, using the same creature-inventing formula as *There's a Wocket in My Pocket!* But instead of being based on an object or place, the creature names fit in with the verse ("Think of black water. / Think up a white sky. / Think up a boat. / Think of BLOOGS blowing by."). Each page focuses on a new idea (and setting and creature or set of them), and while the two-page spreads are not necessarily complex in the way of the architecture and machinery in *The Sleep Book*, they are very much akin to that book in their visual inventiveness. This is so much so that one might wonder if the pictures came before the words. Around this time Ted begun to struggle with his eyesight as a result of cataracts, but one can't see any effect of that in his artwork.

The Cat's Quizzer, meanwhile, also encourages critical thought and imagination. It's a collection of brain-stretching questions and activities: A maze, a seek and find (one hundred things that begin with "h"), challenges ("How long can you play Stare-Eyes without blinking?"), physics and logic puzzlers, and questions, questions, questions. The latter are of all sorts. There's real trivia ("What is Abraham Lincoln's middle name?"), common sense ("Are there a few ducks on the moon?"), and true or false ("There are more doughnut holes in the world than doughnuts."). All of the answers are provided in the back of the book (so you know, Abraham Lincoln didn't have a middle name, there are no ducks on the moon—or elephants either, and there are more doughnuts than doughnut holes if you could count jelly-filled).

Though the book's illustrations are done with high level of draftsmanship, Ted's eyesight troubles seem to have affected him more on *The Cat's Quizzer* than on *Thinks*. Though he drew the illustrations at larger-than-usual size to try to accommodate the shortcomings in his vision, it's still clear Ted's skills were compromised. The ink line is rougher, his typically careful and controlled renderings replaced with something more haphazard. Even the Cat looks off-brand on some pages, as though Ted couldn't quite get him right.

The Cat's Quizzer was the final Beginner Book to be released in the large format (in 1993 it would be issued as a standard-sized Beginner Book and be given the designation B-75), likely because it fits in well with *My Book about Me*, *I Can Draw!*, and *I Can Write!*. Why it wasn't created with the ability to write and draw in the book is up for speculation.

WOULD YOU RATHER BE A BULLFROG? (1975), BE-21

Theo LeSieg and Roy McKie

In theory the either/or questions in *Would You Rather Be a Bullfrog?* are the perfect conversation starters. But like most of Ted and Roy's work together, it has too much forward momentum for its readers to want to stop to chat.

Those who do slow down will have lots to talk about. Like, would you rather be a window or a door? A cactus, a toadstool, or a rose? The book's through line is its first inquiry: "Would you rather be a Dog . . . or be a Cat?" Whether you're a dog person or a cat person is one of those classic get-to-know-you questions, in addition to being one of the ways people define themselves. To have children start this process of outlining their own identity is worthwhile. And though in the end Ted says he still can't make up his mind about whether he'd like to be a dog or a cat, the fact that Roy drew the orange tabby with a large yellow bowtie—a trademark of both Ted and his most famous creation—would seem to indicate otherwise. Roy was an unabashed dog person.

Even if you don't feel like answering the questions, you can get joy out of the way Roy so perfectly visualizes Ted's questions, from the whale and the minnow to the bespectacled mermaid and giant ghost.

HOOPER HUMPERDINK? NOT HIM! (1976), BE-22

Theo LeSieg and Charles E. Martin

Likely because of his love of and sensitivity to the sounds of language, odd and unusual names tickled Ted's funny bone. His proclivity for pseudonyms is evidence enough of that, but as we've seen he also invented names for his imaginary children, names of fake law firms, names of fictional office mates at the Villard Manson, and more. It also shows up in his work over and over again, not just in his invented creatures with odd appellations, but in his animal (Thidwick, Horton) and human (Morris McGurk, Bartholomew Cubbins) characters as well.

Michael Frith says, "I once asked Ted how he came up with all those ridiculous names and he looked at me in surprise. 'They're all right there in my address book,' he said. Not that he knew a 'Bartholomew Cubbins,' but he did know a 'Bartholomew' and a 'Cubbins,' and he said, he just put them together."

So it's surprising that it took him until 1976 to do a whole book about names. *Hooper Humperdink? Not Him!* also doubles as a letter book, with the narrator alphabetically listing everyone he's planning to invite to his party. And it really is everyone, except for Hooper Humperdink. Why? "Somehow, I don't like that guy," the narrator tells us.

As poor Hooper gets passed over we hear about how Babe, Dinny, Elma (a nod to Elma Otto, no doubt), Hedda, Lum, Norton, Olivetta Oppenbeem, Ubb, and Yipper are all getting invites. There are plenty more common names, too, including Mike (Frith?), Bob (Bernstein?), and Ted himself. As this goes along we periodically see poor Hooper looking on forlornly. It would all feel a bit too mean if not for the ending, where the party host relents and invites Hooper in. His excitement and joy is palpable, but the joke might just be that Hooper is the only attendee and that the rest was all wishful thinking (a tiny table with just a few plates and party hats sits outside the door of the house).

Charlie was invited to the party, too, a nod to illustrator Charles E. Martin (1910–1995), who was most known for his work in the *New Yorker* (often signed "CEM"). Martin's career was quite similar to many of the other illustrators who came from the cartooning world to Beginner Books, but unlike Barney Tobey and George Booth, Charles had one other book under his belt before working with Ted. *The Big Orange Thing* was published by Bradbury Press in 1969. Its author was Jerry Juhl, who would make his name working with Jim Henson as a writer on *Sesame Street*, *The Muppet Show*, *Fraggle Rock*, and more.

Charles was born Charles Elmer Mastrangelo in Chelsea, Massachusetts, and grew up one of twelve children (eight survived to adulthood) in the Roxbury neighborhood of Boston. He loved to draw from a young age, but was also very athletic. A big guy, he dropped out during his first year of high school to work in a shoe factory and train as an amateur middleweight boxer, for a time serving in manager Johnny Buckley's prizefight stable. He also played semiprofessional football and hockey.

At age nineteen he started doing set design for the Little Theater in Boston, eventually deciding to try his hand doing set design in New York. He did some acting, too, but to make ends meet would do caricatures in restaurants and nightclubs, "Your likeness guaranteed in three minutes," he recalled. It was during this time he met his future wife, a painter named Florence Taylor (the two would marry in 1934, and have a son, Jared, in 1943).

Feeling that he was stuck in his bohemian theatrical life, Charles took a position as a painting teacher and program supervisor in the Works Progress Administration's Federal Art Project. This was ironic in that he himself was self-taught. He'd spend four years teaching for the WPA, while at the same— just as Ted once had—serving as a political cartoonist for the liberal newspaper *PM* (for his professional career, he'd decided to replace his last name with the more anglicized Martin). From there things snowballed. The *New Yorker* first published his work in the mid-1930s, and it was the start of a fifty-year association with the magazine in which he'd produce not only cartoons, but over two hundred cover images.

Charles's career went on hold during World War II, when he went to work for the Office of War Information as an art director for a mobile leaflet-dropping unit that operated in London, Italy, and France. When the war ended he picked back up on his freelance career, his work appearing in magazines such as *Esquire*, *Life*, *Playboy*, *Punch*, *Sports Illustrated*, and *Time*.

New Yorker art director Lee Lorenz said of Charles: "His most characteristic work was composed with an almost classical sense of balance and executed in a flat, decorative manner, using a muted, sometimes ethereal palette." His humor had a social conscience and awareness, but tended to be gentle, such as a 1960 *New Yorker* cover depicting a winding line of anthropomorphized elephants and donkeys waiting outside a voting booth.

His work in *Hooper Humperdink . . . ? Not Him!* shows off his drafting skills, a clean thin ink line and generous watercolor that fills the page. Though he'd never be a prolific author, he'd publish eight more books in his lifetime. Six of these he wrote himself over a five-year stretch in the 1980s, all based largely on his and Barbara's summer dwelling on Monhegan Island, which is just off the central coast of Maine. These included *Island Winter* (1983) and *For Rent* (1986).

Hooper Humperdink . . . ? Not Him! was only the second Beginner Book—after *Come Over to My House*—to include black characters. Up to this point, Beginner Books' human characters were overwhelmingly white. And this was despite increasingly louder voices calling for picture books to represent the racial diversity of the world (educator and author Nancy Larrick's 1965 *Saturday Review* article "The All-White World of Children's Books" was a particularly bracing call to arms), and despite children's entertainment beginning to answer those calls (*Sesame Street*'s multiracial cast and urban setting). But Ted held fast that Beginner Books would not show black children. In a 1972 interview with Digby Diehl, Ted said:

> We get pressures to integrate our books. But I think that would be another great mistake. Nobody is more sympathetic than I to the desires of the people who want integration, but I think that dropping a picture of a black boy into a book in which he does not logically belong is the wrong way to go about integration. And if you put a black child into a book that is done by a cartoonist—and all of our books are cartoons—you end up with a caricature of a black child. Then, of course, what you'll hear is people complaining, "You've caricatured him."

So the appearance of a black child in *Hooper Humperdink* was both a significant change in policy, and long overdue. Even the Dick and Jane primers Ted hated—once criticized by John Hersey as only depicting "happy middle-class family in ever-clean clothes, straight out of the ads in the magazines"—had introduced black siblings Pam, Penny, and Mike back in 1965. It's no surprise that Ted didn't recognize the harm—both to white children and children of color—in normalizing whiteness. His history of depicting race is a complicated one, as evident not only in the lack of diversity in Beginner Books, but also in the racist caricatures that he created in his *PM* cartoons and in some of his children's books (*If I Ran the Zoo*; *And to Think I Saw It on Mulberry Street*). Even in *Hooper Humperdink* the progress of including black characters is undercut by stereotypical depictions of Native Americans and Inuit people.

In a *Washington Post* interview about his 2017 book *Was the Cat in the Hat Black?: The Hidden Racism of Children's Literature and the Need for Diverse Books* (Oxford University Press), Dr. Philip Nel explained that the seeming paradox of Ted's work containing both racist imagery and antiracist messages (as in "The Sneetches" and *Come Over to My House*) was an example of the insidious and often invisible nature of white privilege. "Seuss is a reminder of how racism infects our minds in ways that we're not aware. He's a reminder that people who say 'I don't have a racist bone in my body' do not understand how racism actually works."

Hopper Humperdink . . . ? Not Him! was reissued in 2006 with new illustrations by Scott Nash.

PLEASE TRY TO REMEMBER THE FIRST OF OCTEMBER (1977), B-63

Theo LeSieg and Art Cumings

Please Try to Remember the First of Octember initially comes off as a lighthearted bit of nonsense designed to practice the names of the months. But it proves to be deeper than its absurdity lets on. In the story we're told in great detail about the first of Octember, a day when your heart's desires, no matter how wild and extravagant, will become a reality. The narrator details all the things you might have to look forward to when this fabulous month begins: "Just say what you want. / You want pickles on trees? / Want to swing through the air on a flying trapeze?"

The book tells of new inventions to be tested and new games to play on October 1, too. A "Jook-a-ma-Zoon" is a jukebox with real automated instruments. A "Jeep-a-Fly kite" looks like a golf cart with a kite connected to a spinner cable. And the "skateboard TV" is pretty much self-explanatory. What adds depth is the fact that many of the virtues of the first of Octember are very much real things both children and adults wish for each day. For example, we're told that there's no work and no school, and that we'll have more time to relax. And that money will rain from the sky.

Most children will read this as a joyful thing, and indeed that's how it's presented, as a celebration of untethered dreaming and hoping. Children and adults both get happiness out of looking forward, even if we know the reality of what's ahead is not likely to meet our imaginings. And while kids will real-ize that Octember is a made-up month, they might not realize the implica-tion. If Octember is not real, then the first of Octember is never going to arrive. That would mean Ted is telling us that our dreams are never going to come true, an unlikely lesson for an early reader.

More likely he's saying that our time spent pining for material things and excess would be better used elsewhere. This is similar to the moral of *How the Grinch Stole Christmas* ("'Maybe Christmas,' he thought, 'Doesn't come from a store.'"), especially since the first of Octember is like Christmas on steroids.

Octember first could be a metaphor for Christmas, but it could just as well be a metaphor for the afterlife and the paradise that many religions believe await the faithful. Had Ted been a religious man, this may have been the most convincing reading of the story.

The book's jaunty, heavily watercolored illustrations were done by Art Cumings (1922–2012), once described by a fellow cartoonist as "a quiet genius." Born and raised in Barre, Vermont, he was the third child and only son of Leon and Nora Cummings (Art appears to have dropped the second "m" in his professional career). Leon worked as a stonecutter, but passed away when Art was only eight years old. According to the 1940 census, Art took up stonecutting himself during high school. He graduated in 1940, and did some work as a draftsman in the auto industry before enrolling at the Pratt Institute in Brooklyn. There he met a fellow art student named Alda Pica. The two became an item.

In 1942 Art enlisted in the US Army, serving as an engineer in the China-Burma-India theater. Upon his discharge in early 1946, he and Alda mar-ried. They settled on Long Island, where Alda had grown up, and Art finished his degree at Pratt. Eventually Art began doing cartooning and illustration work for magazines, including *Sunday Pictorial Review*, *Motor*, *Collier's*, and *Saturday Evening Post*. In 1952 he parlayed his success into his first book, *Cartooning: New Easy Way of Drawing Cartoons That Sell*.

Alda and Art would have three boys, Brian, Peter, and Steven, and Art's career would continue to flourish. His first children's book appeared in 1965, Jean Bethell's *Silly Sidney*, about an elephant who wants to try out being other animals. It wasn't until 1970 that Art really began doing children's books in earnest, and from that point forward he'd do a dozen more books stretching into the early 1980s. He'd also do illustrations for a vocabulary-building cur-riculum called Words in Action.

The 1970s and 1980s would prove to be Art's most productive decades. Besides his book work, he also developed two ongoing magazine features. To

Penthouse he contributed "Balloonheads," one-panel gag cartoons featuring balloons in all sorts of suggestive shapes and positions. "The Artist," featuring musings on the creative process, appeared in *Omni*. From 1976 to 1977 Art did a daily syndicated strip called "Henny" based on the groaners and one-liners of comedian Henny Youngman.

A member of the distinguished Burndt Toast Gang—the Long Island branch of the National Cartoonists Society that has counted Mort Drucker, Jules Feiffer, and John Buscema among its membership—Art loved nothing more than discussing and dissecting his craft and the art of being a humorist.

I CAN READ WITH MY EYES SHUT! (1978), B-64; *OH SAY CAN YOU SAY?* (1979), B-65

Dr. Seuss

Two years passed between the publication of *The Cat's Quizzer* and *I Can Read with My Eyes Shut!*, the longest interval without a new Dr. Seuss book in over a decade. Much of that was due to Ted's declining eyesight. While working on the book he was in the middle of a "five-year series of cataract surgeries, lens implants, and treatments for glaucoma."

Thus, *I Can Read with My Eyes Shut!* is a celebration of one of the most powerful things we do with our eyes—and perhaps one of the things Ted missed most: Reading. And not just reading, but the knowledge it brings, and the way that knowledge empowers us. While rattling off all the things one can learn and do by reading ("You can read about trees . . . and bees . . . and knees. / And knees on trees! / And bees on knees!"), Ted uses the idea of closing one's eyes as a metaphor for willful ignorance. "There are so many things you can learn about, BUT . . ." the Cat in the Hat says to his young Cat, "you'll miss the best things if you keep your eyes shut."

As with *Oh, the Thinks You Can Think!* and *The Cat's Quizzer*, *I Can Read with My Eyes Shut!* is also a celebration of the power of a curious mind. In fact, the lines "The more that you read, / the more things you will know. / The more that you learn, / the more places you'll go," besides gracing many a school bulletin board, presage Ted's farewell book, *Oh, the Places You'll Go!* (1990).

The fact that Ted went ahead with the book despite diminished powers of illustration indicates how strongly he felt about his message. As with *The Cat's Quizzer*, the art is not quite to his usual standard. The ink lines are scratchy, and the compositions simplified. Lest one think Ted's perfectionism was waning, a 1978 profile in the *Christian Science Monitor* while the book was in production revealed that it was "being finished with scrupulous detail for the printer, with each color carefully labeled and numbered on every inch of page."

Ted's eyesight eventually improved, and he was extremely grateful to his ophthalmologist for getting everything sorted out. So grateful, in fact, that he dedicated *I Can Read with My Eyes Shut!* to him: "For David Worthen, E.G. (Eye Guy)."

Oh Say Can You Say?, in contrast to the wisdom-imparting of *I Can Read with My Eyes Shut!*, is a throwback to the 100 percent playful Dr. Seuss of old. This book of "terrible tongue twisters" is a spiritual sequel to *Fox in Socks*. And while nothing quite matches the virtuoso linguistics of the Beedle Beetle Battle sequence in that earlier book, there are quite a few fun moments. These include "How to tell a Klotz from a Glotz" ("So first you have to spot / who the one with the dots is. / Then it's easy to tell / who the Klotz or the Glotz is.") and "West Beast East Beast" ("Then I looked again from the west to the east / and I liked the beast on the east beach least."). The two books also share a through line. *Fox in Socks* had been dedicated in part to Audrey. This one was dedicated to Audrey's daughter Leagray, who apparently inherited her mother's facility with tongue twisters. In the dedication, Ted dubbed her "Lee Groo, the Enunciator."

Ted's eye surgeries and treatments seem to have had a positive effect on his art. Compared to *I Can Read with My Eyes Shut!*, the pages are more ambitious and detailed, and Ted shows much better control of his line. His ink work is still looser than it had been in the past, and one wonders if this was not an effect of eyesight. Perhaps it was hand control (Ted was pushing toward eighty, after all), or maybe he'd been inspired by the more liberated lines of artists he worked with in the mid-1970s such as George Booth and Quentin Blake. Ted had to relearn color after his cataract surgery, but he did so quickly. He ended up requesting the printers create a shade of green for the parrot in the book when the precise one he wanted wasn't on their chart.

THE BERENSTAIN BEARS AND THE SPOOKY OLD TREE (1978), BE-23

Stan and Jan Berenstain

The Berenstain Bears and the Spooky Old Tree takes the same prepositional ideas explored in *Inside Outside Upside Down* and *Bears in the Night* and incorporates them into something with atmosphere, thrills, and drama.

The story concerns three bears (Brother, Sister, and a nameless younger friend) as they set out on an expedition that leads them to the spooky old tree of the title. Once they go inside they end up on a hair-raising adventure that uses a lot of the tropes of classic horror movies: spiderwebs, twisted staircases, hidden passages, haunted suits of armor, and a slumbering beast.

Though the book is two hundred words in total, the number of unique words is much lower because there are two different repeating choruses that trade off to tell the story. The first instance reads like this:

> Three little bears.
> One with a light. One with a stick. One with a rope.
> A spooky old tree.
> Do they dare go into that spooky old tree?
> Yes. They dare.

As the story's events progress the pictures show what happens and the words tell the after-effects, following the pattern above but changing pertinent details. After the smallest bear loses his rope to a crocodile, the story reads:

> Three little bears.
> One with a light. One with a stick. And one with the shivers.
> A giant key.
> A moving wall.
> Will the three little bears go through that wall?
> Do they dare go into that spooky old hall?
> Yes. They dare.

This repetition provides a predictable structure, but the reader has to use the picture and perhaps even look at the words to keep moving forward, which is exactly what an early reader should learn to do. The repeated questions also encourage pre-readers to be active participants. Before the book's climactic moment, when the cubs must choose whether or not to walk over Great Sleeping Bear, there's even a summary of what has happened so far. Taken in whole it's a story that reads very simply, but has complicated structure and mechanics underneath.

The illustrations are also a revelation. Instead of flat color and cross-hatched pen and ink, the pictures are done with watercolor, with black ink outlines defining the characters and other key elements on each page. The result is a lush, moody look that suits the story perfectly. From the ill-boding fog as the bears approach the tree, to the way the yellow light from Brother Bear's flashlight plays on his face, to the texture of the tree Stan and Jan's classical art training is in full evidence.

This style suited the book, but it was also the result of a change in the printing process Random House employed. In the mid-1970s technology had advanced enough that it was cheaper to print in full color than it was using the old color separation process. Artists were now required to do one black line sheet and one color sheet, which allowed for the visual complexity of *The Berenstain Bears and the Spooky Old Tree* (just a couple years later things would advance enough that the entire illustration could be done on just one sheet).

As a testament to *Spooky Old Tree*'s enduring popularity and appeal, the story his lived on in other formats. In 1989 it was made into a board game, and in 2005 it became a video game for the Nintendo Game Boy Advance.

THE HAIR BOOK (1979), BE-24

Graham Tether and Roy McKie

The Hair Book celebrates our follicles with a bouncy verse that covers location, style, color, and shape in just twenty-six pages. It also imagines briefly what might happen if you let your hair grow: "You could make a ladder with your hair . . . or be the maypole at the fair. And if you grew a long goatee . . . you could use your hair to water-ski!"

The first "body" Bright and Early Book since 1970's *The Nose Book* featured a veteran artist (Roy McKie) paired with a Beginner Book beginner. Graham Tether (born 1950) is a pseudonym for Cynthia (Cindy) Graham Tether. She has the distinction of being the first Beginner Book author from outside of Ted's inner circle since Laurent de Brunhoff in 1967, as well as the first female author not named Jan Berenstain since 1965. She was also the youngest Beginner Book author to date, young enough to have actually read Beginner Books as a child.

Cindy grew up in Bronxville, New York, the second child of Willard and Doris Tether. When she was young she loved animals, reading, and music, all interests she carried with her into adulthood. She graduated from Mount Holyoke College in 1972 with her teaching certificate. While doing graduate work at New York University, she began writing stories and poems for children's magazines such as *My Weekly Reader* and *Golden*, and got a job as an editorial assistant at Harper & Row. Her first published book, *Fudge Dream*

Supreme, was released in 1975 with illustrations by Carl Kock. *The Hair Book* was actually her second publication of 1979. Earlier that year, Houghton-Mifflin put out *Skunk and Possum*, featuring pictures by Lucinda McQueen.

But a career in children's books wasn't in the cards. Cindy left Harper in 1978 and enrolled in the MBA program at Columbia University. She graduated in 1980 and got a job as a financial analyst at IBM. Her next children's book—*The Knee Book*—wouldn't appear until 2005.

The 1980s

THE BERENSTAIN BEARS AND
THE MISSING DINOSAUR BONE (1980), B-66

Stan and Jan Berenstain

The Berenstain Bears and the Missing Dinosaur Bone combines elements of *The Bear Detectives* and *The Spooky Old Tree*. As in the former book there's a mystery to solve—in this case a stolen T-Rex femur at the Bear Museum—and Papa Bear's dog Snuff is along for the ride. But the detectives themselves are the same team of three (Brother, Sister, and an unnamed younger bear) that braved the spooky old tree. The lush watercolor art style is also akin to the second book.

One major difference is the (almost) complete absence of Papa Bear (you might spot him in the line waiting to get into the museum). The Berenstain Bright and Early Books had explored other nooks and crannies of Bear Country, but none of their Beginner Books before this one had strayed from the Papa-Bear-slapstick formula.

And more than the other Berenstain Beginner Books, the *Missing Dinosaur Bone* shows just how much the line had relaxed its vocabulary limitations. Words like "wonder," "valuable," "famous," and "wrong" are all difficult for a beginning reader to decode, and none of them are illustratable. Even so, Stan and Jan's verse is as jaunty as ever: "It's getting late / but still they look. / And still no bone, / And still no crook." And the ending is very satisfying, with a solution that was in front of their faces all along—turns out it was Snuff who took the bone and buried it!

MAYBE YOU SHOULD FLY A JET!
MAYBE YOU SHOULD BE A VET! (1980), B-67

Theo LeSieg and Michael J. Smollin

Maybe You Should Fly a Jet! is a dizzying survey of occupations for children to consider. Much like the Bright and Early Book *Would You Rather Be a Bullfrog?*, the narrative centers around the reader making a choice, and has the potential for both conversation and self-discovery. "What do you want to be when you grow up?" is a question children face from many a well-meaning adult, and they typically stick to the expected script with their answer: teacher, firefighter, police officer, doctor.

All of those options are here, but Ted provides quite a few more for kids to think about, and he draws from all categories of jobs: professional, trades, blue collar, service. And he includes both the very common (dentist, tailor, plumber, barista) and the very unusual (diamond miner, jester, lion tamer, spy). Both men and women are pictured doing these varied occupations. Besides the way it opens up a child's future, perhaps the most impressive thing about the book is the way Ted makes it all rhyme: "Tennis pro . . . / Optometrist / Hockey pro . . . / Podiatrist / Chemist / Lepidopterist" goes one 2-page spread.

Every occupation gets a picture, which means sometimes there are four or five illustrations per page, a far cry from the two-page spreads that were the standard in Beginner Books for so long. Illustrator Michael J. Smollin (1925–2010) had made his name doing pictures for Sesame Street books, including the 1971 best-selling classic *The Monster at the End of This Book*, written by Jon Stone. Michael grew up in East Hampton, on Long Island. During high school he was in the marching band and worked doing set design for the theater department. He attended Cornell, but his education was interrupted by World War II. Michael joined the army, taking shrapnel in the Battle of the Bulge.

After his recovery, he attended the Pratt Institute on the G.I. Bill, completing a three-year course in advertising design. At Pratt he met fellow student Cornelia Mueller, and the two became a couple, marrying in 1950. Michael's career in advertising started at Hazard Advertising and would eventually wind through several agencies and work for many prominent accounts such as Ford, Mercedes, IBM, and Gillette. He worked in both print and in animation, and eventually rose to the executive level.

But he missed the act of drawing and creating, and made the decision to go freelance. After some lean times, he found an agent and began landing work in the likes of *TV Guide* and *Time*, and doing design work for Milton Bradley. He started illustrating books. In addition to his popular work for Sesame Street, he'd do joke books for *The Electric Company*, and licensed Strawberry Shortcake and Lego titles, adding up to sixty-two total books. He did animation design as well, winning an Emmy for his work on the trippy syndicated kids' show *The Great Space Coaster* (1981–1986).

Michael and Cornelia settled in Westport, Connecticut, in 1953 (if you've been following, this means Westport was a regular Beginner Book creator colony—Ward Brackett, P. D. Eastman, Leonard Shortall, the Gurneys, Rowland Wilson also lived there), and had four children: Mark, Elizabeth, Steven, and Jennifer. When he died in 2010, Michael's obituary said he was "a devoted father, a generous and charismatic soul, avid reader, ruthless card player, great gardener, antique collector, interior decorator, practical jokester and gourmet cook."

In 2020, the book was reissued with new illustrations by California-based artist Kelly Kennedy.

THE TOOTH BOOK (1981), BE-25

Theo LeSieg and Roy McKie

Ted and Roy's final book together—their ninth collaboration—arrived exactly twenty years after their first. It was a milestone in multiple ways. It was the last book credited to Theo LeSieg, and it was Roy's last original work for Beginner Books (in the early 1990s he was called on to do new pictures for *A Big Ball of String*). And while *The Tooth Book* doesn't quite live up to *Ten Apples Up on Top!*, it's still a fun example of the chemistry of the two creators.

The book is a surprisingly thorough survey of its subject. It covers where you might find teeth ("All Ruths are toothy"), what they're good for, toothless creatures such as snails and chickens, and what not to do with your chompers. The book ends with praise for dentists, something that would prove to be prescient when Ted's own dentist discovered a lesion on his tongue, catching his oral cancer early.

Ted completely disregards the idea of controlled vocabulary, using words such as "huckleberry," "worthwhile," and "broadcaster," and names like Quincy Quack and Donald Driscoll Drew. He was basically un-editable at this point. Janet Schulman once recalled asking Ted to remove the reference to Spam from the book, feeling it was too dated. He told her he'd work on something else, but a few days later told her that was the only word that fit. "I knew you were going to say that," she replied.

Roy's figures and animals are more exaggerated even than usual, with his seemingly effortless line perhaps a bit too effortless in places (character's hands often look more like rooster wattles than actual functioning fingers). The colors are rich almost to the point of garishness. But his expressive way of filling a page is still on full display.

WINGS ON THINGS (1982), BE-26; *SPOOKY RIDDLES* (1983), B-69

Marc Brown

Marc Brown (born 1946) is currently one of the most recognized names in children's literature, with a prolific forty-plus-year career and a long-running PBS show based on his character Arthur. But when he first met with Janet Schulman circa 1980 to discuss publishing his work at Random House, he was a fresh-faced newcomer. He'd completed the first two books in the Arthur series that would eventually make him famous, but that didn't spare him from Janet's characteristic frankness. After the meeting, he recalls, "I felt like roadkill."

But after a few more meetings and a few more rejections, Janet zeroed in on the idea that would become *Wings on Things*. "The Wing Book" in all but name, the idea came to Marc from his son Tolon (who was about ten years old at the time, and whose name shows up on the spine of a book on the "Wings on chairs / Never on bears." page), and was inspired—as his bio in the back of the book indicates humorously—by his own childhood desire to fly. With Ted and Janet as his editors he completed what he calls "my graduate course in making picture books."

Unlike the two Bright and Early Books that sandwiched it (*The Tooth Book* and *The Berenstain Bears on the Moon*), *Wings on Things* adheres closely to the philosophy of limited vocabulary and a low word count; all of the tough words are illustrated. The rounded, cartoony pictures—in a style indebted to Tomie dePaola and Maurice Sendak—are given depth and richness by a mixture of watercolor and colored pencil.

Marc's second work for the publisher, *Spooky Riddles*, was Beginner Books' first collection of jokes since 1964's *Animal Riddles*. One has to assume Bennett Cerf himself would have approved of the Halloween-themed puns (Q: "What do bats need after a shower?" A: "A bat mat."), wordplay (Q: "Why don't skeletons go to scary movies?" A: "They don't have the guts."), and groaners (Q: "What time is it when a ghost comes to dinner?" A: "Time to go."). Like the jokes themselves, the illustrations are a kid-friendly level of macabre. The ghosts smile happily and the witches are lumpy and friendly. Marc credited his son Tucker for the idea for the book (his name appears at the bottom of the sidewalk sign for the Vampire Pig movie the skeleton is too scared to see), and also claims to have collected many of the jokes while traveling to elementary schools around the country.

Born in 1946 in Erie, Pennsylvania, and raised in Mill Creek, Pennsylvania, Marc has described his childhood as "modest" and "no frills." His grandma Thora was a storyteller who encouraged her grandson's love of drawing. In high school he began painting too, taking up watercolors under the guidance of his art teacher. He attended the Cleveland Institute of Art, majoring in painting. While still at school he began working as an art director at WICU-TV in Erie. He married dancer and teacher Stephanie Mariani in 1968 and graduated the following year. The young couple moved to Boston, and Marc took a job as an assistant professor of art at Garland Junior College.

But he had in mind to become an illustrator, and upon presenting samples to Houghton-Mifflin began getting work doing pictures for textbooks. It was steady work, but it wasn't creatively fulfilling. Marc began branching out into book illustration in the early 1970s, doing about ten books for other authors before trying to write his own. That book, *Arthur's Nose*, began life as a bedtime story for Tolon, and was shepherded into published form by Little, Brown editor Emilie McLeod, who encouraged Marc to put the tale to paper. "I learned so much from her," Marc recalled, "about balancing the elements of words and pictures and using the words to do what pictures can't do, and vice versa."

From there Marc would produce a steady stream of books about Arthur and his family, leading to the 1996 debut of the PBS show. Marc and Stephanie divorced in 1977 (he turned the experience into a book, *Dinosaurs Divorce: A Guide for Changing Families*), and in 1983 he married psychologist Laurie Krasny. The couple would do several books together, and have a daughter, Eliza. Marc now lives in a house on Martha's Vineyard that was built in 1735, and does his work in a converted sheep barn.

WHAT DO SMURFS DO ALL DAY? (1983), B-70

Peyo

What Do Smurfs Do All Day? presents a day in the life of the tiny blue creatures that took America by storm in the early 1980s, detailing all the Smurfy ways they work and play.

The Smurfs were created in 1958 by Belgian cartoonist Pierre Culliford (1928–1992), who used the pen name Peyo. They spun off into their own series of comic adventures in 1963, gaining enough popularity to appear in a feature film, *La Flute a Six Schtroumpfs* in 1976. While traveling in Belgium, entrepreneur Stuart R. Ross became aware of the Smurfs, acquired North American rights, and began producing dolls and figurines in the United States. As it happened, the head of NBC, Fred Silverman, bought his daughter one of those very dolls. Seeing her delight with it gave him an inkling that the characters might make a good Saturday morning cartoon. So in 1981, *The Smurfs*, produced by Hanna-Barbera, debuted. It was an instant hit.

Depending on how you classify the Doctor Dolittle and Chitty Chitty Bang Bang books, this is really the first licensed property to be featured in a Beginner Book. Certainly it was the first one to cash in on the popularity of a television show, though Random House had been in the Smurf business since they first came to the United States, publishing four *Smurf Adventures* comics between 1977 and 1980, and an eight book-series of mini storybooks in 1981. Many of these were translations of the Belgian comic album stories from the 1960s and 1970s.

A Beginner Book was a natural step, though unlike Random House's previous Smurfs books, *What Do Smurfs Do All Day?* appears to be original material. The question is who actually created it. The book is credited to Peyo, but Pierre by this point was consumed with the business side of his empire and with approving scripts for the cartoon with his writing partner Yvan Delporte. He rarely did cartooning himself anymore, deferring instead to Studio Peyo, comprised of assistants who produced Smurf material under his name. As for the text of the book, it's unlikely that originated with Peyo or his studio, given that their work was produced in their native French (English translations were often done by the team of Anthea Bell and Derek Hockridge, but rhyming verse does not translate without rewriting). What seems most likely is that someone on staff at Random House wrote the verse, and the studio produced the pictures to match.

A French-language version of the book—*Que Font Les Schtroumpfs Toute La Journee*—was released by Peyo's Belgian publisher Dupuis in 1984. The text of the book made an appearance in the 2013 film *The Smurfs 2*, read as a poem.

IT'S NOT EASY BEING A BUNNY (1983), B-68;
THE VERY BAD BUNNY (1984), B-71

Marilyn Sadler and Roger Bollen

At the start of *It's Not Easy Being a Bunny*, P. J. Funnybunny is fed up with being a rabbit. He's sick of carrots and his big ears and having so many brothers and sisters. So he goes off on a journey of discovery in which he tries out what it's like to be a bear, a beaver, a possum, and several other animals.

As an early reader, the book does a lot of things right. There's a predictable pattern to P. J.'s explorations ("I don't want to be a . . . I want to be a . . .") and the text is also progressive, so the list of animals P. J. doesn't want to be grows by one after each episode. The pictures illustrate the words but also embellish them, such as when P. J. tries to be a bird. "P. J. liked being a bird—until he tried to fly," the text tells us, while the picture shows him falling from a branch, furiously waving his arms.

In the end P. J. discovers that being a bunny isn't really all that bad. In its construction and moral the story is similar to *I Wish That I Had Duck Feet*, with the main character trying on different identities until realizing they should just be themselves. But *It's Not Easy Being a Bunny* has the added layer of P. J. having to go away from home to realize how lucky he truly is.

The first sequel, *The Very Bad Bunny*, also centers on a perspective-changing event, but in this case the change comes in how P. J.'s family views him. As it turns out, P. J. causes trouble from time to time, largely out of thoughtlessness (using his dad's newspaper to make paper dolls) and clumsiness (spilling the syrup). His family is hard on him until the arrival of cousin Binky, an impulsive, destructive, and mean-spirited little rabbit who does things like glue all the checkers together, put bubble gum on chairs, and lock everyone out of the house. When Binky finally leaves, P. J. says: "Now THAT was a very bad bunny" and his family agrees wholeheartedly.

There's no repetition or rhyming to guide the reader in this second book, so its readability is mostly due to the short sentences and the close connection to the illustrations. Despite a few tricky words such as "finally" and "believe" it hews very close to the spirit and philosophy of the original Beginner Books.

Into the fine tradition of married Beginner Book creators stepped wife and husband Marilyn Sadler (born 1950) and Roger Bollen (1941–2015). Roger was born in Cleveland, Ohio. "I was one of those kids who couldn't leave a pencil alone," he recalled in a 1977 interview. "I think I was constantly doodling." He attended nearby Kent State University, earning a bachelor's of fine arts in 1963. After graduation, he did design and advertising work in Akron for three years,

Roger Bollen in 1981, as photographed by Marilyn Sadler. Courtesy
Melissa Bollen Ellsworth.

developing a clean, classic style inspired by Walt Kelly (*Pogo*) and Johnny Hart
(*B.C.*). But his real ambition was to do a comic strip, and he got his wish in spades.

In 1966 Roger landed his first syndicated comic strip, *Funny Business*.
He'd submitted a different idea, a strip called *Ripple Falls*, to the Newspapers
Enterprise Associates syndicate, but they rejected it and instead asked Roger to
try out for a one-panel comic for the business page. They already had the title,
they just needed the cartoonist. Roger got the gig, and within a year he'd landed
a second strip, *Animal Crackers*, focusing on a group of jungle creatures. That
same year, he and wife Georgianna welcomed a daughter, Melissa.

Courtesy Marilyn Sadler.

In 1973, along with Gary Peterman, Roger started up the western-themed *Catfish*, meaning he had three simultaneously running daily comics when most cartoonists find it difficult to keep up with just one. He pulled this triple-duty for five years until *Funny Business* wrapped up in 1980.

Marilyn June Sadler was born in Pittsburgh but grew up about one hundred twenty miles west in Coshocton, Ohio. She majored in fine arts at Ohio State University with a goal of becoming an illustrator, graduating in 1972. For three years she worked as a registrar at the Cleveland Institute of Art while at the same time attending classes at Case Western Reserve University to earn a degree in special education. She would end up teaching only one year before her life and career took a different turn.

Upon meeting, Marilyn and Roger not only began a romantic relationship (they'd marry on New Year's Eve, 1979), but a creative partnership as well. Their first project, as odd as it sounds, was an annual report for the children of stockholders at Figgie International, released under the Seussian title *Ump's*

Fwat. With Marilyn dreaming up with the stories and Roger doing the illustrations, they started developing ideas for children's books. Their first book, *Alistair's Elephant*, was published by Simon and Schuster in 1983. Almost simultaneously, *It's Not Easy Being a Bunny* landed at Beginner Books, and the team of Marilyn and Roger was off and hopping. In all, they would produce over fifty books over the course of the next twenty-five years.

As one might expect, their stories always originated from the funny bone. Marilyn commented, "I am attracted to the silliest things in life and feel most comfortable when I tell my stories from a humorous point of view." She also drew from her own experience. "I take bits and pieces from my childhood memories, mix them all together, then pull out different combinations of experiences in order to piece together new story ideas," she wrote on her blog. "It's a bit like pulling a rabbit out of a hat." And in the case of P. J. Funnybunny, literally.

THE BERENSTAIN BEARS ON THE MOON (1985), BE-27

Stan and Jan Berenstain

The Berenstain Bears on the Moon is an odd book in a few ways. For one, its timing seems off, as the last manned moon mission by the United States had occurred thirteen years earlier in 1972. Space travel was relevant again with the *Challenger* orbiting missions launching in 1983, but they weren't moon landings. Also, the Bears' universe is a malleable place, but it nearly always operates within the realm of reason. A story in which Brother Bear, Sister Bear, and Snuff go on a moon mission that takes off from their own front yard pretty clearly violates that.

The verse in *The Berenstain Bears on the Moon* is written more like a Beginner Book than a Bright and Early. Though the distinctions between the two had blurred considerably in the 1980s, the difference between this and other Berenstain Bright and Early Books such as *Inside Outside Upside Down* and *The Spooky Old Tree* is stark. Those books had low word counts, with sometimes just a word or two per page. *On the Moon* features two sentences per page, and no vocabulary limitations, with terms like "meteor shower" and "moonmobile."

By the release of this book, Stan and Jan had become superstars of children's literature with the First Time books selling millions and their Bears pervading popular culture. It's no surprise, then, that *The Berenstain Bears on the Moon* would be their last Beginner Book work for a dozen years.

I WANT TO BE SOMEBODY NEW! (1986), B-72

Robert Lopshire

In 1986 Robert Lopshire returned to Beginner Books after a twenty-two-year hiatus, though he hadn't intended to be gone so long. After 1964's *How to Make Flibbers, Etc.* Bob was contracted to illustrate Benjamin Elkin's *Magic Tricks and Foolers*. This intriguing pairing of two Beginner Book veterans was to be centered on the "Abba Dabba Magic Club" consisting of a rabbit and three other animals. These characters would present the tricks, with an antagonist monkey pulling the "foolers." But the book was never released.

Elkin completed the script, but Bob struggled to bring it to life. In an October 1965 letter to Bob Bernstein he says he was only able to get fourteen pages worth of material out of what Elkin had given him. By December Bob was speaking of the book in the past tense, writing cryptically to Anne Johnson, "I've been wondering when word would drift through from old Random House about the giant Elkin fiasco or 'Magic, Magic, Who has the Magic?'" He followed with a mention of "legal suits" that are holding him up from the "process of money-making." In his own letters about the book, Elkin took issue with the royalty rate, especially as it pertained to the Grolier Book Club. He had signed the contract, but declared that it would be his final Beginner Book. All this would seem to indicate that either Random House or Elkin sued to break his contract, leaving the project in limbo.

In the meantime, Bob had illustrated Kin Platt's *Big Max*, published by Harper & Row as an I Can Read! book in 1965. He'd do two more I Can Read! books, writing and drawing *I Am Better Than You* (1968) and illustrating Betty Baker's tale of the American Revolution, *The Pig War* (1969). Also in 1969 he put out *It's Magic*, which featured instructions on how to do fourteen different tricks. It hardly seems a coincidence that this followed so close after the failed Elkin book (a sequel, *The Crazy Paper and Other Magic*, appeared in 1977).

The mid-1960s would prove a time of change for Bob. He and Jane divorced, and he returned to Sarasota to live. There he met and married Ina Schutten. He continued to work steadily, providing pictures for another Big Max book (*Big Max and the Mystery of the Missing Moose*, 1977) and two Big Bear books for Richard Margolis (in 1972 and 1977). He also did a handful of instructional books (*A Beginner's Guide to Building and Flying Model Airplanes*, 1967; *Radio Control Miniature Aircraft*, 1972; *How to Make Snop Snappers and Other Fine Things*, 1977).

In the two decades that had passed since its publication, *Put Me in the Zoo* had achieved the status of a classic for at least two generations of young readers. Bob went into semiretirement in the early 1980s, but the lure of being a Beginner Book author again coaxed him back to Spot, Dick, and Jane. He'd stayed friendly with Ted through the years, even despite decamping for I Can Read!.

The new story picks up not all that long after the first book, with Spot feeling restless and deciding to give up his "spot tricks" in favor of becoming something new. He here displays a previously unknown ability to transform, morphing into an elephant, a giraffe, and a mouse (though he remains yellow with red spots no matter his shape). For each animal he tries, the children explain all the drawbacks to his new form. As an elephant, he can't walk on a fence; as a giraffe, he has birds flying into his head; and as a mouse, he has to watch out for cats. They summarize, "We did not like you fat or tall, and now you know what's wrong with small!" And so Spot decides it feels best to be himself.

Ted despised overt lessons in his books, but Bob felt differently, telling *Contemporary Authors*, "In that I am still old-fashioned enough to believe that every story must have a moral, this is a point always welded in." The moral in *I Want to be Somebody New!* was unavoidable: appreciate yourself for what you are. But the way this lesson is put across had unintended consequences. *School Library Journal* took issue with Spot's revelation coming only after he discovers the setbacks of being fat, tall, or small: "Those children who see themselves in the above descriptions," reviewer Tom S. Hurlburt wrote, "might actually be getting the reverse message from what the story is trying to convey." One assumes, given his deep caring for his audience, that Bob didn't intend to write a book that might shame young readers, though his word and story choices made his message easy to misinterpret.

Consider an earlier Beginner with the same moral, *I Wish I Had Duck Feet*. Like *I Want to Be Somebody New!*, the story follows a main character as he tries out different identities and realizes he likes himself just the way he is. But the earlier book disguises its main idea in the absurdity and difficulty of a boy having a trunk, antlers, or a tail, and his revelation comes from within, not from the judgments of others. The same could be said of *It's Not Easy Being a Bunny*.

Not everyone noticed or cared about the book's questionable lesson. *Publishers Weekly* called *I Want to Be Somebody New!* an "intelligent, cheerful sequel" and the book was chosen for the International Reading Association's Booklist of 1987.

THE BLACK STALLION (1987), B-73

Walter Farley and Sandy Rabinowitz

Just as Robert Lopshire made a return to Beginner Books in the 1980s after a long absence, so did Walter Farley. In Walter's case, it had been twenty-four years since the publication of *Little Black Goes to the Circus!*. He returned to adapt his first and best-known work into an easy-to-read book, but how and why exactly this happened is up for speculation. There had been a film version of the book that reignited interest in the Black Stallion series, but that was in 1979. At that time, Random House released a picture book version of the story using stills from the movie.

The Beginner Book version adapts the first part of the novel, leading up to Alex bringing the Black home after they're rescued from the desert island. Though not vocabulary controlled, it's told in simple, declarative sentences that are bolstered by dynamic watercolor illustrations.

Illustrator Sandy Rabinowitz (born 1954) was born into a family of artists in New Haven, Connecticut. When she was nine years old, she won a pony in a contest. Sponsored by a drive-in theater, the entrants had to complete the statement, "I should win this pony because." Sandy wrote, "I love, love, love, love, love, love, love, love, love, love, love horses and have a grassy pasture and big family to help care for him." She added a picture of herself and her siblings taking care of the pony.

Sandy attended both Cooper Union and Parsons School of Design in New York City where she studied art. Her first book—*The Red Horse and the Bluebird*—was published by Harper & Row while she was still in school. Three more books followed over the next six years, all based on Sandy's experiences raising and training horses. In the early 1980s she became serious about competition and won several championships with her horse Sunny.

Sandy began illustrating for horse magazines around this same time, and starting in 1985 she began periodically illustrating books for other authors, both children's books and manuals on dressage. She works steadily, but doesn't consider herself an author or illustrator. "I am a fulltime horsewoman," she told *Contemporary Authors Online*. "I illustrate and write children's books in order to buy hay and grain."

Walter Farley died of a heart attack in 1989, before he could see the publication of *The Young Black Stallion*, which was written with his son Steven, the very same son he had credited for helping write *Little Black, A Pony*. By the time of his death, his books had sold over 12 million copies. Through the years, Walter visited countless schools, and his message was usually a variation on the same theme: "The main thing I want to do is to encourage young children to fantasize, to dream and to put their dreams to paper."

I AM NOT GOING TO GET UP TODAY! (1987), B-74

Dr. Seuss and James Stevenson

Ted's first Beginner Book, *The Cat in the Hat,* was about being stuck inside. His last one, thirty years later, was about choosing to stay inside. In the mid-1980s Ted's health was precarious. While working on what would turn out to be his final Beginner Book, Ted was fighting both cancer and gout, and was pretty much exhausted all the time.

So the premise—a boy who just can't bring himself to get out of bed—came from personal experience. But instead of making it something sad and resigned, Ted turns the refusal into a liberating act of defiance. "I don't choose to be up walking. / I don't choose to be up talking," the boy tells us confidently. "The only thing I'm choosing / is to lie here woozy snoozing."

Ted's vocabulary choices in *I Am Not Going to Get Up Today!* also show a stark contrast to *The Cat in the Hat.* On the latter he had twisted himself into fits using only his 223 preapproved words, but thirty years later he gave himself no limitations. There's a whole segment full of place names likely to stump early readers (e.g., Massachussetts, Connecticut, London), and a sentence like "I guess he really means it" would also be a big challenge, with all of those double-vowel digraphs. Clearly Ted was doing exactly what he pleased at this point.

Because of his physical state, Ted couldn't do the illustrations. Instead he called on yet another *New Yorker* cartoonist, James Stevenson (1929–2017). Unlike George Booth, Barney Tobey, and Charles Martin, James was a writer first, publishing three novels between 1962 and 1967. At the *New Yorker* he was just as likely to contribute features or short pieces for the "Talk of the Town" section as he was cartoons. Sometimes he even fed other artists ideas. He was also well established in children's literature, having published over fifty books for kids by 1987.

James grew up in Croton-on-Hudson, a village in Westchester County, New York, and credited his elementary education with giving him the confidence to follow a creative path. His school, Hessian Hills, had a child-centered philosophy that landed it in a documentary about progressive education that was shown at the 1939 World's Fair. James recalled to *Publishers Weekly* that the school empowered its students. "Everybody could sing, dance, act, play musical instruments, write stories, make pictures and change the world."

From a young age he wrote and drew, encouraged by his artist father and fueled by the movies and comic books that captivated him. James attended Yale and majored in English. He began selling cartoon ideas to the *New Yorker* when he was still in school, but didn't head to work there right away. After graduating in 1951 he enlisted in the US Marine Corps, and then after two years of service he worked for *Life* magazine as a reporter for another two years. In 1956 he got a staff position at the *New Yorker*, and would eventually produce 1,988 cartoons and 79 covers for the magazine in addition to his writing contributions. Art director Lee Lorenz wrote, "A colleague at *The New Yorker* once suggested that, with the possible exception of poetry, James Stevenson could have produced the magazine single-handedly."

James's early cartoons and writings were heavy on social and political commentary, but as he and his wife, Jane (they'd married in 1953), began a family that would eventually grow nine children large, James found his attentions turning toward the interests of young people. His first children's book came when he said to his then-eight-year-old son, James: "Tell me a story and we'll make a book." The younger James obliged, and the older James took it down and then added pictures. *If I Owned a Candy Factory* came out from Little, Brown in 1968. In all, James would publish over 150 books for children in his career, sometimes several in one year. His books are split equally between ones he wrote himself and ones he drew for others. The latter included three books about a homeless man called Jack the Bum in 1977 and 1978 written by none other than Janet Schulman.

And that's how James ended up doing *I Am Not Going to Get Up Today!* He was a great fit, with his light-hearted style keeping the text from seeming too strident or serious. Like Quentin Blake, James had a knack for pictures that look as though they were thought up on the spot (though they're much too well composed to be), and he is unafraid of the occasional stray or jagged line. He often finished his pictures off with a carefully sloppy application of watercolor.

The book was released under the Dr. Seuss name instead of Theo LeSieg. This is likely—as was the case with *My Book about Me* and *Great Day for Up!*—an indication of how proud Ted was of the final result.

The 1990s

SNUG HOUSE, BUG HOUSE! (1994), BE-28;
SNOW BUGS (1996), BE-29

Susan Schade and Jon Buller

Snug House, Bug House! had the distinction of being the first original Beginner / Bright and Early Book in seven years, but it wasn't Susan Schade and Jon Buller's first book with the Cat on the cover. Their Step Into Reading books *Toad on the Road* and *Railroad Toad* were issued in Beginner Book format for the Grolier Book Club in the early 1990s.

Snug House, Bug House! follows six insects as they design, build, and settle into a new home. The first two-thirds of the book follows the construction process, while the final part provides a tour of the bugs' individual and communal rooms. The story is ingenious in a couple of ways.

One is in its balance of text and pictures. The text is written exclusively in two-word labels that follow a pattern. As the bugs build their house, the sentences consist of a verb and noun ("Cut it / Nail it"). When they show off the rooms the labels are a possessive noun and "room" ("Ann's room / Fran's room"). And the communal rooms are presented using an adjective and "room" ("Crazy room / Lazy room"). Though the text is certainly complementary to the pictures, the illustrations do nearly all the work. The book could be entirely wordless without any loss of narrative.

The other innovation is in the way the insects use everyday items from the human world—this was four years before Pixar's *A Bug's Life* did a similar thing. So the house itself is a tennis ball. A double-A battery is their power source. The bugs squeeze the juice from blueberries to use as paint. A credit card becomes a table top.

Two years later a sequel, *Snow Bugs*, appeared. This time the bugs cavort in wintertime, fondly echoing P. D. Eastman and Roy McKie's *Snow*. Though its rhyme is more traditional, the sentences are still very short, and often with implied subjects ("Roll over and slide. / Throw snowballs and hide."). This is made possible again by the clear and precise storytelling of the illustrations. There are even more household objects to spot, too, such as crayons, buttons, a thimble, a popsicle stick, and a broken spoon (the latter two used as sleds).

Author Susan Schade (born 1947) and illustrator Jon Buller (born 1943) are yet another set of married Beginner Book creators. Jon is a New York native who fell in love with cartooning when he was five years old and his uncle Joe taught him to draw a picture of a man looking over a fence. In third grade he created the adventures of a spacefaring ghost named Herman. But as he got older he decided not to pursue cartooning or illustration, instead working as a clerk in the New York City Department of Housing and Development after graduating with a degree in English.

In 1968 he took a vacation to Martha's Vineyard. While eating at Ralph's Restaurant in Edgarton, he met Susan, who was working there as a waitress. Originally from the coastal towns of Groton and Lyme, Connecticut, Susan graduated from Cornell University with a degree in Fine Arts.

Susan and Jon fell in love, took a cross-country road trip together, got married, and settled in Susan's hometown. Jon got a job at the post office while Susan became the children's librarian at the Old Lyme–Phoebe Griffen Noyes Library. In 1974, Jon began doing a comic—"Bob Blob"—for the *Gazette*, a local weekly, something he says felt like the fulfillment of his childhood dream. One of Jon and Susan's neighbors, Lucinda McQueen, was a successful children's illustrator (in a roundabout Beginner Book connection, she had illustrated Graham Tether's book, *Skunk and Possum*, in 1979). She noticed Jon's work and encouraged him to consider illustrating children's books. He wrote some stories and took them to meetings with publishers in New York. No work came from those meetings, but Jon was encouraged enough to keep trying.

In 1982 Jon replaced "Bob Blob" with "Captain Connecticut," a tongue-in-cheek superhero dedicated to "truth, justice, and the Connecticut way." The strip would last for several years as the *Gazette* merged with another weekly and became the *Pictorial Gazette*.

It took seven years for Jon's first book to be accepted. During that time he'd left the post office and began working as a bartender at Anthony's Steam Carriage in the New London train station. He was able to parlay that experience into *Buller's Professional Course in Home Bartending for Home Study*, which was released in 1983 by Harvard Common Press. His first children's book, *Fanny and May*, came out in 1984. Susan had helped out with that book, but it wasn't until *The Noisy Counting Book* that their collaboration fell fully into place. Released by Random House in 1987, it led to a steady stream of publications that has now grown over sixty books long and includes the Danger Show Joe series and a three-book fantasy epic, *The Fog Mound*. Their most successful book, a tooth fairy tale called *No Tooth, No Quarter* (Random House, 1989), has sold well over 700,000 copies.

For many years the couple lived and work in a family home in Lyme that was built by impressionist painter Louis Paul Dessar in 1905. They eventually built another house on the property where they still reside.

NEW TRICKS I CAN DO! (1996), B-77

Robert Lopshire

Ten years after their previous Beginner Book, Robert Lopshire and Spot returned with another sequel to *Put Me in the Zoo*. In this last installment, Spot has been fired from the circus because his act has become stale and overly familiar. But, in a play on the idiom "you can't teach an old dog new tricks," Spot has been working on some additional skills, which he shows off for Dick and Jane. These include completely changing color and manifesting lively patterns on his body. After his display, the children recommend that he give up on the circus and go on TV instead.

Though it follows the same basic plot of *Put Me in the Zoo, New Tricks I Can Do!* finds delight in the details. There's the final punchline, of course, bringing Spot into the modern age. But there's also the obvious joy Bob took in creating the visuals. Spot's various changes, especially when compared to the somewhat pedestrian shape-shifting of *I Want to Be Somebody New!*, are just plain fun. There's a black-and-yellow checkerboard Spot, American flag Spot, rainbow Spot, and Jackson Pollock Spot. Throughout the book, Bob's composition and ink line are as strong as ever.

Another fun aspect is a background detail near the end of the book. Just outside the circus, Spot leans against a fence adorned with three posters. The first advertises "The Amazing Klimo Klowns," the second "Goldsmith the Juggler." Much like Bob paid tribute to Ted by putting the Cat in the crowd in *Put Me in the Zoo*, here he honored his collaborators Kate Klimo and Cathy Goldsmith.

Critics from *Publishers Weekly* and *School Library Journal* didn't like the book, calling it "stale," "flat," and "uninspired." Not that it probably mattered one whit to Bob, "I ignore the critics," he told *Contemporary Authors Online*, "Be they kind or cutting."

Robert Lopshire circa 1997. Courtesy the Lopshire family.

Bob would do two more books for the line. In 1997 and 1998 Random House tried out a new Beginner Book offshoot called Beginner Workbooks. They were comprised of original material designed to explicitly teach and practice specific concepts. So *I Want to Count Something New!* featured Spot-led mazes, matching puzzles, and coloring activities; and *Put Me in the Alphabet!* finds Spot doing a new trick for each letter of the alphabet. These two books would be Bob's last published works.

Bob died in 2002 of emphysema and congestive heart failure. The nurses who cared for him brought their childhood copies of his books for him to sign, and said they were now reading them to their own children. Despite his decreased production in the 1980s and 1990s Bob kept creating: "He never retired," Selma Lopshire—his third wife, whom he married in 1974—told the *Sarasota Herald-Tribune*. "Bob had a massive imagination. Right up until the end, he had intricate model airplanes on one table and was working on another book at his desk."

In 2020 Random House published *Shut the Door!*, the story of a young bear who keeps forgetting to close the door when he leaves the house. Initially published in 1993 as a First Little Golden Book, the Beginner Book edition replaced Bob's original illustrations with new ones by German artist Maria Karipidou.

ANTHONY THE PERFECT MONSTER (1996), B-78

Angelo DeCesare

Anthony the Perfect Monster is a play on the classic monster transformation story, but with a kid-focused, emotional twist. At heart, the book is about the negative effects of repressing your true feelings in order to please others, but it's also about how adults sometimes place unrealistic expectations on children.

Anthony likes being thought of as perfect, but it doesn't necessarily come naturally to him. Sometimes he wants to be loud, say he hates spinach, and not wear his raincoat. But he suppresses all that because he likes to please the adults in his life. This changes when he goes to school for the first time. There, the other kids think he's strange and the teacher finds him too eager. After a mostly sleepless night—thanks in large part to the glimpse he catches of the monster movie his babysitter is watching—Anthony wakes up unable to keep up any pretense of perfection. He becomes a hairy, sharp-toothed monster, and runs rampant through his school day. When he finds that his teacher and mom both still love him despite his destruction and defiance, Anthony is relieved. "So that's how Anthony stopped trying to be the most perfect kid," the story tells us. "He became, instead, a kid who was sometimes angry, sometimes sad, sometimes happy. But always perfectly . . . himself!"

It's a tale taken nearly directly from its creator's own experience. Angelo DeCesare (born 1955) had a difficult childhood growing up in the Bronx. Neither of his parents made it past eighth grade, and the family didn't have much money. When Angelo was five, his father died of cancer. When he was eight, one of his best friends died. The two tragedies tore him up. "It made me really angry," he says. "I was filled with rage and I didn't know what to do with it. My mother's response was to make my sister and I the best kids she could make us be."

The Universal Monsters (Dracula, Frankenstein, Creature from the Black Lagoon, etc.) were at peak popularity in the 1960s, and Angelo found himself fascinated by the Wolf Man. "That was the coolest of all the monsters," he says.

> I would run around pretending to be the Wolf Man. And that was one of the ways I let out my feelings. On the outside I was a very polite nice little boy, but I would also get a little violent now and then. I once took my sister's record player and flung it across the room. I pushed a friend of mine down a flight of steps. I was way too aggressive during games and would say and do hurtful things. I had this rage inside me that was the opposite of what I appeared to be. That's where *Anthony* came from.

Books and comic books were also an escape from the unhappiness. Angleo's apartment building was near a library, so Angelo and his sister made frequent trips there. He recalls how popular Beginner Books were, and like nothing else in the children's department. "The artwork was out there," he recalls, "and the wordplay was just so amazing." It wasn't long before Angelo was creating his own stories and comic books.

After high school, he'd enrolled at Pratt Institute, but dropped out midway into his second year. At the age of twenty-four he got his first professional job, writing and drawing *Richie Rich* comics at Harvey. After a couple of years there, he headed to King Features Syndicate, where he would work for eight years. For four of those years, he did the *Katzenjammer Kids* Sunday feature. The strip was one of very first newspaper comics, having debuted in 1897 in William Randolph Hearst's *New York Journal*. It had a low circulation but was kept going by the Hearst family as a tribute to their grandfather. Angelo calls it a valuable learning experience.

At King Features he also met his future wife, Maria Carmicino, who worked in the editorial department.

Angelo became a freelancer in 1988, starting out at Marvel's Star Comics line, doing work on licensed properties such as *Heathcliff*, *Barbie*, and *Care Bears*. He also did a significant amount of scripting for Archie Comics as well, handling not only the usual Riverdale gang, but also some of the earliest Sonic the Hedgehog comics. He loved doing comics, but Maria had been encouraging him to do a children's book. The notion didn't really take hold until the couple's daughter, Gina, came along, and Angelo began reading to her. He was disappointed with the quality of so many of the kids' books and began to think that he could do better.

He knew he wanted to write a book with a positive message for children, and thought back on his (mostly) suppressed childhood anger. "I wanted to tell kids, be yourself, accept yourself for who you are. Don't be afraid to show your feelings. If you make a mistake, it doesn't make you a monster. If you get angry, it doesn't make you a monster. It means you're a human being." Angleo got about two-thirds through his story, but ended up setting it aside due to a lack of motivation. Then he heard about the contest.

In the summer of 1992, less than a year after Ted's death, Random House announced the Dr. Seuss Picture-Book Award contest. Aspiring children's book authors were asked to send in their best story idea for a chance to earn $25,000 and a contract to publish their book. The publisher specified that they weren't looking for Dr. Seuss imitators, but instead "the new talents who will create the great picture books for future generations of children—and their parents."

Two friends—artist Rick Parker and his wife, writer Lisa Trusiani—told Angelo about the contest at dinner, and he was intrigued. He picked up *Anthony the Perfect Monster* again, reworked it into a sixty-four-page manuscript, sent it in, and waited to hear. The contest results were announced on Ted's birthday, March 2, 1993, and the winner was . . . *Fast Friends—A Tail and Tongue Tale* by Lisa Horstman.

Angelo was disappointed. The contest rules had specified that authors had to ask for their manuscripts back, so he called Random House. They informed him that they couldn't find his book. He was devastated, and even now calls it a low point in his life and artistic career. Not only had he lost the contest, all of his work was gone. But a few days later he received a call from Random House and they said, "Oh, we found your book. One of the editors had it—a woman named Mallory Loehr—and we want to publish it." The contest had received twelve hundred entries. *Anthony and the Perfect Monster* was the only submission besides Horstman's to be chosen for publication.

When Angelo spoke to Mallory (who herself would become a Beginner Book author with 1999's *Babe: A Little Pig Goes a Long Way*), she said she liked the story and that Angelo's cartoony style reminded her of I Can Read! stalwart Syd Hoff. She asked that he cut down the length considerably, which he did, and then she did a revision of her own cutting it down even more. Angelo worked with Cathy Goldsmith on the layout and final art, which Angelo did with pencil and painstaking watercolor. When he was done, Cathy told him, "Ted would have liked this book."

Though this all happened circa 1993, the book didn't come out until 1996. Angelo says they were waiting and waiting for a release date and then Mallory called and said, "I have good news and bad news. The bad news is we have to delay your book. The good news is we want to publish it as a Beginner Book." Angelo was thrilled. He says, "It was a great moment. Here was a boy who had a father and mother who barely had schooling. My father was an immigrant who couldn't speak, read or write the language when he arrived in America. And there was my book on the bookshelves, next to Dr. Seuss."

Anthony and the Perfect Monster got mixed reviews, but it sold well—over 100,000 copies—and in 1997 was picked as a Children's Choice award winner. Angelo jokes that the honor was a joint effort of the "Children's Book Council, the International Reading Group, and my mom." But Angelo's next book—an interactive journal featuring a dog named Flip—wasn't to Random House's liking; they said it was too much like a school book.

Meanwhile, Angelo had created a school program through the Center for Educational Change at Brooklyn College in which he would read *Anthony the*

At school, when the teacher asked, "Who would like to be the first to read their book report in front of the class," Anthony always volunteered, even though it made him nervous when the other kids stared at him.

On some nights, Anthony's big sister stayed up late watching scary monster movies on TV. Anthony NEVER watched monster movies, but always went to bed early, like the perfect kid that he was.

In the schoolyard, Anthony would have liked to run wild and yell, like the other kids. Instead, he played nice games like "Tippy-toe tag" and "Let's see who can sit still the longest."

YOU BLINKED, FREDDY! YOU'RE OUT

Two pages from Angelo's original contest submission. The text especially illustrates how much revision had to be done to turn the book into an early reader. Courtesy Angelo DeCesare.

An alternate cover idea for *Anthony the Perfect Monster*. Courtesy Angelo DeCesare.

Perfect Monster to kids, show them the original illustrations, and draw with the kids. He worked in ten schools the first year, and twenty his second year, which led to him joining up with Brooklyn-based Puppetry in Practice, a not-for-profit that promotes literacy through the arts. The organization's director, Dr. Tova Ackerman, encouraged Angelo to use *Flip's Fantastic Journal* as a basis for a writing and drawing program. Puppetry in Practice also published the book (it was given a wider release by Dutton in 1999).

The book and the program have both connected deeply with kids, especially reluctant readers and writers. There have been seven sequels featuring Flip and his friends, all focused on different aspects of the school curriculum and different kid-centered emotions, and "Mr. Angelo" is in his twenty-second

Angelo and his wife, Maria, at Barnes and Noble on *Anthony's* release day. "It was Maria's encouragement that led to this moment," he says. Courtesy Angelo DeCesare.

year in schools, not just in the five boroughs, but in Rockland County, Long Island, and New Jersey as well.

"I'm doing what I love," he says. "All of this was to get me to the classroom where I really belong. My life has been a succession of wonderful days because of that. Even when I've wanted to jump out of the window because the kids were so difficult, I still know every day I have a chance to do some good in the world."

FOUR PUPS AND A WORM (1996), B-78

Eric Seltzer

Beginner Books had a cozy relationship with advertising from the beginning, with so many of its creators—including Ted himself—having spent time working on Madison Avenue. As Kate Klimo somewhat glibly put it, Beginner Books was comprised of "ad guys who sold reading to kids." Picture book legend Eric Carle also got his start in advertising, and he saw a clear connection between marketing and storytelling: "Like it or not, there is an affinity between the discipline and the art of creating picture books; both place a premium on terseness and clarity, on making every word and image not only count but resonate—and all with a deceptive lightness of touch."

Beginner Books was certainly built on these principles, but there had never been a title in the line that actually *read* and *felt* like a commercial until *Four Pups and a Worm*.

The book is an absurdly fun bit of nonsense promoting the services provided by four dogs (A. J., Rex, Digger, and Goober) and a worm named Sherm. They do delivery, party planning, childcare, handy work, lawn maintenance, and many other things. They even appear to be trained as EMTs. After spending the first two-thirds of the book introducing the company, we get to see the team in action as they rescue Bernice Bee, who got stuck in a flower. Their pitch also includes some mild disparagement of their competition, which includes a goat and seven crows, nine pigs and a bat, and three cats and a slug.

Told in perfectly rhythmic and snappy rhyme—"If a pet frog sounds like fun, / would 3 Cats and a Slug lend you one? / (Never, no, never! / They're just not that clever.)"—and with boldy stylized, idiosyncratic drawings, the book captures the madcap spirit of the best 1960s Beginner Books.

It should be no surprise that Michigan native Eric Seltzer (born 1960) had been in the advertising business for over ten years by the time *Four Pups and a Worm* was published. He says he'd been so entrenched in his work as an advertising art director that he didn't even consciously realize he was writing the story as a commercial. He also didn't purposefully write it as an early reader. "At the time I didn't even know specifically what an early reader was," he says.

He'd graduated in 1982 from the College for Creative Studies in Detroit. From there he kicked around at various positions, working at General Motors in visual presentation, and in on-air promotions at Channel 20, as well as designing and marketing his own line of designer sweatshirts called Le'flirte. In 1986 he landed at Doner Advertising, where he would spend four years. Having grown up loving books and especially admiring the work of author/illustrators such as Arnold Lobel, James Marshall, and (later on) Sandra Boynton, he'd long held a dream of making children's books himself.

In the early 1990s he began making dummies of his story ideas and sending them out to publishers. He says he had dozens of dummies floating around when Kate Klimo called him about *Four Pups and a Worm*. She liked the idea, and saw its potential as an early reader. With her guidance, Eric developed the book into its final form. Then Kate told him she wanted to publish it as a Beginner Book. "I thought that was a big honor," he says. He also felt a strong connection with Ted, having, in 1989, received a personal note and a signed book as part of getting Ted's permission to use The Cat in the Hat for an ad for a literacy program sponsored by the *Detroit Free Press* called the Gift of Reading.

Portrait by Naturally Photography (Naturallymonni.com). Courtesy Eric Seltzer.

Though it didn't happen right away, *Four Pups and a Worm* has led Eric to a robust career in writing early readers. Since 2005 he's published books with Penguin Young Readers (*Bake, Mice, Bake!* and *Dog on His Bus*), Scholastic Readers (*The Long Dog*), and Simon and Schuster's Ready to Read line (*Space Cows, Party Pigs, Knight Owls,* and *Sea Sheep*).

Not only have these all been early readers, they've all been at level one. Many writers find writing within those limits to be a daunting challenge, but for Eric it comes naturally. He has an innate knack for telling funny stories in short, simple rhyming verse. "I don't take any credit for it," he says humbly. "That particular [discipline] happens to work for me."

He's currently at work on his first picture book, for Amazon's Two Lions imprint, and also hopes to one day do another Beginner Book.

HONEY BUNNY FUNNYBUNNY (1997), B-80

Marilyn Sadler and Roger Bollen

Fourteen years after P. J. Funnybunny's debut, the rabbit returned to Beginner Books. His stories had continued outside of the line, in Step Into Reading books, Golden Look-Look Books, and on three ABC weekend specials.

Honey Bunny Funnybunny focuses on the relationship between P. J. and his little sister, Honey Bunny, whom he joyfully antagonizes. He ties knots in the sleeves of her dresses, pours orange juice on her cornflakes, switches the heads on her dolls, and smashes mashed carrots on her head. Eventually P. J. gets caught and punished by their parents. As a result, P. J. starts to ignore Honey Bunny. She's confused and believes this means her brother no longer loves her. So when P. J. returns to his old ways by painting Honey Bunny's face blue with yellow polka dots, she surprises him with a grateful hug.

Sibling relationships can be both joyful and painful, fun and infuriating, and this book captures that dichotomy. Marilyn based the story on her own family. She writes,

> My dad was a funny dad with a silly sense of humor, so there was a lot of joking and laughter in my family . . . including a great deal of teasing. The story itself was influenced by a childhood memory of my younger brother drawing polka dots all over my older brother's face while he was sleeping. In my story, I simply changed the younger sibling to a girl as Honey Bunny was actually me in my mind and I wanted her to be a bigger part of P. J.'s world.

The book was the cause of some minor controversy. Nationally syndicated newspaper columnist Ellen Goodman—whose laudatory quote about *The Cat in the Hat* was featured on the back of Beginner Books for many years—was taken aback when a friend brought the book to her attention. She wrote in her column: "Our little sister learns her lesson: that the wrong kind of attention is better than no attention. That you can either be abused or neglected." Marilyn responds, "I was simply having fun with the tendency of siblings to tease one another. And because boys have a harder time showing their affection, teasing is an avenue for expressing that love." She also points out that P. J. gets punished for his actions.

Honey Bunny would get one more Beginner Book to herself (see the entry for *Money Money Honey Bunny* later in this chapter), but one year after *Honey Bunny Funnybunny*, Marilyn and Roger created two Beginner Workbooks. *Match This, P. J. Funnybunny!* focused on matching activities, and *What's Next, P. J. Funnybunny?*, which gave kids practice with patterns. Along with Robert Lopshire's two workbooks, these comprised the entirety of the Beginner Workbook line, as it was discontinued after 1998.

COME DOWN NOW, FLYING COW! (1997), B-81

Timothy Roland

Come Down Now, Flying Cow! is the story of Beth, a cow looking for an adventure beyond her pasture, which leads her to hijack a hot-air balloon and take off into the sky. In the tradition of earlier Beginner Books like *A Fly Went By* and *Because a Little Bug Went Ka-Choo!*, this story is all forward motion and cumulative chaos. As Beth soars through the countryside she gathers passengers both live and inanimate (a dog, a fish, a clothesline) and leaves a wake of confusion. The kinetic illustrations and snappy rhyme ("A girls jumps up. / Her hat flies high. / 'Come back!' she yells. / But on we fly.") keep the reader going. In the end of the story, Beth comes back to earth, only to immediately zoom away in a red convertible.

Author-illustrator Timothy Roland (born 1956) got the idea for *Come Down Now, Flying Cow!* while watching a hot-air balloon land in a farmer's field not far from his home in Emmaus, Pennsylvania. He began to wonder what the cows thought of the sight, which led to him imagining what would happen if one of those cows climbed in the basket and took off. He named his bold, imaginary cow Beth after his oldest niece, and the seed of a story was planted.

Tim grew up in Emmaus and studied art at Alfred University in New York. Before becoming an author he'd worked as both a corporate designer and as an elementary art school teacher. By 1996 he was an established author, having written and illustrated a four-book early reader mystery series about a character called Detective Dan (published by Zondervan in 1993), and the cheese-shaped board book *Ten Hungry Mice* (Random House, 1995).

Tim initially wrote *Come Down Now, Flying Cow!* in prose, and sent a dummy to Kate Klimo, who asked him to consider reworking it into a forty-eight-page Beginner Book. Tim was thrilled at the prospect, since, as he says, "Like most children who grew up in the 1960's, I was raised on a steady diet of Beginner Books, which helped teach me to read, laugh and imagine." And the book itself, he says, was "influenced by the cartoony art and zaniness of Dr. Seuss and P. D. Eastman."

Under the guidance initially of editor Sue Kassirer, and then Alice Jonaitis, Tim reworked his story, changing the prose to verse to make it more early reader friendly, and adding a nervous bird as Beth's companion (perhaps a subconscious nod to the fish in *The Cat in the Hat*). Cathy Goldsmith, Tim says, was a great help in the layout of the book. You can see the trademark Seussian movement, with large two-page spreads that consistently move the

Courtesy Timothy Roland.

eye from left to right. Tim's style is bright and clean, showing the influence of some of his artistic heroes, Charles Schulz, Walt Kelly, Bill Watterson, and Disney. There's also a touch of Michael Frith in there as well.

Since the publication of *Come Down Now, Flying Cow!* Tim has completed two separate series for Scholastic, Comic Guy (three books, 2007–2008) and Monkey Me (four books, 2014). He says of being an author, "I love letting my imagination fly, thinking divergently, exploring and expressing ideas, creating something (a book) that entertains, educates and inspires." He says he hopes that Beth's story has "encouraged, and will continue to encourage children to be curious and explore their world."

THE A BOOK (1997), BE-30

Stan and Jan Berenstain

Though they likely would never have characterized it that way, the publication of *The A Book* and *That Stump Must Go!* was the Berenstains' gentle revenge on Ted for rejecting those two books back in the 1960s and 1970s.

When renegotiating their contract with Random House in the mid-1990s, Stan added those two books into the deal.

This is understandable. Stan and Jan had put considerable time and energy into both books before Ted finally directed them to pack it in. Mike Berenstain recalls that *The A Book* went through many, many versions before getting the final ax from Ted. Seeing the final product, one wonders why. Perhaps it was the non-illustratable, outsized vocabulary required to make the story work ("advance across"), but as has been made clear, by the late 1960s, Ted played fast and loose with those rules.

The stars of the book are an army of angry ants who are on the march. Where exactly they're headed is kept a mystery until the end, but along the way they encounter all manner of items and creatures that start with "A" (an ax, an alligator, an apartment building full of apes, and an angleworm played by Richard Scarry's Lowly Worm). After traveling across all of Arizona, the ants reach their purpose: attacking an anteater about to eat another colony. In *The B Book*, the text was cumulative, building on each page. Here, Stan and Jan instead present the events one by one, saving a recap of all of the events for the second-to-last page: "That's why angry ants advanced across an apple, an acorn, an apricot, an ax . . ."

MONSTER MUNCHIES (1998), B-84

Laura Numeroff and Nate Evans

Monster Munchies is a counting book that guides the reader from one to twenty using a set of colorful, ravenously destructive monsters. They eat their toys, balls, roofs, beds, pants, and many other everyday items. They eat so much that one wonders how much monster money they spend each week replacing their stuff! Told in peppy four-line rhyme—like most classic rhyming Beginner Books—the story moves toward a satisfying, interactive conclusion in which the reader herself becomes a target of the creatures' hunger: "Twenty hungry monsters / with nothing left to chew. / Better close this book up tight . . . / Before they chew on you!" As illustrated, the monsters strike the exact balance of being weird and odd without being scary.

Laura Numeroff (born 1953), with her penchant for rhythm and rhyme and a silly sense of humor, was a great fit for Beginner Books. She also happens to be one of the very rare cases of an already well-established author doing a book for the line. By 1998, when *Monster Munchies* was released, Laura had been

Courtesy Laura Numeroff.

publishing children's books for over twenty years, and had a massive hit series springing from 1985's *If You Give a Mouse a Cookie* (with illustrator Felicia Bond).

Born in Brooklyn to an artist and a teacher, Laura grew up an avid reader and prolific artist. After high school, she attended Pratt Institute, starting out in the fashion department until she found it just wasn't to her liking. A class called "Writing and Illustrating for Children's Books," however, was inspiring, and one of her assignments ended up being her first published book, *Amy for Short* (Macmillan, 1975). From there she was on her way, writing and illustrating eight more books before her 1985 breakthrough.

As of this writing, Laura has forty-six books to her name, including her parody of *If You Give a Mouse a Cookie* called *If You Give a Man a Cookie*. Ten of those were done in collaboration with her *Monster Munchies* illustrator, Nate Evans (born 1959). Nate grew up in Colorado and California, where, like Laura, his childhood world centered on reading and drawing (and occasional secret agent missions). After college he worked for many years at Hallmark. He enjoyed the work and his fellow artists, but realized that his real dream was to write and draw children's books.

His first published book illustrations appeared in 1997, in an early reader by Roberta Edwards called *Space Kid*. It was followed shortly by Mary Packard's *I Am Not a Dinosaur*. *Monster Munchies* came next, and it would be the start of a productive run with Laura. In 2002 they next did another monster book, *Laura Numeroff's Ten Step Guide to Living with Your Monster*, and followed that up by cowriting *Sherman Crunchley* the next year (with pictures by Tim Bowers). In 2008 they started the four-book Jellybeans series and in 2011 published Ponyella, a retelling of Cinderella with an equine lead. All of these books were done with illustrator Lynn Munsinger.

In all, Nate has now created over forty books. In recent years he has become a teacher. He currently teaches art to elementary students in Gilbert, Arizona.

MAMA LOVES (1999), BE-32

Molly Goode and Lisa McCue

Mama Loves is a sweet ode to the power of animal mothers to protect, instruct, play with, and provide for their young ones. Told in an eight-line rhyme, the book showcases dogs, cats, otters, elephants, raccoons, seals, among other animals. With its cute, sentimental subject matter and semi-realistic painted illustrations akin to Garth Williams's work, the book reads and looks more like a Little Golden Book than a Bright and Early.

Perhaps there's good reason for that. Molly Goode was a pseudonym for editor Kate Klimo (born 1950) who happened to also be in charge of Little Golden Books following Random House's acquisition of the line. More than that, she'd grown up reading Little Golden Books, and her family was friendly with authors Kathryn and Byron Jackson (*The Saggy Baggy Elephant*, *A Day at the Seashore*, *Brave Cowboy Bill*). Kate is also an avowed animal lover.

So is illustrator Lisa McCue (born 1959), whose oeuvre of nearly two hundred books largely feature animal protagonists. Lisa was born in Brooklyn and grew up in Tappan, New York. Her father worked in television, and her mother was an artist who encouraged Lisa's own talents. She had lots of interests—music, dance, track, soccer, skiing—but zeroed in on art while attending Southeastern Massachusetts University. At first her ambition was to do greeting cards, but a fateful encounter with Dutch author Loek Kessels changed that. Kessels was a McCue family friend, and during a visit to the family one winter break, she saw Lisa's work and essentially chose the young artist to illustrate her next book. It would be published during her senior year.

From there Lisa began to focus on book illustration. Her first US publications appeared in 1982—Marguerite Muntean Corsello's *Who Says That?*, and the first of the Sebastian (Super Slueth) series by Mary Christian Blount.

In addition to books, Lisa has designed fabric patterns, wrapping paper, and greeting cards. When she was in high school, she was asked to describe a day in her life twenty-five years in the future. She says, "I described myself as married with 2 children, working in my studio overlooking the ocean and designing greeting cards with a dog at my feet." It nearly all came to pass. Lisa is married to electrical engineer Kenneth Karsten Jr., with whom she has two grown sons. They live in Annapolis, Maryland, so her studio doesn't overlook the ocean, but the Chesapeake Bay instead.

The 2000s

THAT STUMP MUST GO! (2000), B-89

Stan and Jan Berenstain

That Stump Must Go! is a return to the formula of the early Berenstain Beginner Books, with Papa's overzealous nature getting the best of him. This time it's a seemingly tiny tree stump that he decides to extract, only to find its roots are much deeper and longer than he'd anticipated. Instead of giving up or seeking professional help, Papa Bear's obstinacy kicks in. As the ever-admiring Brother Bear puts it, "When he starts, / he does not stop. / That's one good thing / about my pop."

In the other books that follow this formula, Papa's destruction is typically limited to his own self, but here he ends up destroying a whole section of his neighborhood.

That Stump Must Go! began life in the mid-1960s as *The Little Stump*. As the entry for *The Bears' Picnic* detailed, Ted finally killed the project after putting Stan and Jan through revision after revision. As part of the renewal of their deal with Random House, Stan and Jan revisited their original idea, providing a comforting reminder of what made the Berenstains so good at writing early readers—fitting, since it would be their twentieth and final book for the line.

PAWS AND CLAWS (2001), B-90

Erica Farber and J. R. Sansevere

Billy Steers, John Lund, Diane Dubreuil

Paws and Claws are a puppy and a kitten who live on a farm. As this rhyming story begins they're called to the barn to investigate a large green egg that has mysteriously appeared there. First, all the barn animals take turns sitting on the egg, then Paws and Claws head out to investigate. They look at the eggs of green creatures (frogs, a snake, turtles) and find that none are a match. Then they go into the house, grab an encyclopedia, and find their answer: It's an emu egg. The egg hatches shortly after, and Paws and Claws take the newborn up the road to a nearby emu farm to be reunited with its parents.

Paws and Claws wasn't the first Beginner Book for New York–based writers John R. Sansevere (born 1953) and Erica Farber (born 1961). Their first was *Roast & Toast* (B-83, 1998), which was part of Mercer Mayer's Critters of the Night series. John and Erica wrote all of those, most of which were released as Step Into Reading books. John himself had a long history with Mayer, having teamed up with the author/illustrator in the early 1980s to form a software company called Angelsoft, a pioneer in educational games for the Atari, Apple, IBM, and Commodore systems. A 1984 series of games called *Tink! Tonk! Tales* required a player to move through the story by making choices for the character and playing mini-games designed to build various skills such as map reading, counting, logic, letter knowledge, and spelling. John and Mayer also produced text games for licensed properties such as Indiana Jones and James Bond.

As Mayer's Little Critter books began to gain popularity in the 1980s, John's efforts in software development became less about developing outside properties and more about creating multimedia based on the books. In 1993 he wrote an animated home video adaptation of the 1977 book, *Just Me and My Dad*. His writing partner was Erica Farber, who had previously worked as a children's book editor. It was the beginning of a partnership both creative and romantic. Much of their work was with Mayer, not only writing the Critters in the Night books but another spin-off series called L. C. and the Critter Kids, and developing PC games based on the Little Monster, Private Eye character.

John and Erica also branched out on their own, writing pop culture nonfiction titles for Western (*Bad Boyz of Rap*; *Divas: Today's Megamodels*), and a series of fantasy novels called Tales of the Nine Charms. In 2003, the couple had a son, Niko. In recent years as their relationship has ended, Erica has moved into writing on her own. She's worked with Huck Scarry (Richard's son) on the Great Big Schoolhouse line of early readers, and created the Fish Finelli series with illustrator Jason Beene. She also teaches writing to middle schoolers. John, meanwhile, has moved forward with the technology of the times. He continues to work with Mercer Mayer, and focuses on writing and producing apps centered on Little Critter.

The illustrations for *Paws and Claws*—in the big-eyed cutesy style similar to Mayer's—were done unconventionally for a children's book. They were created comic book style, with a different artist responsible for each stage of the art. Billy Steers, an author/illustrator who created the popular Tractor Mac series for Macmillan, did the pencil layouts. John Lund inked the illustrations, and Diane Dubreuil added the color. None of the artists are credited on the cover or title page.

FLAP YOUR WINGS (2000), B-88;
BIG DOG . . . LITTLE DOG (2003), B-92;
FRED AND TED GO CAMPING (2005), B-94;
FRED AND TED LIKE TO FLY (2007), B-96;
FRED AND TED'S ROAD TRIP (2011), B-100;
THE ALPHABET BOOK (2015), BE-41

P. D. Eastman

Peter Eastman

In 2000, Random House converted the original Pictureback edition of *Flap Your Wings* into a Beginner Book. The next book they wanted to adapt was Phil's book of opposites, *Big Dog . . . Little Dog*, but the original had been conceived in a square format and needed reformatting. The publisher got in touch with Phil's son, Tony, who ended up creating several pieces of new artwork based on his father's original drawings. The book was released in 2003 as Beginner Book B-92.

This led to Tony doing three new Beginner Books featuring the dog characters Fred and Ted. In 2005 he released *Fred and Ted Go Camping*. It was followed by *Fred and Ted Like to Fly* and *Fred and Ted's Road Trip*. Each book follows a similar pattern: The two friends go on a journey together but have contrasting approaches and experiences, highlighting opposites such as "Ted stayed dry. Fred got wet." Tony works in an artistic similar style to his father's, and his background in animation shines through in his strong composition and expressive character work.

The books are credited to Peter Eastman because Tony's full name is Peter Anthony Eastman (1942–2020). In addition to creating Beginner Books, Tony has followed in his father's footsteps through a long career in animation. As a youth Tony created flip books and short animated films with a 16 mm Bolex movie camera his father had bought for him. He worked at animation studio Gene Deitch Associates his senior year of high school. Here he met Gene's son, Kim Deitch, who became a lifelong friend. Tony and Kim shot a live action film, "Dial M for Monster" that summer with the Bolex.

He later attended Carnegie Tech (now Carnegie Mellon University). While there he produced/directed/animated a short film titled "For the Love of Phoebe" for Tech's Scotch and Soda Club's 1961 production. After graduation he worked as a designer of on-air graphics for the CBS network. He struck out on his own in the early 1970s, teaching animation at Philadelphia College of Art and working at a variety of New York City animation studios before settling in at R. O. Blechman's Ink Tank in 1981. There he created animation for PBS and Children's Television Workshop, as well and many commercials. He also animated on R. O. Blechman's 1984 Emmy Award–winning, "The Soldier's Tale."

Starting in 1989 Tony directed (first through Jerry Lieberman Productions and later with Jumbo Pictures) six Richard Scarry "Best Ever" Random House Home Videos—"Best ABC Video Ever," "Best Counting Video Ever," for example—animated adaptations of Richard Scarry's work. He went on to direct the pilot and was supervising director on Nickelodeon's *Doug*.

In the mid-1990s he reconnected with J. J. Sedelmaier, whom Tony had given his start in animation, at J. J. Sedelmaier Productions, Inc. Here Tony was head animator the first season of *Beavis and Butthead*, and animated the memorable Saturday TV Funhouse segments on *Saturday Night Live*. He also worked on various TV commercials for companies such as Old Navy, Northern Tissue, Ortho, and 7UP. Tony also did work as a storyboard consultant on the Beavis spin-off "Daria" and Cartoon Network's "Codename: Kid's Next Door." Tony is widely venerated in the animation world, typified by Michael Sporn's description of him as "a talent with a sensitive style and a smile in his work."

THE KNEE BOOK (2005), BE-35

Cindy Graham Tether and Sylvie Wickstrom

In 1979 Cindy Graham Tether gave us *The Hair Book*. Twenty-six years later she returned to put a spotlight on our all-important leg joints. An enthusiastic rhyme tells us where we see knees, what they allow us to do (jump, crouch, hike, bike, skip, run, dance, etc.), how they look different on different creatures, and which animals don't have them (sharks, whales, worms, etc.).

The book's illustrations are done in a minimalist style that matches the loose and fun aesthetic of the Bright and Early Books of the 1970s. Characters rendered in thick wobbly ink lines caper across a stark white background on most pages. The painted color is done in a way that emphasizes the fact that you're looking at an illustration. In some cases you can see the brushstrokes.

Sylvie (Wickstrom) Kantorovitz (born 1960) was born in Casablanca, Morocco, and grew up in Chantilly, France. She studied both at the École des Beaux Arts in Paris, and for a year at the Art Students League in New York. While at the latter she met fellow artist and Florida native Thor Wickstrom. He returned with her to France, and the two were married there. Sylvie worked as a schoolteacher before the couple decided to return to the United States in 1985. They settled in New Jersey at first, but eventually made their way to New York. They'd have one child, daughter Sam.

During her studies, Sylvie had "rediscovered the magic of children's books" and turned her attention toward a career as an illustrator. Her first published work was 1988's *Wheels on the Bus*, featuring children's musician Raffi's take on the classic singalong. Over the next twenty years Sylvie produced work steadily, amounting to twenty-five books. Three of these—*Mothers Can't Get Sick* (1989), *Turkey on the Loose* (1990), and *I Love You, Mister Bear* (2004)— she wrote herself. Since 2008 her work has slowed, but in 2014 she released *The Very Tiny Baby*. She continues to live and work in Albany, New York. She writes, "Besides reading and drawing, I like comics, music, theater, movies, art shows, picnics and dreaming. Daydreaming is a special talent of mine."

Cindy, meanwhile, still lives in Bronxville, New York, where she writes poetry, loves to travel, is heavily involved with her church, and plays violin in local orchestras and chamber ensembles.

MRS. WOW NEVER WANTED A COW (2006), B-95

Martha Freeman and Steven Salerno

When this story starts, things aren't going especially well for Mrs. Wow: her cat is too lazy to catch mice, her dog is more interested in eating than guarding the house, her property has a large expanse of grass that she has to keep mowed, and an unwanted cow has wandered onto her land. Seeing opportunity, the cat (Meow) and the Dog (Bow-Wow) try to train the cow to take over their responsibilities, with comically ineffective results. Mrs. Wow gently reminds them that cows are only good at eating grass and giving milk, and this gives her an idea. The cow can take over keeping the grass short, and her milk can be made into ice cream. The ice cream can then be used to bribe

Meow and Bow-Wow into doing their chores. It's an elegant solution that's pleasing and beneficial to all.

It's fitting that Mrs. Wow and her pets form an unconventional family, because author Martha Freeman (born 1956) is known for her middle-grade novels about quirky domestic situations. She grew up in Southern California in the Los Angeles suburb of Whittier. Not long after graduating from Stanford University, she moved east to Sonora, California. She worked at times as a substitute teacher and advertising copywriter before settling in as a newspaper editor and reporter. In 1995 she moved with her family (husband, Russell Frank, and children Sylvie, Rosa, and Ethan) across country to State College, Pennsylvania. The very next year Delacorte published Martha's first novel, *Stink Bomb Mom*.

Over the course of the ensuing two decades, Martha has produced several more standalone novels, picture books, and multiple novel series (First Kids, Chickadee Court Mysteries, and the Secret Cookie Club). Her latest, with illustrator Violet Kim, is a kids' guide to attending a protest, called *If You're Going to a March*. Martha now lives in Boulder, Colorado.

Mrs. Wow Never Wanted a Cow's illustrations are dynamic and bold, done in a modern retro style that emphasizes the shape and motion of its lines. The colors pop, with visible brushstrokes that push the eye through the pictures. They're the work of New York–based illustrator Steven Salerno (born 1958), whose style *Publishers Weekly* likened to a synthesis of H. A. Rey (*Curious George*) and Ludwig Bemelmans (*Madeline*).

Steven grew up in a small town in Vermont near the Canadian border. He says, "At the early age of five I already knew I was an artist and becoming an illustrator was my path so when I read any picture books as a child I was always absorbing how the artist interpreted the text." Some of the artists who captivated him included Virginia Lee Burton (*Mike Mulligan and His Steam Shovel*), E. H. Shepard (*Winnie-the-Pooh*), and, yes, Dr. Seuss and P. D. Eastman. He recalls being "engulfed" by the images in books such as *The Cat in the Hat* and *Go, Dog. Go!*

After high school, Steven headed to New York City, where he attended Parsons School of Design. There, he took an intensive class in children's book illustration with Maurice Sendak. Though he knew his path and was prepared for it, it would be many years before Steven published his first children's book. After graduating from Parsons in 1979 he worked briefly in animation, then began doing editorial and advertising illustrations, his work appearing in major magazines, advertisements, and on product packaging. In 2000 he was called upon to reillustrate Bill Martin Jr.'s 1946 story *Chicken Chuck*, which was originally published as a magazine story in 1939 under the title "How the Animals Took a Bath" in 1939. The next year he created new pictures for Margaret Wise Brown's *The Dirty Little Boy*.

Since then he's illustrated twenty-eight more picture books, both fiction and nonfiction. On five of these—*Little Tumbo* (2003, Marshall Cavendish), *Coco the Carrot* (2005, Marshall Cavendish), *Harry Hungry* (2009, Harcourt), *Wild Child* (2015, Abrams), and *Tim's Goodbye* (2018, Farrar Straus Giroux)—he is also the author. Though he now incorporates more digital drawing and painting into his work, *Mrs. Wow* was illustrated, he says, "in the traditional manner of drawing and painting by hand directly on paper using gouache, crayon, inks, etc."

MONEY MONEY HONEY BUNNY (2006), BE-37

Marilyn Sadler and Roger Bollen

Honey Bunny's second starring role is a Bright and Early Book focused on the joy of giving. At the story's start, Honey Bunny gathers all of her money for a shopping spree. She buys a couple of things for herself (a ball, a bat, and a "pretty hat"), but for the most part the generous rabbit gets things for her friends and family. This gives Marilyn a chance to do some fun rhyming and Roger to draw some silly pictures, such as a pig in an Elvis wig and a hen with a pen. There's also a sly allusion to Beginner Books past, with the fox getting a pair of socks. And not only is Honey Bunny thoughtful, she's also prudent. The final line reads, "Honey Bunny gave and gave, but still has money left to save" (Roger's picture shows her putting a single coin into her piggy bank).

In the twelve-year interim between *Honey Bunny Funnybunny* and *Money Money Honey Bunny*, Roger and Marilyn continued to make books together, but had turned their eye toward television. P. J. Funnybunny had been the star of ABC weekend specials in 1989, 1993, and 1996. Alistair had a BBC special, and two of his books were featured on *Reading Rainbow*. Things really picked up, though when *Zenon, Girl of the 21st Century* served as the basis for three successful Disney Channel films between 1999 and 2004. This led, in 2006, to Roger and Marilyn creating and developing the hit Disney Jr. show *Handy Manny*, about a young man and his anthropomorphized tools.

Roger and Marilyn divorced not long after the show wrapped up in 2009. *Money Money Honey Bunny* would be their last Beginner Book together.

Roger married Audrey Curran and continued to make his home in the Cleveland area. He passed away in 2015 at the age of seventy-four.

Marilyn has continued to write children's books, including the Beginner Book *Ten Eggs in a Nest* (2014).

THE BELLY BOOK (2008), B-97

Joe Harris

Feet, eyes, ears, hands, noses, teeth, hair, wings, knees, and ... bellies? The latest Beginner Books body part book focuses on an unlikely part of the anatomy, but one that plays an important role in our everyday health and well-being. *The Belly Book* takes its reader on a tour of the different kinds, sizes, and locations of bellies on various humans and animals. It humorously points out a belly's usefulness ("A belly's a good place / for resting your cup. / It also works well / for a chat with your pup."), and gives a pointed message about taking care of your stomach with a healthy, balanced diet.

Presented in four-line rhyme with cartoony pen-and-ink illustrations, *The Belly Book* feels very much like a throwback to the Beginner and Bright and Early Books of the 1960s and 1970s. There's good reason for that. Author/illustrator Joe Harris (1928–2017) was from the same generation and background as many of the first wave of Beginner Book creators. Born in Jersey City, New Jersey, to parents Charlie and Gladys, Joe served in both the United States Navy and the United States Marine Corps after high school. Upon completion of his service he enrolled at Pratt Institute in Brooklyn studying design and illustration.

Not long after his graduation, Joe landed at the ad agency Dancer Fitzgerald Sample, doing work for print and television. One of Dancer Fitzgerald Sample's big clients was General Mills, and in the late 1950s the agency was charged with coming up with a mascot and tagline for a new fruit-flavored cereal called Trix. It was Joe who designed a long-eared white rabbit, and came up with the tagline, "Silly rabbit! Trix are for kids!" It's rare for an ad campaign to survive a couple of years, let alone the sixty years that one has.

Around 1959 Joe and the exquisitely named Buck Biggers, Chet Stover, and Thread Covington teamed up to form a studio called Total TeleVision. The idea had come directly from General Mills, who wanted to sponsor an animated Saturday morning TV show. Total TeleVisions's first show, *King Leonardo and His Short Subjects*, debuted on NBC in 1960. Most of the look of the characters and their backstories came from Joe, who was responsible for design and storyboarding at the studio. Total TeleVision would add two new shows in 1964, *Tennessee Tuxedo and His Tales*, about a wisecracking penguin who plots escapes from the zoo, and *Underdog*, following the adventures of a canine superhero. The latter proved to be their most popular creation by far, even inspiring a balloon in the Macy's Thanksgiving Day Parade that debuted in 1965 and appeared in the parade in each of the following twenty years.

Total TeleVision would only last until 1968 when General Mills ended their sponsorship. Joe returned to the ad business, but his most famous creations will live on and on. In a 2007 interview promoting the live action Underdog film, he shared, "Anytime I'm out in public, people always say, 'Here's a piece of paper, draw Underdog for me, will you?'"

Joe was married twice; first to Janet Opel from 1957 until her death in 1981 and then to Vanessa Campbell from 1983 until her death in 2002. He had three daughters, Joelle, Sophie, and Merrie. Upon Joe's death at the age of eighty-nine at his home in Stamford, Connecticut, Merrie wrote, "May heaven be a big studio."

The Belly Book was Joe's only published work.

The 2010s

HAVE YOU SEEN MY DINOSAUR? (2010), B-99

Jon Surgal and Joe Mathieu

Have You Seen My Dinosaur? is the story of a boy looking for his prehistoric friend. The people he consults—his mom, a fisherman, a police officer, a zookeeper, a paleontologist, and a museum tour guide—are either gently patronizing or dismissive, but the reader knows better because we can see the dinosaur hiding in the background of every page. In the end our hero is clever enough to ask the reader: "I think who I should ask is . . . you! / Have YOU seen my dinosaur? / You have? / He's where? / Say that once more!" It turns out the reader was witnessing an epic game of hide-and-seek.

With its simple, interactive premise and momentum-sustaining couplets, *Have You Seen My Dinosaur?* is very much infused with the Beginner Book spirit. As an early reader, however, it has a few too many fancy turns of phrase, especially in the zoo section that lists some of the animals there: "Plus two gnu. A kinkajou. / Camels with a hump or two. / A big black bear from Baden-Baden. / A Scottish beastie from Culloden." While Seussian, clever, and great fun for read alouds, this is a tough mountain to climb for a first grader.

Writer Jon Surgal (born 1949) has a varied and colorful resume. He was born in New York City to Florence and Alan Surgal. His father worked as a scriptwriter for radio and television and would become best known for the screenplay for *Mickey One*, a 1965 film starring Warren Beatty. Jon followed his father's footsteps. In his twenties he wrote and created for television (the short-lived Saturday morning NBC show *Muggsey* and "The Big Game Hunt" animated segments on the PBS series *Vegetable Soup*). Over the years he's also worked on the Canadian show *Emily of New Moon* and with puppeteer Shari Lewis on *The Shari Show*.

He is a professor of literature, writing, and film studies, and holds a PhD from Columbia University. As a playwright and performer, he is also heavily involved in Manhattan theater, and founded the outdoor performance troupe Theater on the Rocks. *Have You Seen My Dinosaur?* is his first—and so far, only—children's book.

Have You Seen My Dinosaur?'s vivid illustrations were done by Joe Mathieu (born 1949). Though he'd been involved with Beginner Books since 1997, this was Joe's first non-licensed (in 1997 he did the pictures for *Can You Tell Me How to Get to Sesame Street?* by Eleanor Hudson), non-reillustrated (in the late 1990s and early 2000s he provided new illustrations for *The Eye Book*, *The Nose Book*, and *The Tooth Book*) Beginner Book.

Born in Springfield, Vermont, Joe discovered a love of making funny drawings at a very early age. "I was never interested in drawing completely straight," he told *Contemporary Authors Online*. "It's almost impossible for me to avoid humor, caricature and lots of action." He attended day school in Connecticut, got his BFA from the Rhode Island School of Design, and began working as an illustrator immediately after. His first published works began to appear in 1973.

Though he has built a career working with a wide variety of authors—including fellow Beginner Book creator Laura Numeroff—Joe is best known for his Sesame Street books. Since 1972, he's done over seventy-five books featuring those characters, as well as art and designs for hundreds of licensed Sesame Street products. It's fitting because Joe fell under Jim Henson's spell early on. He explains, "As a youngster, I became enamored of Jim Henson and the Muppets long before they were really famous. I would beg permission to miss the bus if they were going to appear on *The Dave Garroway Show* or I'd get special permission to stay up late if they were scheduled for Jack Parr."

When Random House began looking for illustrators to do Sesame Street books, Joe was a natural fit. He made a reverent study of Michael Frith's pioneering work in turning Henson's puppets into drawings (in fact, at a glance one could easily mistake Joe's work on *Can You Tell Me How to Get to Sesame Street?* for Michael's). His work on *Have You Seen My Dinosaur?* is in his own style, but one can still see the Muppet influences in his loose-limbed character work, especially in Professor Pew, the tour guide, and the zoo animals. Though he sometimes still starts with pencil on paper, in 2002 Joe began coloring his work digitally in Photoshop, as he did on *Have You Seen My Dinosaur?*

Joe also works with fellow artist Aristides Ruiz to do most of the artwork for The Cat in the Hat Learning Library books. A jazz and ragtime enthusiast, Joe creates album covers for Stomp Off Records, which puts out new albums and reisssues in those genres. He lives in Massachusetts with his wife, Melanie.

A PET NAMED SNEAKER (2013), B-101

Joan Heilbroner and Pascal Lemaitre

A Pet Named Sneaker is a tale of an exceptional snake who comes to live with a boy named Pete. Sneaker the snake does tricks, attends school with Pete, and even becomes a lifeguard.

Setting a record for the longest time elapsed between published Beginner Books, Joan Heilbroner's second Beginner Book arrived fifty-one years after the still-in-print *Robert the Rose Horse*. Following her impressive 1962 publishing flurry, Joan slowed down. In 1965 she published *Meet George Washington*, a Random House Step-Up book (her sister Barbara provided a companion volume, *Meet Abraham Lincoln*). But her next book wouldn't appear for nearly twenty years. *Tom the TV Cat*, with illustrations by Sal Murdocca, was published in 1984 as a Random House Step Into Reading book.

The long break between books was mostly a matter of being otherwise occupied. After her first three books, she had tried doing some writing for adults, but with both of her sons—Peter and David—attending the Town School on East 76th Street, Joan began volunteering in the school library. Eventually, she enrolled at Columbia University and got a degree in library science, and began a long career as a school librarian.

In her retirement, with no intention of returning to authorhood, Joan was charmed by a story told to her by her grandchildren, David's children Quinten and Katrina. The siblings had a pet snake named Plato. "They were just crazy about that snake," Joan told *Publishers Weekly* in 2013, "and they would play with it endlessly, twisting and turning it. One day, Quentin and Katrina took it to a fair on Martha's Vineyard and the fair director asked if the snake could do tricks. Quentin replied, 'Certainly! He can make figure eights and handcuffs.'" This led, of course, to Sneaker's story, which contains a scene wherein the snake plays a necktie, a hat, and handcuffs.

Underlying her amusement at her grandchildren's story was the fact that Joan herself has no love for snakes. "When I was about 8 or 9 years old," she recalls, "I was in the country and I walked down the hill into the woods and I saw a snake and I screamed. I was just terrified." So, she acknowledges, perhaps writing a book about a snake was her way of coming to peace with her fears.

A Pet Named Sneaker was illustrated by Pascal Lemaitre (born 1967) in a pen-and-ink style not far removed from the work of Roy McKie, with a sense of composition akin to P. D. Eastman (the final pool scene recalls *Go, Dog. Go!*). Pascal grew up in Belgium and was not especially crazy about reading, at least not text. "I was an image-and-drawings eater," he told the blog *Seven Impossible Things before Breakfast*. As a child he adored the comic strips of Belgian cartoonist André Franquin, creator of Gaston and Marsupilami. As an adult his two major heroes are André François and William Steig, both *New Yorker* artists who did children's books, and both influenced by Saul Steinberg (who also influenced Roy McKie). Pascal attended the National School of Visual Art, La Cambre in Brussels, Belgium.

He started landing work in various publications in his home country and France, and eventually got an agent in the United States to help find work here. Since then he's done illustrations for *Time*, the *New Yorker*, and the *New York Times* and has provided the pictures for books by Tony and Slade Morrison, Andrea Beaty, and Kate McMullan, among others.

Pascal, his wife, and daughter Maëlle divide their time between Belgium and New York City.

SQUIRRELS ON SKIS (2013), B-102

J. Hamilton Ray and Pascal Lemaitre

Squirrels on Skis is the tale of a sleepy New England hamlet that's invaded by dozens of skiing squirrels. It seems someone has equipped the bushy-tailed rodents with popsicle sticks and toothpicks, and now they're running—or rather skiing—amok. The town is divided on how to get rid of them. Some would prefer that exterminator Stanley Powers vacuum them up in his new contraption, while others find that to be inhumane.

Young Sally Sue Breeze is in the latter camp, and points out that the squirrels are so occupied with skiing that they aren't eating or coming in from the cold. She gets to the bottom of the problem (a greedy rabbit who has taken advantage of the squirrels) and comes up with a clever solution (a new ski lodge just for the squirrels—the Bushy Tail Great Ski Chalet).

Squirrels on Skis comes on like a classic Beginner Book madcap romp. But whereas with Ted as writer or editor the squirrels might have simply run wild with no consequence or explanation, this story reads more like one of his big books, very much concerned with problem and solution and right and wrong. The result is that the absurd premise has something more serious underneath. One might even be tempted to view it as an immigration allegory: A large group of unwanted outsiders descend upon a town and are seemingly

Courtesy Pascal Lemaitre.

menacing, but are actually in need of help. And if this is a bit of a stretch, at the very least the story promotes the message of compassion and cooperation.

Something else that makes *Squirrels on Skis* read more like *The Lorax* or *How the Grinch Stole Christmas* than a Beginner Book is that while the story has rhythm and four-line rhyme, it is very wordy both in volume (it has perhaps the highest word count of any Beginner Book to date) and difficulty (lots of non-decodable words such as "disposal" and "chalet").

J. Hamilton Ray is a pseudonym for writer Raymond Messecar (born 1952) who was born in New Brunswick, Canada, and grew up in both Connecticut and Maine. His mother was a high school English teacher and his father worked with the National Ski Patrol, so Ray learned to ski at a very young age. As an adult he started out working for the ABC news show *20/20*, and then later branched out into his own production company, Praxis Media Inc., where among other things he did animated adaptations of Beginner Books, including three P. D. Eastman books and *I Am Not Going to Get Up Today!* From there he began writing and directing various shows for PBS Kids, including Chris Cerf and Michael Frith's *Between the Lions*.

Despite his Beginner Book pedigree, Ray didn't consciously write *Squirrels on Skis* as a Beginner Book or a Dr. Seuss homage. He says, instead, he was trying to write a comedy mystery story with a classic feel that kids would want to hear repeatedly. The idea had arrived to him when he and his wife (novelist C. A. Belmond) saw some squirrels sliding down the snowy slopes of their Redding, Connecticut, backyard. The idea stuck with him and he wrote it up. When he read the manuscript aloud to Kate Klimo and Cathy Goldsmith, they both immediately pegged it as a Beginner Book, praising the fact that it honored Ted's spirit without imitating him. Though Ray did imitate Ted in one major way: "I gave my publisher a full storyboard, in which I drew sketches of the entire book, and made decisions of page layouts and scenes."

Of course, illustrator Pascal Lemaitre took this and made it his own. He approaches a picture book the way a film or stage director might: "It's like preparing a theater piece, but you have to draw the casting of actors you would pick, then create the props, think about the lighting, etc." For *Squirrels on Skis* specifically he says, "I felt I needed bold colors as it was like an action movie with squirrels going crazy." Ray says, "Pascal brought his considerable talent and humor to the book, so it was a very successful collaboration."

TEN EGGS IN A NEST (2014), BE-40

Marilyn Sadler and Michael Fleming

Following her split from Roger Bollen, which was the end not only of a marriage but of a fruitful creative partnership, Marilyn has continued to put out books at a steady pace, including *Pass It On* (with Michael Slack, 2012), *Alice from Dallas* (with Ard Hyod, 2014), and three Charlie Piechart books (with Eric Comstock, 2015–2018). The latter books introduce math concepts like graphs, time, fractions, and geometry.

Marilyn's latest Bright and Early Book is also a math book. *Ten Eggs in a Nest* is a one-to-ten counting book with a clever twist. Gwen the Hen and Red the Rooster are expectant parents. When the first chick emerges, Red heads to Worm World to buy a worm from Pinky Pig, but discovers upon his return that two more chicks have hatched. This back and forth continues as more chicks arrive, not one-by-one, but exponentially. So the reader counts not 1, 2, 3, 4, . . . , but 1, 3, 6, 10.

Besides the opportunity to practice math concepts, the book is also an introduction to some common bird-related idioms. In the beginning, Red wants to know how many chicks to expect, but Gwen reminds him, "It's bad luck to count your eggs before they hatch." Later, Marilyn uses "you could have knocked him over with a feather" and "peck on the cheek." It's all very clever, and the book's only real drawback is that the word count and vocabulary feel more like a Beginner Book than a Bright and Early. Though, admittedly, that's a distinction that has blurred over the years, dating back even to when Ted was still in charge.

Illustrator Michael Fleming (born 1969) grew up in the San Francisco Bay area. He headed to the East coast briefly to study film at the Massachusetts College of Art and Design, and then went back to California to finish a degree in experimental animation at Cal Arts. In 2003 he began a career as a freelance illustrator. His focus has primarily been on child-centered media, including design and illustration for toys, games, and animation, working with clients such as JibJab, Scholastic, Independent Film Channel, and American Greetings. Michael's picture book career started in 2003 with Kate Klimo's Step Into Reading book *Twinky the Dinky Dog*.

The whimsical animal world of *Ten Eggs in a Nest* fell into place once Michael came up with the design for Red the Rooster. He then drew and painted the illustrations in Photoshop using a Cintiq tablet. Working with art director Jan Gerardi, Michael decided to keep the inked outline on the characters, which was something he hadn't done before. This has the effect of providing a visual throwback to earlier Beginner Book artists with strong ink lines, such as Roy McKie and Fritz Siebel, and Michael says he believes it "suits the comic-book-like antics in the book very well."

Michael followed *Ten Eggs in a Nest* work with illustrations for *Ten Busy Brooms* (Carole Gerber, 2016) and *Time for School, Little Dinosaur* (Gail Herman, 2017). He currently lives on the island of Alameda with his two dogs, and draws inspiration from his creative friends.

Marilyn continues to work on new books, new television projects, and new story ideas, and looks both back and forward with gratitude. "I love what I do. I feel so very lucky to be able to create characters and tell their stories while getting lost in the worlds of my own design."

A SKUNK IN MY BUNK (2019), B-107

Christopher Cerf and Nicola Slater

The first new, non-licensed Beginner or Bright and Early Book in five years comes from someone with unmatched Beginner Book credentials. Of course, his mom helped start the line, his dad wrote four of them, and he helped out with their production in the 1960s, but Christopher Cerf's (born 1941) non-Beginner Book experiences qualify him even more. Though he started in the "nonbroadcast materials division" of the *Electric Company* and *Sesame*

Street, he spent many more years as a songwriter for Sesame Street and other Children's Television Workshop productions. To the former he contributed over two hundred songs including the classics "Count It Higher" (a 1973 take-off of "Twist and Shout" sung by a Muppet based on Chris himself), 1986's "Put Down the Duckie" and 1989's "Monster in the Mirror" (the latter two with cowriter Norman Stiles).

Chris also, along with Michael Frith and Stiles, created *Between the Lions* for PBS. The show ran from 2000 to 2010, with a primary mission—like Beginner Books—of awakening the joy of literacy in children. Using puppets, animated segments, and songs, the series focused on a family of lions that live in a library. The show won ten Emmys in the course of its run and was hailed by both the National Education Association and the International Reading Association.

In short, Chris knows well how to take educational content and deliver it in a fun way. When Barbara Marcus brought up the idea of doing a Beginner Book to Chris, he didn't hesitate. "Oh my god, yes!" were his exact words. He decided to go back to the original method of creating Beginner Books, working from a word list. Additionally, he used his experience writing for *Sesame Street*: "If I had to write a song about the letter J, I would write down everything that begins with 'J' and all the words that rhyme with those . . . so I was looking for words that rhymed and went together in a funny way, and that's where the idea of a skunk in my bunk came."

The book uses the *Hop on Pop* format, with each segment introducing a set of rhyming family words in all caps, and presenting them used together in a sentence. Thus you end up with "A goat in a coat in a boat" and "A cop in a shop with a bottle of pop." Each of the eight segments escalates from sentences that use one or two of the rhyming words to ones that use three or four. And in the end, all of the characters come together in one of those grand two-page Beginner Book moments.

The illustrations are by Manchester-based artist Nicola Slater (born circa 1977). Born in northern Britain, Nicola attended Buckinghamshire Chilterns University, where she studied graphic design and illustration. There, a love of children's books blossomed. Her career in children's books began in the early 2000s illustrating middle grade novels. By the middle of the decade she began to do picture books as well and since then has illustrated nearly twenty books, including *Where's My Jumper?* (2017) and its sequel *Where's My Pink Sweater?* (2019), both of which she also wrote.

Nicola says she's influenced by old Disney concept art, mid-century modern design, and nature. This all adds up to a style that recalls the golden age of Golden Book artists, specifically Mary Blair. Nicola works with pencils

Christopher Cerf in 2019. The antlers above his head are
part of a sculpture by Ted called "Blue Green Abelard."
Photograph by and courtesy Richard Hine.

and India ink, scanning her drawings into Photoshop and then adding color
and other effects using a Wacom tablet. Her pictures for *A Skunk in My Bunk*
show some little tributes to her Beginner Book forebears, most notably the
rough-line charcoal-effect rendering on the characters that brings to mind
P. D. Eastman and Fritz Siebel.

CAN YOU SEE ME? (2019), B-108

Bob Staake

Can You See Me? is the tale of a giant lizard with the ability to blend in wherever it goes. The book follows this unnamed creature as it hides various
places—the clouds, a brick wall, a field of flowers—and challenges a young

Color sketch for *Can You See Me*. Courtesy Bob Staake.

boy and girl to find it. This premise gives the book a clear kinship to *Put Me in the Zoo*, with a talented animal proudly showing off for two children.

The book utilizes all of the classic Beginner Book tricks well. It's written in simple four-line rhyme, using repetition ("We can see you hiding there! We can see you ANYwhere!") and an interactive structure. Like many of the early Beginner Books, it teaches a simple concept (in this case, colors) and is essentially a romp, with no problem-solution or moral. And much of the joy of reading the book comes from the vividly colored and immaculately composed two-page spreads.

Author-illustrator Bob Staake (born 1957) grew up in Los Angeles, California, with an insatiable appetite for picture books, Hanna-Barbera cartoons, and *MAD Magazine*. A constant doodler, he won an editorial cartooning contest when he was attending West Torrance High School, with the prize of having his work printed in *People* magazine. This led to Bob being taken under the mentorship of *Los Angeles Times* cartoonist Paul Conrad. Though Bob already had contract offers from syndicates, Conrad encouraged him to get an education before jumping right into professional work. Having taken every art class available in high school, Bob chose instead to study journalism and international relations at the University of Southern California.

Bob Staake's self-portrait. Courtesy Bob Staake.

His career as a freelance illustrator started soon after graduation. From the start Bob realized that what was more important to him than the aesthetic value of his work was what message it conveyed. "The drawings became subservient to the expression of my ideas," he says.

This is the perfect mindset for an illustrator, so it's no surprise that that's the path Bob followed. His resume now boosts covers for the *New Yorker* and *Time*, design work for Cartoon Network and Nickelodeon, and a spot among "the usual gang of idiots" of his childhood favorite, *MAD Magazine*. Since 1989 he's illustrated over sixty books, many of which he wrote himself. These include *The Red Lemon*, which the *New York Times* placed on their Top 10 Illustrated Books of 2006; and *The First Pup* (2010), which is about the Obamas' dog, Bo.

Though always in service to the story, Bob's illustrations are highly graphic. For his children's books, he often builds his work in Photoshop with overlapping geometrical shapes, lending a modernist feel to the final result. He cites a long list of influences on his work, but looming large among them are many classic Little Golden Book illustrators, J. P. Miller, Mary Blair, Tibor Gergeley, and Richard Scarry. Also on the list are Dr. Seuss and UPA animation, both having obvious ties to Beginner Books. In fact, Bob says of Beginner Books, "They were not only essential to my development as a reader and looker, but ultimately as an author/illustrator of my own children's books. That I was weaned on the books of Seuss, McKie, Lopshire, et al, to create my own 50 plus years later is simply bizarre."

Bob is married to Paulette Fehlig. They have two grown sons, and live in Chatham, Massachusetts, in a two-hundred-year-old house on Cape Cod. He's currently at work on his second Beginner Book, a sequel to *Can You See Me?* titled *I Can Be Anything*.

Acknowledgments

For sharing their stories and insights: Sally Allen, Michael Berenstain, Bob Bernstein, Stu Bloom, Melissa Bollen Ellsworth, Jon Buller, Christopher Cerf, Rawli Davis, Angelo DeCesare, Tony Eastman, Susan Eastman, Corey Lynn Fayman, Michael Fleming, Michael Frith, Joan Heilbroner, Kathy Shortall Hensley, Becky Holland, Carol Jaffe, Kate Klimo, Pascal Lemaitre, Lee Liebek, Andy Low, Kathy Low, Chris Lyerly, June McKie, Todd McKie, Laura Numeroff, Timothy Roland, Marilyn Sadler, Steven Salerno, Susan Schade, Emily Brewton Schilling, Eric Seltzer, Bob Staake, Barbara Thomas, and Terry Lopshire Tigue.

For their assistance with my research: Arjuna Anday, Lassie Barille, Sandra Boynton, Joanne Coleman, Cliff Erickson, Eleanor Farley, Gayle Feldman, J. Christian FitzGerald, Sandy Green, David Heilbroner, Peter Heilbroner, Brian Jay Jones, Sherri Marmon, Zoe O'Brian, Tish Rabe, and David Tobey.

To Katie Keene, Mary Heath, Jennifer Mixon, Laura Strong, Debbie Upton, and the rest of the staff at University Press of Mississippi for their fantastic work on the book.

And, as always, to my family—especially Wendy, Peter, and Theo—for their love and support. I love you all.

Notes

ABBREVIATIONS

PVA . . . . Paul V. Allen
RHA/CU . . . . Random House Archives, Columbia University
TG. . . . . Ted Geisel

INTRODUCTION

4   "writes his own books": Robert Lopshire to Bob Bernstein, June 26, 1965, RHA/CU (699).

CHAPTER 1

10   "reason should prevail": Chall, Jeanne. *Learning to Read: The Great Debate.* 2nd ed. McGraw-Hill: New York, 1983. p7.

11   "correspond with reality": Hersey, John. "Why Do Children Bog Down on the First 'R'?" *Life,* May 24, 1954.

11   "artificial sequences of words": Flesch, Rudolf. *Why Johnny Can't Read.* Harper & Row: New York, 1955.

12   "strung-out prose": Flesch, Rudolf. *Why Johnny Can't Read.* Harper & Row: New York, 1955.

12   "terribly literal": Hersey, John. "Why Do Children Bog Down on the First 'R'?" *Life,* May 24, 1954.

12   "associative richness": Hersey, John. "Why Do Children Bog Down on the First 'R'?" *Life,* May 24, 1954.

CHAPTER 2

15   "juxtaposition of words": Morgan, Judith and Neil. *Dr. Seuss and Mr. Geisel.* Random House: New York, 1995. p109.

15   "no sense whatever": See, Carolyn. "Dr. Seuss and the Naked Ladies." *Esquire,* June 1974.

16   "can't put down": Morgan, Judith and Neil. *Dr. Seuss and Mr. Geisel.* Random House: New York, 1995. p154.

16 "subsequent swift acclaim": Cohen, Charles D. *The Seuss, the Whole Seuss, and Nothing but the Seuss*. Random House: New York, 2004. p301.

16 "kids that young": Cohen, Charles D. *The Seuss, the Whole Seuss, and Nothing but the Seuss*. Random House: New York, 2004. p301.

19 "with a doodle": Sadler, Glenn Edward. "Maurice Sendak and Dr. Seuss: A Conversation." In *Of Sneetches and Whos and the Good Dr. Seuss: Essays on the Writings and Life of Theodor Geisel*. Thomas Fensch, ed. New Century Books: Chesterfield, VA, 1997.

19 "a secret smile": Morgan, Judith and Neil. *Dr. Seuss and Mr. Geisel*. Random House: New York, 1995. p153.

19 "no adjectives": Morgan, Judith and Neil. *Dr. Seuss and Mr. Geisel*. Random House: New York, 1995. p154.

19 "an adult book": Nel, Philip. *The Annotated Cat: Under the Hats of Seuss and His Cats*. Random House: New York, 2007. p52.

20 "demanding audience": Nel, Philip. *The Annotated Cat: Under the Hats of Seuss and His Cats*. Random House: New York, 2007. p17.

20 "time and sweat": Ford, Carin T. *Dr. Seuss: Best-Loved Author*. Enslow: Berkeley Heights, NJ, 2003. p49.

20 "only genius": Kahn Jr., E. J. "Children's Friend." *New Yorker*, December 17, 1960.

20 "pangs of birth": Nel, Philip. *Dr. Seuss: American Icon*. Continuum: New York, 2004. p35.

20 "exhausted children": Weidt, Maryann N. *Oh, the Places He Went: A Story about Dr. Seuss*. Carolrhoda Books, Minneapolis, 1994. p40.

21 "they are boulevardier": Michael Frith, interview with PVA, November 5, 2017.

21 "feels unfulfilled": Nel, Philip. *Dr. Seuss: American Icon*. Continuum: New York, 2004. p18.

23 "kind of reader": Morgan, Judith and Neil. *Dr. Seuss and Mr. Geisel*. Random House: New York, 1995. p156.

23 "word of mouth": Morgan, Judith and Neil. *Dr. Seuss and Mr. Geisel*. Random House: New York, 1995. p156.

23 "foot-dragging": Roth, Rita. "On Beyond Zebra with Dr. Seuss." *New Advocate*, Fall 1989.

23 "pure and simple": Kahn Jr., E. J. "Children's Friend." *New Yorker*, December 17, 1960.

23 "art of reading": Kahn Jr., E. J. "Children's Friend." *New Yorker*, December 17, 1960.

CHAPTER 3

26 "kid cousin": Hawkins, Robin. "Notable New Yorkers: Bennett Cerf" (interview; session 10, January 5, 1968). Columbia University Libraries Oral History Research Office. http://www.columbia.edu/cu/lweb/digital/collections/nny/cerfb/transcripts/cerfb_1_10_428.htm

26 "cutest-looking kid": Cerf, Bennett. *At Random: The Reminiscences of Bennett Cerf*. Random House: New York, 1977. p149.

26 "smacked me": Hawkins, Robin. "Notable New Yorkers: Bennett Cerf" (interview; session 10, January 5, 1968). Columbia University Libraries Oral History Research Office. http://www.columbia.edu/cu/lweb/digital/collections/nny/cerfb/transcripts/cerfb_1_10_428.htm

28 "reading progress": Christopher Cerf, Interview with PVA, August 30, 2018.

28   "hole in your sock": Hawkins, Robin. "Notable New Yorkers: Bennett Cerf" (interview; session 10, January 5, 1968). Columbia University Libraries Oral History Research Office. http://www.columbia.edu/cu/lweb/digital/collections/nny/cerfb/transcripts /cerfb_1_10_428.htm

29   "anxiously await": Cerf, Bennett. *At Random: The Reminiscences of Bennett Cerf.* Random House: New York, 1977. p153.

29   "find the key": Morgan, Judith and Neil. *Dr. Seuss and Mr. Geisel.* Random House: New York, 1995. p157.

30   "a lopsided smile": Ford, Carin T. *Dr. Seuss: Best-Loved Author.* Enslow Publishing: Berkeley Heights, NJ, 2003. p36.

30   "what you really want": Pease, Donald E. *Theodor Seuss Geisel.* Oxford University Press: Oxford, 2010. p40.

31   "editor and condenser": Pease, Donald E. *Theodor Seuss Geisel.* Oxford University Press: Oxford, 2010. p114.

CHAPTER 4

34   "textbooks leave off": "Beginner Books: New Trade Learn-to-Read Juveniles." *Publishers Weekly*, June 2, 1958. pp116–17.

34   "dramatic conflict and suspense": "Word List and General Instructions." Beginner Books, Inc. Random House internal document. Courtesy of Michael Frith.

35   "good warm smile": "Word List and General Instructions." Beginner Books, Inc. Random House internal document. Courtesy of Michael Frith.

35   "how kids see things": Cott, Jonathan. *Pipers at the Gates of Dawn: The Wisdom of Children's Literature.* McGraw-Hill: New York, 1983.

35   "suspended and wanting more": "A Few Suggestions for Authors Working on Their First Beginner Books." Beginner Books, Inc. Random House internal document. Courtesy of Michael Frith.

35   "throw away the story": "Word List and General Instructions." Beginner Books, Inc. Random House internal document. Courtesy of Michael Frith.

37   "believable, and consistent": Ford, Carin T. *Dr. Seuss: Best-Loved Author.* Enslow Publishing: Berkeley Heights, NJ, 2003. p74.

37   "inherent moral": Bunzel, Peter. "The Wacky World of Dr. Seuss Delights the Child— and Adult—Readers of His Books." *Life*, April 6, 1959.

37   "bunny, bunny books": Gorney, Cynthia. "Dr. Seuss at 75: Grinch, Cat in Hat, Wocket and Generations of Kids in His Pocket." *Washington Post*, May 21, 1979.

37   "you lose him": "Word List and General Instructions." Beginner Books, Inc. Random House internal document. Courtesy of Michael Frith.

37   "systemize and formulate": "Beginner Books: New Trade Learn-to-Read Juveniles." *Publishers Weekly*, June 2, 1958. p117.

37   "younger and younger readers": Morgan, Judith and Neil. *Dr. Seuss and Mr. Geisel.* Random House: New York, 1995. p160.

38   "extraordinarily charming": Christopher Cerf, Interview with PVA, August 30, 2018.

38   "U.S. Steel-Corporation-and-wife": TG to Bennett Cerf, June 8, 1960. RHA/CA (box 42, Beginner Books 1).

38   "the biggest thing": Fadiman, Clifton. *Holiday* 25, no. 4 (April 15, 1959).

39   "I can read": "An Interview with William C. Morris." *Horn Book* 71, no. 1 (January/February 1995).

39   "measure of repetition": Guilfoile, Elizabeth. *Books for Beginning Readers*. National Council of Teachers of English: Champaign, IL, 1962. p. v.

40   "self-conscious children": Nel, Philip. *The Annotated Cat: Under the Hats of Seuss and His Cats*. Random House: New York, 2007. p10.

40   "flood of income": Morgan, Judith and Neil. *Dr. Seuss and Mr. Geisel*. Random House: New York, 1995. p162.

40   "most profitable": Morgan, Judith and Neil. *Dr. Seuss and Mr. Geisel*. Random House: New York, 1995. p159.

40   "becoming embarrassing": Hawkins, Robin. "Notable New Yorkers: Bennett Cerf" (interview; session 10, January 5, 1968). Columbia University Libraries Oral History Research Office.

41   "get the money anyway": Christopher Cerf, Interview with PVA, August 30, 2018.

41   "a great glory": Helen Geisel to Donald Klopfer, September 19, 1960. RHA/CU (Box 42, Beginner Books 2).

42   "still yapping": Hawkins, Robin. "Notable New Yorkers: Bennett Cerf" (interview; session 10, January 5, 1968). Columbia University Libraries Oral History Research Office.

P. D. EASTMAN, PART 1

43   "other moving elements": Sporn, Michael. "Mary Louise Witham Eastman." *Michael Sporn Animation.com*. March 9, 2013. http://www.michaelspornanimation.com/splog /?p=4577.

44   "get left behind": Abraham, Adam. *When Magoo Flew: The Rise and Fall of Animation Studio UPA*. University of Wesleyan Press: Middletown, CT, 2012. p90.

45   "a study in contrast": Abraham, Adam. *When Magoo Flew: The Rise and Fall of Animation Studio UPA*. University of Wesleyan Press: Middletown, CT, 2012. p82.

45   "they fired me too": Stern, Fredric. "Bill Scott of Tujunga: Life Isn't Rocky for Bullwinkle Anymore." *Los Angeles Times*, September 23, 1977.

47   "ever informed": Cohen, Karl F. *Forbidden Information: Censored Cartoons and Blacklisted Animators in America*. McFarland: Jefferson, NC, 2004.

CHAPTER 5

48   "the floodgates opened": "Golden Years and Time of Tumult: 1920–1967." *A Critical History of Children's Literature*. Cornelia Meigs, ed. Macmillan Company: London, 1969. pp393–668.

49   "high dive": Morgan, Judith and Neil. *Dr. Seuss and Mr. Geisel*. Random House: New York, 1995. p187.

50   "new-found reading ability": "What Went Into the Planning of Beginner Books." RHA/
      CU (Box 870, Beginner Books).

50   "can quickly pick up": Beginning Readers' Club advertisement. *Philadelphia Inquirer*,
      September 17, 1961.

ROY MCKIE, PART 1

52   "a tough school": Streetman, Bergin. "Roy McKie: The Early Years." *Vintage Kids' Books
      My Kid Loves* (blog), January 3, 2011. http://www.vintagechildrensbooksmykidloves.
      com/2011/01/roy-mckie-early-years.html.

52   "spend so much time": Streetman, Bergin. "Roy McKie: The Early Years." *Vintage Kids'
      Books My Kid Loves* (blog), January 3, 2011. http://www.vintagechildrensbooksmykid
      loves.com/2011/01/roy-mckie-early-years.html.

52   "next Norman Rockwell": June McKie. Interview with PVA, September 24, 2017.

52   "almost nothing": Streetman, Bergin. "Roy McKie: The Early Years." *Vintage Kids' Books
      My Kid Loves* (blog), January 3, 2011.

55   "just might": Streetman, Bergin. "Roy McKie: The Early Years." *Vintage Kids' Books My
      Kid Loves* (blog), January 3, 2011.

55   "within our institution": TG to Phyllis Cerf, January 11, 1960. RHA/CU (Box 42, Begin-
      ner Books 2).

55   "could and couldn't do": Streetman, Bergin. "Roy McKie: The Later Years." *Vintage Kids'
      Books My Kid Loves* (blog), January 4, 2011. http://www.vintagechildrensbooksmykid
      loves.com/2011/01/roy-mckie-later-years.html.

55   "how many lines": Greene, Jo-Ann. "Illustrator Roy McKie Recalls His Collaboration
      with Dr. Seuss." *Lancaster Online*, February 23, 2013.

STAN AND JAN BERENSTAIN, PART 1

57   "come back rejected": Berenstain, Stan and Jan. *Down a Sunny Dirt Road: An Autobio-
      graphy*. Random House: New York, 2002. p117.

57   "family magazine": Berenstain, Stan and Jan. *Down a Sunny Dirt Road: An Autobio-
      graphy*. Random House: New York, 2002. p119.

58   "more fan mail": Berenstain, Mike. *Child's Play: Cartoon Art of Stan and Jan Berenstain*.
      Abrams: New York, 2008. p45.

58   "Frank Lloyd Wrightish": Berenstain, Mike. *Child's Play: Cartoon Art of Stan and Jan
      Berenstain*. Abrams: New York, 2008. p45.

59   "aren't good for them": Berenstain, Stan and Jan. *Down a Sunny Dirt Road: An Autobio-
      graphy*. Random House: New York, 2002. p137.

59   "helluva lot wrong": Berenstain, Stan and Jan. *Down a Sunny Dirt Road: An Autobio-
      graphy*. Random House: New York, 2002. p148.

59   "get up and go": Berenstain, Stan and Jan. *Down a Sunny Dirt Road: An Autobiography*.
      Random House: New York, 2002. p150.

60   "just as seriously": Berenstain, Stan and Jan. *Down a Sunny Dirt Road: An Autobiography*. Random House: New York, 2002. p146.

60   "sell this to Harper": Berenstain, Stan and Jan. *Down a Sunny Dirt Road: An Autobiography*. Random House: New York, 2002. p152.

60   "terrible-looking book": Mike Berenstain. Interview with PVA. September 21, 2107.

60   "let's back off": Berenstain, Stan and Jan. *Down a Sunny Dirt Road: An Autobiography*. Random House: New York, 2002. p152.

60   "keeping the reader reading": Berenstain, Stan and Jan. *Down a Sunny Dirt Road: An Autobiography*. Random House: New York, 2002. pp152–53.

60   "not every book": Lord, Sterling. *Lord of Publishing*. Open Road Integrated Media: New York, 2013. p214.

60   "tore their hair out": Mike Berenstain. Interview with PVA. September 21, 2107.

60   "he had that charm": Morgan, Judith and Neil. *Dr. Seuss and Mr. Geisel*. Random House: New York, 1995. p216.

CHAPTER 6

62   "eat your turkey": Morgan, Judith and Neil. *Dr. Seuss and Mr. Geisel*. Random House: New York, 1995. p166.

62   "very meaningful": Christopher Cerf, Interview with PVA, August 30, 2018.

62   "serious though sketchy": Greenleaf, Warren T. "How the Grinch Stole Reading: The Serious Nonsense of Dr. Seuss." *Principal*, May 1982.

63   "bad time": TG to Bob Bernstein. September 11, 1961. RHA/CU (Box 605, Beginner Books Sales).

63   "level of brilliance": Christopher Cerf, Interview with PVA, August 30, 2018.

64   "placement of a word": Morgan, Judith and Neil. *Dr. Seuss and Mr. Geisel*. Random House: New York, 1995. p165.

64   "do whatever": Morgan, Judith and Neil. *Dr. Seuss and Mr. Geisel*. Random House: New York, 1995. p179.

64   "if not for Ted": Morgan, Judith and Neil. *Dr. Seuss and Mr. Geisel*. Random House: New York, 1995. p179.

65   "giving in": Hawkins, Robin. "Notable New Yorkers: Bennett Cerf" (interview; session 10, January 5, 1968). Columbia University Libraries Oral History Research Office.

65   "how dare you": Christopher Cerf, Interview with PVA, August 30, 2018.

65   "so wonderful": Hawkins, Robin. "Notable New Yorkers: Bennett Cerf" (interview; session 10, January 5, 1968). Columbia University Libraries Oral History Research Office.

CHAPTER 7

67   "many millions": Morgan, Judith and Neil. *Dr. Seuss and Mr. Geisel*. Random House: New York, 1995. p188.

67   "he's stronger": Hawkins, Robin. "Notable New Yorkers: Bennett Cerf" (interview; session 19, February 5, 1968). Columbia University Libraries Oral History Research Office.

68   "three other books": Benjamin Elkin to TG. August 18, 1965. RHA/CU (Box 696, Elkin—Magic and Foolers 1).

68   "our point of view": TG to Barney Tobey, November 1, 1965. RHA/CU (Box 704, Tobey Duck Feet).

69   "hogwash": "Teaching: The Logical Insanity of Dr. Seuss." *Time*, August 11, 1967.

69   "pendulum is swinging": Diehl, Digby. "The Loose Dr. Seuss." *Philadelphia Inquirer*, November 12, 1972.

69   "unnecessary long words": Frutig, Judith. "Dr. Seuss's Green-Eggs-and-Ham World." *Christian Science Monitor*, May 12, 1978.

70   "your young reader": Edwin H. Bakal to Bob Bernstein, March 29, 1965. RHA/CU (Box 697, Beginner Books 4).

70   "distance himself": Pease, Donald E. *Theodor Seuss Geisel*. Oxford University Press: Oxford, 2010. p130.

70   "mink stole": Morgan, Judith and Neil. *Dr. Seuss and Mr. Geisel*. Random House: New York, 1995. p182.

70   "life without you": Morgan, Judith and Neil. *Dr. Seuss and Mr. Geisel*. Random House: New York, 1995. p195.

71   "unselfish person": Morgan, Judith and Neil. *Dr. Seuss and Mr. Geisel*. Random House: New York, 1995. p198.

71   "meter scanned": Gordon, Arthur. "The Wonderful Wizard of Soledad Hill." *Women's Day*, September 1965.

71   "some of them": Morgan, Judith and Neil. *Dr. Seuss and Mr. Geisel*. Random House: New York, 1995. p95.

71   "they loved Helen": Mike Berenstain. Interview with PVA. September 21, 2017.

71   "great partnership": Mike Berenstain. Interview with PVA. September 21, 2017.

71   "Helen Palmer; Author's Wife": "Helen Palmer; Author's Wife." *Los Angeles Times*, October 27, 1967.

72   "her own right": Jones, Brian Jay. *Becoming Dr. Seuss*. Dutton: New York, 2019. p345.

AL PERKINS

72   "stories about them": "Albert Rogers Perkins." *Contemporary Authors Online*, Gale, 2007. link.galegroup.com/apps/doc/H1000077377/BIC1?u=ramsey_main&xid=ce5e8e9b. Accessed August 28, 2017.

72   "funniest fellow": Morgan, Judith and Neil. *Dr. Seuss and Mr. Geisel*. Random House: New York, 1995. p64.

75   "keep him at work": Helen Geisel to Bob Bernstein, July 27, 1965. RHA/CU (Box 696, Dictionary in French).

78   "might have done that": Sally Allen. Interview with PVA, November 7, 2017.

78   "way with words": Sally Allen. Interview with PVA, November 7, 2017.

78   "just adored him": Sally Allen. Interview with PVA, November 7, 2017.

CHAPTER 8

79   "get lost": Morgan, Judith and Neil. *Dr. Seuss and Mr. Geisel*. Random House: New York, 1995. p195.

80   "pick them up": Michael Frith. Interview with PVA, November 5, 2017.

80   "try this": Michael Frith. Interview with PVA, November 5, 2017.

80   "Harvard and Yale": Michael Frith. Interview with PVA, November 5, 2017.

81   "next natural door": Michael Frith. Interview with PVA, November 5, 2017.

81   "speak to them": Michael Frith. Interview with PVA, November 5, 2017.

81   "for the readership": Michael Frith. Interview with PVA, November 5, 2017.

BRIGHT AND EARLY BOOKS

83   "learning to read": Russell, David H. "An Evaluation of Some Easy-to-Read Trade Books for Children." *Elementary English* 38, no. 7 (November 1961): 475–82.

83   "Prenatal Books": Cott, Jonathan. *Pipers at the Gates of Dawn: The Wisdom of Children's Literature*. McGraw-Hill, New York, 1983.

84   "Ted knew better": Michael Frith. Interview with PVA, November 5, 2017.

84   "authors to sign": Nel, Philip. "Children's Literature Goes to War: Dr. Seuss, P. D. Eastman, Munro Leaf, and the Private SNAFU Films (1943–46)." *Journal of Popular Culture* 40, no. 3 (2007): 469.

85   "Beginner Book meat grinder": Michael Frith. Interview with PVA, November 5, 2017.

85   "just a joy": Michael Frith. Interview with PVA, November 5, 2017.

85   "sweat instead of fun": Morgan, Judith and Neil. *Dr. Seuss and Mr. Geisel*. Random House: New York, 1995. p215.

85   "artistic mind and playfulness": Morgan, Judith and Neil. *Dr. Seuss and Mr. Geisel*. Random House: New York, 1995. p200.

85   "two grown men": Kaufman, Leslie. "The Author Himself Was a Cat in the Hat." *New York Times*, February 4, 2013.

86   "Number 4 lass": Morgan, Judith and Neil. *Dr. Seuss and Mr. Geisel*. Random House: New York, 1995. p217.

86   "giving him candy": Michael Frith. Interview with PVA, November 5, 2017.

P. D. EASTMAN, PART 2

86   "Eastman, Mary." *Stamford Advocate*, 20, March 2013. https://www.legacy.com/obituaries/stamfordadvocate/obituary.aspx?n=mary-eastman&pid=163728279.

86   "P. D. Eastman." *New York Times*, January 11, 1986. http://www.nytimes.com/1986/01/11/obituaries/p-d-eastman.html?mcubz=3.

86   "again and again": *Oneonta Star*, November 13, 1969, newspaper ad.

87   "his old friend": Michael Frith. Interview with PVA, November 5, 2017.

87   "posed studio pictures": Backalenick, Irene. "Tots Steered to Happy Reading in Easy Books by Westporter." *Bridgeport Post*, February 28, 1965.

88   "most satisfying to me": Backalenick, Irene. "Tots Steered to Happy Reading in Easy Books by Westporter." *Bridgeport Post*, February 28, 1965.

CHAPTER 9

89   "some synergy there": Frith, Michael. "12/-/1975—'Michael Frith Joins Us.'" *Jim Henson's Red Book*, December 5, 2011.

91   "almost choked off": Morgan, Judith and Neil. *Dr. Seuss and Mr. Geisel*. Random House: New York, 1995. p225.

92   "minting money": Bernstein, Robert. *Speaking Freely*. New Press: New York. 2016. p161.

92   "president, policymaker, and editor": Diehl, Digby. "The Loose Dr. Seuss." *Philadelphia Inquirer*, November 12, 1972.

92   "fierce and fearless": MacRae, Julia. "Remembering Janet Schulman." *Publishers Weekly*, February 24, 2011. https://www.publishersweekly.com/pw/by-topic/childrens/childrens -industry-news/article/46278-remembering-janet-schulman.html.

93   "very inexpensive": Maughan, Shannon. "Readers for Early Readers." *Publishers Weekly*, May 22, 2000.

ROY MCKIE, PART 2

94   "charming and irresistible": June McKie. Interview with PVA, September 24, 2017.

94   "facial expressions": June McKie. Interview with PVA, September 24, 2017.

94   "Woof! Woof!": June McKie. Interview with PVA, September 24, 2017.

94   "center of my life": Greene, Jo-Ann. "Illustrator Roy McKie Recalls His Collaboration with Dr. Seuss." *Lancaster Online*, February 23, 2013.

95   "a different way": June McKie. Interview with PVA, September 24, 2017.

95   "getting away with it": Greene, Jo-Ann. "Illustrator Roy McKie Recalls His Collaboration with Dr. Seuss." *Lancaster Online*, February 23, 2013.

95   "100 years from now": Greene, Jo-Ann. "Illustrator Roy McKie Recalls His Collaboration with Dr. Seuss." *Lancaster Online*, February 23, 2013.

CHAPTER 10

97   "fulfilled in their work": Bernstein, Robert. *Speaking Freely*. New Press: New York, 2016. p246.

97   "Random House mystique": McDowell, Edwin. "Robert Bernstein Is out as President of Random House." *New York Times*, November 6, 1989.

97   "knew the authors personally": Bernstein, Robert. *Speaking Freely*. New Press: New York, 2016. p227.

97   "eye on profits": Knufinke, Joana Costa. "Ex-RH CEO Still Has a Lot to Say about Publishing." *Publishing Perspectives*. June 27, 2012. https://publishingperspectives.com /2012/06/ex-rh-ceo-alberto-vitale-sill-has-a-lot-to-say-about-publishing/.

98   "Seussian Flame": Kate Klimo. Interview with PVA, October 8, 2017.

98   "near as easily": Kate Klimo. Interview with PVA, October 8, 2017.

98   "really ungodly": Kate Klimo. Interview with PVA, October 8, 2017.

99   "one and only Dr. Seuss": Kate Klimo. Interview with PVA, October 8, 2017.

STAN AND JAN BERENSTAIN, PART 2

100   "ad hoc collaboration": Mike Berenstain. Interview with PVA, September 21, 2107.

100   "except for Ted": Berenstain, Stan and Jan. *Down a Sunny Dirt Road: An Autobiography*. Random House: New York, 2002. p174.

101   "demanding of themselves": Lord, Sterling. *Lord of Publishing*. Open Road Integrated Media: New York, 2013. p217.

101   "joie de vivre": "Dr. Seuss Remembered." *Publishers Weekly*. October 25, 1991.

101   "very productive": Jussel, Amy. "The Berenstain Bears Legacy Lives On through Sons Mike and Leo." *Shaping Youth.org*, February 27, 2012. http://shapingyouth.org/the-berenstain -bears-legacy-lives-on-through-sons-mike-and-leo/.

103   "in the right spirit": Kate Klimo. Interview with PVA, October 8, 2017.

103   "with a good thing": Streetman, Burgin. "The Nose Book." *Vintage Kids' Books My Kid Loves* (blog), February 21, 2008. http://www.vintagechildrensbooksmykidloves.com /search?q=%22roy+mckie%22.

103   "dirty pool": June McKie. Interview with PVA, September 24, 2017.

105   "not a chore": Nichols, Lewis. "Then I Doodled a Tree." *New York Times Book Review*, November 11, 1962.

105   "always made her proudest": Lyman, Rick. November 26, 2006, "Phyllis Cerf Wagner, 90, Socialite and Collaborator with Dr. Seuss, Dies." *New York Times*, November 26, 2006.

105   "unrealistic and unimaginative": Bailey Jr., John P. "Three Decades of Dr. Seuss." *Elementary English* 42, no. 1 (January 1965): 7–12.

106   "add very little": Bader, Barbara. *American Picture Books from Noah's Ark to the Beast Within*. Macmillan: New York, 1976. p312.

106   "up to his quality": "He Makes C-A-T Spell Big Money." *Business Week* July 18, 1964.

106   "no way measure up": Morgan, Judith and Neil. *Dr. Seuss and Mr. Geisel*. Random House: New York, 1995. p231.

106   "a CRASH!ing bore": "Tubby and the Poo-Bah." *Kirkus Reviews*, October 23, 1972.

106   "a pain in my": "There's a Wocket in My Pocket." *Kirkus Reviews*, September 1, 1974. "to these gatekeepers": Goodman, Ellen. "Dr. Seuss Knew How to Talk to Children." *Sioux City Journal*, October 4, 1991.

106   "breakthrough artist": Michael Frith. Interview with PVA, November 5, 2017.

107   "educational expertise": Maughan, Shannon. "Readers for Early Readers." *Publishers Weekly*, May 22, 2000.

107   "engage children in reading": Suen, Anastasia. "15 Classic Easy Readers." *Book Links*, July 2006.

108   "tell the story": Smith, Robin. "Early Readers vs. Picture Books." Calling Caldecott (blog), November 7, 2011. https://www.hbook.com/2011/11/blogs/calling-caldecott /early-readers-vs-picture-books/.

PART 2: THE 1950s

The Cat in the Hat Comes Back

111   "nested sets, infinitesimals": Silvey, Anita, ed. *Everything I Need to Know I Learned from a Children's Book*. Roaring Book Press: New York, 2009. p147.

111   "locutions of advertising": Nel, Philip. *The Annotated Cat: Under the Hats of Seuss and His Cats*. Random House: New York, 2007. p154.

112   "satisfyingly resolved": Greenleaf, Warren T. "How the Grinch Stole Reading: The Serious Nonsense of Dr. Seuss." *Principal*, May 1982.

112   "be in whack": Nel, Philip. *Dr. Seuss: American Icon*. Continuum: New York, 2004. p38.

A Fly Went By

113   "home to burn": Ford, Sterling. *Lord of Publishing*. Open Road Integrated Media: New York, 2013. p13.

The Big Jump

116   "chick just hatched": Savoy, Maggie. "Tots Sharp Readers: Writer Finds Children Challenging Audience." *Arizona Republic*, November 2, 1962.

116   "humorous vein": *Coronado Eagle and Journal*, March 17, 1988.

118   "understand it independently": "Six Foolish Fishermen." *Kirkus Reviews*, October 1, 1957. https://www.kirkusreviews.com/book-reviews/benjamin-elkin/six-foolish-fishermen/.

118   "really, really loved": "Throwback Thursday: The Big Jump and Other Stories." Sturdy for Common Things.com. March 7, 2103. http://www.sturdyforcommonthings.com/2013/03/throwback-thursday-the-big-jump-and-other-stories/.

A Big Ball of String

120   "Senators fan": Grimes, William. "Barbara Holland, Defender of Small Vices, Dies at 77." *New York Times*, September 13, 2010. https://www.nytimes.com/2010/09/14/books/14holland.html.

Sam and the Firefly

123   "rip this book off": "Jon Klassen Shares the Books Which Inspire Him." Playing By the Book.net. September 20, 2011. http://www.playingbythebook.net/2011/09/20/jon-klassen-shares-the-books-which-inspire-him/.

123   "contribution to make": P. D. Eastman to TG, February 10, 1959. Courtesy of Tony and Susan Eastman.

You Will Go to the Moon

125   "images from this book": Streetman, Burgin. "You Will Go to the Moon." *Vintage Kids' Books My Kid Loves*" (blog), September 23, 2007.

The Whales Go By

128   "such permanence": "Paul Galdone." *Major Authors and Illustrators for Children and Young Adults.* Gale, 2002. link.galegroup.com/apps/doc/K1617001299/BIC1?u=ramsey _main&xid=0b510a83. Accessed September 15, 2017.

Stop That Ball!

129   "unpleasant explosions": Cohen, Charles D. *The Seuss, the Whole Seuss, and Nothing but the Seuss.* Random House: New York, 2004. p345.

THE 1960s

One Fish, Two Fish, Red Fish, Blue Fish

133   "unfortunately can't define": Kahn Jr., E. J. "Children's Friend." *New Yorker*, December 17, 1960.
134   "it is no good": Morgan, Judith and Neil. *Dr. Seuss and Mr. Geisel.* Random House: New York, 1995. p165.

The King's Wish

135   "soaring minds": Savoy, Maggie. "Tots Sharp Readers: Writer Finds Children Challenging Audience." *Arizona Republic*, November 2, 1962.

Bennett Cerf's Book of Riddles

136   "absolute ultimate degree": Hawkins, Robin. "Notable New Yorkers: Bennett Cerf" (interview; session 20, February 8, 1968). Columbia University Libraries Oral History Research Office.
136   "impolitic": Hawkins, Robin. "Notable New Yorkers: Bennett Cerf" (interview; session 20, February 8, 1968). Columbia University Libraries Oral History Research Office.

Green Eggs and Ham

137   "on a tree": Nel, Philip. *Dr. Seuss: American Icon.* Continuum: New York, 2004. p33.

Put Me in the Zoo

142   "extravagant humor": Guilfoile, Elizabeth. *Books for Beginning Readers.* National Council of Teachers of English: Champaign, IL, 1962. p10.

Are You My Mother?

143 "of all time": "Story Time: Children's Book Authors Remember Their Favorite Books." Target.com. October 2, 2012. https://corporate.target.com/article/2012/10/childrens -book-authors-remember-their-favorite-boo.

143 "arrant nonsense": Guilfoile, Elizabeth. *Books for Beginning Readers.* National Council of Teachers of English: Champaign, IL, 1962. p10.

143 "capture its essence": Susan Eastman. Email to PVA, April 8, 2019.

143 "psychic distress": Parielle, Ken. "Six Observations About Alison Bechdel's Graphic Archive Are You My Mother?" *Comics Journal,* May 30, 2012. http://www.tcj.com/six -observations-about-alison-bechdel%E2%80%99s-graphic-archive-are-you-my-mother/.

Ten Apples Up on Top!

144 "illustrate myself": Gough, John. "The Unsung Dr. Seuss: Theo. LeSieg." *Children's Literature Association Quarterly* 11, no. 4 (1986): 182–83.

144 "more comfortable": Steinberg, Sybil. *Publishers Weekly,* 1978.

145 "cooperation over conflict": Gough, John. "The Unsung Dr. Seuss: Theo. LeSieg." *Children's Literature Association Quarterly* 11, no. 4 (1986): 182–83.

145 "chaos theory": Handy, Bruce. *Wild Things: The Joy of Reading Children's Literature as an Adult.* Simon and Schuster: New York, 2018. pp134, 108.

Go, Dog. Go!

146 "conjunctions, and adjectives": Backalenick, Irene. "Tots Steered to Happy Reading in Easy Books by Westporter." *Bridgeport Post,* February 28, 1965.

147 "makes me laugh now": Biedenharn, Isabella. "Pop Culture of My Life: Jamie Lee Curtis." *Entertainment Weekly.* September 30, 2016. http://ew.com/article/2016/09/30/pop -culture-my-life-jamie-lee-curtis/.

148 "gnarly zen koan": Silvey, Anita, ed. *Everything I Need to Know I Learned from a Children's Book.* Roaring Book Press: New York, 2009. p149.

148 "party in a tree": Silvey, Anita, ed. *Everything I Need to Know I Learned from a Children's Book.* Roaring Book Press: New York, 2009. p149.

Little Black, A Pony

148 "never owned one": "Walter Farley, Wrote 'Black Stallion' Books." *Tampa Bay Times,* October 19, 1989.

Look Out for Pirates!

150 "skillful promotion": Vinton, Iris. "Today's Boys Can and Do Read—Reports Boys Club Leader." *Reading Teacher* 7, no. 2 (December 1953): 105–7.

151 "heroic merchant mariner": Nelson, Todd R. "The Treasure of a Pirate Tale." *Christian Science Monitor,* January 31, 2013.

A Fish Out of Water

153   "the 9,373rd version": Morgan, Judith and Neil. *Dr. Seuss and Mr. Geisel*. Random House: New York, 1995. p174.

Robert the Rose Horse

155   "stern and unpleasant": Joan Heilbroner. Interview with PVA, October 12, 2018.
155   "lots of servants": Joan Heilbroner. Interview with PVA, October 12, 2018.
156   "wasn't as good": Joan Heilbroner. Interview with PVA, October 12, 2018.
158   "where we lived": Joan Heilbroner. Interview with PVA, October 12, 2018.

I Was Kissed by a Seal at the Zoo

159   "a best-seller": Morgan, Judith and Neil. *Dr. Seuss and Mr. Geisel*. Random House: New York, 1995. p165.
160   "no visible object": "Lynn Fayman (1904–1968)." *Modern San Diego*. http://www.modern sandiego.com/FaymanLynn.html.

The Big Honey Hunt

163   "forgotten how to draw": Berenstain, Stan and Jan. *Down a Sunny Dirt Road: An Autobiography*. Random House: New York, 2002. p156.
163   "haystack wearing overalls": Berenstain, Stan and Jan. *Down a Sunny Dirt Road: An Autobiography*. Random House: New York, 2002. p156.
163   "action and humor": Black, Irma Simonton. "Beginners: Easy Reading." *New York Times Book Review*, November 11, 1962.

Hop on Pop

164   "spelling-pattern principle": Chall, Jeanne. *Learning to Read: The Great Debate*. 2nd ed. McGraw-Hill: New York, 1983. p96.
164   "meaning of words": Ford, Carin T. *Dr. Seuss: Best-Loved Author*. Enslow Publishing: Berkeley Heights, NJ, 2003. p86.
164   "Kan Ga Roo": Morgan, Judith and Neil. *Dr. Seuss and Mr. Geisel*. Random House: New York, 1995. p178.
164   "humorous and well-loved": O'Neil, Lauren. "Toronto Library Asked to Ban 'Violent' Dr. Seuss Book *Hop on Pop*." CBC News, April 30, 2014.

Dr. Seuss's ABC

166   "someday, kiddies": Neal, Rome. "Dr. Seuss: Fun with Words." CBS News, March 4, 2004.

Do You Know What I'm Going to Do Next Saturday?

168   "best juvenile books": Morgan, Judith and Neil. *Dr. Seuss and Mr. Geisel.* Random House: New York, 1995. p182.

168   "least bit unwholesome": "Banned Dr. Seuss Book." Snopes.com, July 12, 2007. http://www.snopes.com/language/literary/seussban.asp.

168   "lively photographs": Goodwin, Polly. "Reading Made Easy—and a Delight." *Chicago Tribune*, November 10, 1963.

Summer

169   "non-photographic blues": Michael Frith. Email to PVA, June 19, 2019.

170   "advance the story": Andy Low. Email to PVA, October 16, 2018.

170   "time per word": Andy Low. Email to PVA, October 16, 2018.

170   "Woods Hole": Andy Low. Email to PVA, October 16, 2018.

Why I Built the Boogle House

173   "really into it": Chris Lyery. Phone interview with PVA, August 18, 2018.

173   "unbridled enthusiasm": Elzey, David. "Why I Built the Boogle House." The Excelsior File (blog), April 4, 2011. http://excelsiorfile.blogspot.com/2011/04/why-i-built-boogle-house|.html.

174   "instantly tell": Streetman, Burgin. "Why I Built the Boogle House." Vintage Kids Books My Kid Loves. July 25, 2007. http://www.vintagechildrensbooksmykidloves.com/2007/07/why-i-built-boogle-house.html.

175   "only good memories": Fayman, Corey Lynn. "My Dad, Photographer and Artist." *Sunburned Fedora*. http://www.coreylynnfayman.com/my-dad-photographer-and-artist/.

175   "unlimited opportunity": "Lynn Fayman (1904–1968)." *Modern San Diego*. http://www.modernsandiego.com/FaymanLynn.html.

The Bike Lesson

175   "around your necks": Berenstain, Stan and Jan. *Down a Sunny Dirt Road: An Autobiography.* Random House: New York, 2002. p158.

176   "whole bear series": Andy Low. Email to PVA, October 16, 2018.

How to Make Flibbers, Etc.

177   "he would encourage it": Terry Lopshire Tigue. Interview with PVA, June 29, 2018.

178   "media or appearance hype": "Robert M(artin) Lopshire." *Major Authors and Illustrators for Children and Young Adults.* Gale, 2002. link.galegroup.com/apps/doc/K1617001556/BIC1?u=ramsey_main&xid=c1491ca8. Accessed September 15, 2017.

178   "stealing books from libraries": "Robert M(artin) Lopshire." *Major Authors and Illustrators for Children and Young Adults.* Gale, 2002. link.galegroup.com/apps/doc/K1617001556/BIC1?u=ramsey_main&xid=c1491ca8. Accessed September 15, 2017.

The Cat in the Hat Beginner Book Dictionary

179   "its own sake": Backalenick, Irene. "Tots Steered to Happy Reading in Easy Books by
       Westporter." *Bridgeport Post*, February 28, 1965.

180   "working on it solo": Lindemann, Richard A. F. *The Dr. Seuss Catalog*. McFarland &
       Company: Jefferson, NC, 2005.

180   "trampled to death": Nel, Snafu article, "Children's Literature Goes to War: Dr. Seuss,
       P. D. Eastman, Munro Leaf, and the Private SNAFU Films (1943–46)," *Journal of Popular
       Culture* 40, no. 3 (June 2007): 468–87.

180   "retired useless country squire": Nel, Snafu article, "Children's Literature Goes to War:
       Dr. Seuss, P. D. Eastman, Munro Leaf, and the Private SNAFU Films (1943–46)," *Journal
       of Popular Culture* 40, no. 3: 468–87.

Fox in Socks

180   "couple of trial runs": Armour, L. "Approach with Care!" *Tennesseean*, May 9, 1965.

181   "the only adult": Morgan, Judith and Neil. *Dr. Seuss and Mr. Geisel*. Random House:
       New York, 1995. p185.

The King, the Mice, and the Cheese

182   "modest menagerie": Gurney, Eric. *Gilbert*. Prentice-Hall: New York, 1963.

184   "MOST CONSTRUCTIVE EDITING": Eric Gurney Author Questionnaire, 1965. RHA/
       CU (Box 696, Gurney).

184   "enjoy it themselves": Bob Bernstein to Eric Gurney, June 28, 1965. RHA/CU (Box 696,
       Gurney).

I Wish That I Had Duck Feet

185   "perfect equilibrium": Collinsmarch, Glenn. "Barney Tobey, 82, a Cartoonist in the New
       Yorker for 5 Decades." *New York Times*. March 28, 1989.

186   "simply delighted": Helen Geisel to Ray Freiman, February 18, 1965. RHA/CU (Box 696,
       Geisel, Helen and Ted 5).

The Bears' Picnic

187   "a big deal": Mike Berenstain. Interview with PVA, September 21, 2107.

187   "enthusiasm and anxiety": Anne MarcoVecchio to TG and Helen Geisel, August 4, 1965.
       RHA/CU (Box 696, Geisel, Helen and Ted 2).

188   "do something else": Berenstain, Stan and Jan. *Down a Sunny Dirt Road: An Autobio-
       graphy*. Random House: New York, 2002. p166.

Don and Donna Go to Bat

190 "Donna's success": "Don and Donna Go to Bat." *Kirkus Reviews*, September 30, 1966. https://www.kirkusreviews.com/book-reviews/al-perkins-2/don-and-donna-go-to -bat-an-i-can-read-it-all-by/.

190 "wholly satisfying": Greenberg, Linda Delvental. "Children's Books No Longer All Sexist." *Newark Advocate*, August 19, 1974.

You Will Live under the Sea

191 "striking resemblance": Karlow, Monty. "A Young Reader's Classic from the 'Wonder Years.'" September 11, 2012. https://www.amazon.com/You-Will-Live-Under-Sea/dp /039490043X.

193 "completely altered": Tyler, Betty. "Commercial Illustrators Meet Challenges of Change in Styles from 'Slick' to 'Arty.'" *Bridgeport Post*, February 11, 1962.

193 "other techniques": "How Far Is Far?" *Kirkus Reviews*, March 23, 1964. https://www .kirkusreviews.com/book-reviews/alvin-illus-ward-brackett-tressel/how-far-is-far/.

Come Over to My House

194 "truly lovely": Ray Freiman to TG, October 5, 1965. RHA/CU (Box 696, Come Over to My House).

194 "adventures and travel": Dill-Shakleford, Karen E. "Come Over to My House." *Psychology Today*, August 28, 2013. https://www.psychologytoday.com/us/blog/how-fantasy -becomes-reality/201308/come-over-my-house.

194 "someone new with imagination": TG to Ray Freiman, Sepember 22, 1965. RHA/CU (Box 696, Come Over to my House).

195 "American Indian reservations": "Richard Erdoes." *Contemporary Authors Online*. Gale, 2007. http://link.galegroup.com/apps/doc/H1000029619/BIC?u=stpaul_main&sid =BIC&xid=da92386a. Accessed November 8, 2018.

196 "communications center": Rijmes, Joanne. "Richard and Jean Erdoes." *Santa Fe Living Treasures*—Elder Stories, 1997. http://sflivingtreasures.org/index.php/treasures/114 -erdoes-richard-a-jean-.html.

196 "tickle my fancy": "Richard Erdoes." *Contemporary Authors Online*. Gale, 2007. http:// link. galegroup.com/apps/doc/H1000029619/BIC?u=stpaul_main&sid=BIC&xid =da92386a. Accessed November 8, 2018.

196 "future generations": Beauvais, Archie B. and Amanda Takes War Bonnett. "Author Richard Erdoes Dies at Home at Age 96." *Lakota County Times*, July 24, 2008. http:// www.lakotacountrytimes.com/news/2008-07-24/front_page/004.html.

196 "introduction to sociology": Walter Retan to Anne MarcoVecchio, August 17, 1965. RHA/ CU (Box 696, The Cat in the Hat's Wide, Wide World).

196 "a light touch": Walter Retan to Anne MarcoVecchio, August 17, 1965. RHA/CU (Box 696, The Cat in the Hat's Wide, Wide World).

Babar Loses His Crown

197 "to make money": "Laurent de Brunhoff." *Major Authors and Illustrators for Children and Young Adults*. Gale, 2002. link.galegroup.com/apps/doc/K1617001078/BIC1?u =ramsey_main&xid=4c6cdba7. Accessed September 18, 2017.

198 "made me happy": Varadarajan, Tunku. "Babar the Elephant Takes His Final Bow." *Wall Street Journal*, November 24, 2017.

The Bear Scouts

196 "outrageous jokes": Berenstain, Stan and Jan. *Down a Sunny Dirt Road: An Autobiography*. Random House: New York, 2002. p166.

200 "don't really do that": Berenstain, Stan and Jan. *Down a Sunny Dirt Road: An Autobiography*. Random House: New York, 2002. p167.

The Digging-est Dog

200 "idea for a book": Sally Allen. Interview with PVA, November 7, 2017.

201 "all-right world": Wildy, Katherine. "Reading and the Family." *Courier News*, February 2, 1972.

Doctor Dolittle

203 "motives are questionable": "Philip Wende." *Contemporary Authors Online*. Gale, 2002. Biography in Context, link.galegroup.com/apps/doc/H1000104872/BIC1?u=ramsey _main&xid=3a79ea7f. Accessed September 18, 2017.

Off to the Races

206 "comic-art storytelling": Chaykin, Howard. "Foreword." *Creepy Archives*, Volume 13. Dark Horse Books: Milwaukie, OR, 2012.

207 "two-wheeled adventures": Nunemaker, Jame T. "Book Review: Off to the Races." *The Cycle* (blog). December 27, 2009. http://cyclescribe.blogspot.com/2009/12/book-review -off-to-races.html.

The Best Nest

207 "quite unsatisfactory": Helen Geisel to Bob Bernstein, February 3, 1965. RHA/CU (Box 696, Dictionary in French 2).

207 "character development": Phil Eastman to Bob Bernstein, February 14, 1965. RHA/CU (Box 696, Eastman, Phil).

THE 1970s

The Bears' Vacation

208 "influenced by that": Mike Berenstain. Interview with PVA, September 21, 2107.

209   "impulsive, funny, and antic": Mike Berenstain. Interview with PVA, September 21, 2107.

209   "Papa Bear resonates": Mike Berenstain. Interview with PVA, September 21, 2107.

Chitty Chitty Bang Bang

210   "wall of his store": Weatherby, W. J. "A Gentle New Yorker." *Guardian*, April 3, 1989.

Inside Outside Upside Down

212   "trip to town": Berenstain, Stan and Jan. *Down a Sunny Dirt Road: An Autobiography.* Random House: New York, 2002. pp170–71.

213   "whole new bear version": Berenstain, Stan and Jan. *Down a Sunny Dirt Road: An Autobiography.* Random House: New York, 2002. pp171–72.

My Book about Me

215   "centers on ME": "Hopefully, Junior Will Accept Mom's Choice." *Indianapolis Star*, November 23, 1969.

215   "as a memento": Kent, June. "Prized Gifts for Children." *Express and News*, November 23, 1969.

Hand, Hand, Fingers, Thumb

216   "sitting on the floor": Michael Frith. Email to PVA, June 19, 2019.

216   "gleefully crazed monkeys": Michael Frith. Email to PVA, June 19, 2019.

216   "very humorous": "Eric Gurney Dies at 82." *Arizona Daily Star*, November 19, 1992.

I Can Draw!

219   "revolt against coloring books": Morgan, Judith and Neil. *Dr. Seuss and Mr. Geisel.* Random House: New York, 1995. p207.

The B Book

221   "immense frustration": Mike Berenstain. Interview with PVA, September 21, 2107.

Tubby

224   "portray their business": O'Mera Lowenstein, Sheila. "Death, Truth and Other cartoon subjects." *Westport News*, August 1, 1980.

224   "cartoonist's cartoonist": Peng, Lief. "'Rowland Wilson (the cartoonist's cartoonist)'—Bill Peckmann." Today's Inspiration (blog), May 18, 2011. http://todaysinspiration. blogspot .com/2011/05/rowland-wilson-cartoonists-cartoonist.html.

Some of Us Walk . . .

225 "no nature channel": Michael Frith. Interview with PVA, November 5, 2017.
225 "about the bongo": Michael Frith. Interview with PVA, November 5, 2017.

I Can Write!

226 "only book he disliked": Morgan, Judith and Neil. *Dr. Seuss and Mr. Geisel*. Random House: New York, 1995. p277.

Marvin K. Mooney

227 "collaborated sooner": Morgan, Judith and Neil. *Dr. Seuss and Mr. Geisel*. Random House: New York, 1995. p221.

Shape of Me

229 "strongest illustrations": Morgan, Judith and Neil. *Dr. Seuss and Mr. Geisel*. Random House: New York, 1995. p220.

Wacky Wednesday

232 "Hjalmar Bonstable Jr.": Lindemann, Richard A. F. *The Dr. Seuss Catalog*. McFarland & Company: Jefferson, NC, 2005.
233 "a part of me": Salie, Faith. "New Yorker Cartoonist George Booth." *CBS Sunday Morning*, November 12, 2017.
234 "but it's true": Stewart, Laura. "The Gently Bizarre World of George Booth 'Gels' from His Experiences." *Democrat and Chronicle*, October 21, 1980.

Great Day for Up!

235 "what a special thing": Michael Frith. Interview with PVA, November 5, 2017.
236 "placed in a scene": "Quentin (Saxby) Blake." *Major Authors and Illustrators for Children and Young Adults*. Gale, 2002. http://link.galegroup.com/apps/doc/K1617001023/BIC?u =stpaul_main&sid=BIC&xid=d4714c78. Accessed January 1, 2019.
236 "something else": Blake, Quentin. "Creating My Own Picture Books and Illustrating a Book for Dr. Seuss (41/65)." *Web of Stories—Life Stories of Remarkable People*, July 14, 2017. https://www.youtube.com/watch?v=ijzdhWxuK4U).
236 "wild assurance": "Quentin (Saxby) Blake." *Major Authors and Illustrators for Children and Young Adults*. Gale, 2002. http://link.galegroup.com/apps/doc/K1617001023 /BIC?u=stpaul_main&sid=BIC&xid=d4714c78. Accessed January 1, 2019.

He Bear She Bear

237 "where are the laughs": Morgan, Judith and Neil. *Dr. Seuss and Mr. Geisel*. Random House: New York, 1995. p216.

Because a Little Bug . . .

238   "twice as many": Michael Frith. Email to PVA, June 19, 2019.

240   "relatively obscure": Michael Frith. Email to PVA, June 19, 2019.

Hooper Humperdink

242   "my address book": Michael Frith. Email to PVA, June 19, 2019.

243   "three minutes": Casey, Phil. "New Yorker Artist: From Roxbury to the Top." *Boston Globe*, September 7, 1970.

244   "ethereal palette": Lorenz, Lee. "Postscript." *New Yorker*, July 10, 1995. p7.

244   "you've caricatured him": Diehl, Digby. "The Loose Dr. Seuss." *Philadelphia Inquirer*, November 12, 1972.

244   "happy middle-class family": Hersey, John. "Why Do Children Bog Down on the First 'R'?" *Life*, May 24, 1954.

245   "infects our minds": Strauss, Valerie. "Just How Racist Is Children's Literature? The Author of *Was the Cat in the Hat Black*? Explains." *Washington Post*. December 11, 2017. https://www.washingtonpost.com/news/answer-sheet/wp/2017/12/11/just-how-racist-is -childrens-literature-the-author-of-was-the-cat-in-the-hat-black-explains/.

Please Try to Remember the First of Octember

246   "a quiet genius": Lynch, Mike. "Art Cumings June 9, 1922–August 28, 2012." *Mike Lynch Cartoons* (blog), September 6, 2012. http://mikelynchcartoons.blogspot.com/2012/09 /art-cumings-june-9-1922-august-28-2012.html.

I Can Read with My Eyes Shut!

247   "treatments for glaucoma": "There's So So Much to Read." Dr. Seuss Art.com. http:// www.drseussart.com/sosomuchtoread/.

248   "inch of page": Frutig, Judith. "Dr. Seuss's Green-Eggs-and-Ham World." *Christian Science Monitor*, May 12, 1978.

Oh Say Can You Say?

248   "facility for tongue twisters": Morgan, Judith and Neil. *Dr. Seuss and Mr. Geisel*. Random House: New York, 1995. p241.

248   "on their chart": Gorney, Cynthia. "Dr. Seuss at 75: Grinch, Cat in Hat, Wocket and Generations of Kids in His Pocket." *Washington Post*, May 21, 1979.

THE 1980s

Maybe You Should Fly a Jet

254   "gourmet cook": "Michael Smollin." *Westport News*, September 30, 2010. https://www .westport-news.com/news/article/Michael-Smollin-680627.php#page-1.

The Tooth Book

254   "going to say that": Morgan, Judith and Neil. *Dr. Seuss and Mr. Geisel*. Random House: New York, 1995. p275.

Wings on Things

255   "like roadkill": Brown, Marc. "Remembering Janet Schulman." *Publishers Weekly*, February 24, 2011. https://www.publishersweekly.com/pw/by-topic/childrens/childrens-industry-news/article/46278-remembering-janet-schulman.html.

255   "making picture books": Brown, Marc. "Remembering Janet Schulman." *Publishers Weekly*, February 24, 2011. https://www.publishersweekly.com/pw/by-topic/childrens/childrens-industry-news/article/46278-remembering-janet-schulman.html.

255   "no frills": "Marc Brown." *Contemporary Authors Online*. Gale, 2016. http://link.gale group.com/apps/doc/H1000012904/BIC?u=stpaul_main&sid=BIC&xid=893a48e1. Accessed January 20, 2019.

256   "vice versa": "Marc Brown." *Contemporary Authors Online*. Gale, 2016. http://link.gale group.com/apps/doc/H1000012904/BIC?u=stpaul_main&sid=BIC&xid=893a48e1. Accessed January 20, 2019.

It's Not Easy . . .

258   "constantly doodling": Roskin, R. Terrance. "Doodling Leads to 'Funny Business.'" *Desert Sun*, January 15, 1977.

261   "out of a hat": Sadler, Marilyn. "A Childless Children's Book Author." *Marilyn Sadler.net*, October 28, 2018. https://marilynsadler.net/blog/f/a-childless-childrens-book-author

I Want to Be Somebody New

262   "giant Elkin fiasco": Robert Lopshire to Anne MarcoVecchio, December 1965. RHA/CU (Box 699, Robert Lopshire 1).

Black Stallion

264   "help care for him": "About the artist." Sandyhorse.com. https://web.archive.org/web/20150324200400/http://www.sandyhorse.com/sandy-bio.html.

264   "hay and grain": "Sandy Rabinowitz." *Contemporary Authors Online*. Gale, 2006. http://link.galegroup.com/apps/doc/H1000080570/BIC?u=stpaul_main&sid=BIC&xid=fa9ace12. Accessed January 22, 2019.

265   "dreams to paper": Debnam, Betty. "Meet the 'Black Stallion' author, Walter Farley." *Saint Cloud Times*, July 19, 1980.

I Am Not Going to Get Up Today!

266   "change the world": "James Stevenson." *Contemporary Authors Online*. Gale, 2016. http://link.galegroup.com/apps/doc/H1000095151/BIC?u=stpaul_main&sid=BIC&xid=632c08ac. Accessed January 22, 2019.

266   "single-handedly": Lorenz, Lee. "Postscript: James Stevenson." *New Yorker*. February 24, 2017. https://www.newyorker.com/culture/culture-desk/postscript-james-stevenson.

266   "make a book": "James Stevenson." *Contemporary Authors Online*. Gale, 2016. http://link .galegroup.com/apps/doc/H1000095151/BIC?u=stpaul_main&sid=BIC&xid=632c08ac . Accessed January 22, 2019.

THE 1990s

New Tricks I Can Do!

269   "kind or cutting": "Robert Martin Lopshire." *Contemporary Authors Online*. Gale, 2011. link.galegroup.com/apps/doc/H1000061284/BIC1?u=ramsey_main&xid=fcd8b7d7. Accessed September 15, 2017.

270   "book at his desk": "Obituaries." *Sarasota Herald-Tribune*. Accessed March 4, 2017.

Anthony the Perfect Monster

271   "my mother's response": Angelo Decesare. Interview with PVA, February 1, 2019.

271   "rage inside me": Angelo Decesare. Interview with PVA, February 1, 2019.

272   "just so amazing": Angelo Decesare. Interview with PVA, February 1, 2019.

272   "human being": Angelo Decesare. Interview with PVA, February 1, 2019.

272   "great picture books": "Oh, the Places You'll Go if You Win New Seuss Picture-book Award." *Honolulu Star-Bulletin*, June 28, 1992.

273   "next to Dr. Seuss": Angelo Decesare. Interview with PVA, February 1, 2019.

273   "and my mom": "About." *Flip and Muzz.com*. http://www.flipandmuzz.com/about.html.

276   "good in the world": Angelo Decesare. Interview with PVA. February 1, 2019.

Four Pups and a Worm

276   "sold reading to kids": Kate Klimo. Interview with PVA, October 8, 2017.

277   "deceptive lightness of touch": Handy, Bruce. *Wild Things: The Joy of Reading Children's Literature as an Adult*. Simon and Schuster: New York, 2018. p116.

277   "know specifically": Eric Seltzer. Interview with PVA, February 2, 2019.

278   "work for me": Eric Seltzer. Interview with PVA, February 2, 2019.

Honey Bunny

279   "P. J.'s world": Marilyn Sadler. Email to PVA, February 9, 2019.

279   "abused and neglected": Goodman, Ellen. "I'm getting upset, I am, I am." *Baltimore Sun*, May 9, 2000.

279   "expressing that love": Marilyn Sadler. Email to PVA, February 8, 2019.

Come Down Now, Flying Cow!

280   "read, laugh and imagine": Timothy Roland. Email to PVA, February 2, 2019.

280   "cartoony art and zaniness": Timothy Roland. Email to PVA, February 2, 2019.

281   "educates, entertains and explores": Green, Sandy. "Writing with Pictures, Drawing with Words—An Interview with Writer/Illustrator Timothy Roland." *The Sandy Side of Life*, October 3, 2012. https://sandydgreen.wordpress.com/2012/10/03/writing-with-pictures -drawing-with-words-an-interview-with-writerillustrator-timothy-roland/.

281   "explore their world": Timothy Roland. Email to PVA, February 2, 2019.

Mama Loves

285   "dog at my feet": McCue, Lisa. "A Personal Note." Lisa McCue Illustrator.com. http:// www.lisamccueillustrator.com/Lisa_McCue/Home.html.

THE 2000s

Flap Your Wings

289   "sensitive style": Sporn, Michael. "Tony Goes Flying." Michael Sporn Animation.com, June 12, 2007. http://www.michaelspornanimation.com/splog/?p=1097.

The Knee Book

290   "magic of children's books": "About Me." Sylvie Kantorovitz.com, 2017. http://www.sylvie kantorovitz.com/sylviekantorovitz.com/about_me.html.

290   "special talent of mine": "About Me." Sylvie Kantorovitz.com, 2017. http://www.sylvie kantorovitz.com/sylviekantorovitz.com/about_me.html.

Mrs. Wow

291   "interpreted the text": Steven Salerno. Email to PVA, February 19, 2019.

292   "directly on paper": Steven Salerno. Email to PVA, February 19, 2019.

The Belly Book

294   "draw Underdog for me": Slotnik, Daniel E. "Joe Harris, Illustrator Behind Underdog and Trix Rabbit, Dies at 89." *New York Times*, April 4, 2017.

294   "a big studio": Evans, Greg. "Joe Harris Dies: 'Silly Rabbit' Creator, 'Underdog' Animator Was 89." *Deadline Hollywood*, April 6, 2017.

THE 2010s

Have You Seen My Dinosaur?

296   "lots of action": "Joseph P. Mathieu." *Contemporary Authors Online*. Gale, 2006. http:// link.galegroup.com/apps/doc/H1000065130/BIC?u=stpaul_main&sid=BIC&xid =15896cdc. Accessed January 28, 2019.

296   "special permission": "Joseph P. Mathieu." *Contemporary Authors Online*. Gale, 2006. http://link.galegroup.com/apps/doc/H1000065130/BIC?u=stpaul_main&sid=BIC&xid =15896cdc. Accessed January 28, 2019.

A Pet Named Sneaker

297   "crazy about that snake": Hartman, Liz. "'Robert the Rose Horse' Author Back on the Scene." *Publishers Weekly*, July 28, 2011.

297   "just terrified": Joan Heilbroner. Interview with PVA, October 12, 2018.

298   "image and drawings eater": Danielson, Julie. "Seven Questions Over Breakfast with Pascal Lemaitre." Seven Impossible Things Before Breakfast, August 18, 2009. http:// blaine.org/sevenimpossiblethings/?p=1764.

Squirrels on Skis

300   "page layouts and scenes": Taylor, Derek. "Squirrels on Skis: J. Hamilton Ray Discusses the New Children's Book." *Adventure Sports Network*, January 22, 2014. https://www. adventuresportsnetwork.com/sport/skiing/squirrels-on-skis-j-hamilton-ray-discusses -the-new-childrens-book/.

300   "squirrels going crazy": Pascal Lemaitre. Email to PVA, August 1, 2018.

300   "successful collaboration": Taylor, Derek. "Squirrels on Skis: J. Hamilton Ray Discusses the New Children's Book." *Adventure Sports Network*, January 22, 2014. https://www. adventuresportsnetwork.com/sport/skiing/squirrels-on-skis-j-hamilton-ray-discusses -the-new-childrens-book/.

Ten Eggs in a Nest

301   "comic-book-like antics": Michael Fleming. Email to PVA, April 6, 2019.

301   "my own design": Sadler, Marilyn. "A Life Filled with Gratitude." *Marilyn Sadler.net*, October 29, 2018. https://marilynsadler.net/blog/f/a-life-filled-with-gratitude.

A Skunk in My Bunk

302   "oh my god": Christopher Cerf. Interview with PVA, August 30, 2018.

302   "in a funny way": Christopher Cerf. Interview with PVA, August 30, 2018.

Can You See Me?

305   "expression of my ideas": Arber, Jason. "Bob Staake." *Pixelsurgeon*, 2002. https://web .archive.org/web/20080328060829/http://pixelsurgeon.com/interviews/interview .php?id=192.

306   "simply bizarre": Bob Staake. Email to PVA, February 22, 2019.

References

INTRODUCTION

Bird, Elizabeth. "Top 100 Picture Books #28: *Go, Dog. Go!* by P. D. Eastman." A Fuse #8 Production. June 5, 2012. http://blogs.slj.com/afuse8production/2012/06/05/top-100-childrens-novels-28-go-dog-go-by-p-d-eastman/.

Brezzo, Steven L. "Introduction." *Dr. Seuss from Then to Now*. Random House: New York, 1986.

Chall, Jeanne. *Learning to Read: The Great Debate*. 2nd ed. McGraw-Hill: New York, 1983. p191.

"Hitch a Ride! We've Got Road Trip Reads for Every Passenger." *NPR*. June 17, 2014. http://www.npr.org/2014/06/17/318601961/hitch-a-ride-weve-got-road-trip-reads-for-every-passenger.

Turvey, Debbie Hochman. "All-Time Bestselling Children's Books." Diane Roback, ed. *Publishers Weekly*. December 17, 2001. https://www.publishersweekly.com/pw/by-topic/childrens/childrens-industry-news/article/28595-all-time-bestselling-children-s-books.html.

CHAPTER 1

Caponegro, Ramona. "From the *New England Primer* to *The Cat in the Hat*: Big Steps in the Growth and Development of Early Readers." In *The Early Reader in Children's Literature and Culture: Theorizing Books for Beginning Readers*. Jennifer Miskec and Annette Wannamaker, eds. Routledge: New York, 2015.

Cormack, Phillip Anton, et al. "The Child, the Text and the Teacher: Reading Primers and Reading Instruction." *Paedegogia Historica* 48, no. 2 (April 1, 2012): 185–96.

Kelly, Kate. "Dick and Jane: Story of These Early Readers." America Comes Alive.com. June 2, 2017. http://americacomesalive.com/2017/06/02/dick-and-jane-story-of-these-early-readers/.

Stedman, L. C., and C. F. Kaestle. "Literacy and Reading Performance in the United States from 1880 to the Present." In *Literacy in the United States*. C. Kaestle, ed. Vail-Ballou Press: Binghamton, NY, 1991.

CHAPTER 2

Buchwald, Art. "It Isn't So: Dr. Seuss Will Never Go." *Palm Beach Post*, October 3, 1991.

Cahn, Robert. "The Wonderful World of Dr. Seuss." *Saturday Evening Post*, July 6, 1957.

Cerf, Christopher. "A Gift Worth Waiting For." In *Your Favorite Seuss*. Janet Schulman and Cathy Goldsmith, eds. Random House: New York, 2004. p84.

Culbert, David H. "Walt Disney's Private Snafu: The Use of Humor in World War II Army Film." *Prospects: An Annual Journal of American Culture* 1, no. 81–96 (1976): 82.

"Dr. Seuss Remembered." *Publishers Weekly*, October 25, 1991.

Fitzsimmons, Rebekah. "Creating and Marketing Early Reader Picture Books." In *The Early Reader in Children's Literature and Culture: Theorizing Books for Beginning Readers*. Jennifer Miskec and Annette Wannamaker, eds. Routledge: New York, 2015.

Ford, Carin T. *Dr. Seuss: Best-Loved Author*. Enslow Publishing: Berkeley Heights, NJ, 2003.

Frutig, Judith. "Dr. Seuss's Green-Eggs-and-Ham World." *Christian Science Monitor*, May 12, 1978.

Goodman, Ellen. "Dr. Seuss Knew How to Talk to Children." *Sioux City Journal*, October 4, 1991.

Greenleaf, Warren T. "How the Grinch Stole Reading: The Serious Nonsense of Dr. Seuss." *Principal*, May 1982.

Harper, Hilliard. "The Private World of Dr. Seuss: A Visit to Theodor Geisel's La Jolla Mountaintop." *Los Angeles Times Magazine*, May 25, 1986.

Kahn, E. J., Jr. "Children's Friend." *New Yorker*, December 17, 1960.

Menand, Louis. "Cat People." *New Yorker*. December 23, 2002. https://www.newyorker.com/magazine/2002/12/23/cat-people.

Nel, Philip. *The Annotated Cat: Under the Hats of Seuss and His Cats*. Random House: New York, 2007.

Nel, Philip. "Children's Literature Goes to War: Dr. Seuss, P. D. Eastman, Munro Leaf, and the Private SNAFU Films (1943–46)." *Journal of Popular Culture* 40, no. 3 (2007): 468–85.

Pease, Donald E. *Theodor Seuss Geisel*. Oxford University Press: Oxford. 2010.

Seigel, Master Sergeant George J. "Hollywood's Army: The First Motion Picture Unit, US Army Air Forces, Culver City, California." Military Museum.org. http://www.militarymuseum.org/1stmpu.html.

Weidt, Maryann N. *Oh, the Places He Went: A Story about Dr. Seuss*. Carolrhoda Books, Minneapolis, 1994.

CHAPTER 3

"Chautauqua Movement History." Chautauqua.com. https://www.chautauqua.com/about-us/history/chautauqua-movement-history/).

Del Barco, Mandalit. "What Walt Disney Learned from South America." *Tell Me More*. September 17, 2009. https://www.npr.org/templates/story/story.php?storyId=112916523).

"Helen Palmer, Children's Writer and Wife of Dr. Seuss, Is Dead." *New York Times*, October 24, 1967. p46.

"The History of I Can Read!" *I Can Read.com*. https://web.archive.org/web/20120819073316/http://www.icanread.com/history.cfm.

Jones, Malcom. "It Took Dr. Seuss a Year to Write 'The Cat in the Hat'—and It Changed Kids' Lit Forever." *Daily Beast*. March 2, 2016. http://www.thedailybeast.com/it-took-dr-seuss-a-year-to-write-the-cat-in-the-hatand-it-changed-kids-lit-forever.

Jones, Brian Jay. *Becoming Dr. Seuss*. Dutton: New York, 2019.

Kane, George. "And, Dear Dr. Seuss, the Whole World's in Love with Yeuss." *Rocky Mountain News*, February 15, 1976.

Klein, Christopher. "Nine Things You May Not Know about Dr. Seuss." *History.com.* March 1, 2012. http://www.history.com/news/9-things-you-may-not-know-about-dr-seuss.

Lambert, Craig. "Channel Cerfing." *Harvard Magazine.* July/August 2011. harvardmagazine. com/2011/07/channel-cerfing, July–August 2011.

Latham, Edward Connery. "The Beginnings of Dr. Seuss: A Conversation with Theodor S. Geisel." *Dartmouth Alumni Magazine,* April 1976.

Lyman, Rick. "Phyllis Cerf Wagner, 90, Socialite and Collaborator with Dr. Seuss, Dies." *New York Times.* November 26, 2006.

Marcus, Leonard S. "He Left Us Smiles." *Parenting,* December/January 1992.

Nichols, Lewis. "Then I Doodled a Tree." *New York Times Book Review,* November 11, 1962.

"One Killed and Ten Injured." *Jasper News,* March 29, 1917.

Pascal, Janet. *Who Was Dr. Seuss?* Grossett & Dunlap: New York, 2011.

"Phyllis Wagner; Small-Town Girl Made Her Mark in Two Big Cities." Washington Post, November 27, 2006.

Renthal, Helen. "25 Years of Working Wonder with Words." Chicago Tribune, November 11, 1962.

Roth, Rita. "On Beyond Zebra with Dr. Seuss." *New Advocate,* Fall 1989.

Schuetz, Kari. *Children's Storytellers: Dr. Seuss.* Bellweather, 2016.

Seuss, Dr. "My Hassle with the First-Grade Language." *Chicago Tribune,* November 17, 1957.

Seuss, Dr. "How Orlo Got His Book." *New York Times,* November 17, 1957.

"'Somebody's Got to Win' in Kids' Books: An Interview with Dr. Seuss on His Books for Children, Young and Old." *U.S. News and World Report,* April 14, 1986.

"Teaching: The Logical Insanity of Dr. Seuss." *Time,* August 11, 1967.

Woods, Mae. *Dr. Seuss.* Abdo: Edina, MN, 2000.

CHAPTER 4

Bader, Barbara. *American Picture Books from Noah's Ark to the Beast Within.* Macmillan: New York, 1976. p499.

"Beginner Books: New Trade Learn-to-Read Juveniles." *Publishers Weekly,* June 2, 1958. p117.

Caponegro, Jennifer. "From the *New England Primer* to *The Cat in the Hat*: Big Steps in the Growth and Development of Early Readers." In *The Early Reader in Children's Literature and Culture: Theorizing Books for Beginning Readers.* Jennifer Miskec and Annette Wannamaker, eds. Routledge: New York, 2015.

Kahn, E. J., Jr. "Children's Friend." *New Yorker.* December 17, 1960.

Ozirny, Shannon. "The Big Shoes of Little Bear: The Publication History, Emergence, and Literary Potential of the Easy Reader" (Master's thesis in children's literature. University of British Columbia, April 2008. p73.)

P. D. EASTMAN, PART 1

Denning, Michael. *The Cultural Front: The Laboring of American Culture in the Twentieth Century.* Verso: New York, 1998.

Johnson, Lisa. "The Disney Strike of 1941: From the Animators' Perspective." Honors Projects Overview, 2008. https://digitalcommons.ric.edu/cgi/viewcontent.cgi?referer=https://www.google.com/&httpsredir=1&article=1017&context=honors_projects).

"Philip Eastman, testimony, March 23, 1953." Communist Methods of Infiltration (Education), Hearings before the Committee on Un-American Activities, House of Representatives, 83rd Congress, First Session.

"P(hilip) D(ey) Eastman." *Major Authors and Illustrators for Children and Young Adults*. Gale, 2002. link.galegroup.com/apps/doc/K1617001241/BIC1?u=ramsey_main&xid=o6c65f8e. Accessed August 28, 2017.

"Tree Honors Fine Memory of Peter Dey." *Iowa City Press-Citizen*, October 11, 1922.

CHAPTER 5

Grolier Royalty Statement. RHA/CU (Box 696, Geisel, Helen and Ted).

Maughan, Shannon. "Readers for Early Readers." *Publishers Weekly*, May 22, 2000. p40.

ROY MCKIE, PART 1

Farmer, Brett. "Time for Another My Fair Lady Tale . . ." The Parallel Julieverse (blog), 2016. http://paralleljulieverse.tumblr.com/post/142178794099/time-for-another-my-fair-lady-tale-in-honour-of.

Giambarba, Paul. "Roy McKie." 100 Years of Illustration (blog), November 2011. http://giam.typepad.com/100_years_of_illustration/2011/10/roy-mckie.html).

Maughan, Shannon. "Obituary: Roy McKie." *Publishers Weekly*, March 12, 2015. https://www.publishersweekly.com/pw/by-topic/childrens/childrens-authors/article/65852-obituary-roy-mckie.html).

McKie, Todd. Interview with PVA, September 16, 2017.

"Roy McKie, Jr." *New York Times*. March 9, 2015.

STAN AND JAN BERENSTAIN, PART 1

Sims, Gayle Ronan. "Stanley Berenstain Dies at 82." *Philadelphia Inquirer*, November 30, 2005.

"Stan and Jan Berenstain." *Encyclopedia of World Biography*, vol. 33. Gale, 2013. link.galegroup.com/apps/doc/K1631009865/BIC1?u=ramsey_main&xid=95c1fob3. Accessed August 28, 2017.

Woo, Elaine. "Jan Berenstain of Berenstain Bears Empire, Dies at 88." *Tallahassee Democrat*, February 29, 2012.

Woods, Mae. *Stan & Jan Berenstain*. Abdo: Minneapolis, MN, 2000.

CHAPTER 6

Bob Bernstein. Interview with PVA, September 26, 2018.

"'Somebody's Got to Win' in Kids' Books: An Interview with Dr. Seuss on His Books for Children, Young and Old." *U.S. News and World Report*, April 14, 1986.

The Pig That Wouldn't Fly: "A Forgotten Capote Work." *Buffalo News*, July 22, 1993. https://buffalonews.com/1993/07/23/a-forgotten-capote-work/.

CHAPTER 7

Arnold, Thomas K. "Critics Pan Green Morgan and Ham." *San Diego Union-Tribune*, June 8, 1995. https://www.sandiegoreader.com/news/1995/jun/08/critics-pan-green-morgan-and-ham/#.

"Beginning Readers' Schedule of Net Units Sold Fourth Quarter Ended December 31, 1964." RHA/CU (Box 696, Geisel, Helen and Ted 6).

"Helen Geisel, Children's Author, Dies." *San Francisco Examiner*, October 24, 1967.

"To Discuss with Geisels—October 1965" (memo). RHA/CU (Box 697, Beginner Books 1).

AL PERKINS

Helen Geisel to Anne MarcoVecchio, August 9, 1965. RHA/CU (Box 701, Perkins, Al).

CHAPTER 8

Beck, David L. "The Seuss Is Loose!" *Pensacola News Journal*, November 19, 2000.

Bernstein, Robert. *Speaking Freely*. New Press: New York, 2016. p92.

P. D. EASTMAN, PART 2

"A Protégé of Dr. Seuss." *Allison's Book Bag* (blog), September 8, 2014. https://allisonsbookbag.wordpress.com/2014/09/08/a-protege-of-dr-seuss/.

CHAPTER 9

Schulman, Janet. "Looking Back: The 1974 Macmillan Massacre." *Publishers Weekly*, April 10, 2008.

"Western Picks Graphics VP." *Journal Times*, January 29, 1980.

CHAPTER 10

"New for New Readers: An Easy Reader Renaissance." *Horn Book*, February 26, 2018.

Roback, Diane. "Obituary: Gerald Harrison." *Publishers Weekly*, February 2, 2012.

Ross Lipson, Eden. "The Little Industry That Could." *New York Times*, December 3, 1989.

"U.S. SEC Form 10-K, Scholastic Corporation," May 31, 2004. http://investor.scholastic.com
/static-files/4e7c5c89-6175-4859-a6a8-3c3fdf320ad1.

PART 2: THE 1950s

A Fly Went By

Peng, Leif. "Fritz Siebel: "never felt that he needed to be recognized . . . but he was always
proud." *Today's Inspiration* (blog), October 11, 2012. http://todaysinspiration.blogspot.com
/2012/10/fritz-siebel-never-felt-that-he-needed.html.

"The Restless Illustrator: Frederick 'Fritz' Siebel." *Of All Arts* (blog). March 11, 2009.

Thomas, Barbara. Email to PVA, July 27, 2018.

A Big Ball of String

"Children's Author-Illustrator Marion Hall Holland Dies at 81." *Washington Post*, April 8, 1989.

Schilling, Emily Brewton. "Marion Hall Holland" *Art and Honor*. https://www.artandhonor
.com/bio--marion.html.

The Big Jump

"Benjamin Elkin." *Contemporary Authors Online*. Gale, 2001. link.galegroup.com/apps/
docH1000028891/BIC1?u=ramsey_main&xid=15fee05a. Accessed August 28, 2017.

Bloom, Stu. "A Lifetime of Elementary Schools, Part 1." Live Long and Prosper . . . (blog), March
16, 2011. https://bloom-at.blogspot.com/2011/05/lifetime-of-elementary-schools-part-1
.html?m=0.

Bloom, Stu. Email to PVA, June 3, 2018.

Evans, Katie and David. "Artist Profile: Katherine Evans." *Art and Nature Center*, March 18, 2012.
https://www.wianc.org/blog/artist-profile-katherine-evans).

Jaffe, Carol. Email to PVA, July 24, 2018.

"Jon Klassen Reads *The Big Jump* in Bed." https://www.youtube.com/watch?v=pYJvn5XkJnc.

"Katherine (Floyd) Evans." *Contemporary Authors Online*. Gale, 2002. link.galegroup.com/apps
/doc/H1000030045/BIC1?u=ramsey_main&xid=7dc9cdf0. Accessed September 15, 2017.

"Library Receives Books by Mrs. Evans," *Manitowoc Herald-Times*, September 30, 1964.

Liebek, Lee. Email to PVA, June 17, 2018.

Savoy, Maggie. "Tots Sharp Readers: Writer Finds Children Challenging Audience." *Arizona
Republic*, November 2, 1962.

You Will Go to the Moon

Baker, Melinda, and Amy Stumpfl. "Portrait Artist Everett Raymond Kinstler at Lipscomb,
Vanderbilt." *Tennessean*, March 16, 2018.

Elmgren, Ainur. "Bathing Beauty." *1920 A.D.* (blog), April 28, 2008. http://goldenbirdsings
.blogspot.com/2008/04/bathing-beauty.html.

"Mae Freeman." *Contemporary Authors Online*, Gale, 2009. link.galegroup.com/apps/doc
/H1000033974/BIC1?u=ramsey_main&xid=49c6a423. Accessed September 15, 2017.

"Robert Patterson (1898–1981)." *American Art Archives*. http://www.americanartarchives.com
/patterson,ro.htm.

Weidner, Richard T. "Ira M. Freeman." *Physics Today* 41, no. 5 (1988): 116. https://physicstoday
.scitation.org/doi/pdf/10.1063/1.2811433.

Cowboy Andy

"Edna Walker Chandler." *Contemporary Authors Online*. Gale, 2002. link.galegroup.com/apps
/doc/H1000017037/BIC1?u=ramsey_main&xid=96fe2b75. Accessed September 15, 2017.

"Edna Walker Chandler." *Map of Kansas Literature* (Washburn University), 2015. http://www
.washburn.edu/reference/cks/mapping/chandler/.

"Everett Raymond Kinstler." *Contemporary Authors Online*. Gale, 2001. link.galegroup.com/apps
/doc/H1000054363/BIC1?u=ramsey_main&xid=5ebe3425. Accessed September 15, 2017.

Nott, Robert. "The Fine Lines of Everett Kinstler." *Santa Fe New Mexican*, October 6, 2006.

Russell, David H. "An Evaluation of Some Easy-to-Read Trade Books for Children." *Elementary
English* 38, no. 7 (November 1961): 475–82.

Vadeboncoeur, Jim, Jr., and Everett Raymond Kinstler. *Everett Raymond Kinstler: The Artist's
Journey through Popular Culture, 1942–1962*. Underwood Books: Nevada City, CA, 2005.

The Whales Go By

Berger, Wolfgang H. "Memorial to Fred B. Phelger." Geological Society of America, June 1994.
https://www.geosociety.org/gsa/Memorials/v25/Phleger-FB.pdf.

"Fred Phelger Biography." University of California–San Diego. http://scilib.ucsd.edu/sio/biogr
/Phleger_Biogr.pdf.

Sutherland, Sandra Wright. *Rainbow Quest: The Adventurous Life of Audrey McElmury*. Iris
Press: Bozeman, MT, 2016.

Stop That Ball!

"Children's Author Dies." *Star Press*, December 10, 1989. Donald Klopfer to TG, March 1, 1960.
RHA/CU (Box 42, Beginner Books 2).

Siebel, Gretchen. Email to Barbara Thomas, September 11, 2018.

Thomas, Barbara. Interview with PVA, July 30, 2018.

Phyllis Cerf to Donald Klopfer, February 17, 1960. RHA/CU (Box 42, Beginner Books 2).

Bennett Cerf's Book of Laughs

Charlton, Linda. "Carl Rose, Cartoonist, Is Dead at 68." *New York Times*, June 22, 1971.

Ann Can Fly

"Audrey McElmury First U.S. Citizen to Win World Title." *Central New Jersey Home News*,
August 24, 1969.

"Robert Martin Lopshire." *Contemporary Authors Online*. Gale, 2011. link.galegroup.com/apps
    /doc/H1000061284/BIC1?u=ramsey_main&xid=fcd8b7d7. Accessed September 15, 2017.

THE 1960s

The King's Wish

"Leonard W. Shortall." *Contemporary Authors Online*. Gale, 2002. http://link.galegroup.com/apps
    /doc/H1000090797/BIC?u=stpaul_main&sid=BIC&xid=bc4459a7. Accessed June 21, 2018.
"PTA Plans Book Fair." *Bridgeport Post*, November 5, 1961.

Green Eggs and Ham

Adil, Janeen R. *Dr. Seuss: Great Story Teller*. Mitchell Lane Publishers: Hockessin, Delaware,
    2005. p19.
Moje, Elizabeth B., and Woan-Ru Shyu. "Oh, the Places You've Taken Us: The Reading Teacher's
    Tribute to Dr. Seuss." *The Reading Teacher*, May 1992.
Wheeler, Jill C. *Dr. Seuss*. Abdo & Daughters: Edina, MN, 1992.

Put Me in the Zoo

"Robert Martin Lopshire." *Contemporary Authors Online*. Gale, 2011. link.galegroup.com/apps
    /doc/H1000061284/BIC1?u=ramsey_main&xid=fcd8b7d7. Accessed September 15, 2017.

Go, Dog. Go!

Bird, Elizabeth. "Top 100 Picture Books #28: *Go, Dog. Go!* by P. D. Eastman." A Fuse #8 Produc-
    tion. June 5, 2012. http://blogs.slj.com/afuse8production/2012/06/05/top-100-childrens-novels
    -28-go-dog-go-by-p-d-eastman/).

Little Black, A Pony

Scaggs, Jim. "Hall of Fame Ceremonies Nearing." *Daily Republican-Register*, April 30, 1982.
Scardino, Albert. "Walter Farley, 74, a Writer on a Series on a Black Stallion." *New York Times*,
    October 18, 1989.
Sharp, Sonya. "Illustrator Turns to Doing Portraits." *Morning Call*, February 18, 1963.
"Walter (Lorimer) Farley." *Major Authors and Illustrators for Children and Young Adults*. Gale,
    2002. link.galegroup.com/apps/doc/K1617001262/BIC1?u=ramsey_main&xid=59152ba5.
    Accessed September 18, 2017.

Look Out for Pirates!

"Iris Vinton, 82, Author of Novels for Children." *New York Times*, February 9, 1988.

Peng, Leif. "H.B. Vestal (1916–2007)." Today's Inspiration (blog), March 9, 2012. http://todays inspiration.blogspot.com/2012/03/hb-vestal-1916-2007.html.

Saunders, David. "Herman Vestal (1916–2007)." Pulp Artists.com, 2011. https://www.pulpartists .com/Vestal.html.

Robert the Rose Horse

Ainslie, Betty. "Children's Books Have Excellent Illustrations." *Daily Herald*, November 1, 1962.

Albanese, Andrew. "Human Rights Watcher: PW Talks with Former Random House President Robert Bernstein." *Publishers Weekly*, May 13, 2016.

Hartman, Liz. "Robert the Rose Horse Author Back on the Scene." *Publishers Weekly*, July 28, 2011. https://www.publishersweekly.com/pw/by-topic/childrens/childrens-book-news /article/48151-robert-the-rose-horse-author-back-on-the-scene.html.

Heilbroner, Joan. Interview with PVA, September 20, 2018.

"Joan Knapp Heilbroner." *Contemporary Authors Online*. Gale, 2002. link.galegroup.com/apps /doc/H1000044098/BIC1?u=ramsey_main&xid=f8c6ae1d. Accessed August 28, 2017.

Oliver, Myrna. "Robert Heilbroner, 85; Economics Texts Were Praised for Lively Writing Style." *Los Angeles Times*, January 11, 2005.

I Was Kissed by a Seal at the Zoo

Corey Lynn Fayman. Interview with PVA, August 13, 2018.

"Lynn Fayman—'Red Feather.'" *Objects USA*. http://www.objectsusa.com/?jw_portfolio=lynn -fayman-red-feather.

"Lynn G. Fayman." *Kansas City Times*, June 18, 1968.

"Mrs. Ruth A. Fayman." *Kansas City Times*, October 26, 1955.

Varga, George. "Danah Fayman, Longtime San Diego Arts Champion, Has Died at 97." *San Diego Union-Tribune*, June 22, 2017.

Hop on Pop

Mangione, Kendra. "Toronto Public Library asked to pull Dr. Seuss book 'Hop on Pop.'" Toronto CTV News, April 29, 2014. https://toronto.ctvnews.ca/toronto-public-library-asked -to-pull-dr-seuss-book-hop-on-pop-1.1797204.

"Teachers' Top 100 Books for Children." National Education Association, 2007.

Dr. Seuss's ABC

Hill, Joanne. "ABC—A History of Alphabet Books." *Stella and Rose's Books*. https://stellabooks .com/article/abc-a-history-of-alphabet-books.

Do You Know What I'm Going to Do Next Saturday?

Davis, Rawli. Emails to PVA, February 25, 2018, and August 23, 2018.

"Do You Know What I'm Going to Do Next Saturday?" *The Haunted Closet* (blog), February 21, 2010. http://the-haunted-closet.blogspot.com/2010/02/do-you-know-what-im-going-to-do-next.html.

Summer

"Alice Low." *Contemporary Authors Online*. Gale, 2007. link.galegroup.com/apps/doc/H1000061577/BIC1?u=ramsey_main&xid=2070ae11. Accessed September 4, 2017.

Marcus, Leonard. *Golden Legacy*. Random House: New York, 2017.

The King, the Mice, and the Cheese

"J. Eric Gurney." *Contemporary Authors Online*. Gale, 2001. link.galegroup.com/apps/doc/H1000040545/BIC1?u=ramsey_main&xid=5dc349e7. Accessed August 28, 2017.

Donnelly, Lucia. "Westport's Eric Gurney Real Cool Sketching Life with Calculating Cats." *Bridgeport Post*, September 30, 1962.

"Eric Gurney Dies at 82." *Arizona Daily Star*, November 19, 1992.

I Wish That I Had Duck Feet

"Barney Tobey; New Yorker Cartoonist." *Hartford Courant*, March 28, 1989.

Don and Donna Go to Bat

Bunis, Dena. "Court Leaves Schools Alone on Book Bans." *Democrat and Chronicle*, July 3, 1982.

You Will Live under the Sea

Erodes, Richard. *The Saloons of the Old West*. Knopf: New York, 1979.

Gavidor, Leorah. "50th Anniversary of Sealab II." *San Diego Reader*, October 12, 2015. https://www.sandiegoreader.com/news/2015/oct/12/waterfront-50th-anniversary-sealab-ii/#.

Walter Retan to Helen Geisel, February 5, 1965. RHA/CU (Box 696, Geisel, Helen and Ted 6).

"Ward Brackett." In *The Illustrator in America 1880–1980*. Walt and Roger Reed, eds. Madison Square Press: New York, 1984. p257.

"Ward G. Brackett, 92." *Westport Now*, February 19, 2008. https://westportnow.com/index.php?/v2/comments/ward_g_brackett_93/.

The Digging-est Dog

Phil Eastman to Helen and Ted Geisel, 1966. Courtesy of Susan and Tony Eastman.

Anne Johnson to E. E. Harper, October 28, 1965. RHA/CU (Box 700, The Dog That Wouldn't Dig).

The Cat in the Hat Songbook

Opie, Iona and Peter. *The Lore and Language of School Children*. Oxford University Press: Oxford, 1959.

Off to the Races

Ashley, Mike. "The AMAZING Story: The Sixties—The Goose-Flesh Factor." *Pulpfest.com*, March 3, 2016. http://www.pulpfest.com/tag/leo-summers/.

"Audrey McElmury First U.S. Citizen to Win World Title." *Central New Jersey Home News*, August 24, 1969.

Levin, Dan. "What Makes Audrey Pedal? Tiga Mik." *Sports Illustrated*, November 24, 1969.

Von Ruff, Al. "Summary Bibliography: Leo Summers." *The Internet Speculative Fiction Database.* http://www.isfdb.org/cgi-bin/ea.cgi?7792.

My Book about Me

Michael Frith. Interview with PVA, November 5, 2017.

The Best Nest

Gutierrez, Thomas D. "The Best Nest." *Pretty Blue Glow* (blog), January 9, 2016.

Sally Allen. Interview with PVA, November 7, 2017.

Susan Eastman. Emails to PVA, December 9, 2018, and December 13, 2018.

THE 1970s

The Bears' Vacation

Woo, Elaine. "Jan Berenstain of Berenstain Bears Empire, Dies at 88." *Tallahassee Democrat*, February 29, 2012.

King Midas and the Golden Touch

"Harold Berson." *Contemporary Authors Online.* Gale, 2001. http://link.galegroup.com/apps/doc/H1000008187/BIC?u=stpaul_main&sid=BIC&xid=5398ed94. Accessed November 30, 2018.

Sally Allen. Interview with PVA, November 7, 2017.

The Ear Book

Larson, C. "Illustrator—William O'Brian." All About Oscar (blog). https://oscartheseal.wordpress.com/about/illustrator-william-obrian/.

Walter Retan to Bob Bernstein, March 9, 1965. RHA/CU (Box 696, Editorial Report).

Zoe O'Brian. Email to PVA, December 6, 2018.

Tubby

Crouch, Bill, Jr. "Rowland B. Wilson." *Cartoonist Profiles* 34 (June 1977).

Hoare, Philip. "Rowland B. Wilson, 'Playboy' Cartoonist and Disney Animator." *Independent Online*, July 13, 2005. http://www.independent.co.uk/news/obituaries/rowland-b-wilson -498685.html.

Koppel, Lily. "Rowland B. Wilson, 74, Creator of Wry Cartoons." *New York Times*, July 10, 2005.

Wacky Wednesday

Duke, Sara. *Biographical Sketches of Cartoonists & Illustrators in the Swann Collection of the Library of Congress*. ComicsDC: Arlington, VA, 2017.

Gehr, Richard. "George Booth: Semper Fi." *Comics Journal*, August 12, 2013. http://www.tcj.com /george-booth-semper-fi/.

Johns, Paul. "Mozarks Moments: The Missouri Man Who Draws Cats and Dogs." *CC Headliner*, March 25, 2018.

Marvin K. Mooney

Coover, Robert. "Robert Coover's Long Lost Seussian Satire of American Politics: The Cat in the Hat for President (would be better than what we have now)." *Literary Hub*, April 10, 2018. https://lithub.com/robert-coovers-long-lost-seussian-satire-of-american-politics /Harper, Hilliard.

Krull, Kathleen. *The Boy on Fairfield Street: How Ted Geisel Grew Up to Become Dr. Seuss*. Random House: New York, 2007.

"The Private World of Dr. Seuss: A Visit to Theodor Geisel's La Jolla Mountaintop." *Los Angeles Times Magazine*, May 25, 1986.

October

"Arthur Cumings Weds Long Island Girl." *Burlington Free Press*, February 8, 1946.

"Arthur E. Cumings, 1922–2012." *Comics Reporter*, September 10, 2012. http://www.comics reporter.com/index.php/art_cumings_1922_2012/.

"Motor Illustrator: Art Cumings." Second Chance Garage.com, 2018. http://www.second chancegarage.com/motor-covers/MoTor-Cover-Artist-Art-Cumings.cfm.

Hooper

"Charles E. Mastrangelo." *Contemporary Authors Online*. Gale, 2002.

Saxon, Wolfgang. "Charles Elmer Martin, or CEM, New Yorker Artist, Dies at 85." *New York Times*, June 20, 1995.

The Hair Book

"Cynthia Graham Tether." *Contemporary Authors Online*. Gale, 2007. http://link.galegroup.com /apps/doc/H1000098032/BIC?u=stpaul_main&sid=BIC&xid=0d4d82c9. Accessed January 12, 2019.

Smith, Mildred Ann. "Books for the Young." *Santa Cruz Sentinel*, September 30, 1978.

THE 1980s

Maybe You Should Fly a Jet

"Michael Smollin—Artist Profile." *Smollin.com.* http://smollin.com/michael/bio/bio.htm.

Wings on Things

Barbanel, Josh. "Would an Aardvark Live Here?" *New York Times,* September 17, 2006.

Smurfs

Folkart, Burt A. "Pierre Culliford; Created the Widely Popular Smurfs." *Los Angeles Times,* December 25, 1992. http://articles.latimes.com/1992-12-25/news/mn-2392_1_pierre-culliford.
"Peyo—Pierre Culliford (25 June 1928–24 December 1992, Belgium)." *Lambiek Comiclopedia.* https://www.lambiek.net/artists/p/peyo.htm.

It's Not Easy . . .

Belanus, George. "Author Returns to Tell Her Story." *Tribune* (Coshocton, OH), March 12, 1989.
Downing, Bob. "Doubts of an Animal Cracker." *Akron Beacon Journal,* January 20, 1974.
Seagall, Grant. "From Rocky River, Marilyn Sadler Entertains Children Far and Wide: My Cleveland." *Plains Dealer,* September 12, 2014.

Snug House Bug House!

Buller, Jon. "Buller's Story." *Bullersooz.com,* 1998. http://www.bullersooz.com/buller1.html.
Libby, Sam. "Talents of Couple Illustrated." *Hartford Courant,* June 23, 1988.
"Susan Schade." *Contemporary Authors Online.* Gale, 2008. http://link.galegroup.com/apps/doc/H1000181270/BIC?u=stpaul_main&sid=BIC&xid=ad98eb56. Accessed January 28, 2019.
Warchut Day, Katie. "A Cat in Hand: Cartooning with Jon Buller." *The Day,* November 21, 2010.

Anthony the Perfect Monster

"Angelo Decesare." Lambeik Comiclopedia, January 7, 2018. https://www.lambiek.net/artists/d/decesare_a.htm.

Four Pups and a Worm

Cat in the Hat Gift of Reading ad. Detroit Free Press, 1989. https://www.newspapers.com/image/99928713/?terms=the%2Bgift%2Bof%2Breading%2Bseuss.
Lannon, Linnea. "These Sweatshirts Take a Flirty Twist." *Detroit Free Press,* December 9, 1982.

Monster Munchies

"About." Nate Evans.com, 2017. http://nateevans.com/my-page-21/.

Evans, Nate. "The Kindness of Illustrators." Nate Evans, Janice Hardy's Fiction University, September 28, 2012. http://blog.janicehardy.com/2012/09/guest-author-nate-evans-kindness-of. html?fbclid=IwAR1FzDoCQfoKroGgK63ZYMMmW-nPZ5jzpNZaIM5ve7K-NwLgpZr XeJree2o.

"Laura Numeroff." *Contemporary Authors Online.* Gale, 2010. http://link.galegroup.com/apps /doc/H1000073779/BIC?u=stpaul_main&sid=BIC&xid=b385cd31. Accessed January 28, 2019.

Maryniak, Paul. "Two Ahwatukee Authors' Book Presents Different Cookie Monster." *Ahwatukee Foothills News,* September 21, 2017.

The A Book

Kate Klimo. Interview with PVA, October 8, 2017.

Mama Loves

"Lisa (Emiline) McCue." *Contemporary Authors Online.* Gale, 2002. http://link.galegroup.com /apps/doc/H1000066162/BIC?u=stpaul_main&sid=BIC&xid=2cdfo42c. Accessed February 15, 2019.

THE 2000s

Paws and Claws

Comstock, Lori. "Author/Illustrator Brings Love of Tractors to Children." New Jersey Herald, August 12, 2017.

Maney, Kevin. "Winning the Video Game." Journal News, December 9, 1984.

"Young Writers' Workshop, Erica Farber: What's Your Point of View." *New York Society Library,* 2016. https://www.nysoclib.org/events/young-writers-farber-whats-your -point-view.

The Knee Book

Hall, Alice. "Vacationing Artists." Tampa Tribune, August 4, 1986.

Money Money

"Marilyn (June) Sadler." *Major Authors and Illustrators for Children and Young Adults.* Gale, 2002. http://link.galegroup.com/apps/doc/K1617001788/BIC?u=stpaul_main&sid=BIC &xid=do84de35. Accessed January 21, 2019.

Sangiacomo, Michael. "Roger Bollen, Creator of 'Animal Crackers' Comic Strip, Dies at 74." *Plains Dealer*, October 8, 2015. https://www.cleveland.com/metro/index.ssf/2015/10/roger _bollen_creator_of_animal_crackers_comic_strip_dies_at_74_photos.html.

Mrs. Wow

Danielson, Julie. "7-Imp's 7 Kicks #270: Featuring Steven Salerno." *Seven Impossible Things before Breakfast* (blog), February 26, 2012.

"Martha Freeman." *Contemporary Authors Online*. Gale, 2009. http://link.galegroup.com/apps /doc/H1000127842/BIC?u=stpaul_main&sid=BIC&xid=41108464. Accessed February 15, 2019.

"Meet Martha." *Martha Freeman.com*. http://www.marthafreeman.com/meet-martha.

"Salerno, Steven." *Something about the Author*, February 18, 2019. https://www.encyclopedia .com/children/scholarly-magazines/salerno-steven.

"Steven's Bio." *Steven Salerno.com*. https://www.stevensalerno.com/bio.

The Belly Book

Heintjes, Tom. "Hogan's Alley, Whatever Happened to Total TeleVision Productions?" *Cartoonician.com*, February 20, 2013. http://cartoonician.com/whatever-happened-to-total -television-productions/.

THE 2010s

Have You Seen My Dinosaur?

Surgal, Jon. LinkedIn. https://www.linkedin.com/in/jon-surgal-13269716/. Accessed February 21, 2019.

"About Joe Mathieu." *Joe Mathieu.com*. https://joemathieu.com/about/. Accessed February 22, 2019.

Squirrels on Skis

Ray, J. Hamilton. "Bio." www.squirrelsonskis.com. Accessed February 24, 2019.

A Skunk in My Bunk

"Christopher Bennett Cerf." *Contemporary Authors Online*. Gale, 2014. http://link.galegroup .com/apps/doc/H1000016791/BIC?u=stpaul_main&sid=BIC&xid=90f7a854. Accessed December 13, 2018.

Goldberg, Beverly. "The Lionization of Libraryland." *American Libraries*, October 1998.

"Nicola Slater." *Children's Illustrators*. http://childrensillustrators.com/nslater/about. Accessed February 21, 2019.

"Nicola Slater." *Nosy Crow*. https://nosycrow.com/contributors/nicola-slater/. Accessed February 21, 2019.

Can You See Me?

"Biography." Bob Staake.com., 2018. http://www.bobstaake.com/biography.shtml.

"Bob Staake." *Contemporary Authors Online*. Gale, 2010. http://link.galegroup.com/apps/doc/H1000152981/BIC?u=stpaul_main&sid=BIC&xid=a4937541. Accessed February 22, 2019.

Driggs, Alexis. "Cartoonist Bob Staake Began His Career at USC." *Daily Trojan*, April 12, 2012.

Index

About the Author

Photo courtesy of the author

Paul V. Allen learned to read on Beginner Books and now uses them in his work as an elementary literacy specialist. He is the author of two previous books about creative people and their work, *Eleanor Cameron: Dimensions of Amazement* and *The Hopefuls: Chasing a Rock 'n' Roll Dream in the Minnesota Music Scene*. He lives in Normal, Illinois, with his wife and two sons.

CPSIA information can be obtained
at www.ICGtesting.com
Printed in the USA
BVHW032255230421
605451BV00003B/9

9 781496 834058